Agent Provocateur for Hitler or Churchill?

*To my sister, Anne Thompson,
who has been my lifeline when times got tough*

Agent Provocateur for Hitler or Churchill?

The Mysterious Life of Stella Lonsdale

David Tremain

First published in Great Britain in 2021 by
Pen & Sword History
An imprint of
Pen & Sword Books Ltd
Yorkshire – Philadelphia

Copyright © David Tremain 2021

ISBN 978 1 52677 962 5

The right of David Tremain to be identified as Author of this work has been asserted by him in accordance with the Copyright, Designs and Patents Act 1988.

A CIP catalogue record for this book is
available from the British Library.

All rights reserved. No part of this book may be reproduced or transmitted in any form or by any means, electronic or mechanical including photocopying, recording or by any information storage and retrieval system, without permission from the Publisher in writing.

Typeset by Mac Style
Printed and bound by CPI Group (UK) Ltd,
Croydon, CR0 4YY

Pen & Sword Books Limited incorporates the imprints of Atlas, Archaeology, Aviation, Discovery, Family History, Fiction, History, Maritime, Military, Military Classics, Politics, Select, Transport, True Crime, Air World, Frontline Publishing, Leo Cooper, Remember When, Seaforth Publishing, The Praetorian Press, Wharncliffe Local History, Wharncliffe Transport, Wharncliffe True Crime and White Owl.

For a complete list of Pen & Sword titles please contact

PEN & SWORD BOOKS LIMITED
47 Church Street, Barnsley, South Yorkshire, S70 2AS, England
E-mail: enquiries@pen-and-sword.co.uk
Website: www.pen-and-sword.co.uk

Or

PEN AND SWORD BOOKS
1950 Lawrence Rd, Havertown, PA 19083, USA
E-mail: Uspen-and-sword@casematepublishers.com
Website: www.penandswordbooks.com

Contents

Author's Note   vii
Acknowledgements   viii
Abbreviations and Acronyms   x
Introduction   xvi

Chapter 1	The Beginnings of a Covert Life	1
Chapter 2	The Mayfair Playboy	9
Chapter 3	'Some Interesting Work'	17
Chapter 4	Capture and Recruitment	21
Chapter 5	'Pat O'Leary'	29
Chapter 6	The Gifted Liar	39
Chapter 7	The Man in Grey	47
Chapter 8	Flight from France	51
Chapter 9	The RENÉ Enigma	55
Chapter 10	'Keeping the Lady on Tap'	68
Chapter 11	Telegrams and Telephone Checks	91
Chapter 12	Major Masterman's Report	97
Chapter 13	'Damn the Torpedoes!'	100
Chapter 14	Jean Castelain	107
Chapter 15	A Parting of the Ways	112
Chapter 16	Declarations of Love	118
Chapter 17	'A Person of Hostile Associations'	121
Chapter 18	'Well, There is Only One Lie …'	129

Chapter 19	Aylesbury or Bust!	138
Chapter 20	'A Very Cheap Specimen of a Human Being'	146
Chapter 21	The 'Pot Calling the Kettle Black'	156
Chapter 22	Stella's Circle	162
Chapter 23	The Advisory Committee	168
Chapter 24	'If I Had Been a Nasty Piece of Work …'	176
Chapter 25	'A Fog of Falsehood and Misrepresentation'	184
Chapter 26	The Advisory Committee's Report	191
Chapter 27	'The Woman Who Laughs Like a Horse'	198
Chapter 28	Stella's Statement to the Abwehr	208
Chapter 29	The *Sunday Express* Affair	217
Chapter 30	'A Champagne-loving Brunette'	234
Afterword		237
Appendix I: Mrs Lonsdale's Secret Ink & Code		241
Appendix II: The 'Siegfried' Letters		243
Appendix III: Notes for Purposes of Investigation in France		249
Notes		252
Selected Bibliography		277
Index		279

Author's Note

Unless otherwise specified in the notes, all quotes and extracts have been taken from files at the National Archives at Kew (TNA). When quoting from these files some minor formatting changes have occasionally been made to ensure the text flows better, and accents added to French and German words where they were missed out in the original text because the typewriters of the time lacked those keys; otherwise, no changes have been made to the original punctuation or spelling. In these files many MI5 documents use the term 'German S.S'. In this context it is generally meant as a generic name for the German Secret Service rather than Schutzstaffel, the Nazi Party's paramilitary organization, or the Sicherheitsdienst (SD), the Nazi Party's intelligence service. Likewise, the terms 'MI6' and 'SIS' are frequently used interchangeably to mean the British Secret Intelligence Service. Unless MI6 is specifically used in a quote or a bibliographic reference, the term 'SIS' will be used in this book. Codenames or aliases are prefixed using the symbol @. Stella's codename was MICHAEL.

Acknowledgements

All files in the National Archives are © Crown Copyright and are reproduced with permission under the terms of the Open Government Licence. Quotes from Hansard contain Parliamentary information licensed under the Open Parliament Licence v3.0. Every attempt has been made to seek and obtain permission for copyright material used in this book. In certain cases, this has not been possible. However, if we have inadvertently used copyright material without permission/acknowledgements, we apologise and we will make the necessary correction at the first opportunity. The author and publisher would like to gratefully acknowledge the following for permission to reproduce copyright material: Mark Beynon, The History Press, for material quoted from *Cloak of Enemies*; Bloomsbury Publishing, © Adam Sisman, 2015, *John le Carré: The Biography*, Bloomsbury Publishing Plc; Suzi Feay, *The Independent on Sunday*; Dr Peter Geiger, for material quoted from *Kriegzeit: Liechtenstein 1939 bis 1945*; Bradley W. Hart, for material quoted from *George Pitt-Rivers and the Nazis*; Keith Janes, to quote from his website, *Conscript Heroes*; Natalie Jones, Express Syndication & Licencing, Reach plc, Daily Express/Express Syndication for a *Daily Express* article on Stella Lonsdale, 20 April 1947; Simon Kitson, for material quoted from *The Hunt for Nazi Spies: Fighting Espionage in Vichy France*; Emma & Neill Lochery, for material quoted from *Lisbon: War in the Shadows of the City of Light, 1939–1945*; Mark McCormick, University Press of Kentucky, for material quoted from *Silent Heroes: Downed Airmen and the French Underground*; F. Landis MacKellar, for material quoted from 'Captain George Henry Lane-Fox Pitt-Rivers and the origins of the IUSSP'; Richard and William Neave, and the Hon. Mrs William Webb (*née* Marigold Neave) for permission to quote from *Saturday at MI9* by their father, the late Airey Neave; Liisa Qureshi, Vapaa Sana Press Limited, to quote from an article in *Vapaa Sana*; Royal Aero Club Trust for photograph of Cyril Mills; Stacey Thidrickson for articles in the *Winnipeg Free Press*; Nigel West, for material quoted from *The Guy Liddell Diaries Vol.1, 1939–1942*, and *MI6: British Secret Intelligence Service Operations 1909–45*; Wesley Wilson, Coordinator of Archives & Special Collections, DePauw University, Indiana; Wiley-Blackwell, for permission to quote from

Anthony Masters' *The Man Who Was M*, © Anthony Masters, 1984: All rights reserved.

The author would also like to thank the House of Commons Enquiries; the National Archives, Kew; and the Security Service (MI5) Enquiries Team. In addition, the following individuals for their assistance: David Armstrong; Tracy Barber, Registrar, University of Colorado; Pierre Casque; Marie-Noël Challan-Belval, for information on her father; Judith Curthoys, Archivist, Christ Church College, Oxford; Andrew Dawrant, Trustee, Royal Aero Club for information on George Hicks; Jane Down; Madelin Evans, Churchill Archives Centre, Churchill College, Cambridge; Helen Fisher, University of Birmingham Archives; Dr Helen Fry; Margaret Barnard Hankey; Amanda Ingram, Archivist, Pembroke College, Oxford; Joyce Hutton and Alan 'Fred' Judge, Military Intelligence Museum, Chicksands; Dr Giselle K. Jakobs for her translation of Dr Geiger's material; Christopher Long; Richard Kemball-Cook; Steven Kippax; Robin Libert, Councillor general, Academic Outreach & Partnerships of the Belgian Veiligheid van de Staat/Sûreté de l'Etat. President RUSRA-KUIAD (Royal Union of the Intelligence and Action Services); Andrew and Angela Lownie; Charles Lyttleton, the Viscount Cobham; Bernard O'Connor; Professor Eunan O'Halpin; Edward Paine; Linda Pietronigro, Wellington Shields & Co., LLC; Jeffrey Pilkington, Christie's; Anthony Pitt-Rivers; Charles Platiau; Very Rev. Fr. Richard Reid, CSsR, The Redemptorist Community, St. Mary's Monastery, Clapham; Dr Donald P. Steury; Francis Suttill Jr.; Phil Tomaselli; Chantal Trubert; Peter Verstraeten; Nigel West; Elisabeth Alsop Winthrop; Wesley Wilson and Taylor Zartman, Archives & Special Collections, DePauw University. Finally, I would like to thank Claire Hopkins, Laura Hirst, Chris Cox and all the team at Pen & Sword for making this book possible.

Abbreviations and Acronyms

A5	Occupied France, Gibraltar, Tangier; section supporting Gaullists (SIS)
A/CD	Air Cdre Archie Boyle (SOE)
A/DP	Lt. Cmdr John Senter (SOE)
AI1(Z)	Air Intelligence
AMPC	Auxilliary Military Pioneer Corps (British Army)
ARA	Agent de Renseignements et d'Action (Belgium)
ATS	Auxillary Territorial Service
AWS	Aliens War Service
BEF	British Expeditionary Force
BEM	British Empire Medal
BLISS	OSS code word
BM	British Movement *q.v.* BUF
Bn	Battalion
BOAC	British Overseas Airways Corporation (now British Airways)
BSC	British Security Coordination
BUF	British Union of Fascists *q.v.* BM
CE	Counter-espionage
CEGESOMA	Centre for Historical Research and Documentation on War and Contemporary Society (Belgium)
CIA	Central Intelligence Agency
CIB	SHAEF Counter-Intelligence Branch
CO	Commanding Officer
Coy	Company (British Army)
CRA	Commander, Royal Artillery
CRD	Controller of Research & Development
CRUSADE	OSS field unit in France
CSDIC	Combined Services Detailed Interrogation Centre
CSsR	Congregatio Sanctissimi Redemptoris (Congregation of the Most Holy Redeemer)
CSW Black List	Central Security War Black List
CX	Reports generated by SIS

D/CE	Maj. Gen. Lakin, Security section (SOE)
DDPL	Deputy Director Pioneer & Labour
DMI	Director(ate) of Military Intelligence
FBGB	Forces Belges en Grand Bretagne
GIS	German Intelligence Service
GSO	General Staff Officer
HMT	His Majesty's Troopship
HOW	Home Office Warrant
H/TD	Head of Training & Development (SIS)
IB List	Investigation Branch (General Post Office)
IO	Intelligence Officer
IS9	Section of MI9
IVz	MI9 designation for J.M. Langley
ISOS	Intelligence Service Oliver Strachey
ISRB	Inter-Services Research Bureau (cover name for SOE)
JP	Justice of the Peace
KLM	Royal Dutch Airlines
KRRC	King's Royal Rifle Corps (British Army)
LAC	Leading Aircraftman (RAF)
LRC	London Reception Centre q.v. RVPS
MAP	Ministry of Aircraft Production
MI1a	Military Intelligence, Organization & Coordination
MI1x	Part of the War Office Directorate of Military Intelligence
MI6	British Secret Intelligence Service q.v. SIS
MI8	Radio Security Service (RSS)
MI9	British intelligence organization responsible for escape and evasion
MI14d	Sub-section responsible for compiling the German order of battle; formerly MI3b
MEF	Middle East Forces
MEW	Ministry of Economic Warfare
MPO	Military Permit Office
MSS	Most Secret Sources (ULTRA)
MTC	Motor Transport Corps
NLT	No living trace
NSA	National Security Agency (USA)
NT	No trace
OC	Officer Commanding
OSS	Office of Strategic Services (USA)
P.15	Sub-section of MI9

PAIR	OSS codename for ULTRA
PII	Public interest immunity
POW/PW	prisoner of war
POWAS	Prisoner-of-War Assistance Society
P&PO	Passport & Permit Office
PTC	put through the cards (vetted)
PWE	Political Warfare Executive
RAeC	Royal Aero Club
RAF	Royal Air Force
RAuxAF	Royal Auxiliary Air Force
RASC	Royal Army Service Corps
RCMP	Royal Canadian Mounted Police
RE	Royal Engineers (British Army)
REME	Royal Electrical & Mechanical Engineers (British Army)
RMS	Royal Mail Ship
RNVR	Royal Naval Volunteer Reserve
RVPS	Royal Victoria Patriotic School *q.v.* LRC
SCI	Special Counter-Intelligence (OSS) (104 SCI was a British unit)
Section V	SIS counterintelligence
SHAEF	Supreme Headquarters Allied Expeditionary Force
SIFE	Security Intelligence Far East
SIS	British Secret Intelligence Service *q.v.* MI6
SOE	Special Operations Executive
SPEARHEAD	Codename for OSS
SPU	Special Parachute Unit
STS	Special Training School
TD	Territorial Decoration
TDU	Torpedo Development Unit
TRE	Telecommunications Research Establishment
USAAF	United States Army Air Forces
USFET	US Forces, European Theater
VB5a	SIS sub-section
VCB	SIS section
VD	SIS sub-section dealing with Iberian Peninsula
VSSE	Veiligheid van der staat/Sûreté de l'État (Belgian Security Service)
WO	War Office
WPC	Women's Police Constable
WRNS	Women's Royal Naval Service

X-2	OSS Counterintelligence
ZB	Section of SIS
ZEBRA	OSS codename for Field Detachment 55 in Germany 1945

MI5 Sections

A6	Scientific analysis
ASCO	Assistant Security Control Officer
B1a	Special Agents
B1b	Espionage, Special Sources
B26	Section V, SIS (honorary MI5 section)
B4b	Espionage, Industry and Commerce
B6	'Watcher' Service
D4	Security and Travel Control: Security Control at Sea and Air Ports
D4a4	Exit Permits and Military Permits
D4b	Traffic Control and Security at Ports
DSO	Defence Security Officer
E2a	Finland, Poland, Baltic States
E2b	U.S. Citizens; Hungary & Balkan States (after 1943)
E7	Alien Control
F3	Fascists and right-wing organizations
RSLO	Regional Security Liaison Officer
SCO	Security Control Officer
SLA	Legal Section
SLB	Legal Section
SLO	Security Liaison Officer
WRC1d	War Room
WRCd	War Room

French Abbreviations

BCRA	Bureau Centrale de Renseignments et d'Action
BDOC	Bureau de Documentation
BSM	Bureau de Sécurité militaire
BST	Brigade de Surveillance du Territoire
DSDOC	Direction des Services de Documentation (or DSDoc)
FFC	Forces Françaises Combattantes
FFI	Forces Françaises de l'Intérieur
FNFL	Les Forces Navales Françaises Libres – Free French Naval Forces
FTPF	Francs-Tireurs et Partisans Français

FTP-MOI   Francs-Tireurs et Partisans Main-d'oeuvre imigrée
LVF   Légion des Volontaires Français
PPF   Parti Populaire Français
RGPP   Renseignements généraux de la prefecture de police parisienne
SCR   Section de Centralisation du Renseignement
SFIO   Section française de l'Internationale ouvrière (French Section of the Workers' International)
SRA   Service de Renseignements et d'Action
SSM   Service de sécurité militaire
TR   Travaux Ruraux

German Abbreviations

FAK   Frontaufklarungskommando (front reconnaissance [spy] command)
FAT   Frontaufklarungstrupp (front reconnaissance [spy] troop)
Fw.   Feldwebel (Sergeant)
GFP   Geheime feldpolizei
Hilfs Off   Auxilliary Officer
KO   Kriegsorganization
Korv.Kptn.   Korvettenkapitän (Lieutenant Commander, Kriegsmarine)
Leiter   Leader
MK   Meldekopf (Advanced message centre)
NSDAP   NationalSozialistische Deutsche ArbeiterPartei (National Socialist German Workers' Party) Nazi Party
O/Faehnr.   Oberfähnrich (Officer Cadet)
O/Gef.   Obergefreiter (Acting Corporal)
O/Lt.   Oberleutnant (Senior Lieutenant)
Obst/Lt.   Oberstleutnant (Lieutenant Colonel)
OKW   Oberkommando der Wehrmacht
RSHA   Reichssicherheitshauptamt (Reich Main Security Office)
Rittm.   Rittmeister (Captain, Cavalry)
SD   Sicherheitsdienst (SS intelligence service)
Sdf.   Sonderführer (Specialist Leader)
Sdf.Uffz.   Sonderführer Unteroffizier (Specialist Leader, NCO)
Sold.   Soldat (Soldier)
Studienrat   Educational councillor
Uffz.   Unteroffizier (NCO, Sergeant)
V-Mann   Vertrauensmänn or confidential person (pl. Männen)
V-Mannführer   Leader of V-Männen

Abwehr Abbreviations

Abt	Abteilung (Abwehr branch)
Abt IIIF	(Feind) Abteilung III F (Counter-espionage; penetration of enemy intelligence services; the largest and most important section)
Alst	Abwehrleitstelle (head Abwehr station)
Ast	Abwehrstelle (Abwehr station)
Nest	Nebenstelle (Abwehr sub-station)

Introduction

Of all the stories emerging from the Second World War, Stella Lonsdale's is a fascinating tale involving three marriages – the first, to a spurious White Russian prince; the second, to a playboy-turned-criminal involved in a major jewellery robbery in the heart of London's Mayfair in the late Thirties; finally, after the war, to another notorious criminal whom she had met earlier during the war, as well being romantically involved with a well-known former British Fascist. It was even claimed that she was an ex-mistress of Joachim von Ribbentrop, the German Foreign Minister (1938–45) while he was ambassador to Britain (1936–8), although this remains doubtful and unproven.

Some who encountered her described her as 'remarkable' and 'quite ravishing', while most were less enthusiastic:

'a woman whose loose living would make her an object of shame on any farm-yard';[1]

'a woman of no morals whatever, who frequently changed her lover and cared little as to his nationality';

'a very cheap specimen of a human being';

'she collects lovers as other people do postage stamps'; and

'the better class prostitute type'.

Sir David Petrie, the wartime Director General of MI5, said of her, 'She is utterly a-moral, sexually unbalanced, a glib and practised liar, unscrupulous in money matters, and selfish to the core … She is the type of person who would sell us to the Germans without a scruple.'[2]

All of these remarks derived from her notorious lifestyle of short-term relationships with a motley assortment of male suitors, all spiced with what one infers to be a risqué sex life. In today's apparent need for salacious news these relationships would certainly make the front pages of the tabloid press and social media, but during the war MI5 were too squeamish to include any of the sordid details in her files, so they must be left to our imagination!

When the Germans invaded France in May 1940 she stayed behind and lived in Nantes, a city on the Loire. Later, in Marseille she became involved with a major escape line established to help downed airmen, and soldiers stranded after Dunkirk to escape back to Britain. During this time, she claimed to be working for British Intelligence and the French Deuxième Bureau, but it was alleged that she had also worked for the Abwehr (German military intelligence). If so, did she betray anyone to them?

MI5 found inconsistencies in her story whenever she gave a statement. Facts emerged which either clarified or muddied the waters and were sometimes embellished for better effect; yet, at the same time, many others proved to be correct when checked against the interrogation reports of her associates. Was any of the intelligence that she had provided to British Intelligence believable or acted upon, or was it discounted as merely the boasting of a delusional woman? One key piece of intelligence was ignored in favour of that obtained from another dubious source which was considered more reliable. But whatever work she claimed to have done for British Intelligence had not been sanctioned by them. Was she really a spy, and if so, for whom, or was she simply a fantasist? The tall tales she recounted to MI5 caused them to believe that she was a pathological liar and to suspect that perhaps she *had* actually been working for the Abwehr, although it was never resolved entirely to their satisfaction, and for some historians, 'the jury is still out'.

One person who featured so prominently throughout her time in France was the mysterious RENÉ. Did he really exist, or was he, as some suggested, a composite of many characters? Was he committed to the Nazi ideology, or was he in fact, as they both claimed, really sympathetic to Britain? Stella went to great pains to conceal his identity, but later in this book his true identity will be revealed.

Until Matthew Sweet's *The West End Front* appeared in 2011 detailing the 'Wartime Secrets of London's Grand Hotels',[3] in which he devotes an entire chapter to Stella, very little had been recorded about her life. She doesn't even merit a mention in the two official histories of MI5,[4] and Guy Liddell makes only a few brief entries in his wartime diaries. With the release of her MI5 files to the National Archives at Kew in 2002, a whole new episode in the intriguing world of wartime intelligence has been opened up which begged to be explored further.

This book forms the final part of a trilogy conceived about three lesser-known women spies during the Second World War, the first about Mathilde Carré (*Double Agent Victoire*) and the second about Vera Eriksen (*The Beautiful Spy*). Each volume can be read in any order, or on its own, without reference to the others. Together they complement one another because, inevitably, some of the same familiar figures – MI5 officers, members of the Abwehr, and certain British, French and German agents – reappear in each volume. Together, they tell an intriguing account of how these three women dominated the resources of British Intelligence throughout the war in trying to get at the truth of their stories. And as we shall see, truth is often stranger than fiction.

David Tremain
Ottawa, 2021

Chapter 1

The Beginnings of a Covert Life

On 23 January 1942 there was a knock at the door of Stella Lonsdale's London flat. Special Branch officers had come to arrest her. She was taken to Holloway prison where she would rub shoulders with a quintet of other women spies – Mathilde Carré, Vera Eriksen, Mathilde Krafft, My Eriksson and the Duchesse de Château-Thierry – as well as others who had been supporters of Sir Oswald Mosley. What had led to her arrest and brought MI5 to charge her under Defence Regulation 18B (hostile associations) was a whole sequence of events, beginning with her life in France before and after the Occupation; her association with various individuals involved in an escape line; her friendship with an Abwehr intelligence officer; and her escape back to England, all of which caused them to suspect that there was more to her than met the eye.

* * *

Stella Lonsdale was born Stella Edith Howson Clive on 9 January 1913 at 42 Lyndon Road, Olton, Warwickshire, a suburb of Solihull, to Ernest Robert George Clive, a confectioner, who died in 1929 when she was 16 of an inflammation of the lungs, leaving her Lithuanian mother, Stella Howson Clive (*née* Allcock), the 'usufruct' of the entire estate for life,[1] meaning that Stella was dependent on her for financial support. During the Second World War her brother Dennis served as a Leading Aircraftman (LAC) in the operations room at RAF Bramscote near Nuneaton, Warwickshire, while another brother, John Norman Clive, suffered from dementia praecox. Her younger sister, Norah Janet Clive, lived at home with her mother at 44 Reservoir Road, Olton.

Of medium height (5 feet 7 inches), with dark brown hair and blue-grey eyes, she needed glasses for reading. Given her somewhat humble origins, for most of her adult life she inhabited the *demi-monde* of the upper-class – a world of Mayfair 'playboys', endless parties, loose living and a voracious appetite for sex, possibly bordering on nymphomania ('she is sex-fanatical') – and attracted a variety of unsavoury characters. She once told her sister-in-law, the actress Diana Vernon, 'And if you see your friend, tell him I am still looking for a nice clean man ... With French technique.' Men came and went with the frequency of a revolving door, falling for her sexual charms and tolerating her histrionics, even though her attentions to them were often short-lived and rarely reciprocated in equal measure. She lived for danger and derived vicarious pleasure from the thrill-seeking adventures in which she became involved.

In 1942 MI5's Legal Section (SLA) prepared 'a careful appreciation of Mrs. LONSDALE's character by a person who has had the distasteful task of listening to a great deal of her conversation':

> Owing to the fact that much of Mrs. LONSDALE's conversation cannot possibly be submitted in a report owing to its indescribably filthy nature, I am giving below a short summary of her character so far as I have been able to study it.
>
> (a) She is a liar of such convincingness as I would not have believed existed. Unless one had actually heard her make statements that appeared to bear every ring of truth, and then, shortly afterwards, gloating over the way in which she had put them over, one could have sworn that she was sincere. Even knowing her so well, there have been times when one has – against one's will – believed her, only to learn a little later that there was not a single grain of truth or honesty.
>
> (b) Her histrionic powers are of the first water. On one occasion she indulged in violent bouts of weeping and hysteria for an hour and a quarter that seemed to shake her whole being. When the man for whose benefit they were staged departed, within one minute – in fact, instantaneously – she was laughing and congratulating herself on the success of her act. Her emotions cannot be so much as skin deep.
>
> (c) She has an unshakable conviction that every man on earth finds her completely irresistible. This amounts to a virtual obsession, beside which Cleopatra and Helen of Troy fade into nothingness. That her husband has deserted her for another woman causes her constant and nagging pique.
>
> (d) The sole aim of her life is to amass as much money as possible, and she gives the impression that she would stick at nothing to achieve this. No sooner has she extracted money from one victim than she was discussing plans to get some from another. She is utterly unscrupulous and without loyalty. She probably has a certain careless generosity when it costs her nothing.

(e) Her mind is – simply and frankly – a cesspool. Without going into details, she held forth for 40 minutes on the difference in love-making of a Frenchman and an Englishman in terms that defy description. On another occasion she expatiated on the theme of animals. She apparently knows not the meaning of either decency or reticence. She is sex-fanatical.

(f) Trying to find some point in her favour, one can only say that she has a certain gaiety – though it is all directed to one end. In toto, she appears to be an utterly worthless character – unscrupulous, unbalanced, and wholly selfish.[2]

In 1930 Stella matriculated from the Royal High School for Girls, Warwick, whereupon she claimed to have been sent to London to be presented at Court. Given that she would have been 17 and considered too young – one had to be 18 to be a debutante and 'come out' – this seems highly unlikely.

Her mother made various attempts to marry her off, first to a journalist named Meredith, who may have been the financier and journalist, later RAF Wing Commander, Hubert Angelo Meredith.[3] However, this arrangement didn't suit Stella's plans; she was indifferent to him and had seen how unhappy her sister Norah was. There were also several alleged engagements, first in 1934 to Lord Cobham's son, Tony Littleton [sic] and the following year, when she was 22, to Lieutenant Derek McCardie with whom she spent the night before he went off to Suez prior to the Abyssinian crisis in 1935.[4] However, there do not appear to be any scions of the Viscounts Cobham branch of the Lyttleton family called Tony or Anthony, and the present Lord Cobham has confirmed that his father was not engaged to Stella Lonsdale.[5]

Mrs Clive was against Stella studying in London so she opted to spend two years studying commerce at the University of Birmingham before taking the Bachelor's exam. However, the University of Birmingham's Alumni office and the Cadbury Research Library have been unable to find any record of her being a student there, let alone graduating.[6]

With £25 she'd managed to save she bought a second-hand typewriter and set up the Phoenix Bureau, Typewriting and Copying, registered in the name of Stella Clive, at 1 Albert Street, Edgbaston, with the help of the first of a series of shady characters with whom she was to become associated – a 42-year-old Danish architect named Paul Christian Boeg Holme whom she had allegedly met in 1934 when she was 22.

Holme was born in Copenhagen on 10 October 1889 and first came to the United Kingdom in 1916.[7] In 1925 he began working as an agent for Danish Provision Merchants of 31 Castle Street, trading as Paul Holme & Co. and living at various addresses in Birmingham. Two other business ventures – a partnership with fellow Dane Henrik Edward Weis Soelberg, and the United Produce Company at 1 Albert Street, Edgbaston, the same address as Stella's company – both foundered. Since 13 March 1935 he was registered as living with Stella at 16 Beaufort Road, Edgbaston, and apparently engaged to her. But what he hadn't told her was that he was already married to a British-born woman named Nancy, from whom he was separated, having tried unsuccessfully to divorce her.

The work at the Phoenix Bureau came from solicitors and architects and before long Stella was making a profit of £30 a week, employing five people and three shorthand typists. This enabled her to move the business to 73 Colmore Row, but many of their suppliers of typewriters had difficulty in getting paid, which also became apparent when the business was sold in July 1935 for £300 and money was owing on them. One supplier even had to get a warrant of committal in default to get his money,[8] although another, while not always getting paid for goods supplied, found Holme to be 'honest and straightforward'! Stella later told the Abwehr that the reason she had sold her typing business was because it was affecting her eyesight too much and that she'd sold it for £2,500!

Stella's mother didn't approve of her daughter's relationship with Holme, so in 1936 she decamped to London, according to a statement given to Detective Sergeant Rhodes of Special Branch at New Scotland Yard on 10 January 1942. Prior to 1936 she had been living in an expensive boarding house at Bexhill-on-Sea, Sussex; exactly why or whether it was with Holme is unclear, but it may have been to escape their creditors. SLA's 1942 summary of the case noted, 'Though HOLME has maintained an interest in Mrs. LONSDALE down to the present time, it does not appear that they have lived together since 1936 at latest.'[9] In the meantime, Stella continued to have affairs with other men.

In 1937 Holme was still taking care of her debts and living at 32 Belsize Avenue, London NW3, working as the London manager for Eli Pearson & Company of Coventry, listed in 1929 as contractors of 33 King Street, Coventry. But by then the company was on the verge of bankruptcy. An advertisement appeared in the *Coventry Evening Telegraph* on 10 July 1937 offering for sale a variety of building materials, and a notice appeared in the *London Gazette* on 17 August dissolving the partnership. Holme told the police that he had known Stella Clive for many years and had become engaged to her, but then she'd gone off to Monte Carlo. At this time, he had incurred a debt on her behalf and was due to appear at Bow Street Magistrates' Court.

In March 1936 (later changed to September) Stella met the second of her ne'er-do-well men friends – a stateless White Russian named Nickolas

Sideroff @ Sederoff @ Warner @ Nicholas @ Prince Magaloff – at a seaside resort where she had gone to convalesce after receiving a kick in the stomach from a horse while out riding. Susan Barton, the cover name for Austrian-born Gisela Ashley, who worked in MI5's B1a, stated in 1941 that the couple were in Casablanca at one time, although no specific date was given, and a report from the Chief Constable for Warwickshire's office also stated that she had met Sideroff there.

Sideroff was born in Petrograd (now St. Petersburg) on 21 or 31 August 1914, the nephew of Vladimir Bashkiroff of the stockbroking firm Shields and Co. of New York founded in 1923.[10] Stella claimed that her mother knew his family as she was also Russian (some sources say Lithuanian). The Sideroffs were actually of Georgian nobility named Maghalashvili. This period of his life is full of inconsistencies. For example, at the age of 4 he accompanied his parents to America, and then in 1937 to France. However, this date cannot be correct for reasons which will shortly become apparent, and is possibly meant to be 1927 because on 24 February 1934 he was expelled from France.

The young Nickolas ran away from every school that he attended, resulting in his being sent to a reformatory school to mend his ways. Such was his bad behaviour that his mother refused to have anything to do with him. While in France he befriended a Roman Catholic bishop at Chambéry and stole several thousand francs from him,[11] resulting in a conviction and prison sentence. On his release he tried to travel back to America as a stowaway but was discovered and repatriated to France.

In December 1935 he allegedly stole a gold watch from a ship's captain, but to avoid being caught he stowed away on a ship at Cherbourg and travelled illegally to Southampton where he was refused leave to land by the immigration officer and failed to register with the immigration authorities as an alien. Somehow this illegal entry into Britain didn't come to the attention of the police until September 1938 when they received an anonymous tip-off, leading to his being charged in November with landing without the permission of an immigration officer and sentenced to two months' imprisonment. On 21 August 1939 he was fined twenty shillings (£1) for failing to notify the authorities of a change of address. Stella's file records that while he was in England he worked as an assistant to his uncle, L.W. Smith, who owned Irfé, a 'scent shop' at 45 Dover Street, in London's West End.

In November 1936 they travelled first to Paris, she as Miss Stella Clive, then on to Monte Carlo as Prince and Princess Magaloff, a name Sideroff claimed he'd borrowed from his mother Tania's second husband, Prince Magaloff. He also claimed to be the son of Prince Nikita Magaloff and Barbara Bachkiroff or Bashkiroff.[12] Travelling under this alias might help to explain how after his deportation from France in 1934 he was able to return there in 1936. While in Paris, on 21 November 1936 they stayed at the 'Hôtel Basle' (most likely the Hôtel Basile, 23, rue Godot de Mauroy in the 9th *arrondissement*) where Stella claimed to have met a German whom she would refer to as RENÉ, who would later play a significant rôle in her life. In December 1936 she and Sideroff were married in Monte Carlo on a boat just outside the three-mile limit. However, the marriage was later declared invalid since there had been only a religious ceremony, but no civil one, mandatory under French law.

As with everything in Stella's story, there were more inconsistencies: when they were both interrogated on 10 January 1942, she told that she had gone through a religious ceremony as Stella Clive and he as Prince Magaloff, whereas Sideroff told Rhodes that they were married in a church, *not* on a boat. She claimed that a man named Adamoff had first introduced her in Monte Carlo to RENÉ, but Sideroff said he'd met RENÉ in a bar on the Champs-Élysées the day after he'd arrived in France in 1936, along with his friends Adamoff and Jacques Chatelain. He also said that Stella had been secretary to the Hon. Arthur Wentworth Roebuck, KC, Attorney-General of Canada [*sic*] when he came to the UK for a meeting of the Privy Council, whereas Roebuck was actually Attorney-General of the province of Ontario from 1934–7.

As well as supposedly working for the *Encyclopedia Britannica*, from about February 1938 to May 1939 Stella claimed to have been the secretary to a Member of Parliament referred to in her file as 'Major Graham Gill' [*sic*] to whom she gave the codename 'Kommandant John Graham Gillam' in a letter dated simply 'Sunday' (7 September) sent from Marseille, and postmarked 9 September 1941, addressed to 'Mr Nicholas M.O.T.P.', the Cleveland Club, 87 Priory Road, London NW6. This was obviously Sideroff as she addresses him as 'Kaliouschka', one of her pet names for him. Elsewhere Gillam is referred to as John Graham Gillham, and by Sideroff as 'Graham Gill'. If this was Major John Graham Gillam, late of the Royal Army Service Corps (RASC), and author of *Gallipoli Diary* in 1918, there appears to be no record of his ever being a British Member of Parliament.[13] As reported in *The Times* on 10 February 1938, when Sideroff appeared in November 1938 at Marylebone Police Court, charged under the Aliens Order (1920), he claimed that Mr John Graham Gillam had offered him a job. It emerged that while in France he had also accumulated five convictions for unknown crimes and been sentenced to five months' imprisonment.

In spite of Stella having an annual allowance of £120 and Sideroff receiving one from his uncle, the couple still managed to get into debt owing to Sideroff's frequent gambling at the casinos. This resulted in their borrowing 3,661 francs from the British Consul in Nice, which Stella thought was sometime after their 'marriage'. When Holme found out about this, he repaid the debt, not realizing that Stella and Sideroff had 'married' in Monte Carlo, and thinking that he was still engaged to her. She also received a letter from the Foreign Office on 25 November 1941 requesting the repayment of 3,341.80 francs (£19.1s.4d) 'covering relief payments during the period August 1940 to November 1940', and whether she was prepared to refund amounts advanced by the US authorities.

Stella told Rhodes that when she had returned to England in February 1937 she was pregnant. Sideroff undertook to discharge a debt for her and accommodate them at his home at 87 Priory Road, London NW6 until the child was born. After that, they planned to send the child to New York to be taken care of by Bashkiroff's mother, and he would find employment with his uncle. She would also go to New York, obtain a divorce, then return to England and marry Holme. It seems callous and hypocritical that no sooner had the child been born than she should want to part with it so that she could continue her life unburdened by having to bring it up. That being said, with the impending war, it would have been safer for the child to be brought up in New York than London.

On 11 October 1937 Stella gave birth to a baby boy who was registered as Felix Nikita Karl Warner; his parents' names were given as Nicholas Noel Warner and Stella Edith Warner, the names under which they were living at that time. Sadly, the child died on 12 February 1938. Yet in spite of this being an illegal registration (and presumably also the death registration), the Director of Public Prosecutions decided to take no action against them. She later claimed that the baby's godfather was 'Prince Yourupoff' [*sic*], the man who shot Rasputin and involved in plotting his murder.[14] She must have meant Oxford-educated Prince Felix Felixovich Yusupov, also known as Count Sumarokov-Elston, who had married Princess Irina Alexandrovna, the niece of Tsar Nicholas II.[15] Yulia Dehn, the Tsarina's friend, described Yusupov as 'that effeminate and elegantly dressed young man' who had had a homosexual affair with Grand Duke Dmitri Pavlovich Romanov and had also been slapped by Rasputin for dressing up as a woman.[16]

Stella also claimed that Sideroff, his aunt Barbara Lithgow-Smith, Prince Felix and Princess Irina Yusupov had all come to London and set up a perfume business in Dover Street; that her own grandmother was a Russian princess, and that Sideroff's rich uncle in America was 'Prince Buiskarkoff' (Bashkiroff). The prince and princess came to London shortly after the October Revolution in 1917 and only stayed in London until 1920 when they went to Paris and lived there for the rest of their lives.[17]

An unnamed SIS source, referred to in a report dated 23 January 1945 from VB5a at SIS to Edward Cussen at MI5, confirmed that Magaloff (Sideroff) and Stella parted company in June 1939 'on amicable terms', although Stella kept in touch with him throughout the war. The source was an American woman who was married to a Frenchman whose house had been searched by 'MEGALOFF's gang' [*sic*]. Megaloff is reputed to have worked with members of the Carbone gang for the Marseille Gestapo.[18] However, it is questionable whether this was the same man with whom Stella associated, as apart from being a White Russian, his gambling, and his mother being associated with Elsa Schiaparelli, the famous fashion designer, Sideroff does not seem to have been the gang member type.

In May 1944 Sideroff applied to work for the BBC and required a security clearance from MI5. They declared that 'we do not want to have more discussion about her [Stella] than we can help'. J.L.S. Hale in SLA, the Legal Section added that:

> it occurs to me to suggest that perhaps Nicholas SIDEROFF's criminal record and general appalling disreputability is sufficient to disqualify him from any form of public service. He is a very poor degenerate type, quite incapable of anything except cards and dog racing, both of which things he is really quite good at, funnily enough. I personally would not have him in any show of any sort in which I had any concern.[19]

Chapter 2

The Mayfair Playboy

Exactly when Stella met her future husband, John Lonsdale, is unclear. She claimed it was while she was visiting Sideroff in Wandsworth prison, but Sideroff claimed to have introduced her to him at the Dorchester Hotel after his release from Wandsworth. John later thought that she'd gone to see him in prison.[1] She'd felt sorry for him and taken him fruit and books, as well as written to him. It was only when she was in hospital, and Sideroff had brought in a newspaper with an article about the robbery, that she'd found out about his crime. McLaren states in his book that it was at a party three years earlier,[2] but she told the Abwehr that she had known John since childhood.

John Christopher Mainwaring Lonsdale was a Mayfair playboy and 'born crook', born in Calgary, Alberta, on 22 October 1913 (according to Special Branch), although Stella claimed it to be on 24 October 1913 in Camberley, Surrey.[3] In 1942 Cyril Mills in B1a of MI5 stated that John had made a false claim on his application for a passport on 11 November 1939. John's mother, Georgina Beatrice Lonsdale, and father, John Claude Jardine Lonsdale, had immigrated to Canada in 1900 and 1908 respectively, and lived in Macleod, Alberta (now Fort Macleod). Lonsdale senior returned to England to serve in the 3rd Battalion, the Dorsetshire Regiment during the First World War. His family were partners in Glyn, Mills & Co., the bank handling all the remittances for the British Army, which became part of the Royal Bank of Scotland in 1969.

Like Sideroff, the younger Lonsdale appears to have had a misspent youth and was probably expelled from the many schools he attended: Pembroke Lodge School, Southborough, Hampshire; Aldenham School, Radlett, Hertfordshire; and finally Radley College, an English public school in Abingdon, Berkshire (now Oxfordshire) where he remained until he was sixteen. There is no evidence to support his claim that he studied for the Diplomatic Service in Lausanne, Munich, Paris, Berlin and San Sebastian. In about 1931, when he was 18, he returned to England (from where is unspecified). From August 1932 until about the beginning of 1933 he worked as a junior clerk with Messrs. A.T. Chendalls & Co., accountants at 115 Chancery Lane, London WC, but he found the work unsuitable and left 'with a good character'.

For someone so rebellious it seems strange that he should then have dabbled with a career in the armed services. On 4 March 1933 he enlisted in the King's Royal Rifle Corps (KRRC), but was 'bought out' by his father on 15 August 1933, still with a good character. Then on 7 November 1933 he joined the RAF as a short term pilot officer and was posted to No. 4 Flying Training School, Abu Seuir, Egypt, but his short service commission was terminated on 16 February 1934 when he overstayed his leave in Marseille, and for writing bad cheques.[4] While in Egypt his passport was impounded.

When he returned to the UK he worked as an advertising agent for the *Army, Navy and Air Force Gazette*. On 21 June 1934 he enlisted in his father's old regiment under the name 'J. Trevilian' (or 'Trevelyan'), but deserted two months later. Someone named Dennis Trevelyan had been a boarder at Pembroke Lodge School in 1911, which is possibly where he had borrowed the name, but changed the spelling. After leaving the army he worked for about sixteen months as a canvasser for the National League of Airmen at 2 Norfolk Street, in the Strand. He also formed two companies – Lonsdale and Churchill,[5] and Cumulus Pictures Ltd. – which were likely bogus, and were liquidated as there was no business. He then joined General Franco's Foreign Legion in Spain. MI5 thought it likely that he was engaged in arms deals for Franco and the Finnish government (see Chapter 28).

In April 1936 he was involved in a slander suit when 20-year-old 'society girl' Pamela Blake, the daughter of socialite Lady Twysden (Mary Duff Sterling, the muse for Ernest Hemingway's Brett Ashley in *The Sun Also Rises*), spread a rumour that he had contracted venereal disease. He won the case and was awarded £500 damages, but it cost him his engagement to Miss Evelyne Wolseley, daughter of Mr and Mrs Mervyn Wolseley of Sutton Park, Guildford. Ironically, the judge in the case was Lord Chief Justice Hewart, who would confront him again two years later.

While in France in 1937 he was accused of defrauding Czech Rudolf Slavik, the head bartender at the Hotel Georges V, of 1,000 francs.[6] Later that year, on 20 December, he and three other Mayfair 'playboys' – David Wilmer, aged 25, Robert Paul Harley, aged 26, and Peter Martin Jenkins, aged just 21 – lured Étienne Bellenger, the manager of the London branch of Cartier to the Hyde Park Hotel, attacked and robbed him of diamond rings worth £13,000–£16,000, today worth roughly a million pounds. Bellenger was found lying on his back in a pool of blood by Henrietta Gordon, a housemaid at the hotel, and waiter Enrico Laurenti who had come to her assistance and unlocked the door with his master key. The following day the four were arrested in Oxford, with only Lonsdale receiving bail set at £1,000.

All were ex-public schoolboys, from well-to-do families: Wilmer was the son of Brigadier Eric Randle Gordon Wilmer, and educated at Oundle; Harley was the son of a much-decorated army officer, the late Brigadier Henry Kellett Harley and the Hon. Margaret Holland, and educated at Wellington; Jenkins was educated at Harrow, whose father was a wealthy wool merchant and part of Cobb & Jenkins of 11 Great Marlborough Street, London, specializing in ladies' woollens.

Their trial in Court Number One at the Old Bailey, which began on 15 February 1938, was a media sensation and attracted much public attention, with the likes of the Duke of Rutland, Viscount Byng of Vimy, and Lord and Lady Asquith in attendance. The judge, Lord Chief Justice Hewart, declared: 'Each of you, with the exception of Lonsdale, might, but for a small accident, have been indicted here on a charge of murder.' Their sentences were severe: Harley received the stiffest – seven years' hard labour plus twenty strokes of the cat-o'-nine-tails because he had beaten Bellenger over the skull with a 'blackjack' or 'life saver' (something like a cosh). He liked to think of himself as a tough gangster and retained his tough guy image and smiled cynically at the court as he turned and left the dock.[7] Wilmer received five years' hard labour and fifteen strokes, and broke down and 'wept like a child'; Jenkins three years and no strokes; and Lonsdale eighteen months' hard labour for his part as the driver.[8]

Wilmer's punishment provoked George Bernard Shaw to comment, 'sadists and flagello-maniacs who are making the offender's vice an excuse for gratifying their own peculiar form of it on the one hand, and the sympathetic amorists on the other.'[9] During this time John was also under investigation by the French for fraudulently obtaining a diamond ring valued at 85,000 francs from Parisian jeweler Élie Lévy. He had been released on bail, but had fled to England before he could be rearrested.[10] After the war in 1945 Wilmer married heiress Pamela Joyce Phillimore. In his post-war diary entry for 11 November 1947 Guy Liddell, the Director of MI5's B Division, reported that 'ZIG ZAG [Eddie Chapman] is working with WILMER, one of the ex-Mayfair boys'.[11] Jenkins, thought to have served in the Royal Signals, deserted from the army.[12]

When John Lonsdale left Wandsworth prison in 1939, he proposed to Stella and she accepted 'on the spur of the moment'. They were married on 14 July 1939 at Kensington Registry Office, followed by a religious ceremony at Brompton Oratory on 4 August. Sideroff had tried to prevent it, claiming that *he* had married her in Monte Carlo, but Stella denied it. In any case, his claim was moot as that marriage had been declared invalid under French law. Her mother had tried to talk her out of it, but 'she did marry him without any consent from myself and, in fact, without my knowledge ... I was rather upset over this, and even up to the present time I have not met Lonsdale, my son-in-law'.[13]

* * *

Two days after Britain declared war on Germany John enlisted in the Royal Engineers and Stella did not see him again until his embarkation leave in early December. While he was away, she lived with Sideroff: on 29 September 1939 she is shown as living at 41 Tavistock Square, St. Pancras, London, WC1 as a 'secretary typist commercial'; in October at 63 Westbourne Court, London, W2. During that time John wrote to New Scotland Yard accusing Sideroff of blackmailing her, although Stella denied it. As MI5 noted, 'If any weight is to be attached to Mrs. LONSDALE's confession (or boast) that SIDEROFF was present on the night of her wedding, obviously anything is possible in this milieu.'[14] (Stella later told MI5 that on her wedding night she had found herself in bed with John on one side and Sideroff on the other.) Sheer braggodocio perhaps, but it had given rise to the 'farm-yard' comment coined by Susan Barton. John had also known about her relationship with Holme, which had caused many quarrels and enmity between them, so it is unlikely that he would have tolerated Sideroff any differently.

When John returned home on embarkation leave from the BEF he accompanied Stella to the Passport and Permit Office (P&PO) on 11 December so that she could apply for a passport and an exit permit 'for the purpose of visiting my mother-in-law who is resident in Paris' who was supposedly ill and about to undergo an operation. They referred her to the War Office. When she later returned to the P&PO she had with her a letter dated 2 January 1940 signed by Lord Cobham saying that 'the Director of Movements has now ruled that, in the special circumstances of your case, there is no objection'.[15]

Shortly before Christmas John left for France and was posted to the 2nd Base Sub Area of HQ South District, British Expeditionary Force (BEF) in Nantes. Stella's passport was issued on 9 January 1940 and she sailed from Southampton on the 12th, landing at Le Havre the following day. Cyril Mills of MI5's B1a stated that she had made a false claim on her application about not having a previous passport which had been verified by Jasper Jocelyn John Addis, solicitor at 27 Old Bond Street. Leonard Burt, the Special Branch superintendent attached to MI5's B5, wrote that Leslie Crane, Addis's managing clerk, was 'as you know a shady solicitor, in collecting debts from undesirable people connected with the club life in London',[16] and had a dubious association with John Lonsdale. At the general election in 1929

Addis contested the Limehouse constituency as the Liberal candidate against Clement Atlee; in 1933 he was declared bankrupt; in 1936 divorced from his wife, Hilda Agnes Wadnow, on account of her adultery; struck off as a solicitor in 1947; and in 1954 with George Dawson bound over to keep the peace in the sum of £10, and also jailed for two years for fraud.

When Stella arrived at her mother-in-law's flat in Paris at 33, rue Delambre, Montparnasse (now the Hôtel des Bains) she found that '[she] was very glad to see me and very sweet to me', but her best friend, American Nina Conrad, who lived at the Hôtel Lenox in the rue de l'Université (now the Hôtel Lenox Montparnasse, 15 rue Delambre), was staying with her so Stella's presence was unnecessary. 'I seem to be rather de trop,' she remarked.[17]

On 21 January Stella arrived in Nantes and stayed at the Hôtel Moreau in the rue de Gigant. A shortage of money forced her to borrow 2,000 francs from Major Gordon of the Pioneer Corps (of more later). She later told Cyril Mills that she did not have a bank account at that time and was living on her army allowance of thirty shillings, but was really 17/6d, with John making up the difference, and supplemented by his grandmother 'Little Gran', who gave her a total of £60.

On 19 November 1941 MI5's Helenus 'Buster' Milmo interviewed Captain John Wilfred Murray, then serving with the 37th Independent Infantry Brigade Home Forces as a Roman Catholic chaplain, about Stella. At John's suggestion, Father Murray had been the priest who had given her religious instruction and had formed a very high opinion of her intellectual capabilities in understanding complicated theological concepts. Murray stressed that there had been no impropriety between her and Major Gordon. Yet in spite of his reservations – he thought there was something very strange about her – Gordon had persuaded him to accept her into the Roman Catholic Church. He also recalled Stella buying a revolver (in May 1940 when 'everyone was getting very excited') which Gordon had insisted she hand over to him, but before he left Nantes, he returned it to her.

John's commanding officer, Colonel Edward Brydges Willyams, regarded Stella as a nuisance and several times tried to get rid of her by encouraging her to return to England, but she insisted that if she did, her former 'husband' (Sideroff) in England would pour his attentions on her, which she would be unable to resist. So, in spite of Willyams' exhortations, she stayed in Nantes until the Germans occupied the town, with Sapper Lonsdale being posted back to England in March 1940.

When General Otto von Stülpnagel's Second Army marched into Nantes on 19 June 1940 they were, to quote an MI5 report, 'given a disgustingly favourable reception on entering the town. The population, or a large proportion of it, were ready and willing to work for the Germans and consequently one had to be very careful'.[18] As she would explain to the Advisory Committee in 1944, by 24 June 1940 the English had gone: 'Everyone was in an awful turmoil, no one knew what to believe among the people I knew.' The vice-consul at the consulate told her that he would let her know what could be done, so she returned to her lodgings where she was staying with Madame Claire Dugast and her son Michel. The three of them went to the Café de Commerce in the Place Royale. There she was confronted by a Polish engineer, Olgierd Około-Kułak, who'd recognized the Polish eagle she was wearing in her lapel, given to her by an unnamed friend, and spoke a language she didn't understand. When she explained she wasn't Polish but English he asked how she proposed getting back to England, saying: 'I am the Chief Engineer on some ship or other, my ship is in the port now. I am sure if I asked the captain he would be agreeable to giving you a passage back to England because we are going this evening.'[19] He insisted he would only take her and that she should not to tell the consul, nor Albert Jolivet in charge of the Aliens Department of the police in Nantes, nor the priest.

His ship, the 1,942-ton steamship MV *Lewant*, was part of a convoy which sailed from Saint-Nazaire on Tuesday 18 June. Stella was therefore mistaken about 24 June being the date when she met him.[20] She and Claire Dugast were suspicious of Około-Kułak and went away to discuss his offer with Claire's husband, Marcel, promising to give him an answer. Claire warned her not to go on a ship with a complete stranger as he may or may not be genuine, and might not even be going to England. Besides, John would be very annoyed should anything happen to her. Instead, they offered to take her with them to Biarritz, where they had a business, and she could stay with them for as long as necessary.

Why Około-Kułak should have singled out Stella for exfiltration and no one else has never been explained satisfactorily, nor why he was so emphatic that she should tell no one else. It seems too simplistic to accept that it was a chance encounter based merely on her wearing a Polish eagle brooch and that she was in some way sympathetic to the Poles. Had he perhaps been instructed by the Polish TUDOR network in France to arrange for her exfiltration? If so, had she or John made some connection, or had dealings, with them?

Stella's statement to Rhodes in January 1942 about not leaving with Około-Kułak, and the story she would tell the Advisory Committee in 1944 about the Dugasts' offer that she accompany them to Biarritz, were in direct contrast to Marcel Dugast's statement to the French authorities in 1944. In 1944 Stella explained to the Advisory Committee, 'As it happened this fellow was a perfectly honourable man and did go back to England and did post my letter which was received and I could have gone with him and should have been perfectly all right.' In hindsight, she said she 'would have jumped at the chance and gone with him but at that time I was in a more conventional state of mind and did not want to go with someone who would not even let me tell the priest I was going'.

On 8 August 1940 Około-Kułak wrote to Stella enquiring whether she had reached England safely, saying that 'it is a great pity that you didn't come on our ship.' He asked that she write to him at the following address: Mr Olgierd Około-Kułak, M.V. *Lewant*, c/o Messrs. R.F. Sanderson & Co., 8 Peter Street, Manchester.[21] He also wrote to her mother from Manchester on 13 August 1940, this time giving his address as c/o The Polish Steamship Ag. Ltd., Plantation House, Fenchurch Street, London, EC3:

Dear Mrs Lonsdale [*sic*],
It is really a great pity that your daughter did not arrived at England [*sic*] yet. The last time I saw her was at Nantes in the evening on 17th of June. She was quite well and healthy and as far as I know she have had money [*sic*], but she told me that she is expecting some more.

The situation on this evening was very serious and I was afraid that your daughter may fall into enemy hands, so I tried to persuade her to come to England on Polish ship at which I am officer [*sic*]. But Mrs Stella was very optimistic about the actual situation and refused my proposal because on advice of Mr and Mrs Dugast then your daughter wrote to letters [*sic*] – one to you and the second to her husband would leave one day later your daughter would decide to come on it to England because the situation was becoming worse every minute.

Those letters I took and posted them after coming to this country. As far as I know Mrs Stella intended to go to Biarritz and I think that she has gone there after my departure from Nantes.

So let's hope that she managed to get to Spain and Portugal and after she may come to England.

The main cause why Mrs Stella didn't want to come on our ship was that she thought that her husband is still in France.

In any case Mrs Stella considered possibility of departure to England and consulted the British Consul about it on the 17th of June in the morning.

I think that if our ship would leave one day later your daughter would decide to come on it to England because the situation was becoming worse every minute.

I am really sorry that neither I nor the Captain of our ship failed in persuading Mrs Stella to come on our ship. But I am sure that so an intelligent and enterprising a person as Mrs Stella is, was able to leave Nantes southwards before the enemy occupied this town or if not she is now in unoccupied territory of France.

I am sorry but this is all what I can say about my last seeing of your daughter.

I thank you very much for your letter and please be so kind to inform me after receiving news from your daughter.[22]

Chapter 3

'Some Interesting Work'

John Lonsdale returned to France in April 1940 for a fortnight of duty and leave, hoping to transfer to the Deuxième Bureau. When he was interviewed by John Masterman of MI5's B1a on 10 January 1942,[1] Corporal Lonsdale told him that Louis Simon, a commissioner of police who was well known for his work during the First World War, had suggested that he and Stella work for them, a fact Stella also claimed later.[2] She had written to Lord Cobham at the War Office on his behalf, but in the end all it did was cause John to be arrested.

Before he'd left Nantes, John said that a White Russian 'of considerable wealth' whom Stella had known in Paris or Monte Carlo in 1936, referred to only as Loschenski (first name thought to be Nicholas) had contacted her; he'd shown up as a taxi driver and offered her a large sum of money to engage in espionage. She thought he was one of Sideroff's friends, but stressed to MI5 that although she'd met him on five occasions, he was not her lover. The first time she'd met him he'd been shabbily dressed, but after the Occupation he was smartly dressed, so she assumed he must be a fifth columnist. She would later deny meeting him earlier, as well as being pretty certain that John had never met him. John added that Stella was fascinated with espionage, but had warned her not to get involved. It was only when Loschenski had told her that one day the Germans would fight Russia and take it back for the White Russians that she decided to have nothing more to do with him. He'd also told her that he'd served in the French Army, but she didn't think he'd had anything to do with the Deuxième Bureau, and denied that he'd asked her to spy for the French against the Germans. Both she and MI5 believed that he was working for the Germans.

John's passport application and the false birthplace he had given resulted in his having to get a certificate from Canada House to correct it, thinking that Camberley was his sister's birthplace, where his father had been stationed at the time.

Stella's letter, given to Olgierd Około-Kułak to post to her mother, said that 'she was doing some interesting work which she would only be able to tell her about after the war', a reference to the position she'd been offered at the Berlitz School and *not*, she insisted to Rhodes, intelligence work. Her mother told Detective Sergeant Buckley that 'I don't know exactly what my daughter is doing but I surmise that she is working in some secret job, probably for the Secret Service'. An unnamed report, most likely by Cyril Mills, was at pains to stress that she was *not* working for either French or British Intelligence:

> She is unable to offer any satisfactory explanation either for staying on in Nantes when her husband went home or for remaining there when the Germans were immediately threatening the town. It is known that two days before the occupation she was offered, and refused, a passage home. About this time she wrote to her mother hinting that she was engaged in secret service work.³

On 12 January 1942 Mills wrote to Major G.P. Wethered, the MI5 Security Control Officer (SCO) in Birmingham, on behalf of Tar Robertson, saying that Stella had

> admitted to having pretended to work for the German Intelligence Service, but says that she did not begin to do so until early 1941. She was not working for S.I.S. in 1940 and I am therefore particularly anxious to know what was the interesting job to which she referred. She has admitted writing the letter referred to but has denied the statement about the interesting job.⁴

When Mills asked her about that letter on 4 February 1942, she became agitated and very uncomfortable, unable to explain it, then admitted that she'd written it 'because she felt everybody in England was doing war work and she wanted to reassure her mother that she was doing something too'. He asserted that 'We have the best possible reasons for believing that her letter was written on the 16th, 17th or 18th June 1940'. At the bottom of his report he added:

> At this point MICHAEL was told that we had now proved that the letter which she wrote to her mother mentioning her interesting work was written before the German occupation, brought to this country and posted by the Polish ship's officer. She made absolutely no attempt to deny it and adopted an attitude of resignation to the fact that she had been found out. This letter was referred to three times during the interrogation and only at the third mention did Michael make any attempt to explain it away. She was told that her attempt was only pathetic.⁵

When Milmo asked Captain Murray during his interview whether there had been any Poles in the town, he didn't remember any. While not ruling out the possibility, he felt sure that he would have remembered had there been any. He stated that Stella had spun him a yarn about John working for the British

Secret Service and the French Deuxième Bureau. He was also aware of her friendship with a Madame Simon, her landlady, who lived near the Salle des Fêtes, who he believed worked for the Deuxième Bureau and must have been Louis Simon's wife.

John wrote a letter[6] dated 25 November 1940 to Stella's mother from his post at the 24th Bomb Disposal Section, Royal Engineers, 48 Wickham Road, Beckenham, Kent, expressing his bitterness about how she had allegedly treated Stella, and enclosed an undated letter from two soldiers Stella had helped to escape – Privates A. Bibby and G. Ritson of HQ Company (Cooks), 4th Battalion, the Border Regiment, Kington, Herefordshire:

> Dear Mrs S. Lonsdale,
> We are so sorry that we could not write before as we lost your Address and we could not find your Husband at Folkstone House but we have come across your Address by a bit of luck and we certainly thank you for what you did for us in France as we would have never got back but for you. We had a rough time after we left you as we were Bombed and sunk but we were lucky enough to be Picked up again and brought back to St. Nazair [sic] were we got a car to Bordeaux after a two day's travel where we came across a Major who took us to Bayone and we caught the last Boat to England.[sic] We certainly hope you arrived save and sound and that your Husband is in the best of Health as you was a real Nightingale to us and we cannot find words to thank you but we will never forget you as long as we live and that goe's for our Familys' to who also sends there sincere thanks from the Bottom of there Hearts. [sic]
>
> Well we will have to close now hoping this letter find's you in good health and Spirite and hoping to hear from you and your Husband so Thanks once again and Goodluck for the Future and if ever we can do anything for you just name it and we will try our utmost to do it anytime. [sic].
>
> Forever Your Sincere Friends,
> A. Bibby & G. Ritson[7]

The two squaddies were subsequently identified in 1942 by Major Sir Rupert Malise Speir, the RSLO in York, as Private Amos Bibby (army number 3600569), 3rd Maritime AA Battery, Royal Artillery, whose headquarters were at Easby House, Preston, North Shields, Co. Durham; and Corporal George Ritson (army number 3601329), 4th Battalion, The Border Regiment, stationed in the Middle East.[8]

John followed up with another letter on 5 December from the Cheyne Hospital for Children, Cheyne Walk, London, SW3:

My dear Mrs. Clive,

You should by now have received my telegram with the wonderful news of Stella.

The Foreign Office rang up yesterday and told me that she is still living in the same flat in the Place Royale in Nantes with a charming doctor and his wife, that she is well and in receipt of a small allowance from the American consul. As a special favour, I was allowed to send her a short message, but am going to the F.O. shortly to see a friend there who is going to arrange for letters to be sent to her. Please let me know whether it is permitted to send her money over and above what she receives from the consul, but shall find out and will let you know how Little Gran has often tried to get funds through to her, but, up till now, without success. However, lets [*sic*] hope that now it will be possible.

Just one more thing, do lets [*sic*] forget that there has ever been any disagreement between us. After all, we both love Stella so much and all that matters is her happiness.

Yours sincerely,
John Lonsdale

P.S. I was told not to try to get in touch with her direct and ask you not to try either until I hear from the F.O.[9]

The telegram, postmarked 4 December 1940, confirmed that Stella was still in Nantes during November and December: 'STELLA SAFE IN NANTES MESSAGE RECEIVED FOREIGN OFFICE JOHN.' Yet in spite of warning Stella not to get involved in espionage, John had a scheme whereby the pair of them should work together as agents for the Deuxième Bureau and travel to Switzerland where he knew certain German shipping agents, such as Hermann Zollinger of Zurich,[10] and a Dr Stiehl and his business partner, Brennwald. Milmo reported that

> [ab]out a month after John LONSDALE had returned to England he turned up [in] Nantes in civilian clothes. There was an emotional meeting between [them? and] after a week he disappeared and Captain Murray found STELLA [*half a line missing*] [John L]ONSDALE had wanted her to go with him to Switzerland on the mission proposed by the Deuxième Bureau but she had refused as she had not felt up to it. The plan of action was of the Philip OPPENHEIMER variety in which she was to quarrel with her husband and then fall into the waiting arms of the German ship-owners from whom information was to be extracted.[11]

Chapter 4

Capture and Recruitment

There are varying accounts of how Stella was captured by the Germans. She told Detective Sergeant Rhodes at New Scotland Yard on 14 January 1942 that on the day of the Germans' arrival in Nantes (19 June 1940) she had taken a job as an English language teacher at the Berlitz Language School offered to her by Monsieur Martineau, the local manager. Her presence at the school attracted 'the attentions of various Germans who, although they spoke English well came to her for lessons and whom she says were spying on her'.[1] She always refused, saying that because her husband was a British soldier she couldn't possibly go out with the enemy.

One such admirer was Oswald Bendemann, a professor who spoke English fluently and didn't need any lessons. He'd flirted with her and tried to convert her to National Socialism as well as trying to get her to share a bottle of champagne with him.[2] By the middle of August, when she still hadn't fallen for his charms, he abandoned her. She later learned from Karl Meissner that he had been sent by the Gestapo as an *agent provocateur*.

On 23 October 1940, a few minutes after leaving the US Consulate in Nantes, Stella was arrested and charged with espionage. She'd gone there to see the consul, Hassell H. Dick, about a plan of the underground petrol dump at Sainte-Luce-sur-Loire obtained from Jean Platiau – 'an effeminate little Frenchman … not normal and having the mannerisms of a pervert', as well as 'pansyish', who came to the Berlitz School. However, Dick refused to forward the plan to British Intelligence. She later claimed that 'Samson' (who has not been identified) had given it to her, as well as being mistaken about the date of her arrest, which she had originally said was 23 November 1940.

She was taken to the headquarters of Abwehrstelle Angers at 1, Avenue du Maréchal Pétain, the local German intelligence station and headquarters of German Intelligence for northwestern France, where she was interrogated by Oberstleutnant (Lieutenant Colonel) Friedrich 'Fritz' Dernbach whom she described as a cad and a bully, and the stereotypical caricature of a German she'd seen in *Punch*: 'very, very ugly and very rough in his manner', who frightened her and shouted at her a lot.[3]

Dernbach was about 48, of medium build and thickset, height about 5 foot 7 inches (1.7m), dark hair going bald, brown eyes, broad face, healthy complexion and clean-shaven, somewhat coarse and clumsy in appearance, tending to be 'negligent in his dress, but inclined to dress showily', and having a loud, coarse voice.[4] He had been brought in from Oslo to become *Leiter* III-F (head of counter-espionage) when Ast Angers was established in the summer of 1940,[5] to organize their activities in Brittany, Anjou and Normandy west of the Seine. He was 'one of the leading men in German counterintelligence in France from the early days of the occupation until the German armies were driven out in August 1944, and after that was active in Western Germany until March 1945'.[6] In April 1941 he was transferred to Ast Lyons. The SLA summary of the case described him as

> a particularly foul brute who has achieved considerable success in counter-espionage by his bullying methods against small fry and people who can be shouted into submission. DIRNBACH [sic] roared at Mrs. LONSDALE, accusing her of being a de Gaullist. Eventually he snatched at her bag and found the plan of the Sainte Luce petrol installation.[7]

He immediately took the plan down to Karl Meissner, *Leiter* of Ast Angers. Even though he seldom saw prisoners Meissner had Stella brought to him. In complete contrast to Dernbach, he was apologetic and charming. Also present was RENÉ, dressed in plain clothes, a man she claimed to have met socially in Paris in 1936, but he gave no indication that he recognized her. His significance and true identity will become apparent as her story unfolds (see Chapter 9). She explained to Meissner that a stranger, who had recognized her as being English, had come up to her in the street and handed her the plan, saying that the British would be interested in it. But Meissner did not accept such a feeble excuse and turned her back over to Dernbach who put her in prison.

Freegattenkapitän (Commander) Karl Robert Johannes (or Johannes Robert Carl) Meissner @ Hans @ Peter, was born in Dresden on 20 February 1895 (a declassified CIA report gives the year as about 1893). He was 5 foot 11 inches (1.8m), with a heavy build and oval face, large nose, fresh complexion, grey-blond hair and partly bald, with piercing blue eyes. After a First World War career as an Oberleutnant zur See (sub-lieutenant) and a submarine commander, he was recalled to active service in September 1933 and trained in signals. In 1935 he was recruited by a friend, Freegattenkapitän Ruge of Ast Kiel, and posted as III-F and III-L to Nest Swinemünde with the rank of Kapitänleutnant (lieutenant).

In 1938 he was posted to Abwehr headquarters at Tirpitzufer 80 in Berlin as assistant to Oberst (Colonel) Joachim Rohleder, *Gruppenleiter* III-F, and listed as being *Leiter* of III-F1, dealing with France, Belgium and Holland,[8] and a good friend of Admiral Canaris, head of the Abwehr, which may explain how he had been appointed to that position. Meissner's MI5 file mentions that 'MEISNER [*sic*] took every opportunity of travelling to Berlin and on these occasions was always received by the Admiral'. He was in Norway in III-F as *Gruppenleiter* III of Ast Oslo, shortly after Dernbach arrived in March 1940 but was apparently removed owing to a dispute with Oberst (Colonel, later General) Erich Buchenhagen, and posted to Ast Angers in June 1940 where he remained until November 1941, according to Edward Blanchard Stamp of WRC1a, writing on 10 June 1945.

A note from WRC1d (MI5's War Room) dated 19 June 1945 states that, 'The earliest trace on MEISSNER whose PAIR cover-name was PETER shows him at Brest on 21.6.40. By the end of that month he was reported as Leiter Ast Oslo … In February 1941 he was reported as Leiter Ast Angers'.[9] A confidential CIA report on the interrogation of Oberstleutnant Friederich Dernbach lists Meissner as being *Leiter* III-F of Ast Angers from August 1940 to July 1941 and exclusive of III-F.[10]

Meissner's MI5 file records him meeting Stella in Angers, whom he described as 'an unsatisfactory English woman', as well as recruiting Vera Eriksen, whom he had first met in Copenhagen in 1940.[11] In June 1941 he was promoted and moved to Ast Paris to take control of counter-espionage for the whole of France until his move to Bern, Switzerland, in March 1942 as *Leiter* KO (Kriegsorganization) under cover of the Consulate-General, succeeding Oberstleutnant Waag. In May 1945 he was captured by the Americans and held in Milan by G-2, IV Corps, US Army, before being sent to England for interrogation at Camp 020.[12] Stella later alleged to MI5 that her meeting with him was on 2 April 1941, which cannot be correct as she was arrested in either October/November 1940:

> Stella Lonsdale (B.1.b Case) came into contact with MEISSNER who had her imprisoned. RENÉ, assistant to MEISSNER persuaded his Chief to release her and she was supposed to work for the G.I.S. She escaped from Angers into unoccupied France. MEISSNER told Stella LONSDALE that he was operating certain British Wireless sets and was transmitting a considerable amount of true information in order to keep the "sets" alive.[13]

MI5 recorded that 'N.B. Stella LONSDALE's information is not considered reliable'.

Conditions in the prison were appalling and she was forced to sleep on the floor of her cell – there was no bed or pillows, and only two thin, dirty blankets which were taken away from her at 5.30 every morning. Nor did she get much sleep as she was woken up every hour. The food was inadequate and disgusting, and she was given no soap, towel, comb or brush. Except for ten minutes' exercise every day, she was confined to her cell. To intimidate her, Dernbach sent in 'a physically revolting little Bavarian' guard several times a day to exhibit bullets and play-act the drill of a firing squad. At first it didn't bother her, but later it got on her nerves. She later claimed to MI5 that while in prison she kept a loaded revolver wrapped in cottonwool under an elastic suspender belt in the small of her back as the Germans had never searched her properly, which seems highly improbable. Indeed, Nina Myers, the woman MI5 would later place to live with her, disputed this story and told Cyril Mills that she thought Stella had invented it to make the Germans seem incompetent.

On Christmas Day Stella was brought to Dernbach's office where she found him drunk and his secretary, Charlotte-Louise Rieth, on his knee. He ranted and roared at her and stubbed out his cigarette on her forehead. Later he was reprimanded, not so much for his behaviour that day, but because it had upset preparations for the military tribunal before which she was shortly due to appear. RENÉ visited her in prison after Christmas and prior to the tribunal, offering to help her as much as he could and saying that he was 'all for your people'.

The tribunal rejected her story of how she had come to possess the plans and she was returned to prison. RENÉ informed her that she would be shot as a spy but had managed to persuade Meissner to try to get her to work for them and had arranged another tribunal. Before the second tribunal Meissner personally delivered to her a parcel of toiletries and told her that he believed her story. If she worked for them, she could make a lot of money, and he offered to pay her in pounds sterling or dollars instead of French francs. She didn't readily agree to his proposition, but nor was she horrified by it. He also made sure that she was given special privileges and better food.

During the last week of January 1941 RENÉ collected her in his car and instructed her how she should behave and how to answer the second tribunal's questions. He confided that he hated Hitler and had influenced two members of the tribunal in her favour. If she were to agree to work for the Germans, she had three choices: (a) to genuinely work for them, (b) to escape, or (c) to double-cross them.

The tribunal delivered a verdict in her favour and she agreed to work for the Germans. After her release she was taken to a room at the Hôtel de France near Angers railway station. All her expenses were paid and she was given 50,000 francs, but she returned all but 10,000 francs saying that she didn't need the rest. Meissner met with her on an almost daily basis and suggested that they work together, but she refused because of the difficulty of double-crossing if she had a partner. All this time RENÉ remained in the shadows.

Throughout her later interrogations by MI5 she steadfastly refused to disclose RENÉ's true identity. At one point she alleged to MI9's 'Jimmy' Langley[14] that his first name was Raoul, aged 29, that he had been born in France, educated at Oxford University and in America, spoke fifteen languages, had worked as a lawyer in Paris, was a *Graf* (count), owned land in America; was a *Hauptmann* (captain) in the Abwehr, pro-British and had important information which he wished her to pass on to them. However, on 15 January 1942 Susan Barton reported that 'MICHAEL said that she never stated definitely that RENÉ had been to Oxford and she certainly never said that he had been to College there'. She thought that it was an attempt to mislead them about his identity.[15]

The timing of the second tribunal means that MI5's report that Stella was in prison from November 1940 until February 1941 is correct,[16] and concurs with her statement to the Abwehr in January 1941, but contradicts her claim to have been released in Angers two weeks after her arrest in November. When she returned to Nantes to collect all her belongings, she confided in the Abbé Jean-Baptiste Luneau, curé of the church of Sainte-Croix, of her plan to double-cross the Germans with RENÉ's help.[17] She even persuaded RENÉ, an Austrian Roman Catholic, to meet with the Abbé on several occasions. The Abbé was suitably impressed and subsequently advised her to pursue her plan.

Stella told SIS on 12 November 1941 that German counter-espionage (i.e. III-F) was divided into three zones, with headquarters in Paris, Dijon and Angers, and that RENÉ was second-in-command to Meissner (other reports say he was assistant to him). Meissner told her that they were operating a number of wireless sets and sending out information to keep them alive. But when the report was compiled Meissner had become head of counter-espionage in Paris and taken RENÉ with him.

While in Nantes she claimed that she had been introduced to Crown Prince Alois (Louis) of Liechtenstein by either Meissner or RENÉ. She learned of a German scheme, currently in abeyance, to send agents to Britain under the diplomatic cover of Liechtenstein, possibly to include Meissner. She alleged that Prince Alois was working for the Abwehr at Ast Angers in III-F (counter-espionage) and later that he was head of the Paris Leitstelle which sent agents to the UK.[18] Tar Robertson's letter of 10 February 1942 to SIS stated that Prince Alois had been a member of Meissner's organization in Nantes but was now part of the Paris organization.[19]

Adalbert Paulsen's MI5 file appears to support Stella's allegation: 'Hpt. Prinz von LICHTENSTEIN [*sic*]: Leiter der Auswertung [Interpretation] and I.H. Colour of arm: white … Came from Ast. St. Germain. Transferred to Warsaw end 1942. Seen at Angers.'[20] A note on 24 March 1942, most likely from Sir Robert Mackenzie in VB4, the SIS section dealing with

France, Corsica, Andorra, Belgium, the Netherlands and Luxemburg, stated that 'The members of the LIECHTENSTEIN family are ... well-known to be extremely pro-German and Prince Ferdinand figures as Case No. 482 on C.S.W. [Central Security War] Black List'.

In 2001 the Liechtenstein government commissioned historian Dr Peter Geiger to clarify its position during the Second World War. His two-volume report states that the principality, while remaining officially neutral, had done business with the Nazis, but the government's official website claims that Prince Franz-Josef II, the ruler from 1938 until his death in 1989, had a blameless war record.[21] Dr Geiger's research revealed the names of Prinz Hans Moritz von Liechtenstein, Prinz Alois (Louis) von Liechtenstein and Prinz Ferdinand von Liechtenstein, but he pointed out to me that Prinz Alois was *not* a crown prince as Stella had claimed, meaning that he would have been next in line to Franz-Josef II:

> The above mentioned three members of the family von Liechtenstein were German citizens. The remark cited by the MI5 counter-espionage [*sic*]: "The members of the LIECHTENSTEIN family are ... well-known to be extremely pro-German" does not reflect the historical reality, but only activities of some of the members.[22]

His account lists Prinz Alois as 'Parteigenosse und Wehrmachtoffizier' (Nazi Party member and Wehrmacht officer).[23]

Prince Aloys (Alois or Louis) Géza Georg Hubert Maria Liechtenstein was born in Vienna in 1898 and died on 19 February 1943 in Burzowka, Russia, at the start of the Third Battle of Kharkov. On 1 May 1938 he joined the NSDAP. He *was* a member of the Angers Abwehrstelle in July 1942 and a member of Abwehrkommando 302 (FAK 302) in August 1942, confirmed by Leutnant Walter Arthur Speck who states that Hauptmann 'Prinz zer Liechtenstein ... assisted Maj. [Hans] Lips, Leiter I, Ast ANGERS 40–42'.[24] If Stella met Prince Alois when he was attached to Ast Angers it must have been before she left Angers and Nantes and arrived in Lisbon on 3 November 1941.

As Dr Geiger wrote:

> Evidently, in 1938, right after the Anschluss of Austria, Prince Alois became acquainted with, and completed his entry into, National Socialism. In October 1938, in Würzburg, he married Gräfin [Countess] Hertha Marie von Reichenberg (born 1919) [Hertha Maria Wolfskeel von Reichenberg, 31 August 1919–2014]. Shortly after the beginning of the war, in October 1939, Prince Alois enlisted (was conscripted) into the Armed Forces, to the Staff of the Infantry Regiment 282 in Grafenwöhr

in the Bavarian Oberpfalz. He was 41 years old. After four months of training, at the end of February 1940, he joined Infantry Replacement Battalion 481 in Hof (Saale). One month later, on 1 April 1940, Prince Alois was promoted to "Oberleutnant z.V". (zur Verfügung) [in the Reserves]. He was now an officer in the Wehrmacht.

In the summer of 1940, Alois was assigned to the Field Command Headquarters (v) 820 in Wehrkreis XIII (Würzburg). The Field Command Headquarters were used for military administration and control of occupied territories – the Field Command Headquarters (v) 820 was, for the time being, ordered to France. After a few months, in November 1940, Alois was assigned to the OKW in Berlin, apparently with Amt Ausland/Abwehr. They sent him to Abwehrstelle Angers in western France. In August 1941 he was promoted to Hauptmann z.V. [zur Verfügung – available] He stayed in Angers until the summer of 1942.

Regarding Alois' deployment in occupied France, German military archival information now concurs with Secret Services information from England. The English woman, and suspected double agent, Stella Lonsdale, was in France from 1940 to 1941 and also stayed in Angers. Here, in November 1940, she was arrested by the Germans and interrogated until February 1941. In her own words, she was "turned" for German espionage and set free. In the autumn of 1941, she fled from Marseille to England. There she was in turn arrested by the British Intelligence Service (MI5) and questioned extensively. In the process, in November 1941, Stella Lonsdale revealed that the German who controlled all of the German agents, sent from Paris to England, was named "Prince Louis of Liechtenstein". In Angers, Stella Lonsdale might have encountered Prince Alois (Louis) as a German Abwehr Lieutenant, or heard of him. How much of the above account is true, is open (for discussion). Unlikely (however) to have been pulled out of thin air. The German documents confirm his work with the Abwehr and his presence in Angers.

In July 1942, Prince Alois was transferred from Abwehrstelle Angers to OKW Amt Ausland/Abwehr, Befehlsstab Walli Abw. III … which organized counter-espionage on the Eastern Front, under the direction of Canaris, Gehlen, Baun and Schmalschläger. At the end of August 1942, Alois was assigned to Abwehrkommando 302 [in Galați, Romania]. Each Army Group was assigned such an Abwehrkommando. Tasks included front reconnaissance, counter-espionage, infiltration of partisan organizations and evaluation of information.

On 1 February 1943, Alois was promoted to Major z.V. [zur Verfügung – available] – three weeks later he was dead. Just as the Battle of Stalingrad was lost for Germany. A few days later, the Soviets began an attack against Wehrmacht-held Charkow [Kharkov] in East Ukraine. In the course of the "Third Battle of Charkow", in February and March, Prince Alois fell on 19 February 1943, near Krasnograd, 100 km southwest of Charkow; Gustav Wilhelm in the Stammtafel (ancestry table) names the death location as Brazowka. According to a notice from the military hospital "R2/529", Alois was buried on 26 February 1941. The fact that he was in the hospital suggests that he was severely wounded when he was admitted. [He was later reburied in the Military Cemetery Charkow, Block 8, Row 52, Grave 5146.] ... Had Prince Alois not died on the Eastern Front in February 1943, he would, like Prince Hans Moritz, likely also have been dismissed from the Armed Forces due to Hitler's May decree. Prince Alois left behind a wife and two children, one 2 years old and one 5 months old.[25]

Speck's file states that he was accidentally killed by the Gestapo.[26]

Chapter 5

'Pat O'Leary'

In July 1940 Major Donald Robert Darling, the SIS Head of Station in Gibraltar and a former member of Claude Dansey's prewar Z-Network, was sent to Lisbon and Barcelona to establish links with the French and set up escape lines into Spain over the Pyrénées, a task he was eminently capable of doing as he spoke French and Spanish. Airey Neave of MI9 described him as 'dark-haired and well-built – a younger version of the actor Herbert Marshall.' His codename was 'Sunday',[1] which the French referred to as '*Cheri*' (Darling). However, Sir Samuel Hoare, the British ambassador to Spain, himself a former SIS officer during the First World War, forbade him from working in Spain because he didn't want to be embarrassed, or compromise Spain's neutrality.

Hoare had arrived in Madrid 'with a number of prejudices against SIS and imposed severe restrictions on the activities of the local head of station, Mr Hamilton Stokes' who had replaced Lieutenant Colonel Edward de Renzy Martin, expelled from Spain with his secretary over the 'Colonel Martin affair'.[2] Darling was made unwelcome in Madrid and expelled:[3] 'Sir Samuel told me that he had arranged for me to leave by road for Lisbon with a diplomat the next morning and I felt that he would be surprised if I were not murdered in my bed in the meantime.'[4]

In contrast, Sir Walford Selby, Hoare's counterpart in Lisbon, was more sympathetic and told Darling that he would turn a blind eye to his activities, so Darling set up his base there.

Later, when Hoare visited Lisbon and promised to help in any way he could, Darling was 'sickened by his insincerity'. Hoare's change of heart was clearly due to the scathing report Darling had sent Dansey after his removal from Spain:

> The interpretation of the prime minister's directive, in its most extreme form, was tantamount to keeping in with General Franco at the expense of our own evading … Sir Samuel had clearly received a rocket from London for his performance in Madrid over the 'Martin affair', which had put paid to our plans in Spain.[5]

That rocket had most likely come from Dansey himself, who was not a man to be crossed. Many in the intelligence community hated or even feared him. He had, according to Ben Macintyre, 'the sharp, penetrating eyes of a hyperactive ferret'. Hugh Trevor-Roper called him 'an utter shit, corrupt, incompetent, but with a certain low cunning', while another colleague referred to him as 'the only truly evil man I ever met'. He was, as Langley said, 'one of those powerful people who prefer to keep their power hidden: an éminence grise rather than a ruling monarch but a highly influential personage for all that. What Dansey wanted done was done and what he wanted undone was undone'.[6]

When the 51st Highland Division surrendered on 12 June 1940 at Saint Valéry-en-Caux on the Normandy coast, Captain Ian Grant Garrow of the 9th Battalion, Highland Light Infantry[7] and eight of his men went on the run, arriving in Marseille in August. Garrow surrendered to the Vichy authorities, while the others made their various escapes. He was imprisoned in Fort St.Jean, but free to wander around the nearby Vieux Port. During his perambulations he saw many people who were trying to escape which gave him the idea to set up a network, so he established contact with Darling in Marseille. Neave described him as 'a tall, commanding Scotsman; quiet and deliberate in speech and thought [but] He knew little French and his Highland features made disguise impossible among the population of Marseille'.[8]

Garrow set up his escape line in Marseille with 64-year-old Marie-Louise Dissard @ 'Françoise' who ran a series of safe houses in Toulouse, Marseille and Perpignan. He described her as 'almost exactly as I had imagined her to be – a rough-voiced, tough dame with a strong *midi* [*sic*] accent, dressed in a black camisole and smoking constantly through a wooden cigarette holder. She pretended to be a cross-patch but underneath was the kindest of women'.[9] Regarded as eccentric, wherever she went she was accompanied by her cat 'Miff', so she became known as 'the cat lady'. When he and Guérisse were captured she helped them escape.[10]

The 'Pat Line' was named after 'Patrick Albert O'Leary', the *nom de guerre* of Belgian army doctor Albert-Marie Guérisse. Posing as French Canadians, he and the crew of the French merchant ship, *Le Rhin*, renamed *Fidelity*, operated several missions to help people escape from France but became stranded while attempting to bring out some Polish officers and were arrested by the French police in Cerbère. Guérisse escaped from Saint-Hippolyte-du-Fort in the Gard *département* of southern France and made his way to Marseille, where he contacted Garrow. When Garrow was captured in October 1941 he took over the network.

English journalist Elisabeth (Lisa or Lisl) Haden-Guest, born in Königsberg (now Kaliningrad) as Louise Ruth Wolpert on 30 August 1910, was the daughter of wealthy Jews, who as a teenager had joined the Communist Party. In 1939 she married Peter Haden-Guest, 4th Baron Haden-Guest, having previously married English communist journalist Bertie Coker in 1934 as a means of establishing a new nationality. She and her son Anthony were imprisoned in Besançon but escaped across the demarcation line and made their way to Marseille.[11]

Canadian Thomas Edward James Kenny @ 'Lieutenant Johnson' was a 'well-to-do businessman and resident of Marseille',[12] born on 26 April 1910 in Halifax, Nova Scotia. He was 'a good and enthusiastic supporter of Ian Garrow's from the very beginning, though he had no political leanings or affiliations. Nevertheless he was naïve, and had no previous experience of clandestine activities'.[13] His uncle, Captain Patrick William Kenny, had worked closely with Sir Vernon Kell, the Director of MO5 (the precursor to MI5) before the First World War, and as an assistant censor for MI7a during the war.[14] On 29 April 1941 Tom Kenny became engaged to 18-year-old Micheline Digard @ Suzanne Martinez, born Paris 29 April 1923, introduced to him by close friend Nancy Fiocca. On Tuesday 15 July 1941 they were married in Cannes:

> Sue is referred to as Micheline Digard in Russell Braddon's 1956 book 'Nancy Wake'[15] and … called Sue Martinez by most English writers but she was Micheline until her marriage. She is the daughter of Emmanuel Michele Martinez, founder and owner of the fabulous Hotel Martinez on the Boulevard de la Croisette in Cannes. Martinez was an Italian married to Marie Maldiney but in 1919 he had met and fallen in love with Emma Digard … Martinez could not get a divorce and it was Emma who was seventeen year old Suzanne's adopted mother.[16]

He escaped across the Pyrénées on 11 January 1943, was commissioned into the RAF, and became an intelligence officer for the rest of the war.[17]

Louis Henri Nouveau @ 'Saint Jean' was a 60-year-old Marseille businessman who financed the escape line and acted as a courier. He was betrayed by Roger le Neveu @ 'Le Légionnaire' who knew Harold Cole, and was arrested on 13 February 1943 in Saint-Pierre-des-Corps while assisting five American airmen to escape. Nouveau was taken to the Gestapo headquarters at 11, rue des Saussaies, Paris and beaten severely. After spending time in Fresnes, he was sent on 17 January 1944 to Buchenwald where he was executed on 5 October 1944.

The Rev. Donald Caskie had been the resident minister at the Scots Kirk in the rue Bayard, Paris, since 1935, but prudently left there on 11 June 1940 and had headed for Marseille, where he managed the Seamen's Mission at 46, rue de Forbin. He died in 1983.

Dr George 'Rodo' Rodocanachi was a British-born physician of Greek descent who had studied in Marseille. His home in Marseille became a safe house for Garrow's network and he was responsible for helping Allied airmen escape across the Pyrénées, as well as Jews escape to America. His betrayal and subsequent capture on 25 February 1943 resulted in his being sent to a prison in Compiègne, then to Buchenwald where he died in the spring of 1944. His widow, Fannette 'Fanny' Marie Nathalie Vlasto, believed he had been betrayed by one of the concierges at the house.

Nancy Wake, a New Zealand-born journalist along with her husband Henri Fiocca, a wealthy French industrialist whom she had married in 1937, remembered Garrow as 'very impressive, tall, well-built like an athlete, good-looking and [a] charming gentleman'.

Mario Lambros Achilles Prassinos @ 'Convoyeur' was a Greek born in Egypt in 1898, who also worked for the Resistance and joined the 'Pat Line' early on. He was evacuated from France by O'Leary at the end of 1942 (Neave says 1943) when the Vichy authorities were closing in on him and escaped across the Pyrénées with two RAF pilots. Neave described him as, 'A short middle-aged man in the smartest business clothes, carrying a black hat and cane, like a character from some prewar film set on the French Riviera, entered … and introduced himself with care and elegance', and by O'Leary as 'the bravest man I ever knew'.[18] He died of typhus on 4 March 1945 in a concentration camp at Schwerin.

Stella's involvement with the network began with a chance encounter at the American Consulate in Marseille in mid-May 1941 with Canadian Walter Stangroom, the manager of Massey-Harris (later Massey-Ferguson) in Germany before the war who claimed to know someone in British Intelligence and introduced her to Garrow. Her meeting with Stangroom coincided with meeting Jean Jacques Pavie at the post office in Marseille, who claimed to work for Garrow and wanted her to take a message to him. Later he asked her to obtain information about the Dewoitine D.520 dive-bomber for which he offered her 50,000 francs, saying that he would split with her the 5,000,000 francs he would receive from 'my friends in Paris' when they received the information, causing her to suspect that he was working for the Germans. Garrow advised her to have nothing more to do with him. However, she managed to find out 'certain particulars' about the aircraft, possibly from Raymond Claubert, which Garrow told her would be sent to the proper authorities.

A British agent had surrendered to the Germans and was now working for them; it was imperative that British Intelligence be informed as soon as possible. RENÉ insisted that she should obtain assurance from them that they could protect her. Should she decide to act as his agent, she should return and report back to Meissner before 31 May.

* * *

That British agent was Alfred Gaessler @ 'Georges Marty' sent to France by Captain André Dewavrin ('Colonel Passy'), head of the BCRA, with French naval officer Lieutenant Henri Louis Honoré d'Éstienne d'Orves @ 'Châteauvieux', a distant cousin of writer Antoine de Saint-Exupéry. On 21 December 1940 they left Newlyn, Cornwall, for Plogoff, Brittany, aboard the trawler *Marie-Louise*, landing the following day at Pointe du Raz. But on 19 January 1941 Gaessler walked into the *Kommandatur* in Nantes with his wireless transmitter, saying he was an enemy agent and ready to betray all the members of the Nemrod (Nimrod) network to German counter-espionage[19] – Jan Doornik, Maurice Barlier, and d'Éstienne d'Orves. The latter was convicted before a military court martial on 13 May 1941 and executed on 29 August at the Fort de Mont-Valérien, Suresnes.[20] This was later confirmed by RENÉ and Comte André Philippe Marc Lévêque de Vilmorin, the well-known French horticulturalist.

Garrow informed London in May about Gaessler but somehow the message became mutilated during its transmission and SIS was unaware that the Germans were working Gaessler's radio set, *not* that he was working it on their behalf. As a test SIS responded by sending a W/T message requesting the name of his fiancée.[21] After that the Germans appeared to have no further use for Gaessler and threw him into prison where he tried to commit suicide. Mills was surprised, thinking that they would have valued him as a double-cross agent, but Stella told him the Germans would have expected the English were no longer concerned about the transmitter and decided to operate it themselves. However, Mills was loathe to trust her story:

> Either GESSLER was kept at the key of the transmitter, and in that case RENÉ lied to MICHAEL, or the Germans are bigger fools than I dare assume. It seems quite unbelievable that the Germans would do other than take the greatest precautions to keep the GESSLER set operating along the lines of previous operations, and the suggestion that one snap question answered properly would allay English suspicions immediately and forever, is absurd.[22]

Someone purporting to be Gaessler later sent a message requesting more money and more agents to be sent over. SIS informed him that he should get in touch with a barmaid at a café in the rue du Siam in Brest. But the Germans didn't trust him and regarded him as an expensive nuisance, so they sent a Frenchman known as 'Nicois' instead.

With the help of SIS, John Masterman and John Marriott of MI5's B1a compiled a list of questions related to these radio communications, to which they required answers. One of these was whether Gaessler was actually arrested, or whether he had walked into the *Kommandatur*, as Stella claimed. However, Dansey complained that he had never received Milmo's report on the information about Gaessler. Liddell commented in his diary on 18 December that had MI5 seen Dansey's traffic a few months earlier it 'might well have prevented SIS being led up the garden path so long'. But to Robertson, it was perfectly clear that Gaessler was under German control.[23]

* * *

Everywhere Stella went she was given the runaround, with no one particularly interested in what she had to say. The American Consul in Nantes, Hassell H. Dick, told her to contact Hugh S. Fullerton, the American Consul-General in Marseille. There she also saw George M. Abbott, who had been appointed Consul on 28 January 1938. She tried to warn him about the wireless set but he refused to have anything to do with her and sent her to see the British Consul in Cannes, Sir Coleridge Kennard, Bt., who also rebuffed her, telling her to go to Madrid and see David Eccles, First Secretary at the British Embassy, who would put her in touch with the military attaché, Colonel Oswald Smith-Bingham.

A friend of Ian Fleming, David McAdam Eccles was employed by the Ministry of Economic Warfare (MEW) in Madrid and Lisbon (1940–2), under cover as Economic Advisor to the British Ambassadors of Spain and Portugal.[24] All of this Stella considered a futile exercise as by the time she was able to pass on the information it would be too late. She returned to Marseille and saw Major (Ret'd) J.H.M. 'Hugh' Dodds, the British Consul-General attached to the British section of the American Consulate, but he also refused to help her, telling her that she would have to go to Lisbon.

'Grannie' Dodds oversaw conditions at Fort Saint-Jean, as well as caring for the needs of British civilians. MI5 regarded him as 'mildly suspect' owing to his friendship with Sir Lionel Haworth, a member of The Link, and an accusation that he had allowed a highly suspect member of the Sûreté in Marseille to look through the consulate's confidential files, but mainly because of his alleged reluctance to help British soldiers to escape. But as John Day of B1b noted, 'Providing assistance to Garrow ... was another matter as the U.S. State Department prohibited its consular offices from aiding the escape or evasion of British military personnel.'[25] Day thought it would be relatively easy to check Stella's activities in Marseille, and whether her allegation that Jean Castellain had received money from the American Consulate was true.[26]

Hiram 'Harry' Bingham IV, American vice-consul in Marseille, corroborated Stella's account of her visits, reporting that she had called at the consulate between March and April 1941, referred by Fullerton and Dodds, asking for assistance in crossing the border into Spain without the usual visas, and claiming to have valuable information about the Gestapo which she'd obtained while working for them in northern France. She told Bingham that she'd been arrested as a spy, but released after the intervention of a German officer and agreeing to work for them. She also admitted to travelling on a French passport under an assumed name with her British passport sewn into the bottom of her handbag. Bingham was sure that 'warnings were sent to British Authorities at Madrid and Lisbon that she was suspected of being a German in spite of the fact that she was bearer of a British passport':

> She tried unsuccessfully to get us to include her name in a long list of British persons whose applications for exit visas had already been approved by Vichy Government. She even persuaded the office Prefecture to ask us to say that it would be all right if we slipped her name in – causing us to warn Prefecture that we knew nothing about her.
>
> My impression was that she was trying in every possible way to trick Consulate into doing something compromisingly illegal.

Bingham and Dodds cautiously followed the consulate's practice of advising everyone to always obey French laws and regulations. They could only provide her with the same assistance as any woman holding a British passport, so she would have to wait for French exit and Spanish entry visas.[27] Her 'slight foreign accent and manner' invoked suspicion in four members of the consulate, as well as an American relief worker (possibly American journalist Varian Fry) in Marseille who observed her taking notes on a conversation he was having one afternoon with an important Greek statesman in the lobby of the Terminus Hotel where she was staying. Bingham added that 'She was the … most dangerous of a large number of persons suspected of being German agents who called almost daily at Marseille Consulate probably with a view to compromising its activities'.[28] With Fry, he would help over 2,500 Jews flee from France, including artist Marc Chagall and his wife Bella Rosenfeld; artist Max Ernst; Heinrich Mann, brother of author Thomas Mann; and anti-Nazi writer Lion Feuchtwanger and his wife Marta Loeffler.[29]

* * *

Stella had missed her 31 May 1941 deadline to get in touch with Meissner again and become a double-cross agent.[30] RENÉ was annoyed that he'd heard nothing from her about when she would be returning, so he'd written to her expressing his displeasure and received a stiff letter in response.[31] She'd also sent him a telegram from Tours to his flat in Angers, but when she arrived and let herself in she found a note instructing her to proceed to Paris where he was now posted. At the flat that evening 'there was a touching meeting', but he was upset when she told him that it was only for work, and did not intend living with him. He was also angry that she had been unable to establish a means of communicating with British Intelligence, so too late to pass on information regarding Operation *Barbarossa* – the German invasion of Russia – which had originally been scheduled for 6 June, but delayed until 22 June. However, ULTRA decrypts ensured that British Intelligence already knew about it in advance, but Stalin had refused to believe the warnings given to him by H.A.R. 'Kim' Philby.[32]

Stella stayed at RENÉ's flat until they went to a hotel between Tours and Le Mans. She thought that it was during this time he'd told her about the W/T message sent to Gaessler from London asking him for the address of his girlfriend, although she was unclear on dates when RENÉ had passed on certain information. However, she was most insistent that at no time did he ever enquire about her contacts, which seems strange. She would later explain to Milmo that he had always wanted her to give up the spying game and live with him, but 'although RENÉ was very much in love with her he had never made any improper suggestions and he was not the sort of man who would ever suggest living with a woman who he intended to marry'. This is in direct contrast to what she would later tell the Advisory Committee.

In the middle of June 1941 Garrow instructed her to return to the occupied zone and make contact with RENÉ to see what other information he had. Jean Castelain, who lived at 25, rue Roux Alpheran, told her that he had a friend 'in aviation' who could obtain photographs and lists of plans on French aerodromes and wondered whether she could pass it on. She agreed but first consulted Garrow, who considered it to be valuable information. Yet in spite of Garrow expressly telling her to drop Castelain because he was too indiscreet, he accompanied her. During the course of her crossing, using a false *carte d'identité* instead of the one RENÉ had given her, she was shot at several times and in the confusion ended up back in the unoccupied zone, but finally succeeded in getting across.

There were more trips to the occupied zone between June and August, sometimes disguised with blond hair, sometimes red, or as a brunette, but using the *Ausweiss* RENÉ had given her. Once, in July, she'd accompanied him to Brest in the Zone Interdit (forbidden zone). A trip planned for September was aborted when he'd suddenly warned her not to return and to get out of the country as quickly as possible.

Before she left for Marseille, RENÉ had given her the same secret ink recipe and its developer, and a code by which they could communicate, as those given to Gaessler. During September and October, she communicated with him by secret writing, telling him that she was in touch with someone at the American Consulate in Marseille. However, he'd warned her that German agents had infiltrated the ministries in London and the Admiralty and was terrified that one of them would see her reports. Therefore, she should only deal with senior people in British Intelligence.[33]

Pavie was arrested in August by French police for dealing on the black market, as a result of a tip-off from Stella, but he was released on bail shortly afterwards. Even though she'd tried to avoid him he'd got in touch with her and became angry, claiming to know everything about Garrow's organization and its headquarters, and threatened to have all of them arrested. This confirmed her suspicion that he was a German agent and she tried to warn Garrow. He later sent her two telegrams from the occupied zone asking if Garrow could arrange for him to go to England. Failing that, he would make his own way there as he was a good friend of SS-Hauptsturmführer (Captain) Ernst von Alisch @ Ernesto Seiler of the SiPo und SD in France in charge of Abteilung VI-C at the Paris Dienststelle.[34] He also told her that he was double-crossing the Germans. She later told Milmo that she thought Pavie would come to England and that he should be closely watched. Tar Robertson confirmed to Mackenzie of SIS that he was 'undoubtedly identical with René Jean Jacques PAVIE' and that he should be granted a visa and admitted to England 'so that he can be sent to Ham [Camp 020] as soon as he arrives'.[35]

Pavie had visited England illegally a number of times in 1937 between January and May but was refused leave to land as he was suspected of being a German agent. MI5 knew he had been involved 'in shady deals or thefts concerning the sale of commercial aircraft in Spain' before the war, working as a pilot for the Hon. Mrs Victor Bruce *née* Mildred Mary Petre, who had been trafficking in illegal arms, notably aircraft, to Paraguay in 1935, and from September 1936 to November 1937 in the sale of aircraft to Spain.

* * *

The arrests came between 15 and 17 July with police raids on the Hôtel Noailles where various members of the escape organization usually met in room 530, followed by the usual pointing of fingers as to who had betrayed them. Suspects ranged from the concierge, who was an informer for the Service de Renseignments (SR) of the Deuxième Bureau, to Stella, who had sent a message in July to Kenny via Frank Viner who had been using the room, with information about German sabotage agents in North and South America.

She also alleged that she had contracted venereal disease from Garrow and intended to have him arrested.[36]

Elisabeth Haden-Guest claimed that either one of the French policemen, Harold Cole, or the Seamen's Mission on the rue Forbin, had tipped them off. It was common knowledge at the Mission that meetings were held at the hotel.[37] Others suspected were Christine Gorman @ Madame Lombrez and Private (later Captain) Francis George Kerr Mumme of the Gordon Highlanders[38] who was known to Garrow, Captain Murchie who had run the escape line prior to Garrow, and the Rev. Caskie at the Seamen's Mission.

Cole was a petty criminal who had joined 18th Field Park Company, Royal Electrical & Mechanical Engineers (REME) in September 1939 and was posted to France as part of the BEF. After Dunkirk he became a prisoner of war but managed to escape with Henri Duprez[39] and six other British evaders in a stolen car. In Lille he dabbled on the black market and reinvented himself as a former New Scotland Yard detective. Roland Lepers had introduced him to Garrow who told him that Cole was working for the Resistance,[40] but O'Leary suspected that he was working for the Germans, heightened by Garrow's arrest in October. When Cole was brought back over the demarcation line to Dr Rodocanachi's flat in September 1941, O'Leary accused him of using money destined for Duprez to pay for women, which Cole flatly denied, saying that Duprez had been paid. As Neave relates,

> O'Leary then opened the door of the next room. Suddenly confronted with Duprez, Cole went white and moved towards O'Leary, who hit him hard in the mouth. He fell, and lay bleeding and moaning on the floor. He then confessed to having done "something terrible" in a moment of weakness.[41]

While they were all trying to decide what to do Cole escaped through a window and disappeared into the streets of Marseille, then defected to the Geheime Feldpolizei (GFP). That December the Abbé Pierre Carpentier, Corporal Kenneth Bruce Dowding and Duprez were all arrested, brutally tortured, and executed at Dortmund prison in June 1943. Cole was shot and killed by French police on 8 January 1946 while trying to escape.[42]

Chapter 6

The Gifted Liar

After his escape from Spain, Frank Viner, also known as František Wiener, and Boris Melikoff were interrogated in Gibraltar by Captain P.S. Gubbins of 54 Field Security Section, Intelligence Corps, based at the Hotel Cecil.[1] A full report sent to MI5 by the DSO Gibraltar, Major H.C. 'Tito' Medlam, giving details of the activities of Viner, Garrow, and Stella, stated that Viner (referred to as 'Winer') was a Czech, born in Prague on 28 August 1910, who had worked as a journalist for the *New York Herald Tribune* and the *Daily Mail*. During the Sudetenland crisis of 1938 he joined the Czech War Office working as liaison between the British and American press, and the Czech Press Service. During the German occupation he was in Budapest with the Czech Mission:

> Following the German occupation, he went first to Paris; from there he was sent, by the Czech Minister in Paris, to London to fight the Polish and Hungarian press campaign against Czecho-Slovakia. Later, armed with a French passport, he went to the Balkans to report on the political situation.
>
> He returned to Paris on 26.8.39 with advance news of the Russo-German Agreement [the Molotov-Ribbentrop Pact]; he submitted this to high authority but was not believed.
>
> He then reported on 2.9.39, on the instructions of the Czech Minister in Paris to Col. MORABC [*sic* – František Moravec], Chief of the Czech Intelligence Service, in London. He left England on 4.9.39, having been sent to France to join the Czech Army, since he was a political and not a military journalist.
>
> He joined the 2nd Regt. of the Czech Army, was promoted to Sergeant and awarded the French Croix de Guerre.
>
> In mid-July 1940 (i.e. after the Armistice) he was commissioned in the 1er Regiment of Volontaires Étrangers.
>
> He states that his Company Commanders were Lt. MICA and Lt. BECHIME.
>
> In the chaos following the Armistice the identity papers of the personnel of his regiment were destroyed, his among them.

He went to Vichy to meet Major MENARD, Chief of a Department of the Vichy Ministry of War. He then contacted the Czech Representative. At this time he appears to have helped to get officers out of France. He moved freely between Marseille and Vichy, employing forged demobilisation papers to evade restrictions on the movement of demobilised foreigners. Returning to Vichy on 18.10.40, he was denounced for using false papers and spent three months in prison in Marseille. He was released on 15.1.41.

He then asked Mr. Dean and Captain GARROW to get him into the British Intelligence Service, and thereafter worked for Capt. GARROW. To him he submitted a variety of reports mainly on political matters, of which he has a list ... Winer gave the following information about Capt. GARROW and his organisation:-

> Capt. Garrow took over from Capt. Murch [*sic* – Murchie, see below], who was incapable, drunk and indiscreet. At first his job was to get people out of France but he progressively took on Intelligence work as well. He is <u>not</u> a capable Intelligence Officer and gives his subordinates no guidance.
>
> One of these subordinates, a Mrs. LONSDALE, first "turned up" in Angers, having previously been in Paris; she had been condemned to death by the Germans and then set free on the understanding that she would work for them. She gave Garrow information on troop movements in France and on the seizure by the Germans of certain wireless transmitting sets, which they used to transmit <u>valid</u> intelligence to the U.K. with the intention of sending <u>false</u> information at an important moment. These sets had originally been supplied by the British Authorities to their agents.
>
> Mrs. Lonsdale is now trying to obtain the names of two German Agents in Gt. Britain, from an official of the German Intelligence Service who wants British nationality as a reward. He will reveal his name only to the Chief of British Intelligence in London [Sir Stewart Menzies], but Winer knows that his first name is Siegfried, and that he uses the address "Poste Restante, Angers."
>
> Mrs. L. is also trying to get two German official rubber stamps so as to facilitate the supply of false papers to British agents; the lack of such papers is apparently serious.
>
> In both these matters Mrs. L. is following <u>Winer's</u> instructions since Capt. Garrow would not take the responsibility of issuing them!
>
> Mrs. L. and Garrow are now free (having bee[n] again arrested?) and Mrs. L. moves freely between the two zones.

Winer was himself arrested together with a certain Kearney [Kenny] and "Elisabeth" [Elisabeth Haden-Guest] (?Identical with Elisabeth KEEST, Garrow's assistant in Brussels – see report MT of 15.8.41). "K" and "E" were charged with espionage. Winer was released by the French Special Police, who treated him leniently because of their pro-Ally sympathies.

Marseille was henceforth too hot for him, however, and he asked Capt. Garrow to get him across the Spanish frontier. Accordingly he left Marseille with Melikoff and they spent two months in Miranda Concentration camp with him. They were not interrogated by the British Embassy representative from Madrid, and Winer says that this Captain does not bother to listen to prisoners. Winer was in Marseille from 10.8.40 until 28.7.41. He claims to have founded his own organisation in fifteen persons, there, but says that it has been inactive since his departure.

He makes the following comments on the British Intelligence organisation in France and on the measures taken to smuggle men into Spain:-

1. The British Authorities are using men of obvious English appearance, and who do not speak French adequately such men are under suspicion from the first [*sic*].
2. The funds supplied to their agents are hopelessly and ridiculously inadequate, even for their personal expenses. German Agents, however, are well supplied with money and can therefore buy information. French sympathisers are keeping British Intelligence organisations going by gifts.
3. It is extremely difficult to obtain false identity papers for Agents.
4. There is a general lamentable lack of organisation, especially evident in the smuggling of men over the Spanish frontier. Although the journey over the mountains from Perpignan is most arduous there are no arrangements for the supply of food, clothes or footwear, and no rest-houses before Figueras. Men are usually arrested once they leave Figueras. The guides provided to conduct them into Spain are wholly incapable (this agrees with report MT of 15.8.41).

He makes the following criticisms of the attitude of the American Consulate in Marseille:-

1. Mr. Bradford, the American Vice-Consul, is selling visas. [Leonard G. Bradford]
2. Another Consul, in charge of British interests, apparently informs the French police whenever British subjects call at the Consulate,

with the result that they are soon arrested. This man has also handed over diplomatic mail to the Germans.

Finally, Winer says that in the North of France Agents need more guidance and should be told what type of intelligence they should obtain.

He recommends Melikoff as a resolute and capable man who helped him in Marseille.

He wants to return to France to work for British Intelligence.[2]

A suggestion that Viner was actually Karl VI, Prince Schwarzenberg (1911–86), a well-known Czech resistance fighter, was later disbelieved by MI5 as their birthplaces and dates of birth did not concur.

Mills told Lakin that 'we had him brought here for interrogation, both for his own sake and in the hope that he might be able to throw some light on the Stella LONSDALE case'. Viner was held at the Royal Victoria Patriotic Schools (RVPS) on Wandsworth Common for six months and interrogated by Mills on 19 January 1942, after which he was allowed to join the Czech Army. Viner claimed to have worked for SIS in Marseille and was now anxious to meet Stella, even though in France he had considered her untrustworthy and treated her with suspicion. However, it was Mills's opinion that in Marseille

> he succeeded in getting himself attached, if only as an informer, to a British Escape Organization there. He may have done some valuable work for us there, but I do not think S.I.S. trusted him, and the Americans have said quite frankly that they regard him as a double agent.

Ronnie Haylor was trying to find out how Viner had obtained the PO box number for MI5 and written to an officer of the RVPS trying to get a job with British Intelligence.[3] According to Major General J.H.F. Lakin, SOE Security Section (D/CE), he had been introduced to SOE through a 'Major Garrold' (Garrow) who had run the escape organization until he had been imprisoned as a result of his association with Stella. Garrow had given Viner the name of some important member who Mills thought was the head of ISRB, 'a man who would be interested in … VINER's proposals, which … concerned the formation of a band of wreckers who should go to France or Germany on our behalf'.[4] Lakin told Mills that the officer who had interviewed Viner was unconvinced by his story so he was not offered employment with SOE. Mills thought that he was 'really looking for some fairly easy and safe job which will save him from having to serve as a soldier'.

Prior to Marseille, Leonard Bradford had been vice-consul in Genoa (1936–8), and living with an Italian mistress, although another account contradicts this by saying that he did not live with her in Marseille but travelled to Switzerland every weekend to see her. The unnamed girlfriend told Stella that Bradford frequently took his girlfriends to Bern, Switzerland. Journalist Leo Hirsch alleged that the girlfriend had German intelligence connections with the Abwehr, not the SS-Sonderkommando. Fullerton told Stella in confidence that Bradford was very rich and kept $6,000-worth of gold in his bedroom, that his position as vice-consul was only an honorary one – he was really just a clerk – and that he was very dissatisfied with him and had tried to get him removed. Neither Garrow nor Lee (Leigh) D. Randall, another vice-consul in Marseille, trusted him. The Abwehr had obtained Bradford's name from an Italian connection which RENÉ was trying to find out more about and asked Stella whether she knew him. Milmo concluded that 'There is something sinister about this woman and BRADFORD's relations with her'.

Viner was commonly known to frequent the various bars and night clubs in Marseille. When he met Langley in December 1940, he led him to believe that he worked for SIS. But while he never worked in an escape line, he took an active interest in what was going on, leaving Langley to believe that he was in touch with the French or Germans. Langley said he was

> an intelligent man who has lived by his wits for some time; he is, however, weak-minded and easily swayed. He has a great attraction for women, and a large part of his income probably comes from this course. He is one of the most gifted liars I have ever met, and is indiscreet in every language he knows. Personally, I do not think that he was actually employed by the French or Germans, but he may well have earned a little money passing on gossip which he has picked up. I should not credit him with the courage required to undertake active espionage.
>
> I can produce no evidence whatever to show that he has been working against us. I will answer any questions which you may wish to ask, and I should like to interrogate him on P.O.W.s when he reaches the U.K.[5]

Kim Philby, the head of SIS's counter-espionage Iberian sub-section (VD), refutes at least some of the information sent by the DSO Gibraltar. He states that Viner had aroused suspicion since June 1939 when he was the Paris correspondent of the *New York Herald Tribune* and in touch with Eugen Fiehl, the press attaché at the German Embassy in Paris who was well known for his propaganda work. But John Elliott, the permanent representative of the *Herald-Tribune* in Vichy denied Viner's claim that he had been a reporter for that newspaper.[6] Viner also claimed to have been employed by the Czech Intelligence Service, which they denied.[7]

Mary Wesley's biographer, Patrick Marnham, described Melikoff as 'an Armenian communist' with whom she had had an affair and who 'had found it hard to take British Society seriously since the day he found his first wife in bed with his mother – a lady who eventually became editor of Paris Vogue.'[8] Philby reported that Melikoff and his mother had been friendly in 1939 with Lucien Vogel, the editor and director of *Vogue* in Paris: 'VOGEL was in contact with suspect circles in France and the U.S.' He later reported that an unnamed SIS officer knew him, and that Viner was a survivor of the 1st Czech Infantry Division which had fought in France prior to its surrender in May 1940. Melikoff had worked as a hotel manager in Marseille from 20 October 1940 to 27 July 1941 who had helped Stella and Viner by hiding documents and escapees, but he had no connection with Garrow.

Prior to interrogating Viner and Melikoff at the RVPS, Mills left the room, allowing them to chat. Viner asked Melikoff the name of the hotel in Marseille where Stella had left the plans on the night when the police were looking for her, as well as the date of her last arrest sometime between 10 and 15 July. Melikoff said it was l'Hotel de Lyonnais, 32, rue de Ricolettes and that RENÉ's cover name was Serge Richard and his cover address was *poste restante*, Angers. Viner couldn't remember the Canadian's name but Melikoff said it was Stangroom.

When Mills returned Viner revealed that Jean Castellain had given Stella the plans of the aerodrome at Sainte-Luce for 1,000 francs but she'd had to borrow money from various people, including Bosio.[9] Melikoff didn't know Stella very well, only that she'd told him she'd been in prison, but didn't know why or for how long.[10] Viner added that there was an American in the occupied zone from whom she was getting her information, but didn't know his name. Captain Murch – actually Captain Charles Plowman Murchie, Royal Army Service Corps (RASC) – had run the escape line until he escaped in April 1941, whereupon Garrow had taken over.[11]

Robert Coe at the US Embassy in London wrote to Peter Ramsbotham of MI5's E2b on 17 March 1942 stating that Colonel Schow, the US military attaché at Vichy, had formed a very bad opinion of Viner and 'considers [him] to be very slippery, and is suspicious of his German relationships'.[12] His report also stated that Stella had spoken affectionately about Viner and had told Fullerton that he'd been in a Spanish concentration camp after he'd escaped from France without any visas. 'It is not thought likely that their relations were more than casual, due to the above-mentioned attachment, which was about the same time.' Fullerton thought Viner was a refugee seeking to obtain work. Mills passed on Ramsbotham's information to Ronnie Haylor at the RVPS.

The documents reveal that Stella was in Marseille from December 1940 or January 1941 and had been released from prison on or about 17 December. This, of course contradicts the claim that she had been brought to Dernbach on Christmas Day and made it easier for MI5 to believe that immediately after her release she may have started working for the Germans and had gone to the unoccupied zone on their behalf. There she had obviously contacted the Americans, not the British, as Langley was in Marseille at the time and hadn't come across her, but Dodds would be able to confirm Fullerton's statement.

Mills conferred with Jim Hale who felt that the Americans' new evidence, together with Stella's own admission that her original story was untrue, would be sufficient to satisfy the Advisory Committee and enable them to hold her in prison indefinitely. Her story was 'a patchwork of lies and truths and … we are driven to the assumption that she has only told us the truth when it has suited her to do so'. He decided that MI5 should begin to wrap things up while still collecting just enough evidence 'to satisfy a jury that MICHAEL has at some time knowingly worked for the enemy.' However, he felt that it would be difficult to prove that she had been an agent for the Germans.

There was conflicting information about the nature and origin of the map of Sainte-Luce which Stella had shown Dick, the American consul. She'd said that it was of an underground petrol station, whereas Dick had said it was of anti-aircraft batteries. She also said she'd obtained it from a Frenchman, while Dick said it had been stolen from a car. All of this left Mills suspicious that she had had some ulterior motive.

Dick reported that Stella had frequently asked about the location of the British Intelligence organization and their activities in Nantes, leaving Mills to suspect that she was indeed working for the Germans. Trying to give her the benefit of the doubt, he posited that she could have been attempting to pass on information to them, 'but her enquiries about the activities of the American Consulate cannot be fitted into the picture unless they are taken to mean that MICHAEL was at that time working for the Germans and was trying to embarrass the American Consul'.

Indeed, Stella had tried her best to discredit Dick, accusing him of being an 'isolationist', but Mills concluded that Dick was justified in mistrusting her, while at the same time treating her much more fairly than he needed to. It was also significant that, without the Americans' assistance she was able

> without the slightest difficulty and without the knowledge or intervention of the American Consulate in Marseille, to obtain French exit and Spanish and Portuguese transit permits, whereas all other British subjects required the assistance of the American Consulate in these matters. If this statement indicates anything, it is surely that MICHAEL had a good deal of German or Italian backing in Marseille of which she has told us little or nothing.

He added that Fullerton's reports to the British military attaché in Lisbon and Lieutenant Colonel Robert Drummond-Wolff in Madrid in November 1941 had never reached MI5 via Section V of SIS, and had gone astray.[13] But these reports *were* passed to VD, Kim Philby's Iberian sub-section of Section V.

When Mills finally met the now retired Dodds at the Travellers Club on 28 April

> it was evident from the outset that he had formed a very shrewd opinion as to what MICHAEL is and was and in his capacity as an official employed in the U.S. Consulate in Marseille he was of course in a very difficult position when dealing with people like her. It is therefore not surprising that he would have nothing to do with her and this no doubt accounts for the black marks she tried to give him as soon as she arrived in England.[14]

Dodds confirmed much of what MI5 already knew about Stella's activities in France, but nothing much about her connection with Garrow or his organization. He was firmly convinced that her first appearance in Marseille was in April 1941, which concurs with what she'd told MI5, but not with Fullerton. At some point she'd commented: 'I went to see Major Dodds and told him that I had plans from a friend of German Submarine Centre. He kicked me out.'

Stella told MI5 that Fullerton's secretary was 'working either for the French or more probably for the French and the Germans' and that Dodds 'had the gravest suspicions about her and says he told Fullerton that he thought she was not on the level'. Fullerton ignored the warning, most likely because there was no evidence to substantiate Dodds's claim. As Mills pointed out, 'It seems as if there is nothing we can do in the matter at this late stage.'

Following their meeting, Dodds wrote to Mills enclosing a letter from his former chief accountant which mentioned an RAF sergeant who Stella had known, 'who was making a fool of himself by marrying a foreign woman'. This must have been Flight Sergeant Philip Mond, introduced to Stella by Jean Castellain at the Café Pélican opposite the American Consulate. Mond claimed to have important information from a young Englishman, Castelain, 'who had means of passing the information on to what he thought was a very good source but was not sure'. She offered to take it to Madrid or Lisbon since she was going there anyway. RENÉ later warned her not to visit the Café Pélican as it was used by many German agents. Whoever he was, he appears to have been yet another 'walk-on part' in the drama of Stella's complicated life.[15]

Chapter 7

The Man in Grey

After Viner's release from prison in France he and Stella had dined with Gars and Brun of the Deuxième Bureau so that she could tell them about a German agent, the name of whom she wrote on a piece of paper, which immediately identified her as the author of the documents which Viner had had in his possession when he was arrested. When Kenny was arrested, he confirmed Stella's contact with a German officer so Gars and Brun made her a proposition: in return for her protection she should reveal everything she knew about German agents working in France. She agreed and was introduced to 'Guy Leclerc', one of the chiefs of the Deuxième Bureau in Vichy working against collaboration with the Germans, who promised to provide her with visas, transport, and anything else she needed, but before finally agreeing to assist him, she consulted Garrow.

The true identity of 'Leclerc' remains a mystery. Stella described him to Langley as about 38, over six feet tall, straight fair hair but bald in the front, and who always wore light grey. He was *'très sportif'* (very sporty) and drove a black Citroën car with front-wheel drive (Citroën Traction Avant). Paul Paillole's book[1] mentions that he had a *'traction avant'* car, but so did many others in important positions, including the Gestapo, so this doesn't prove anything. She noted that the initials on his pocket-book (wallet) were 'P.P.' suggesting that he could have been Colonel Paul Paillole @ 'Philippe Perrier' @ 'Bernard Billaud', born in 1905, who in 1935 was assigned to the Deuxième Bureau. As of 1940 he was in charge of a French counter-espionage network operating out of Marseille known as TR – Service de Travaux Ruraux (Rural Works) – at their headquarters 'Cambronne' at the Villa Éole at 23 Promenade de la Plage – together with his assistants, Lieutenant Joseph Challan-Belval @ 'Charton' and Captain Roger Laffont @ 'Verneuil'.[2]

When Milmo interviewed her at the Waldorf Hotel in London on 14 November 1941, she provided two slightly different descriptions of 'Leclerc', which mostly concur, apart from the following minor differences:

- colour of hair: dark blond vs. dark brown;
- no ring vs. gold signet ring;
- no perfume vs. use of frangipane or other perfume;
- no mention of gold teeth in second description

Milmo suspected that he was in fact Christian Boulanger.³

Simon Kitson suggests that Paillole was in fact an Anglophobe and 'typified the position of the upper echelons of Vichy secret services, declaring in his 1942 lecture, "Germany is the number one danger"' and '"England is the number two danger ... Everyone is working against us. France is all alone"'.⁴ However, Marie-Noël Challan-Belval, Joseph Challan-Belval's daughter, told me that from what she learned from her father when she was growing up, 'I believe Paillole has been more in opposition to De Gaulle's attitude towards his services than ambivalent towards the British.'⁵ She also didn't believe that 'Leclerc' was Paillole since his pseudonym, Philippe Perrier, took the same initials as his real name, which was a common practice. But if the initials 'P.P.' didn't refer to Paul Paillole, then who was 'Leclerc'?

In order for Stella to travel to the occupied zone she needed to dye her hair blond and provide two photographs for her *carte d'identité*, one showing her wearing glasses, the other without. When RENÉ wrote to her, he reported that the photograph without glasses and her particulars from the *carte d'identité* had been betrayed to the Germans. Meissner issued a warning for all frontier crossings to be on the lookout for someone answering that description.

Another letter from RENÉ, written in secret ink, stating that she'd been betrayed to the Germans in late August, left her to conclude that whoever had done so must have been working for the Deuxième Bureau. She suspected Inspector André Gars, because when she asked him for the second photograph, he became uneasy and claimed not to have it, but offered no further explanation. Yet if she had not trusted him, why would she have asked him to pass on a letter to 'Leclerc' whose address she claimed to have mislaid, after she arrived in England? Both letters sent from the Waldorf on 20 November 1941 – one addressed to Raphael Gars [*sic*] at 15, rue Clovis Hugues, Belle de Mai, Marseille, the other to 'Leclerc' – used her alias Suzanne de la Roche:

Dear André,
You will be astonished to have my news and I regret not having written earlier.

Unfortunately I have mislaid M. Leclerc's address and I ask that you have the kindness to convey this letter to him.

I hope you are well and also your wife, Pierrot, your children and M and Mme Valentin. Do you remember my visits to the Belle de Mai [North African quarter of Marseille] when I came looking for my rings and ate pizza?

My best wishes to everyone for a good and happy year and I wish you well in your new job.

Suzanne⁶

Could the phrase about coming to look for her rings and eating pizza be some sort of code? Otherwise its triviality would not be worth mentioning. The other reads:

> My dear Guy,
> At last I've found a moment to write to you and I hasten to take this opportunity to give you my news.
>   My silence may surprise you but if you knew the many things that I have been through since my arrival, you wouldn't hesitate to dismiss me.
>   I'm very much afraid that I am unable to wish you a happy new year in person, because I don't think I can return before mid-January, but you can count on me around that date. At the moment I'm at my mother's, I will give you the details at our next meeting chou-chou!
>   I'm sorry to miss the Christmas celebrations but we'll make up for it when I arrive. So for now it's goodbye and good luck, and think of me as often as I think of you (and you know that it's a lot!)
>   I'll end with lots of affection and good memories of our time spent together.
>   Suzanne.[7]

Again, is this a coded message? The term '*chou-chou*' (actually *chouchou*) means 'pet' in French.

In October Garrow was arrested on the day Stella was about to go north. She'd also received an inter-zone postcard from RENÉ, written in French as if he were writing to his wife, sister or cousin, and using the Christian name 'Simon':

> "We have lately had news of Simon [*sic*] and she is looking very much better now, and she has pulled herself together" … "she has got a new hair style and done her hair differently, and I must say it looks very pretty with her blond hair, and she is coming to visit Uncle Henry in a few days, and he is impatiently waiting to see her because it is so long since we have seen each other" … Well, that gave me a terrible shock … I am glad to tell you that her eye-sight is very much better and she does not have to wear glasses now except for reading.[8]

'Uncle Henry' was a code which she and RENÉ had devised meaning the German Intelligence Service, confirming to her that there had been a leak. 'Simone' was another of her aliases.

Now that the Gestapo had her new description, she told 'Leclerc' that she would not be going to the north. He claimed that only he and his secretary had seen her new photograph, so she accused his secretary of being a traitor, which shocked him. He swore that neither he nor his secretary had double-crossed her, and suggested that someone must have rifled through his cabinet. Later, he rang her summoning her to see him immediately. When she arrived, he told her that she must get out of Marseille. An order had come down from Vichy for her arrest and extradition, but he would conveniently 'lose' it in a pile of papers until after she had departed for Madrid and Lisbon and onward to England, then he would have to carry out the order. That set the wheels in motion for her departure from France.

As she would later tell the Advisory Committee: 'All that proved to what he was referring, the photograph with my hair up, blond and no glasses, so incontestably the Germans saw that photograph. Whether that man Leclerc was a double-crosser I do not know, but I should imagine that the English Authorities will be able to find all that out, will they not?'[9]

She told Mills on 16 December 1941 that 'Leclerc''s secretary's name was Henry (Henri), that his initials were H.C., 'age[d] about 30–32, height 5 ft. 10, slightly built, clean-shaven, dark brown eyes, dark brown hair, also always dressed in grey [like 'Leclerc']. He is a very ordinary looking man and has none of Leclerc's dash. He is Leclerc's shadow'.[10] Paillole's secretary was Renée Morell and his deputy was Lieutenant Joseph Challan-Belval, 'a young reserve officer who was excellent in our specialty, and had been helping [André] Bonnefous and myself since 1938'.[11] Joseph Challan-Belval also had dark eyes, dark hair, tall and slim and 1.85m (just over six feet), and would have been 30 when Stella met 'Leclerc'. What she neglected to consider was that instead of 'Leclerc''s secretary betraying her, she may have been set up by RENÉ or Meissner, the only other persons to have known her new description.[12]

RENÉ's letter of 10 September informed her that the denunciation had been via the Armistice Commission at Aix, which they had obtained from a Gestapo agent in Marseille – François Fayyang, a director of a wholesale fruit merchants at 3, Quai de la Joliette. The Germans were applying to arrest her, then extradite her. He advised her to get out as soon as possible and not to return to the occupied zone before December. All frontier posts had been alerted and she would be shot if the Germans found her. If they needed to see each other he would come down to the Free Zone.

Chapter 8

Flight from France

It was time for Stella to make plans to get out of France. Richard Tagnard, the Director of Air France in Marseille and a personal friend of hers, could get her on a flight to Madrid, but there was a problem. Since the flight was operated by Lufthansa, he told her that she would not be allowed on the plane. However, at the last minute he was able to 'bump' an Austrian Jewish refugee so that the Germans didn't have the opportunity to check up on her. She noted that the look on the steward's face was priceless when he saw her British passport.

When she arrived in Madrid, she met purely by chance José María de Chávarri, an old acquaintance whom she had met in Cannes some years previously, with whom she dined and danced. Mills concluded that he was just yet another of her lovers.[1] There was also Prince Louis Metternich, on leave from the German Army in France. This must have been Paul Alfons Fürst (Prince) von Metternich-Winneburg, the so-called 'playboy socialite' and racing driver, belonging to a 'circle of opponents of the Nazi regime', who had only recently married Princess Tatiana Vassiltchikova on 6 September 1941. On 3 November 1941 while in the lounge of the five-star Avenida Hotel, Rua 1° Dezembro 123 in Lisbon, she was greeted by Egon Pöhner, who approached her and declared, 'You are Mrs. LONSDALE.'

Egon Adin Pöhner, 28, was born on 4 September 1914 in Hamburg. In Lisbon in 1941 he was posing as a Swede, which was odd considering that when she tried out one or two Danish and Swedish expressions on him, he didn't know them. However, he spoke English very well and was fluent in German and French, as well as a little Bulgarian and Polish, and was learning Portuguese. He claimed to have been in Lisbon on business since May marketing resin and turpentine. Heinz Carl Weber was the German in charge of purchasing minerals in Portugal and someone with whom Pöhner may have done business.

Prior to Lisbon Pöhner had been in Greece, Bucharest, Belgrade, and Sofia, which raised a few red flags with Stella, who recalled that these were the very places in which Meissner had suggested she might operate as an agent. It was also suspicious that Pöhner's passport bore a striking resemblance to a German one, and the photographs of his family bore the stamp of a Hamburg photographer. Undeterred by her suspicions, she subsequently went out with him on several occasions. However, if she had arrived in Lisbon on 3 November as stated in the timeline in her file[2] and not 28 October as stated in Milmo's report,[3] then either Pöhner's letters contradict this, or Milmo's date is wrong. Milmo's statement about Pöhner not staying at the hotel also appears to be incorrect as his addresses, recorded in Stella's address book, were c/o Avenida Palace, Lisbon, and the Banco Espírito Santo e Comercial de Lisboa,[4] run by Baron Oswald Theodor von Hoyningen-Huene, the German ambassador to Portugal (1934–44), which traded heavily with the Germans.[5]

MI5 suspected Pöhner was a German agent. What appears to have clinched it for her was when, after an evening out at various nightclubs in Estoril, a Lisbon suburb famous for its casinos and nightclubs, he and Stella ended up singing national anthems, beginning with 'La Marseillaise', followed by his rendition of 'Deutschland Über Alles'; but after she sang 'God Save the King' and suggested he sing the Swedish anthem, he was unable to do so.

Pöhner was on friendly terms with Saly Mayer, a Swiss Jew and leader of the American Jewish Joint Distribution Committee in Switzerland, known as the 'Joint'. Stella never actually met him but had seen him speak to Pöhner on several occasions and described him as a little taller than Pöhner and aged about probably 45 or 46 (he would have actually been about 59), and living in the Avenida Palace. He kept an office in Lisbon and worked with Rabbi Joseph J. Schwartz in negotiating with the Swiss government over the immigration of Jews to Switzerland.[6]

When Milmo interviewed her, she had two notes from Pöhner written from the Avenida Palace making appointments to see her, the first, to have dinner, and the second, expressing his sorrow that she was leaving for London the following day. In 1942 his name appeared on a list of names blocked by the US State Department.[7] Based on their experience gained in various Hamburg companies, in 1947 Egon and his brother Lothar founded the company Gebrüder Pöhner GmbH, a broker company specializing in 'oilseeds, vegetable oils, animal fats, feedstuffs and oleo-based products', which would fit with his earlier business of marketing resin and turpentine.[8]

Stella's arrival at Whitchurch (Bristol) airport on 5 November 1941 on a KLM flight was noted by the Security Control Officer (SCO), Major E.S. Humphrey:

> Telephone message from B.26 [redacted] to D.4.b at [redacted] 11.15 hrs on 1.11.41.
> B.26 [redacted] rang that Mrs. Stella Clive LONSDALE was expected in from Lisbon by air, and he would like advance information of her journey

if possible, so that he could send down Lieut. Langley, who would be in uniform, had the M.C. and had only one arm, and another officer in civilian clothes, who he wished to be present unobtrusively during the interrogation of Mrs. LONSDALE by the S.C.O. It was entirely for the S.C.O. to decide what he should do with Mrs. LONSDALE. S.C.O. Whitchurch and S.C.O. Poole [Captain C.C. Carter] were informed. Later B.26 rang that they were not sure whether Lieut. Langley would be able to come down. But they would like to be informed as to what happened to Mrs. LONSDALE as soon as she arrived.

Telephone message from B.26 to B4b, 10.15 hours. 5.11.41
Captain Cowgill, B.26, telephoned regarding Mrs. Stella Clive LONSDALE, telephone message no.7 of 1.11.41., and asked that she should be told to go to Room 055a, War Office, and ask for Lt. Le[igh]. If she was not going up to London in the ordinary way, she should be told that the War Office would pay her fare up to London. If she still demurred about going, her address should be taken. Captain Cowgill was told of the previous instructions that we had received and S.C.O. Whitchurch was informed. Later, after 18.00 hours, S.C.O. Whitchurch telephoned that Mrs. LONSDALE had arrived. He was not quite satisfied as regards her being "turned loose" and allowed to proceed before she was interviewed by Lt. Le[igh]. [Leigh or Lee was Langley's cover name] Her story was quite interesting, and she stated that she had been sent over here to work for us and had expected to be met and given instructions and that she had no money. S.C.O. proposed having her looked after for the night at Bristol and sending her up with an F.S.P. [Field Security Policeman] as a guide to Room 055a in the morning. All her papers were taken off her and sealed and Captain Cowgill was consulted and agreed to the procedure.[9]

Humphrey instructed the immigration officer to examine her closely about her movements abroad. When she confessed to having in her possession a torn-up letter from a lover, and also a letter from a German officer this caused the immigration officer (A. Gold) to question her more closely. He concluded that 'Scotland Yard would like to know of the arrival of this lady, who, it is agreed here, is of the better class prostitute type'.[10]

Given that Cowgill's name is linked to B.26 in the second message, it is likely that it is his name which has been redacted from the first. Coincidentally, B.26, an MI5 designation, was also the designation given to Section V of SIS, of which Cowgill was head; D4b (Traffic Control and Security at Ports) was headed by Major (later Lieutenant Colonel) C.H. Burne; B4b (Espionage, Industry and Commerce) was headed by J.G. Craufurd.

As Neill Lochery's book on Lisbon during the Second World War states, 'The passenger lists of the flights were a who's who of the senior network of British spies in the city, as well as shadowy Allied industrialists involved in the trade war with the Germans.'[11] KLM operated four flights per week from Lisbon on behalf of Imperial Airways (later BOAC) using the twin-engined Douglas DC-3.[12]

Stella was put up in a hotel in Bristol for the night. The following day she was personally escorted by the ASCO (Assistant Security Control Officer) to Room 055 at the War Office for interrogation by MI5 and SIS.

Chapter 9

The RENÉ Enigma

RENÉ's true identity would remain an enigma until 1945. Mills and Courtenay Young speculated that he and Meissner might be identical, but Mills observed: 'for what it is worth I came away with the impression that they are not, for STELLA talked first of one, then of the other confidently and in a way that would have been full of pitfalls if in fact she had been discussing one man acting different roles in different parts of the story.'[1] One contender was Ernst von Einem, but when Mills showed her a photograph of him Stella refused to look at it. He commented that while it wouldn't be fair to form a judgement based on the photograph, he and Susan Barton felt that von Einem and RENÉ 'may be identical'.[2] But based on Meissner's movements Young thought that 'The evidence [in] support of this theory is slender in the extreme'.[3]

Ernst August Hermann Guenther Edwin Robert von Einem was born in Vienna on 26 October 1912, the son of Baroness von Einem, Gerta-Louise Anna Lucie Emilie Kitty Antonie Johanna *née* Reiß von Scheurnschloss, and Baron William Ernst Hermann von Einem. Records in the archives of Christ Church College, Oxford, show that he had registered in October 1933, having already been in England since early April receiving a month's tuition in English from a Mr T.E. Gullick of Westgate-on-Sea. He took the entrance examination in April 1933 and was to have taken a diploma in economics, but an operation for acute appendicitis prevented him from sitting the exam. A request to defer the exam was denied as the Statutes did not allow it. He departed for Austria in July 1935 to do ten months' military service in the Austrian Army from 1935–36, but afterwards did not resume his studies.[4]

Mrs Brett-Perring, a DR.18B detainee at Aylesbury prison, would later reveal to Christopher Harmer that Stella had become friends with Mathilde Carré (VICTOIRE) and had confided in her details of her case, including RENÉ's identity:

> Rolf von P. whom she [Stella] had met for the first time on her honeymoon at the Café Georges V, Paris … VICTOIRE is convinced from hearing STELLA's story, and particularly the suggestion made by ROLF that she should bring back a wireless set and operate it for the benefit of the

British, that he was in fact, merely trying to set up a chain of controlled wireless sets in France.[5]

As Harmer pointed out that:

> at the time they hoped to get STELLA back, they were also controlling the WALENTY set [the codename for Roman Garby-Czerniawski], but I doubt actually whether the dates in this respect fit. The other two [W/T sets] were both controlled from 1941 onwards. VICTOIRE thinks she was nearly introduced to Rolf in 1941, but only saw him in the distance in a café.[6]

He suggested that this must be Rolf von Pöel, since Stella had already mentioned a du Pöel as a possible identity for RENÉ. Credence to this claim was added in February 1942 when Stella relented and wrote down a name on a piece of paper, on condition that it would remain between herself, Cyril Mills and Tar Robertson. The note was placed in an envelope, sealed with Tar's signet ring and marked: 'NOT TO BE OPENED WITHOUT THE PERMISSION OF Major ROBERTSON (B.1.A).' Mills wrote underneath, 'The meaning of the enclosure is known to Major Robertson and Major Mills of B.1.A.' and dated it 12.2.42. Whether out of frustration at trying to get to the bottom of the mystery or something else, on 26 August 1942 he opened it and found the name Gerhardt Gunther du Pöel, which proved to be a red herring.[7] As Mills surmised, this was Stella making mischief again because *Zahlmeister* (Paymaster) von Pöel was responsible for purchasing soap for the Abwehr!

In October 1944 when he was in Camp 020 Adalbert Karl Friederich Paulsen @ Paul Kleber @ Paul Roland @ Max Platon @ Koto8 stated that he knew of a Sonderführer Rauch or Rauh who had been attached to Angers III-F for a short while but doubted that he was Meissner's assistant. Nor does his description of a 'small dark man' match with Stella's of RENÉ being aged about 30, 5 feet 11 inches, with blondish-light brown hair and blue eyes.

Paulsen worked as a radio operator in I-i (communications) of Ast Angers from May 1942 to February 1943 at 1, rue de la Manufacture and corresponded with other Abwehrstellen; in January 1943 he was operating out of 73, boulevard Maréchal Foch. During the early part of the summer of 1941 RENÉ's flat was at number 43. In Europe the number '7' is crossed with a downward stroke so it seems likely that it had been mistaken for the number '4'. Strangely, there is no mention of Rauch in Paulsen's MI5 file.[9]

Information from MI5's Registry (RB3) on 27 November 1944 showed that RENÉ had been attached to Angers III-F in December 1942 and appeared 'identical with Sonderführer Rauch @ Rauh ... and possibly identical to Lieutenant Colonel Rauh @ Rauch'. But Young doubted that the two were identical since their descriptions didn't match and their functions – one in III-F (counter-espionage), the other in I-i (communications) – were different. Besides, 'It is possible, of course, that this character changed his trade, but I think it too long a shot, especially having regard to the statement ... that the Lt. Colonel did not consort with woman [sic]. I cannot believe that this description would fit any of Stella's friends!'[10]

Letters addressed to RENÉ were sent c/o Dr Terrenoir, 30 Quai Gambetta, Chalon-sur-Saône, and also c/o Gaston Piedbout in Angers. Charles Terrenoir @ 'Louis', born on 7 July 1913 in Saint-Vallier, Saône-et-Loire, was a member of the FTPF (Francs-Tireurs et Partisans Français), who was arrested in Amboise on 4 April 1943 by French police. After being convicted by a military trial, he was shot by a German firing squad at Saint-Jean-de-la-Ruelle, a commune in the Loiret *département*, on 8 October 1943. Piedbout, born 7 June 1901 in Vitré, Ille-et-Vilaine, a commune in Brittany, was deported from Compiègne on 2 July 1944 and sent to Dachau; he was liberated from Allach, a sub-camp (*Haftstätte*) of Dachau on 30 April 1945.[11]

Mills contacted Lieutenant Commander John Senter, the head of security at SOE to see if he could shed any light on RENÉ's identity, enclosing a photograph of du Pöel obtained from Stella, with brief details of his career, but not revealing the source, only that he was understood to have been Meissner's personal assistant. Du Pöel and Meissner had moved to Paris some time during the summer of 1941, when Meissner had become head of the entire counter-espionage organization in France at that time.[12]

Captain Arthur Maldwyn Baird, SOE's Assistant Police Liaison, Security Section, made extensive enquiries, but could find no trace of anyone named Pöel in any of their country sections, but thought their Fighting French Liaison might know of him. He also drew a blank when it came to Meissner's assistant in Norway and France. Baird assumed that MI5 had already approached SIS who held 'Almost all our information of the type you require ... who will therefore have access to far more information than is available to us'.[13] However, MI5 had not done so. Mills suggested to Tar that an SIS look-up about RENÉ would suffice for the time being until he could get the name from Stella when he next saw her, instead of having to explain how MI5 had got the name and why they hadn't already done something about it.[14]

At a meeting on 10 November 1941 between Dick White, ADB1 (Assistant Director B1), Mackenzie from SIS's Section V, and Langley from MI9 they all agreed that they could not accept RENÉ as a friend of Britain who was acting independently of the German Intelligence Service, because he had given Stella English codes to communicate with him, and allowed himself to be seen with her in the *zone interdite* at Brest. They thought it impossible that someone as careful as RENÉ should run such risks, 'Therefore he must be regarded as a German agent directing Stella along the lines desired by the German Intelligence Service.'[15] White agreed that Langley's conclusions were 'perfectly correct' about the information Stella had supplied regarding SIS's escape organization in the South of France. But their opinion was divided as to whether or not she had been acting in good faith when she agreed to co-operate with the Germans.

RENÉ's part in the whole affair also generated much discussion. Langley believed that her story was not simply an elaborate cover story and was the whole truth since SIS could corroborate much of the detail. White and Milmo begged to differ and shared a distrust of her, but White still believed that RENÉ could have duped her into thinking that he was a genuine friend of Britain who gave her information which would be of use to them:

> An agent of this kind will go a long way to establish that whatever else she is, she is not a fool or has been easily duped. Moreover, her vanity is at stake because she is naturally not unwilling to believe that RENÉ acted in the way he did because he was in love with her. Nevertheless, I see the force of Mr. Milmo's argument that for a clever women not to have been suspicious of him when he handed to her a British code and travelled with her into the Zone interdite is difficult to understand.[16]

Milmo offered three possible scenarios: (1) that her whole story was true and RENÉ was a real person and genuinely pro-British, (2) that she was genuinely a loyal British citizen, but mistaken in her assessment of RENÉ who was using her as a dupe, or (3) that she was and always had been working for the Germans.[17] He discounted (1) because he believed that RENÉ was running her as an agent, and because he found it incredible that he should have given her a code and secret ink taken from Gaessler; and (2) because she continually lied when it suited her, particularly when weaknesses in her story were pointed out to her: 'She is in my view concealing the identity of RENÉ for some reason other than the reason which she gives.' That left (3), but he was not entirely convinced that it had been proven she was a conscious German agent. He believed that she was trying to double-cross both sides 'for her own personal edification and benefit' and dismissed as ridiculous the notion that 'Leclerc' would be compromised if she failed to return. If she returned she would be using false papers; to do otherwise would not help 'Leclerc', and would only cause the Gestapo to arrest her. Langley stated that MI9 also knew that Gaessler was under German control prior to the date which RENÉ had given her.

Guy Liddell felt 'quite certain that RENÉ was using her but I am not entirely convinced that she too was consciously working for the Germans' and that SIS knew Stella was under control at a prior date to the one which RENÉ had told her: 'It would make a good deal of difference if S.I.S. could say that it was clear to the Germans that S.I.S. knew this before RENÉ informed Stella … the more this woman talks the more she will get herself tied up.'

They needed to settle her somewhere so that 'Special Facilities' could be installed – hidden microphones in 'the cupboard above the clothes cupboard outside her bathroom', which was locked and 'no attempt should be made to open it'.[18] Since she was dependent on MI5 for funds it shouldn't be too difficult, but they needed to prevent her from seeing John Lonsdale until the necessary arrangements had been made as their first meeting would be an important one.[19]

Following Mills's interview with Stella on 23 November 1941 he added:

If he [Viner] did not warn her and if RENÉ did not, and if in fact she does not know such things, it would fit with the hypothesis that she is an unconscious agent of RENÉ's as in that case he would not necessarily have told her more than he had to. On the other hand if RENÉ were really acting the part which she says he is he would surely have schooled her in the tricks of the trade and one would expect it to be part of her make-up to profess that she knows them all rather than to act as if she knows nothing of this sort of thing.

If, however, STELLA is a conscious agent of RENÉ and he has invented her whole story about him she probably does know at least the elementary tricks and therefore to pretend that she does not think we have photographed her property does not fit with the supposition that RENÉ would have schooled her properly had he been playing for us.

It seems therefore that whether her attitude in this matter was genuine or feigned it is inconsistent with her story about RENÉ.

The conversation drifted to Nazi beastliness and atrocities including the shooting of hostages and when we had both expressed our loathing of these things STELLA asked me whether I thought RENÉ, who was a good German but one who loathed Hitler, and all the Nazi tyranny stands for [sic], was a traitor. I gave her the answer which the phrasing of her question indicated which seemed to me to be as follows:-

RENÉ hates Nazism and all that it stands for, he knows that if he works against it in Germany or with Germans he will be caught and shot within a few days. He is a German belonging to the upper classes and is determined in some way or another he is going to do something to get rid of Hitler and his gang. He believes that only the English can now restore Germany to the decent minded Germans and therefore he decides to help them. In these circumstances he may be a Nazi traitor but that does not make him a traitor to Germany. This answer seemed to be exactly that which STELLA hoped to receive – it was given because (a) the phrasing of the question indicated the reply she wanted to hear and (b) it is our policy at the moment to let STELLA think that we have swallowed the whole RENÉ story.

She seemed very relieved at this and said she was glad that we were so much alive to the possibilities as not only her own, but RENÉ's life would be forfeit if the Germans ever got hold of the reports.[20]

Milmo reported to Cowgill that White had discussed the matter with Mackenzie and Langley who gave him to understand that SIS was no longer interested in her, and that MI5 had reached the following conclusions:

1) That the man RENÉ, whoever he may be, is acting directly on behalf of the German Intelligence Service, and that the story that he is a friend of Britain and personally interested in Mrs. LONSDALE's position is wholly unacceptable.
2) Mrs. LONSDALE may be RENÉ's accomplice in deceiving us, or she may be RENÉ's dupe. Either hypothesis is consistent with the story as told to us by her, but if she is the dupe, she must be a singularly vain and gullible person, which she does not in fact appear to be.
3) That the Germans wish us to believe Mrs. LONSDALE's story and send her back with instructions to continue her good work. They do not view her as a person through whom they can collect valuable information about the British, but they regard her as an excellent channel through which to feed some grand deception at the right moment. It is possible that the information she supplied concerning the German plans for invading the Peninsula was intended by the Germans to mislead us on this point.[21]

Liddell and White favoured giving the appearance that they were carefully considering her proposed return to France, thereby securing the opportunity of extracting further information from her and 'judging her real position', on which they thought B1a was well suited to advise. But she would not be severely cross-examined without an arrest, which would only make her embittered and 'leave her as a grave source of danger both to your organization and to security here'; arresting her and interning her would give her the right to appeal, 'which might easily be successful'.[22] Meanwhile, MI5 and SIS would be 'keeping the lady on tap at the Waldorf Hotel'.

Masterman's 'Preliminary Observations' of 13 November agreed that Milmo's conclusions were 'thoroughly sound':

1) I entirely agree that RENÉ (presuming his existence) is running Mrs. LONSDALE as an agent. If he were not, he was running impossibly foolish risks. On the presumption that he was genuinely pro-British, he would have quite certainly have got Mrs. LONSDALE out of the country and back to England as soon as he could and have provided her with as much useful information for us, verbally, as he could.

2) It is more doubtful whether Mrs. LONSDALE has been deceived by RENÉ or whether she is in fact herself a German agent. Here again I am inclined to accept Milmo's provisional hypothesis that she has compromised herself with the Germans and played to a certain extent with both sides. The fact that she has lied on a number of important points (according to Milmo's account) tells heavily against her. I do not, for example, understand why she had the trouble over her journeys to the occupied zone when she was in possession of the Identity Card given to her by RENÉ. The last contact with BOHNER suggests very strongly that she was fairly deeply engaged with the Germans.

3) On the practical point involved I feel tolerably clear. I understand that the suggestion is that she might be sent back to France, but this seems to me to be wrong.

   a) If she is to go back, that is in the first instance a business for either S.I.S. or S.O.2 [the earlier designation for SOE], and I understand that S.I.S. will have nothing to do with it.

   b) If, therefore, we are asked to consider this project, we must first have a written request from S.I.S. to do so, and an undertaking of their approval and support. I fancy that the plan will break down here, but if it does not, then –

   c) Is the suggestion to send her back under an assumed name or to send her back as Mrs. LONSDALE, and is she to go to occupied and unoccupied France? If she is to go under an assumed name the project is doomed to disaster, for she has far too many contacts to escape detection. I therefore assume that she is to go as Mrs. LONSDALE.

   d) But in this case also it seems to me that the project is doomed to failure. According to her own story, the Germans have asked for her arrest and extradition in unoccupied France. Her memorandum which was taken off ~~WEINER~~ VINER sufficiently condemns her, and she will be either put in prison or worse, or else persuaded to work entirely for the Germans. There is no likelihood that she will be allowed to return here, unless the Germans decide that that is in their interests.[23]

But he was sceptical whether RENÉ would actually give her information on the agents allegedly communicating with the Germans from Britain, and concluded that he was a 'hundred percent German Intelligence officer'. Mills interrogated Stella (MICHAEL) on 4 December 1941 and reported that:

> MICHAEL was asked what RENÉ was doing in Paris and also at the Hotel between Tours and Le Mans when she stayed with him on the occasion of her first return to occupied France. She replied that his commission was more or less of a roving one and he was just travelling about to various places. MICHAEL has told us that RENÉ is friendly with the man who controls German agents in England and that this man is in Paris. When asked whether she knew anything about him, MICHAEL said that she had not met him and did not know anything about him but that RENÉ had promised to give her details on the occasion of her next visit. This is nothing less than a 'cock and bull' story because RENÉ obviously knew the answer when he last saw MICHAEL and if he was working for us when he told her this, he could have given the details to her then.
>
> Without being questioned about this story MICHAEL has told Nina [Myers] that RENÉ is so keen to get her to go back that he is withholding this information as an inducement. This is also a 'cock and bull' story because MICHAEL has told us that RENÉ has promised to give her the names of all German agents operating in England at the present time and if there are any plums in this pudding, that is the one we are looking for, as we already know who controls German agents in Paris and RENÉ probably knows we do.[24]

RENÉ had told Stella about four British agents dropped into France: Richard van de Walle @ 'Marine'; Albert Thiou (Thioux); Maurice Duclos @ 'Saint Jacques'; and Muelleman @ 'John McLennan'. Muelleman was arrested in June 1941 at the demarcation line and 'turned', betraying Charles Deguy, Marcel Halbout and Lucien Feltesse of the BCRA (Bureau Centrale de Renseignments et d'Action), who were arrested on 8 August 1941.[25] Van de Walle[26] was arrested with Thiou just hours after landing[27] and compelled to send eleven wireless messages as part of a *Funkspiel* (radio game), 'but he deliberately left out the agreed checks, so that we should know that he was working under Pressure, and gave wrong answers to questions we sent him – to confirm this'. Duclos was arrested, but released a month later; Thiou was executed in Schaarbeek on 21 March 1942.

* * *

On 28 September 1944 double-cross agent ZIGZAG (Eddie Chapman) was shown three photographs of RENÉ, but he did not recognize him or the name Siegfried Rauch.

At Young's urgent request, Joseph Lynch, the FBI's legal attaché at the US Embassy in London, looked into whether Siegfried Rauch had studied law at Denver University, Colorado, and if Hilde Bernard, his married sister in Pasadena, existed. Since Lynch could find no record of him at either Denver University or Westminster College, Denver, Young told him that Stella must still be lying to them. Nor could the Rauch family be traced to 107, Rheinestraße in the Wiesbaden telephone book since neither SIS, SOE, nor the Ministry of Economic Warfare had a Wiesbaden street directory.[28] However, MI5 was able to confirm that he had been working at Angers in September 1941,

> so she has this time at least given us a genuine name, but I shrewdly suspect she has attached phoney description … If in fact Mrs. LONSDALE is telling the truth, it is obviously a matter of some interest to you that the sister of a full blown Abwehr agent is living quietly in California, but I place little reliance on Mrs. LONSDALE's story even in this latest and amended version.[29]

A Home Office look-up revealed no traces of anyone named Rauch ever coming to Britain.

It would take until 25 September 1944 when Stella finally revealed to Young that RENÉ's real name *was* Siegfried Rauch @ 'Serge Robin' whose parents did indeed live at 107 Rheinestraße, Wiesbaden. But it took until 24 March 1945 before Lynch was able to confirm the following:

> Investigation by the Los Angeles Field Office developed information to the effect that Hilde Bernard, the subject's sister [Rauch], resides at 1777 Orangewood Drive, Pasadena, California. She arrived in the United States from Germany in 1924 and was naturalized at Los Angeles in 1939. She told associates that the subject, her brother, attended Depauw University, Greencastle, Indiana, as an exchange student in 1935 and 1936. She also indicated that the subject had visited her at Pasadena in 1936. Hilde Bernard's husband, Ervin V. Bernard, is a clerk at the Huntington Library, Pasadena, California. In mentioning her brother to friends, Hilde Bernard has stated that he was an interpreter and officer and not a "fighting man." She also indicated that she had another brother, Walter, in the German Army, who was killed in Russia. She has confided to other associates that she has two brothers, both of whom are in the German Intelligence Service. No information was developed by the Los Angeles Field Division which would indicate that Hilde Bernard or her husband is engaged in subversive activities.

Investigation by the Indianapolis Field Division developed information to [t]he effect that the subject attended Depauw University at Greencastle, Indiana, as a German exchange student for two semesters during 1935–1936. The records of that institution reflected that he was born on April 2, 1917, at Strassburg [*sic*], France. His church was listed as German Protestant. His father was Gerhard Rauch, whose occupation was listed as professor at Wiesbaden High School, Wiesbaden, Germany. Subject graduated from this school on March 2, 1935. He attended the University of Freiburg Law School for two semesters during 1934–1935. His address while at Depauw was listed as the Beta Theta Pi House, Greencastle. At Depauw he was regarded as quiet, a good student, and one of the best of the exchange students. He made talks to several local clubs, admitting Nazi training in youth labor camps and giving the impression of being a local supporter of the Nazi movement, although he made no attempt to convert local associates.[30]

Hilde E. Bernard, aged 37, and her husband Erwin, aged 42, had a 10-year-old son, Ralph, born on 29 April 1929.[31] The US Social Security Death Index 1935–2014 gives Hilde's date of birth as 22 July 1902 and her death as February 1987.[32] Rauch's religion, listed as being German Protestant, was earlier described as being Austrian Catholic when Stella took him to see Abbé Lunau.

An article from DePauw University mentioned that Rauch had also gone to Colorado Springs, Colorado, and attended the University of Colorado or Colorado College.[33] But the Registrar of the University of Colorado has confirmed that 'There is no record of an individual named "Siegfried Rauch" in the University of Colorado student records database. The University of Colorado Colorado Springs (UCCS) campus was founded in 1965 so they could not have been a student at UCCS.'[34] However, DePauw University has confirmed that Rauch *was* an exchange student there in 1935–6, and his photograph appears in *Mirage*, a yearbook for Der Deutsche Bund, a German club on the university campus.[35] Lynch sent a photograph taken of Rauch at DePauw dated 1935–6 (now in Stella's file) to MI5 in 1945. Dr G. Herbert Smith, Dean of the university when Rauch was there considered him 'the only German exchange student that he knows who would have made a good United States citizen … there was no indication that the subject was disseminating Nazi propaganda and the subject was genuinely distressed when he was required to return to Germany'. On 26 December 1939, while serving in Sieradz, central Poland, Rauch wrote a long letter to the university on his daily routine, his impressions of the war, and speculated on its outcome: 'Who of us is going to see the end? Most likely you; most unlikely I.'[36] Prescient words indeed.

RENÉ had stated that he would only reveal his name to the chief of British Intelligence in London (presumably Sir Stewart Menzies), but 'Winer [*sic*] knows that his first name is Siegfried, and that he uses the address "Poste Restante, Angers"'.[37] A look-up at Ryder Street revealed that 'According to M.S.S. [Most Secret Sources – ISOS] of 2.9.41 Sonderführer Dr Siegfried RAUCH is working at Angers. As Paris informs Ast Angers that the financial section at Wiesbaden want to known [*sic*] the decision about his transit. N.T. of ROBIN or of the addresses'.[38]

A declassified CIA report lists him as 'RAUCH, Dr Siegfried @ RICHARD; O/Faehnr [Oberfähnrich – officer candidate]; MK 2 ANGERS and MK TOURS'. Working as his assistant was Elfreide Schneider. He had been a lawyer and assessor, which concurs with what Stella had told MI5. In October 1940 he was transferred from Ast Wiesbaden to III-F, Ast Angers; in April 1943 to MK Perpignan, and in August 1943 to MK Évian. There he lost contact with Abw Leit Truppe 351 under the command of Dernbach during the German withdrawal in August 1944 and was reported missing along with Fraulein Schneider.[39] Meissner's MI5 file also confirms that he was one of his assistants at Ast Angers.[40] Additional evidence on Rauch is provided in an extract of a 12th Army Group report in Speck's MI5 file (as well as Stella's),[41] and concurs with the CIA report from which the information below was obviously obtained (see Figure 1):

RAUCH? Dr Siegfried Robin (1941–42) (ANGERS) RICHARD (TOURS, ANNEMASSE, LYONS) German	
Address	Stayed with his mother WIESBADEN? Rheinstrasse (bomed out) [*sic*]
Status	Sonderfuehrer. Was appointed in absentia Oberfaehnrich FAK 313, missing since Aug 44
Description	Born 2 Apr 1917 in WIESBADEN 5' 7" (170m) slim build; oval face; pale complexion; straight brown hair; brown eyes; dresses carelessly; wears civilian clothes.
Miscellaneous	Spoke French without accent, had French carte d'identité, lawyer in civilian life has studied at US university, has friend in Senate Committee for Foreign Affairs, speaks English fluently as well as Russian. Was friendly with Mrs Stella LONSDALE in ANGERS.
Career	Succeeded Sonderfuehrer SCHIELE as Meldekopf IIIF at ANGERS); transferred LYON Mar 43, was succeeded by Sonderfuehrer BUERVENICH; was Meldekopf IIIF at ANNEMASSE et EVIAN. At ANNEMASSE he use[d] cover of black market operations. Did not obey order of Col DERNBACH to retu[rn] to LYON but stayed in EVIAN with Fraulei[n] SCHNEIDER.

Figure 1.

John Rainsford-Hannay in H4d at MI5 reported that:

> With reference to Hpt.Dr. Siegfried RAUCH appearing in the case of SPECK, he is almost certainly identical with Hpt. RENÉ @ du POEL Gerhardt Gunther @ RAOUL @ SIEGFRIED @ ROBIN Serge @ RAUCH Siegfried @ SIBER RENÉ @ RICHARD Serge, born c.1910, Address in 1941 43 Boulevard Marechal Foch, ANGERS. Lawyer. Nov. 1941 Stated by Stella LONSDALE to be 2nd in command to Hans MEISSNER, chief of Berman [sic] C.E. in France, H.Q. in Paris. That he had spent some time in the U.S.A., speaks 15 languages. He knew she was working for the British and wanted to give her messages for the British S.S. LONSDALE's information is thought to be unreliable.[42]

In 1945 three photographs in CSDIC's possession were returned to B1b from WRC4a (part of MI5's War Room). One showed Rauch with Charlotte-Louise Rieth *née* Pillon, Dernbach's private secretary and mistress, taken at Dernbach's house at 15, rue Haute Pressoir in Angers. (Coincidentally, one of Dernbach's aliases was Pillon.) Dernbach escaped from Lyon on 23 August 1944 before its liberation by Free French Forces on 3 September but was captured by the Americans on 13 March 1945 in Bad Kreuznach and charged with 'moral turpitude' involving relations with Charlotte Rieth. When she became pregnant in 1944 she took part in a fake marriage and sought refuge at her cousin's house in Hauenstein, Rhineland-Palatinate, where she gave birth to her daughter, Oulika. In 1946 she became secretary to the President of the Tribunal intermédiare de la Sarre (Saar) in Saarbrücken and died in Brazil at the age of 95.[43]

The second photograph showed Rauch at work at the Place Champ-de-Mars, Angers; the third was the woman in the car with two Germans in uniform. Speck believed the woman was Stella, but he was unable to make a positive identification. When he'd met her at Rauch's house in Angers in the boulevard Maréchal Foch in October or November of 1940 she'd been living in Nantes and working as a language teacher. She would regularly visit Rauch and together with Sonderführer Bürvenich @ 'Gilles', a member of the local Meldekopf working for III-F, they would have 'fireside chats'. Speck thought that the money she received from Rauch and Meissner came from official sources, although he didn't know what it was used for or any missions they may have assigned her.

But Speck's claim to have met her in October or November of 1940 appears to predate her arrest. She'd claimed to be a descendant of 'Clive of India' and admitted that her husband was a British agent, 'but no definite proof was ever found against her, personally. She disappeared later, and was believed to have gone to PARIS.'[44] That was at the end of 1940/beginning of 1941.

Then she'd appeared on a German 'wanted list', a copy of which was received from 105 SCI Unit on 22 March 1945: 'This woman constitutes a danger to the occupying authorities, as she worked earlier for the English Intelligence Service.'[45] She was next heard of in Paris (probably when she was visiting Rauch), then not again until she resurfaced in Marseille in 1942, although this latter appearance is incorrect as by that time she was in London.

During the early part of 1944 Speck and some friends, including Rauch, had planned to organize a resistance group within Abwehr Leit Truppe 351 in Lyons, the predecessor of Kommando 313, but three other reports suggest that Rauch had surrendered to the Americans and was taken to Évian where he was co-operating with them and recruited by the OSS.[46] A note from Major J.F.E. Stephenson of the MI5 Liaison Section to Mrs Spring of B1b on 18 June 1945 reported that 'I have at last heard from the Americans that Siegfried Rauch, whom she wanted to borrow for interrogation, is reported to have been killed by the F.F.I. [Forces Françaises de l'Intérieur] in September last [1944]'. The MI5 file on FAK 313 agent Antonio Moglia @ Antonio Aristides Moglia @ Jacques Molliani @ Jean Moschetti @ IDOL contains an extract from an interim report on RICHARD, a known cover name for Rauch, who was thought to have been killed by the Maquis. Last seen in Lyons in February 1944, he was rumoured to have been in Évian with his 'wife'. Although Moglia knew nothing about RICHARD's work, he was well thought of but now believed to be a traitor. He described him as:

> German, aged 35, 1m 75 in height, 75kgs. in weight, thick dark brown hair, brushed back, dark blue eyes, rather round fat face, pallid complexion, rather large straight nose, jutting chin, good teeth, cleanshaven, thick lips, nervy hands, untidy appearance, wore civilian clothes (not very smart), loud deep voice. Walks quickly, is always late. Speaks German and perfect French.[47]

A further twist in Rauch's story appeared in DePauw University's records: 'Towards the end of the war, serving as an interpreter with the Nazi forces in France, he attempted escape, but was arrested and shot.'[48] And,

Killed by Nazi Firing Squad
Word has come from the mother of Siegfried Rauch of his death during the war at the hands of the Nazi firing squad. Serving as an interpreter in France, Rauch was cut from his post when a revolt against the Nazis broke out in 1944 where he was stationed. Together with his secretary he attempted to flee into Switzerland but did not succeed in getting across the border and he and his companion were arrested and later shot.[49]

The saga of RENÉ had finally come to an end.

Chapter 10

'Keeping the Lady on Tap'

After her arrival at Whitchurch from Lisbon on 5 November 1941 Stella was not sent to 101 Nightingale Lane, Clapham, the female annex of the London Reception Centre (LRC) in Wandsworth, also known as the Royal Victoria Patriotic School (RVPS).[1] This prompted W.R. Perks of the Home Office Immigration Branch to question whether she should have been dealt with under Article 2 of the Arrival from Enemy or Foreign Territory Order.[2] Major C.H. Burne of D4, Port Security based at Oxford assured him 'that this woman is being taken care of perperly [sic] by us'.

Her first interrogation was conducted by Milmo @ 'Miller', in Room 055 of the War Office. All subsequent interrogations were conducted by him and Mills in room 519 at the Waldorf Hotel in Aldwych, London, where she was accommodated at MI5's and SIS's expense,[3] during which she provided the following snippets of information:

7 November 1941

While in German custody she was visited by Colonel Friederich Alfred Garthe @ Arnold @ Dr Schultz @ Jensen, *Leiter* I-L (head of air intelligence for France, 1940–43) based at Abwehr headquarters at the Hôtel Lutetia in Paris. He tried to persuade her to go to Vichy to contact French aviation circles and discover what they might be concealing from the Germans, but she refused to work for him because going further afield would have meant she couldn't work for Meissner, whose agents only worked in France.[4] HARLEQUIN's MI5 file describes him as being violently anti-Nazi; however, his own file states that he joined the NSDAP (Nazi) party in 1931 and had been a member of the Abwehr since 1935/6.[5]

9 November 1941

She said the German Intelligence Service in occupied France was controlled from a central headquarters at the Hôtel Lutetia in Paris, with three area headquarters:

1. St. Germain, which controls the Paris area;
2. Angers, which controls the whole of the North West Coast. From some date prior to November, 1940 until 20th June MEISSNER was a Head of the Angers Abwehrstelle. Angers was always spoken of as controlling the South-West, which was a code word indicating in fact the North-West.
3. Dijon. In June of 1941 MEISSNER was promoted to Paris, where he became chief of Counter Espionage for the whole of France.

14 November 1941

MI5 returned two of John's letters taken from her at Bristol, 'In order to get her into a favourable state of mind and to lead her to believe that a more favourable view was now being taken of her case'. She clarified that she was no longer estranged from her mother, that Martineau had been acting in self-interest and not out of compassion for her when he'd offered her a job at the Berlitz School, and RENÉ had broken off his engagement to an American girl whose name may have been Elsa, as a result of Stella's involvement with him.

Perversely, her possession of a revolver was not because she'd contemplated suicide but in case at some point, she might need to kill herself (?), or someone else! RENÉ later returned it when she was in Marseille. She had cockily nicknamed Dernbach 'Snooty', which had stuck; now all the *Abwehrstelle* knew him by that name. Hermann Heinemann @ 'Harry', aged between 55 and 58, was someone she'd met on many occasions, sometimes in Angers, but not since March, and will be discussed later.[6]

Her new *carte d'identité* in Marseille enabled her to return to the unoccupied zone without compromising RENÉ if she were captured with a false one while crossing the demarcation line illegally on her outward journey. But it was incorrect that she'd only used the *Ausweiss* twice; in fact, she'd used it on all but two occasions when she'd crossed the border. She now claimed her arrival in Angers was not on Monday 16 June 1941 but Friday 20 June, two days before the Germans invaded Russia. Had she done so earlier, she would have been able to provide Garrow with information from RENÉ about the impending invasion. Milmo noted that 'this is a deliberate departure from her original story as she had previously definitely stated that she had arrived in Angers on the Monday'.

Frank Viner was very indiscreet and exercised poor judgement. Because of this she had very little confidence in him, but she was confident that he wasn't involved with the Germans. Christian Boulanger was trying to find out 'Leclerc's' real name, which of course puts pay to Milmo's earlier supposition that they were one and the same, unless this was a smokescreen. Pavie was arrested again prior to the visit of Admiral Darlan to Marseille during a general swoop on foreigners by the French police.[7] She collaborated with the Deuxième Bureau to procure papers for him, and would have succeeded had she not needed to leave France in such a hurry.

In mid-July RENÉ had given her codenames for the simultaneous attack on England and Gibraltar planned for 1 September 1941: *Unternehmen Seelöwe* (Operation *Sealion*) – originally the codename assigned for the invasion of Britain in September 1940 – and *Unternehmen Seeadler* (Operation *Sea Eagle*) respectively.[8] But it was not until after Meissner was captured on 8 June 1945 that MI5's War Room (WRC4a) was able to verify this and other issues relating to her when he was interrogated at Camp 020 on 7 August 1945. He was asked whether this information had been genuine or a 'plant':

> As regards "Seeadler", MEISNER [*sic*] had heard this name but can no longer state with certainty what operation it was intended to cover ... That a considerable amount of true information was being transmitted over captured wireless sets (presumably S.O.E.) to keep the sets alive. This information was either innocuous or already known to the British but it was eventually intended to use the sets to convey false information when a German invasion of England was about to take place.[9]

He believed that by that time the Germans had abandoned any intention of such an attack; the information sent was meant to keep up pressure on Britain and to cover preparations for the invasion of Russia.[10]

No further details on d'Éstienne d'Orvres would appear until the interim report of 30 July 1945. Other W/T sets being used by Ast Angers were intended to send false information in the event of an impending invasion of England and 'a certain amount of information regarding troop and shipping concentrations in German western and Baltic ports was transmitted', most of which was innocuous or well known. Therefore, the War Room concluded that the information about a forthcoming invasion of England was 'plant material'. Roland Bird of B1b agreed that 'there is nothing sufficiently definite about this to justify the case of Stella LONSDALE being in any way reopened'.[11]

Meissner only remembered meeting Stella on two occasions, having been introduced to her by Dernbach in his office in Angers in November or December 1941, but had apparently also met her in Nantes where he believed she may have been working for Dernbach for some time, but didn't know how much he had told her about their activities. He was sceptical about her claim that she was a member of English society, but Dernbach was convinced that she could prove of great importance. When Meissner met her again, she was living in a flat in one of the main streets of Angers. He maintained that they only discussed general topics and he'd made no arrangements with her. About a fortnight later she'd disappeared into unoccupied France. Since then he'd heard nothing further about her.

All of this contradicts her claim that he'd brought her toiletries while she was in prison and had met with her on an almost daily basis after her release following the second tribunal. As far as Meissner could remember, she was in close contact with Sonderführer Dr Rauch, one of Dernbach's assistants, who may have passed on a certain amount of information to her, but claimed to know no more about Rauch being a member of the Abwehr than he'd already told MI5. As far as he knew, Rauch had never worked in Switzerland.

Stella expressed concern that should an invasion of Britain occur, all MI5's records would be destroyed, something she would echo to Mills on 22 November. Milmo assured her that none would fall into German hands. The interview left him with the impression that 'she was feeling much more confident of her position in relation to this department'.

15 November 1941

The previous meeting had left unfinished business to discuss, but Stella didn't want to see Milmo because she thought she'd already said too much and 'might be getting ambiguous'. When he arrived, she kept him waiting for half an hour, claiming she was dressing. He suspected that she needed more time to co-ordinate her thoughts and corroborate the story she'd already told him. When she deigned to see him, she told him how impressed she'd been by how 'the humble people in this country' had stood up to German air raids and wanted to contribute to the war effort by returning to France. She also wanted to atone for John's misdeeds. John was angry that she hadn't told him about her arrival in Britain or what she'd been up to in France and they'd had a 'first-class row'. She was seeking a divorce from him, after which she no longer wished to see him.

Stella was convinced that if she were to return to France it would be in the next fifteen days and suggested that she could either be landed in unoccupied territory by aircraft, or failing that, by parachute. If neither of these options was viable, she could go to Barcelona and be smuggled across the border and contact 'Leclerc'. He had obtained a false passport for her, currently at the Swiss Consulate in Marseille; she also had the use of a false identity card belonging to an unnamed friend of hers. Milmo informed her that such a trip took time, required careful preparations by SOE, not MI5, and she would need to ensure that all of her details corresponded with those papers in Marseille.

Once she arrived, she replied, the documents used to enter the country could be destroyed. But as he noted, 'she did not like the suggestion that the papers should be produced from Marseille and she refused to give any particulars of the name or identity of the person in possession of the false Identity Card.'

'Leclerc's' interest in her was solely because she'd supplied him with the names of German agents. If she were arrested all she had to do was request that he be contacted. As Milmo pointed out, this was inconsistent with the story she'd originally told about 'Leclerc' only allowing her to leave France 'on condition that she returned within a very short time … otherwise he would get into trouble for having failed to execute the Germans request for her extradition'. This left him with the impression that she had not divulged her real reason for wanting to return.

To avoid giving herself away in Marseille she would have to live in a different quarter of the city and avoid her friends and acquaintants, but Christian would protect her, implying that he and 'Leclerc' were not necessarily the same person. This left Milmo wondering why she should want to live in Marseille at all, rather than anywhere else in unoccupied France, and what useful work she thought she could do.

RENÉ would be waiting for her and she would get in touch with him using an interzone card and secret writing – he only had to request that she go to the occupied zone and she would do so, but it would only be necessary to travel to northern France in December. He would provide her with details of agents in Britain who were in touch with the Germans, and the Luftwaffe's return to northern France. She left Milmo with this parting shot: 'You have always been saying that RENÉ did not give me information about British spies until they were hanged. (This is quite untrue) This just shows that you are quite wrong.'

That same day, Dansey, not one to mince words, and clearly unimpressed with her story, offered his thoughts to Langley on the case:

1. This is an extremely astute young woman, and without seeing a good deal more of her I would not venture to reach a conclusion as to her motives. She is an actress and a glib liar. It is a thousand pities she was not searched on arrival, and had so many opportunities to communicate with people outside this office.
2. I am inclined to have some doubt about the existence of this famous German lover [RENÉ]. She is making herself the centre of an interesting situation, all of which hinges on this man. It was obvious to me she was rather disappointed when I did not ask her questions about him. Indeed, you will remember she went out of her way to speak about him without my ever having asked a single question.

3. I took her up first on her acquaintances and relations with BOSIOT [*sic*] because here is a man whom I know a good deal about, as I do about his family. When I asked her a question about his brother, she embarked on a very long story. It was glib. It seemed pat. It was untrue. Then she realised that her imagination might have run away with her and she quickly switched to a long story of how Bosiot had wanted her to go to Rome to see Mussolini who was going to give her a message for the Prime Minister. I am sure this was all untrue, was done to get me off the questions I was asking her, and to make time also to bring herself forward as a V.I.P. (Very Important Person).
4. I feel fairly certain she did have messages to some persons or person in this country from this Italian. When I asked her that question, you will remember she immediately enumerated half the female members of the peerage and threw in Lord Reading as the single male makeweight.[12] It would be interesting to know who she did have verbal messages for.
5. I thought her story regarding her hurry to get in touch with her first husband extremely thin. You will remember that when I asked her how she could find him so quickly, she said she had had a telegram from him in Marseille. It would be interesting to know how this nebulous Russian knew she was in Marseille and how he could get at her. Her explanation of this was rather thin and requires a lot of checking. I should think the background of the first husband requires careful investigation. There may be some connections there that are well worth going into, considering the background of that type of Russian who frequented Paris and London before the war. On her admission, he was a complete gambler and spendthrift and yet always had money to spend.
6. Again the histroy [*sic*] of her life between '36 and January '40 might be interesting. Her story of how she came to go to Nantes to be near her husband in January 1940 would in my opinion also be worth clearing up. There was something here that did not ring true. It was too pat, and the addition of how as soon as she arrived in Nantes her husband was moved from his military duties there might be worth checking up on.
7. She had a remarkable vocabulary of all the terms employed in espionage and her bland and childish expression when I told her that she knew all the expressions of the trade very well was clearly put on.
8. I would not exclude the possibility that this young woman and either one or both of her two husbands had been engaged in some espionage

9. To turn to an essential part of her story. She did bring and deliver to Garrow 100 per cent correct information about six British agents, who had been arrested, giving details which could be only known to somebody in the German or French contre-espionage services – the German most likely. But at the same time, she delivered an item of information about impending operations against Spain and Gibraltar, which as events turned out was quite misleading, although there is just the possibility that the prolongation of the war in Russia cancelled other plans the Germans had, but on the other hand I find myself asking why an assistant in a German contre-espionage service should know of such details. You will remember that when I put it to her that of the information she delivered to Garrow, 85 per cent was correct but there was 15 per cent incorrect, she very hurriedly asked if that concerned Spain and when I refused to answer her question, she was rather rattled and showed a desire to find out what the untruthful items were. She had a pretty shrewd idea. This on top of the story that the German lover only had one aim and object and that was to supply the British with exact information regarding his country's plans.
10. Although I deliberately tried to lead her to believe that I was seeing her in the guise of the benevolent sugar daddy who was going to try and send her back to France, I never had any intention of this. Indeed, I should resist her return very strongly. Her ideas as to how this return could be effected and how easy it would be were childish and left me with the belief that she must have had some arrangements either with the French or the Germans which would allow her to return with any kind of story, no matter how thin it might be.
11. She is out for notoriety and if she thinks she cannot go back she will not object to publicity. She will seek it. It would be interesting to know all of the contacts she makes within the next week or ten days. She is quite clever enough to delay making any contacts she might have had to make in this country until later on.
12. If her story is all to be believed, it is difficult to understand how her German and French and Italian friends allowed her to go away pennyless. [*sic*] Query: Was she really pennyless? A proper search of her body on arrival would alone have answered this question. The fur coat she was wearing might bear examination too, particularly as to the maker's name. I suppose she will always be ready to explain, if it came from Paris, that the German lover gave it to her.

13. I think she ought to be made to go through the motion of handling the L.M.T. code, which she says she learned from her German lover. I have a strong feeling that the reason her French friend allowed Garrow to come out of prison and meet her in a Café may well have been that she was put on to pump Garrow and report what he said.
14. The appendix to your report dated 12.11.41. should be passed to Section V.[13]

Bosio, who had introduced himself to her, was the only German or Italian friend she had in Marseille, and they saw each other two or three times a week: 'Bosio did not mind being seen with me, he liked it.'[14]

On 18 November 1941 Guy Liddell recorded in his diary:

> We had the famous meeting with SIS: Stewart Menzies, Valentine Vivian, Jasper Harker, Dick White and myself, with the Director-General in the chair … Before the meeting broke up, I referred to the Stella Lonsdale case. It was essential that in a case of this sort we should be given the fullest possible information. It was only by the most detailed collaboration that we could really get at the facts. Stewart said he would be only too pleased to let us have any information about the case that we required.[15]

19 November 1941

Milmo announced that Tar Robertson and Cyril Mills, who introduced themselves as 'Mr Thompson' and 'Mr Martin' respectively, would be taking over. Tar began by praising her work in occupied France and saying that they were considering her return to France but 'we could only lay on plans for her return when we had every detail of her recent history at our finger-tips. We were only interested in a fool-proof plan and one in which her own safety was adequately safeguarded'.

To make things easier for them to see her they would move her into a flat with Nina Myers, a friend of theirs. Stella expressed that the flat not be in Mayfair 'as she knew too many people there and felt it would be better to give some of her earlier acquaintances a wide birth [sic] for the time being'. They told her it would be in the Sloane area, and agreed to give her £10 so that she could go down to Dorset for a few days to stay with John's family, which seemed to satisfy her. Mills thought she was 'anxious to impress her present sense of loyalty on us', even though she told them that before the war she had not been very 'loyalty conscious'. He remarked:

This is hardly surprising having regard to the fact that men have for many years been her main interest in life. As a matter of fact, she is alarmingly frank in her confessions concerning men and I have a feeling that if she has something to keep dark, she will disguise it as another of her immoral affairs.

On the subject of loyalty STELLA said that she felt that a golden chance had fallen into her lap and that it was the least she could do to grab it in order to serve her country even if only in a small way.

STELLA, if only on her past record, must be credited with ability as a man-charmer, and for the reason that she takes as much care to charm as to be convincing, she is difficult to assess. At the same time, I feel very strongly that everything she says now is well rehearsed. I would suggest that if her story contains lies, she has rehearsed them so often that she nearly believes them to be true. I think therefore, that we can only hope for results if we can keep her talking until she has told us everything she has rehearsed and then see how she acts if we are able to break any new ice. She is, in my opinion an extremely clever woman – but she knows it and this very fact may indeed be her undoing. She has all the answers on the tip of her tongue and it will be interesting to see how long she can keep this up if we are able to get her on to some aspect of her case which she has not foreseen and for which she has not rehearsed herself.

Stella had told 'Leclerc' that she was only going to Madrid on family matters so there were things she needed to follow up with him. As Mills summed up, 'The basis of her understanding with him is that he is anti-German and not pro-British – he does not however, mind if she works 98% for the British provided she works 100% for him and for both against the Germans.'

22 November 1941

Over lunch at the Waldorf Mills reported that whatever Stella's other vices, her alcohol consumption on this occasion was moderate:

> She drank one glass of sherry before lunch and plain ginger ale with her meal. Her Lisbon hotel bill shows large consumption of fruit juice and I think liquor is one of the vices she does not possess although she told me that she can sink buckets full of champagne or good brandy and said she hoped I was a cigar smoker as she loves the smell of good cigars. (Oh! what this might cost B.1.A in certain circumstances!!)

25 November 1941

Stella moved into a flat at Queen's Court, Bayswater, where all subsequent interviews were conducted, and stayed there until 23 January 1942. She expressed no objections to living in that neighbourhood because it was where 'her man SIDEROFF usually moves', but she was concerned about having to share the flat with someone else. Mills told her that it was 'our wish that she should and that in any case Nina is lots of fun and that I thought she would like her and that they would get on very well together'.

She let slip that she had been in touch with Paul (Holme), and had also received a cable from Frank Viner now in Gibraltar, seeking news of her. Mills returned various items which she'd given to Milmo earlier, including her two poetry books and some innocuous-looking scraps of paper, but not the railway tickets, which he kept, noting that:

> She affected great surprise at the return of the two letters which POEHNER wrote her in Lisbon saying that she thought we ought to keep them as samples of his handwriting
>
> This latter expression of surprise was either genuine or <u>brilliantly</u> rehearsed for there was not the slightest suggestion of a knowledge that we would obviously have had all these documents photographed. It would be interesting to know whether Garrow ever told her that things are photographed when they fall into hands like ours – he presumably was not in a position either to make or keep records safely at any time and probably would not have mentioned any such thing. If he did not warn her and if RENÉ did not, and if in fact she does not know such things, it would fit with the hypothesis that she is an unconscious agent of RENÉ's as in that case he would not necessarily have told her more than he had to. On the other hand if RENÉ were really acting the part which she says he is he surely would have schooled her in the tricks of the trade and one would expect it to be part of her make-up to profess that she knows them all rather than to act as if she knows nothing of this sort of thing.
>
> If, however, STELLA is a conscious agent of RENÉ and he has invented her whole story about him she probably does know at least the elementary tricks and therefore to pretend that she does not think we have photographed her property does not fit with the supposition that RENÉ would have schooled her properly had he been playing for us.
>
> It seems therefore that whether her attitude in this matter was genuine or feigned, it is inconsistent with her story about RENÉ.
>
> It also has to be remembered that STELLA is not as well schooled as she should be after working for Garrow (who by the way she always refers

to as Ian) even if she has not been schooled by RENÉ for among her property were two documents which would incriminate her in the eyes of the Germans if not in those of the French. One of these documents was a paper bearing some notes in STELLA's handwriting of some enquiries which she was to make for Garrow about a man named KRAFT.[16] I asked her why she had this in her possession and she said that she really thought that by now she was a discreet woman and that she was ashamed that we found this paper among her possessions.

The second such document was a shorthand note (not at that time transposed and even now only partially so). I deliberately did not ask her about this as I wanted to keep it for an occasion when I knew something of its contents.

Meissner had 'acted the perfect gentleman to his prisoners [but] he used them to the best possible advantage and promised nothing worse than imprisonment for the duration and then, when his purposes had been served, had them shot,' she told Mills. She expressed concern at his suggestion that RENÉ might be traitor, so he gave her the reply she wanted to hear: that while he may be a traitor to the Nazis, he was not necessarily a traitor to Germany. He wanted her to think that they had swallowed the whole story about RENÉ so he assured her that he would be studying every detail of her reports and come back to her with more questions in order to produce a completely foolproof plan for her possible return to France.

Much to her annoyance, when she had arrived in Lisbon, Drummond-Wolff, the British military attaché, had not been available, nor was there anyone there who knew anything about her. That, Mills explained, was because information such as hers could only be retained in the head, and not written down, in the event of an invasion of Lisbon, or a burglary. If RENÉ's name got out he would be killed by the Germans, she replied.

The following day Milmo requested that Colonel Robin 'Tin-Eye' Stephens, Commandant of Latchmere House (Camp 020), question Ulrich Graf zu Finckenstein about who had been on Meissner's personal staff in Oslo, but without mentioning von Einem by name. The reply he received was disappointing: while Finckenstein had frequently called on Meissner, he'd never had any dealings with his assistants; consequently he didn't know any of their names and failed to recognize the photograph of von Einem, saying that had he been on Meissner's staff in Oslo, he would probably have remembered him.[17]

4 December 1941

Stella now claimed that she'd forgotten the first name of the man who'd told her about the U-boat base at Lorient and the underground petrol dump at Sainte-Luce, which struck Mills as odd, given 'that all her troubles with the Germans arose out of the information given her by this man'. Realizing she was backed into a corner, she told him that she'd had a lot of French friends in Nantes. Mills's view was that she would never have touched the information had she not known him pretty well and had reason to trust him, in case it had been a plant.[18]

Pavie had claimed to know all about Kenny and Garrow, and as a result, they'd been arrested. Mills asked whether it was he who'd denounced them, since he'd made threats against them, but she said that Kenny's arrest had been due to his clumsiness and that he 'had all sorts of queer people visiting him at his Hotel room'.

Yves Delbar, a White Russian journalist living in Marseille (real name Nicholas Kosyakov/Kosiakov), wrote for *Candide*, an anti-parliamentarian, anti-republican, anti-Communist newspaper; *Life* and *Time* magazines, as well as a Swiss newspaper, and another who Stella had met at the American Consulate and claimed to work for Garrow. She'd mentioned him to Mills and Tar on 19 November, but they'd only caught part of the name.[19] He was eager to work for the British, preferably from Lisbon under cover as a journalist for a London newspaper and could provide good information for them for a monthly fee. Garrow had been unsure whether to trust him but had paid him 50,000 francs for information.

Delbar had provided a report containing the names and addresses of German agents in North and South America,[20] as well as information about a German–Hungarian treaty.[21] He could also get hold of a list of sixteen American factories which were going to be sabotaged between 4 December 1941 and March 1942. A magnesium factory had already been blown up on about 24 October and there were also plans to commit acts of sabotage in Canada.[22] He even claimed he could get copies of Hitler's and Mussolini's speeches before they were made public.

Garrow was arrested on 7 October before he could meet with him. When Viner failed to find him he sent Delbar to the American Consulate claiming to have certain information of interest to the British, but Fullerton told him that the British organization 'had gone to pieces' and that it was run by Garrow, Elisabeth Haden-Guest, Stella and Kenny, adding that Stella was quite an important person in the organization. Mills felt they should follow up on it 'as the man may be mixed up in her espionage affairs – he may, on the other hand, be just another lover!'

But Mills's questions about how she'd obtained the papers waiting for her in Marseille under the name Solange de Leprevier, or about RENÉ's warning to stay away until at least December because she'd been denounced by someone in the Armistice Commission in Aix remained unanswered. A German report announced: 'Edith Lonsdale, under the identy [*sic*] of Simone de Vallier, details given, is a British spy and will be coming into the occupied zone within the next few days or weeks.' She told Mills, 'If Hans Meissner gets his hands on me, I am done and therefore the success or failure of my mission depends on whether the Germans know I am back or not. Meissner is very much influenced by RENÉ and … can make him think what he wants him to think, at least to a great extent.'[23]

Meissner was apparently unaware that she'd been in Paris staying with RENÉ, but during the week of 8–15 August while on a train from Saint-Pierre-des-Corps (Indre-et-Loire) to Paris a German officer had recognized her, so word would have got back to him that she'd returned. At that time, she was living in Marseille but had stayed for a few days in Tours.

Turning to Garrow, she said that the less RENÉ knew about him the better. As far as he was concerned, he was someone at the American Consulate, but didn't know him by name. But if he were to be caught, he would certainly hear about it. The only way to save him would be to collect him from the prison on the pretext of an interrogation, then disappear with him. True to form, she would contradict this when she appeared before the Advisory Committee in 1944.

Stella left France 'unostentatiously but with ostentatious results'. She now claimed that 'Leclerc' had *not* received any orders to arrest her, and all her papers were in order.

> René said he would listen [on the BBC] to Col. Britton's broadcasts [to Austria] at night from the time I left until I came back and we arranged that he should receive news about me in the following way:
>
> The message is for: KARL HEINZ BECKER of VIENNA and you can send any sort of personal message saying how is he and don't be discouraged about the political situation and that means to René that matters are not dropped and going along all right and if any date is mentioned, that means that I should be seeing him about that time. "Aphrodite" (pronounced the German way) [Aphro – dite] should be mentioned in that message which means everything is going well, he is regarded honourably and need have no doubts about it. The message should be repeated three times.[24]

The loquacious Kenny 'talked about a lot of things he need not have talked. He told them ['Leclerc'] everything he knew', such as about a German officer from Angers (RENÉ) with whom she'd been in touch but he didn't know that he was now in Paris. Garrow told her that the French may have threatened him about what they would do to his wife, Micheline, if he didn't co-operate. He instructed Stella to go to Lisbon and report on the deplorable means of communication which currently existed. Viner was arrested when he went to deliver an envelope containing a list of German names to Kenny. As far as the French were concerned, he and Stella were in love and working together. She told Mills:

> Viner was let out but was not to leave Marseille. He asked for permission to go along the coast and skipped it into Spain. He sent me a telegram to say he was at Miranda [de Ebro prison]. With Garrow's permission I told Gars where Viner was to convince the French I was not double-crossing them.
>
> I gave as a reason for going to Madrid that I was going to get Viner out of the prison camp and Leclerc said he knew I would also take a report from Garrow and he was going to have a look at it on the train. Garrow's idea was to give me a written report for the French to see and tell me the rest verbally.[25]

Mills reported, 'Just before I left MICHAEL yesterday … [she] asked me whether I knew anyone called Hans HANKEY.' He denied it and asked her who he was, but later admitted, 'I did know him quite well before the war as he lived near me and I had met him on many occasions when ski-ing in Switzerland.' She said that Hankey came from a very good family and was in 'this racket' (intelligence). Now he was curious to know what Hankey was up to and intended to ask her what she knew about him.[26]

* * *

Old Etonian Hans Mark John Barnard Hankey was born on 31 October 1905 in Fetcham, St. Mary, Surrey, and married three times. During the Second World War he served in the Royal Navy Volunteer Reserve (RNVR) as a temporary lieutenant,[27] and apparently with SOE in France, although no mention of this appears in any of the SOE literature or files. A keen downhill skier, he was active in the Ski Club of Great Britain.[28] Peter Northcote Lunn, a Royal Artillery officer seconded to SIS in 1941, who spent the next thirty years serving in numerous postings overseas, ran the Ski Club for many years and may have recruited him.[29] The Lunn family had a winter home at Mürren, close to Wengen, so it is likely that their pistes crossed:

Hans has always been an elusive figure … He was part of a very racy set who put up for months at a time in Wengen, Switzerland for ski-ing and curling. He was vice president of the DHO (Downhill Only Club) for a number of years. Partying was his life. My husband has said that he soon went through his substantial inheritance owing to his taste for fast living: fast women, fast horses and fine wines.[30]

In keeping with his racy lifestyle, Hankey appears to have been named as a co-respondent in a divorce case in 1930.[31] There is no information in Stella's files of how she came to know him, but given his proclivity for fast women and her loose living, they might have had a 'fling'. Various entries in the *London Gazette* give him as a horse trainer living at Thruxton Farm, near Cholderton, Wiltshire, and relate to discharges granted subject to bankruptcy, hardly surprising given his profligate spending.[32] He died at Mauld, Struy, near Inverness on 11 December 1999.

* * *

10 December 1941

Mills asked for details of the letter Stella had written in plain code to John Lonsdale while she was in occupied France saying she was taking a keen interest in fishing to while away her time and that she had heard there was good fishing for 'big fishes' at Lorient (i.e. U-boats). It was sent to Shields & Company, a firm of Wall Street stockbrokers founded by Cornelius Shields in 1923 (referred to in Chapter 1), one of whose partners was somehow connected with Sidoroff. However, it is unclear why it should have been sent there, unless it was an accommodation address used by the Abwehr in the USA. She had also written to RENÉ *poste restante* at the post office at 12, rue Balzac in the 8th *arrondissement*, off the Champs-Élysées.

She and Christian had established a private code so that prior to returning to France she would send him a cable asking '*Comment va Phillippe*' (How is Phillippe?), indicating her imminent departure and looking for his approval (see next chapter). If there was a problem, he would reply that someone was ill. She maintained that their love affair was 'an empty thing', and only persisted with it because he had a lot of influential friends and was a good link to 'Leclerc'. If the London–Marseille cable route were to break down, MI5 could cable him at any time from Lisbon and sign it 'Solange'.

Her address book contained the names of Elisabeth Haden-Guest, Baron von Rotherman ('Pitzi') and Karl Heinz Ludwig ('Heinzi'). Mills asked that

Elisabeth's name be expunged as it 'has no security interest whatsoever and MICHAEL is the type of person who has been so many different men's mistresses that she assumes every woman is the mistress of any man whom she may be seen speaking to or working for'. The main interest to SIS would be the reference to von Rotherman and Ludwig, thought to have gone to the USA on an espionage mission.[33]

On 2 December Stella sent a telegram to Christian mentioning 'Solange'. Mills commented: 'This is the first sign of a crack. We have never been told that Christian is able to communicate with RENÉ. We know that SOLANGE [Solange de Leprevier] is one of the pseudonyms which Stella uses and one that is known to RENÉ.' From this he inferred that although Christian knew RENÉ and could pass on information about her, it positively confirmed that neither he nor Viner knew RENÉ's identity, a fact she confirmed on 14 January 1942 when interviewed by Detective Sergeant Rhodes about that relationship. Christian had never met RENÉ or knew that he was German; all he knew was that SIBER c/o the *poste restante* address in the rue Balzac, Paris, was somehow involved with intelligence. But if Christian were arrested by the Germans there was a small but improbable chance that he might talk.

The only communication she'd had with RENÉ was indirectly through Christian when she'd sent him a telegram before leaving France. Christian was to say that she was going away around 28 October and expected to return about 15 January and to tell RENÉ that he'd heard from 'Solange', indicating the date of her return. That being said, no one had given her permission to communicate with him, nor had she told anyone she'd done so.[34] Christian would not use secret ink when communicating with RENÉ, so the question MI5 posed was, 'How does Christian get his letters through to René and how would any answer be transmitted?' Liddell commented in his diary on 5 December:

> There has been an interesting development in the Stella Lonsdale case. She has sent a wire to a man called Boulanger in Marseille who she previously told us was her lover and had no connection with intelligence work. She asks of Boulanger whether he has given news of Solange to René. Stella has already told us that she had false papers in the name of Solange. Lonsdale's sister [Diana Vernon] who is a great friend of Stella's has been spending nights with her at the flat. The mike revealed that Stella was nervous about her conversation being overheard. It looks more and more as if she were a German agent. She is undoubtedly a clever woman. She was shown a photograph of von Einem and almost too hurriedly handed it back saying that she had never seen him before.[35]

A telegram signed 'Christian Gerschel' sent from Marseille to Stella, dated 12 November 1941 was collected from the Avenida Palace Hotel in Lisbon. She told Mills that he was Christian's business partner and she had recently sent him a telegram asking why he hadn't replied to her. Mills inferred that Gerschel and Boulanger were one and the same, and that by sending the telegram to Gerschel she had tried to put him off the scent.

16 December 1941

Mills soon realized that Stella was very familiar with the 'Gessler code' that RENÉ had given her (see Appendix 1), and had used it on many occasions. On 19 December he wrote to [*redacted, possibly Mackenzie*] at SIS:

> I think you will be particularly interested in her re-expressed desire to go back to France as soon as possible and also her statement which infers [*sic*] that the future of GARROW, Mrs. Haydn-Guest [*sic*] and other members of the British Organisation is being held in the balance pending her return. I regard this statement as just another of MICHAEL's lies although this one savours very strongly of blackmail. The other interesting part is the reference to the using of Christian's business house for the smuggling of letters into the occupied territory. This, coupled with telegrams which Christian Boulanger has sent to MICHAEL recently, established beyond all possible doubt that Boulanger knows who RENÉ is and that he is in fact a link between MICHAEL and the German Secret Service.[36]

Following a test with a Morse key on 31 December 1941, she had only made two mistakes and

> Mr. [Ronnie] Reed thinks that MICHAEL may have had previous experience with a morse key but says that if she is a very brilliant woman with an extremely retentive memory it is just possible she may have learned since I gave her the key, in spite of the fact that she has only used two dry batteries.[37]

Mills added that she was 'the lowest and trickiest human being that it has ever been my misfortune to encounter. She is indiscreet both on the telephone and at other times and I still hope that she will, before very long, say something which will entitle us at least to lock her up for the duration of the war'.

On 17 December Valentine Vivian, Vice Chief of SIS (VCSS), arranged for Tar and Mills to meet with Dansey at 54 Broadway, the headquarters of

SIS, to discuss Stella's case and Liddell's letter of 17 November to Cowgill, in which Liddell

> set out 13 points upon which we desired to have the fullest information from S.I.S. The original main purpose of our visit was to try to find out whether the Germans knew that we knew GAESSLER was blown. It is clear from the brief history of the case that they have been able to give us that we shall never be able to discover the answer to this question unless the traffic which is referred to later contains something which, upon analysis, enables us to form a definite opinion.

Dansey also provided a short note produced by A5 giving a history of the Gaessler case as far as it was known to SIS, based on statements made by Stella (see below).

Liddell noted that

> After a lengthy discussion with Colonel Dansey chiefly centering round Mrs. LONSDALE it became quite clear that Colonel Dansey had not seen Milmo's memorandum on his interrogations of Mrs. LONSDALE at the Waldorf Hotel between the 4th and 9th November. In connection with this it was agreed that a copy should be sent over to Colonel Dansey as soon as possible so that he and his officers could see for themselves exactly what information Mrs. LONSDALE had given. It was, however, observed that Colonel Dansey had among his papers on the case a copy of a note which Mr. Mills had supplied to Section V.[38]

He expressed that it was a matter of security and a need to discover whether Stella was a German spy or 'an unconscious dupe of MEISSNER's', as well as knowing exactly how the Germans viewed her status. If they were able to solve the first problem, then it 'may open up a promising opportunity for the exercise of the legitimate functions of Robertson's section' (i.e. handing her over to Tar to turn as a double-cross agent). If, on the other hand, they discovered that she was, or had been, a medium-grade agent of the Germans, or if the Germans thought she had been compromised, then returning to France would make any mission 'negligible' and MI5 would have to consider assigning her a mission in the UK meaning 'that her continued liberty would be a danger'.

Liddell's thirteen points covered:

(1) A request to see reports sent by Garrow;
(2) When SIS knew that Gaessler's organization was blown, and how;
(3) Whether the Germans knew about it and when, and a request to see the actual traffic;

(4) Who were the nine agents arrested; whether the names Stella had given were accurate; the 'minor inaccuracies' in the SIS report, and how much of her information was useful;
(5) When Gaessler ceased functioning, and who had initiated it – the Germans or SIS;
(6) When the Germans started running the W/T set themselves, and whether SIS was aware of it;
(7) If there was a transmitter in Brest and confirmation that SIS communicated with Brest, as Stella had claimed;[39]
(8) Whether SIS knew of other sets controlled by the Germans, and if so, whether the Germans suspected that SIS knew. 'If not, the information puts STELLA very high and/or indicates the abandonment of invasions plans';
(9) Details of the van der Walle case and when SIS knew that the transmissions were not genuine;
(10) What SIS knew about Visot and Duclos and whether they had escaped;
(11) Whether the code and secret ink given to Stella by RENÉ was the same as those used by Gaessler;
(12) Whether Garrow's organization was blown because of Stella's activities, or independently, and the grounds for believing either case; and
(13) A request to see other reports by SIS representatives which mentioned Stella.[40]

Access to C's traffic would therefore render some of these questions superfluous. Liddell also wanted clarification of SIS's position regarding the case and whether they had now lost interest in it and no longer had control, as well as answers to their reasoning behind not wanting to send her back to France.

On 6 December 1941 Vivian wrote to Liddell emphasizing that Stella had never been part of SIS and that they and MI9 'would oppose most strenuously any idea of her going back to France'. Liddell's report, prepared by Masterman and Marriott of B1a, commented that ADB1 (Dick White) had ordered that the report on the Lonsdale case be handed over to B1a for examination. On 11 November 1941 Liddell minuted that he was very much in favour of extracting information from Stella by appearing to give careful consideration to her project, but

> It does not appear, however, that a definite decision has been made whether course A or course B (Minute 4) is to be adopted. This decision, of course, does not lie with B.1A. but it would appear that we only come in at all

if course A is decided upon. For the purposes of this note therefore we assume that course A has been, or will be adopted, though we may later be compelled to report that we consider this a mistake and that course B would be preferable.[41]

As White put it, 'the more this woman talks the more she will get herself tied up.'

According to the SIS report on Alfred Gaessler (FORT/A):

1. GAESSLER was a wireless operator on board the "TRIOMPHANT", which ship joined the F.F.F. at the time of the Armistice. He had an excellent record and was chosen for this particular mission by the then Head of the French 2ème Bureau, for whom he was to operate in France and who, as you know, was subsequently arrested and shot. In view of the circumstances in which this man was recruited, I think the charge of deliberate treachery from the outset can be disregarded. What I think is more probable, is that he lost his nerve on arrival in France and then proceded [sic] to "sell out" to the Germans.
2. He, together with FORT, were landed in France on the night of December 21st/22nd, 1940 and shortly afterwards wireless contact was established. We now know from other sources that FORT was arrested just a month later, on January 21st, probably due to the treachery of GAESSLER, although again this is not certain. He might only have gone over to the Germans after his chief had been arrested.
3. From the time wireless contact was first established (25th December, 1940) onwards, there were a constant series of telegrams, mainly concerned with minor bombing targets although on 26th March (therefore after his arrest) a telegram was received in FORT's code indicating the arrival of the "SCHARNHORST" and "GNEISENAU" and a number of captured British merchantmen or their crews.
4. On the 5th June, when we were growing suspicious, a question was 'thought up' concerning FORT/A's fiancée. This is the point when the Germans are supposed to have 'thrown in their hand' but for a long period after this, Section VIII [Communications] have always maintained that there was no doubt that the genuine operator was at the key and that he betrayed nonervousness.
5. It occurs to me that GAESSLER's fiancée is still in this country. She is Miss Ethel SEPHTON of 22 Macauley Street, LIVERPOOL 7. M.I.5 might care to interrogate her, in which case I suggest they obtain the assistance of a member of the F.F.F., as the history is a complicated one and in the absence of Lieut[enant Rh]odes (who handled the scheme) I have no one [words missing] has it at his fingertips.[42]

Tar observed that A5's report failed to answer their questions, but this was likely because 'the section which knows most about GAESSLER's case has not had an opportunity of seeing Milmo's note, but the file shows that a copy was sent to Major Cowgill on 11th November 1941 by Mr. White'.

When the *Scharnhorst* and *Gneisenau* were preparing to put to sea, Resistance leader 'Colonel Rémy' – Lieutenant Colonel Gilbert Renault-Roulier – sent out urgent warnings from Brest. But the Admiralty ignored his signals in favour of a message sent from 'La Chattière' – a spy nest set up at Maisons-Lafite outside Paris, part of a *Funkspiel* (radio game) operated by Hugo Bleicher of the Abwehr and Mathilde Carré, formerly of the Interallié network, which stated that the two ships were too badly damaged to be moved. The Admiralty had regarded previous messages from Interallié about shipping as accurate, so, as a result, the three ships ran the British blockade through the Straits of Dover from Brest to the Elbe between 11 and 13 February 1942 – the so-called 'Channel dash' codenamed *Unternehemen Zerberus* (Operation *Cerberu*s) – right under the noses of, and undetected by, the Royal Navy. This was, Tar said, 'the first intimation that S.I.S. had received about their presence in Brest.' However, the information which Stella had supplied about Gaessler, the German battleships *Scharnhorst* and *Gneisnau*, and battle cruiser *Prinz Eugen* was 'almost certainly accurate, especially with regard to [the] ships'. The *Gneisnau* was badly damaged by the RAF on the night of 26/27 February 1942, and the *Scharnhorst* was sunk by HMS *Duke of York* at the Battle of the North Cape on 26 December 1943.

Major Crawford of SIS (A5) stated that the information in Milmo's report was very accurate. Had he seen it earlier, he would have been able to answer MI5's questions immediately, although as MI5 noted, 'the information at his disposal still does not enable him to answer the all-important questions (a) of dates and (b) of whether the Germans were at that time giving STELLA information which they knew we had already.' Between 10 and 26 January Gaessler went silent, having surrendered to the Germans on 18 January 1941, a date thought to be accurate as SIS records revealed that d'Éstienne d'Orves was arrested on 21 January as a result of Gaessler's treachery. Dansey agreed to give copies of all the relevant traffic to MI5.

On 27 December MI5's Director General, Sir David Petrie, told Robertson that he shared Masterman's doubt about whether 'the impressive amount of work devoted to this case has been justified by results – either actual or prospective ... [I]t would be the merest folly even to think of sending this woman back to France!' He expressed concern about who would collate the information from her and check its reliability, since they would be unable to question her about it. Based on what they already knew, 'her information would not be worth the paper it is written on. She is the type of person who would sell us to the Germans without a scruple, and she knows an uncomfortable amount about us'. He thought it wise to seek legal advice since any further actions by MI5 would be governed by it.[43]

Tar asked Jim Hale (J.L.S. Hale), MI5's legal advisor, to see whether there was 'sufficient evidence to lock this woman up and keep her inside'. Hale responded that as the case stood currently the Advisory Committee would recommend continued detention, nor would it be easy to 'persuade the Home Office to maintain the detention order in the face of a recommendation to the contrary'. Having discussed it with Mills he suggested that 'he should get our tackle in order for a full-dress interrogation, which would aim either at building up a case for detention or at eliciting evidence of an offence in connection with Mrs. L's present passport'.[44]

Mackenzie suggested that Leopold Hirsch be interrogated at Camp 020 about whether von Einem might be in Paris with Meissner, but it failed to produce a positive identification when Hirsch was shown a photograph of him. Hirsch was an Austrian Jew born in Budapest on 15 March 1890, who had been a prominent banker since 1920. He was imprisoned by the French in 1939 for accepting money from Goering to introduce pro-German bias in the French press, but following the fall of France he was released and forced to work for Ernst von Alisch of the Austrian section of the SS-Sonderkommando in Paris,[45] then Ast Paris. He and his wife Olly, née Fuchs, were arrested in Trinidad in October 1941 and interned in November under DR.18:

> According to SS-Sonderkommando, so H. [Hirsch] claims, there is an American Vice-Consul (fairly recently appointed) in Marseille, who has a girl friend connected with a local Polish journalist – this girl friend is a V-woman for the SS-Sonderkommando, and there is considerable leakage of information in this way from the Consulate.[46]

Given MI5's weak legal position, a plan of action was needed. Petrie wanted to discuss with Mills, Tar, Hale and Toby Pilcher the suggestion that:

> if for instance we could have MICHAEL detained and at our disposal for two months before she appeared before the Advisory Committee, we might during that time produce useful results by means of interrogation. Major Robertson said that he hoped it would be possible, if MICHAEL were detained under such circumstances, to have her cell covered in view of the fact that she talks to herself so frequently.

By that he meant installing listening devices, euphemistically known as 'Special Facilities'.

On 1 January 1942, Mackenzie wrote to Mills about the code RENÉ had given Stella saying that 'there is no trace of any of our agents having been given the book or secret number to which she refers'.

* * *

1 January 1942

Gaessler had told Stella that the office of British Intelligence was in room 61, 161 or 661 'Grant (Grand) Buildings, Northumberland Avenue', the first indication that she'd actually been in contact with him. Grand Buildings overlooking Trafalgar Square had connections with British Intelligence and was often used to interview candidates for SOE. He could also have been referring to either the old Victoria Hotel at 8 Northumberland Avenue, or the Metropole Hotel used by MI9, at Whitehall Place in the Strand, but neither was the headquarters of either MI5 or SIS, the former being at 57–58 St. James's Street, and the latter being at 54 Broadway.

It is not known how John Lonsdale had learned about Dolphin Square and Pembroke College. He claimed that he'd heard about Stella's activities in France from Capitaine Le Duc, a Belgian, and also Le Guyon 'who is well known in Dolphin Square'.[47] Maxwell Knight lived at Dolphin Square and conducted his anti-Nazi campaigns from 709 Nelson House; a number of the flats were used by MI5, such as 308 Hood House and 10 Collingwood House; and the Free French occupied Grenville House.[48]

Pembroke College, Oxford, was occupied by the Intelligence Corps from 1940–3 when Captain John Russell, a former Oxford Union President[49]

> obtained ... permission to use two colleges – Pembroke for the Commandant and Oriel for the HQ, training and officer accommodation. This arrangement was approved by the DMI ... During Mid December 1940 the Intelligence Corps depot moved to Oriel College in Oxford. Until 1943, the college was used by the Intelligence Corps as the Staff headquarters for all officers in the Corps and for the training, messing and accommodation. Along with Oriel, Pembroke College was used as the administrative headquarters for the commandant of the Intelligence Corps and his staff who controlled both the officers and other ranks' wings at King Alfred's College [Winchester]... Oxford also hosted one section of the MI Directorate – MI1(x) who occupied the Old Master's Lodging at Pembroke until August 1942 when it moved to London, administered by the Depot and accommodated at Oriel. MI1(x)'s function was to administer the selection, training and appointment of all military intelligence officers apart from Battalion IOs.[50]

Chapter 11

Telegrams and Telephone Checks

MI5 intercepted all Stella's mail and incoming and outgoing telephone calls through a Home Office Warrant (HOW) which covered a number of addresses where she lived (see Figure 2). They revealed that she kept in constant touch with Nickolas Sideroff, as well as members of the Clive and Lonsdale families, most of which contain trivia about her social life. There was also a series of calls to her husband John and his solicitor, Leslie Crane, regarding their forthcoming divorce, and frequent calls to the Waldorf and Dorchester hotels enquiring about any telegrams or letters which may have been sent to her there. During November and December 1941 these were mainly from Christian Boulanger and Frank Viner. Christian's are full of expressions of love for her, even though she had professed not to be in love with him, and in spite of what Liddell had noted in his diary on 5 December.

ADDRESS & TELEPHONE NO	DATE ON	DATE OFF
Waldorf Hotel, Aldwich [*sic*], W.C.2. Tel:- Temple 2400 12A Queens Court, Queensway Tel:- Bays. 4811	5.11.41 25.11.41	25.11.41 23.1.42
Telephone numbers on check: Bayswater 4811	25.11.41	23.1.42
Names and Addresses in this country subject to H.O.W. Under name of Stella Edith Howsen LONSDALE & Miss Stella CLIVE, the following:- 12A Queens Court, Queensway Waldorf Hotel, Aldwich, W.C.2. Dorchester Hotel, London W.1. "The Further House", Wimborne, Dorset 10, Crescent Court, Westbourne Crescent	 25.11.41 26.11.41 26.11.41 30.11.41 15.12.41	 21.8.42
Names and addresses in this country on I.B. List Under name of Stella Edith Howsen LONSDALE & Miss Stella CLIVE, the following:- Dorchester Hotel, London W.1. 12A Queens Court, Queensway Waldorf Hotel, Aldwich, W.C.2. (12A Queens Court, and Dorchester Hotel also confirmed on 26.11.41)	 17.11.41 25.11.41 26.11.41	

Figure 2. Home Office Warrant

Her first call was to Nickolas Sideroff to arrange to meet on 26 November but became very coy when he asked about her present location and refused to tell him over the telephone. The listener transcribing the call inferred that he intended to pay for her train ticket to Birmingham so that she could visit her mother. On another occasion, he called wanting to know why she hadn't kept their date on 4 December. 'I would have to explain everything before you could understand anything and I am not in a position to do so,' she replied. He inferred that possibly her husband John was there at the flat, but in fact, she was being interviewed by Cyril Mills (see Chapter 10).

On 13 December 1941 she called John to ask him about 'a Czeck in London called Wenback [sic]'. He thought the name sounded familiar and asked whether he worked for the Czech government, but she didn't know, only that he was in with 'some queer people'. John replied: 'They are all a most sinister bunch of cut-throats,' having already said that he didn't actually know Otto Wambach. Like many of her friends, it is unclear how she came to know Otto and his wife Olga.[1]

At the last minute she cancelled a dinner party for four she had arranged at the Dorchester for Monday 15 December since Sideroff had obviously not wanted to dine with her and the Wanbachs. She explained that her motive wasn't entirely social: 'it is a question of some work I am doing and I am interested in him from that point of view. I am finding out what I can about him and that is why I have arranged this.' A note underneath says, 'This is obviously Otto WENBACH [sic].' She asked Diana Vernon to phone them and explain that she'd been delayed in Birmingham. The resulting conversation with Sideroff descended into a melodramatic episode worthy of an afternoon TV soap-opera.

The listener recorded that Stella became very unsettled and 'very worried' when Sideroff told her that he had just run into Mrs Kemball-Cook [sic] and told 'Suslick' that he'd just been speaking to Stella. Stella pleaded with him not to tell her that she was in town but still in Birmingham, and that he'd been speaking to her on a long-distance call. He wanted to tell 'Suslick' the truth, but Stella exclaimed that 'Suslick' would kill her if she knew, so he tried to soothe things by inviting her over to the American Bar at Charing Cross, but she refused. At this point Stella rung off in tears, then called him back five minutes later, during which he handed the phone over to 'Suslick'.

Sideroff told her that the Wambachs had arrived and were waiting for her so she'd better come round right away. Stella burst into tears again, claiming that she had no money, not even to get her hair done. He agreed to have a cocktail with the Wambachs and then come over to her flat. During their conversation she told him that she wanted to get a divorce from John.[2] He phoned her again later to say that the Wambachs were 'rather annoyed' that she wasn't there, so she resorted to subterfuge, by ringing up Paul Holme in Birmingham and spinning him a yarn, asking him to send glibly worded telegrams to Lady Kemball-Cook at 39 Hill Street, Mayfair, and Mrs Wambach at 63 Eaton Square, SW1.

Lady Cecile Kemball-Cook *née* Protopopesco was the daughter of General Paul Olenitch of the Imperial Russian Army. At the end of the First World War she had arrived in Paris from Russia. On 7 April 1931 she secretly married Sir Basil Alfred Kemball-Cook at the Guildhall in London.[3] At the outbreak of war in 1939 she returned to England from her holiday in Capri leaving her trunks of clothes behind with Thomas Cook's, the contents of which – mainly designer gowns and handbags – were sold at Christie's South Kensington on 13 November 2013.

Matthew Sweet refers to her as living in 'genteel poverty' in Queen's Gate after Sir Basil died in 1949, with a single-bar electric fire and sleeping on a single mattress in the hallway, but from about 1930 to 1950 she 'moved on the fringes of high society'.[4] According to friends of Susan Barton, she owned a dress shop in Mayfair called Xenia, and was currently living with a young American named Carter who worked at the US Embassy in London.[5] One of Barton's friends described her as looking like 'either an international jewel thief or a spy'. She was also friends with US Army Colonel Bernard B. McMahon who, according to her step-grandson Richard Kemball-Cook, was an intelligence officer before D-Day.[6] Later she befriended Freddie Mercury of the rock band Queen, who used to come round to play her grand piano.[7]

When Stella called Holme in Edgbaston to thank him for his letter MI5 noted, 'Part of this letter was read to John Lonsdale over the phone – see telephone check,' and 'Another one we have not seen.' Before ringing off she told Holme that if he ever needed to contact her he should leave a message at the Waldorf.[8] She then rang Sideroff to apologise for the previous night's episode, saying that she'd been unable to sleep because of it and would have to stay in as she had no money. She sent a telegram to Boulanger, giving Nina's name and address, translated as:

> I've received your telegrams of the 6th and 13th today. Don't worry about Solange she will return mid-January without fail. I'll see Brigos and Sosthene tomorrow. Why do you ask me about 23 November? Give news to René. Be patient a little longer my love I love you so much.[9]

As noted earlier, Solange Léprevier or de Leprevier were two of her aliases.

Sideroff informed her that 'Sissy' was not in a good mood and was furious because of the to-do the night before.[10] 'Sissy's' animosity towards Sideroff continued well into the next few days. He told Stella that she was not entirely to blame; he was fed up with 'Sissy' and thinking of leaving her. Stella became anxious and asked whether it had anything to do with Wandsworth or Brixton prisons, but he assured her that 'Sissy' knew nothing about that.

Stella tried to call 'Mr Martin' (Mills) the following day but got a crossed line and Sideroff answered. She and Sideroff arranged to meet at the Silver Grill for lunch, to which 'Sissy' was also invited, during which they planned to deceive her into believing that they hadn't seen each other for over a week. Late on 22 December when she called him, she said that she'd been to see the doctor and might need to have an operation but was unsure how she would be able to pay for it. Her condition was diagnosed as muscular rheumatism which she explained to Olga Wambach was due to her never being well since the birth of Nickolas's son.

When Sideroff asked her what she wanted for Christmas she asked for money. Her answer was the same when he called her the next day, but then she suggested a nightdress or some underwear, and a pair of silk stockings for Nina. On Christmas Eve she informed him that she'd cancelled her doctor's appointment that day because she had guests coming round. When they spoke again, he invited her over to the club, but she refused because she expected 'Sissy' to make a scene. Acting on his suggestion and instructions, she then called 'Sissy' and told her that she hadn't heard from Sideroff all day.

At her Boxing Day party, she invited Sideroff, saying that Natasha Tchermoieff, the widow of a Russian refugee was there,[11] but he told her it was impossible. Stella, Jimmy Bruce, Diana and Ina all phoned him later that evening to say what fun they were having. After that, whenever she called him, he said he was too busy to talk. As an interesting aside, Nina rang Stella on 27 December to tell her that Cyril (Mills) would be coming round at six o'clock with a 'new buzzer for her "toy"' – a sex toy perhaps? When Nina returned to the flat that day, she found to her annoyance that her bedroom and bathroom had been used. As Susan Barton reported:

> In order not to give the [Special Facilities] away, it was arranged that Nina should point out to Michael that she had found traces that her room had been used and that she strongly objected to it. In case Michael became difficult it was further arranged that Nina should have told Louise [Green] about her objections who in turn handed the information to C.M. [Cyril Mills]

> When Nina confronted Michael with her suspicions Michael immediately called Ina and Diana as witnesses that nobody else except them had spent the night at the flat, in fact she seems to have acted injured innocence to such an extent that Ina, who in fact seems to know nothing about all this, suggested that Michael's best course under the

circumstances would be to pack her bags and leave the flat at once, and Michael started packing. This again was learned from the [Special Facilities] and C.M. and Louise went round to clear the matter up. Meanwhile, Michael seems to have seen Diana alone for a few minutes in the kitchen and arranged the necessary story.[12]

MI5 also recorded and copied a series of letters and telegrams from Frank Viner and Christian Boulanger. The first of these from Viner at the Grand Hotel, Gibraltar, postmarked 3 November 1941, said, 'I did my very best to introduce you and FRIEDL to London.' MI5 posed the question, 'Who is Friedl?' According to Stella, this was the name she and Viner used when referring to RENÉ – 'it is short for Siegfried which seemed a good old German name to use in connection with RENÉ.' Exactly what was meant by introducing her and FRIEDL to 'London' was not explained, but likely meant British Intelligence.

Christian Boulanger also wrote to her on what appears to be the same day:

> I have never told you, but now I can no longer make my jealousy keep silence – what does the 23rd November mean in your life? You tell me that life is pleasant, cheerful and easy at Lisbon? How do you expect me to fight against that? Later at London you will find your friends – and what friends! A background which is familiar to you and which will absorb you. What then will become of me?[13]

Their telegrams exchanged between 16 November and mid-January 1942 mostly featured him bemoaning his separation from her. A message sent on 6 December but not received in London until the 16th mentioned that 'René has been advised of the return of Solange in January confirm date', indicating that she was ready to leave.

The telegrams were a definite indication that Christian was acting as a courier for RENÉ, but tend to contradict Stella's pronouncement that she was not really in love with him, unless she was simply stringing him along, which is quite possible. Further professions of Christian's love would follow in the various letters he wrote to her. As with all these telegrams, there is no interpretation by MI5 as to whether any were legitimate messages or ones sent in code, except '*comment va Phillippe*' (how is Philippe?) which suggests that it might have been.

An undated letter from Christian stated that he had given her ring to a young lady – Madame Roland Bandinel – who was leaving for Lisbon and could give it to her at the British Embassy or room 168 at the Avenida Palace Hotel where she was staying. Madame Bandinel delivered the ruby ring to the embassy, with an accompanying note asking where she could give it to her. Her visiting card found in Stella's possession gave her address as 89, Avenue

Paul Doumer. Suzanne (or Susanne) Marguerite 'Tante Suzy' Bourgeois was married to banker Roland Bandinel. His death notice in the *London Gazette* confirms the abovementioned Paris address, and his former address as 144 Swan Court, Chelsea Manor Street, London.[14]

On 17 December 1941 Stella received a letter sent c/o the Waldorf Hotel from Maurice Bauer, The Manor House, Shutford, Banbury, Oxfordshire, who seemed to know something about her:

> Dear Mrs Lonsdale,
> Thanks to the information you gave me in the train I telegraphed to my sister – Miss Clara Bauer, Roc Fleuri, 231 Boulevard Carnot, Nice asking her if she was willing to fly home and have today received a note from the P/O [post office?] via American Embassy transmitting telegram dated 2 Dec. that 'she is still in convalescent stage and intends remaining Nice'.[15] All the same should you be writing to your friends in Marseille, I should be glad if you would inform them of her existence as things may change very much and very quickly, also if you would let me know the name and address of your friends, I would pass it on to my sister. Permit me to express the hope that you will spend a pleasant Xmas in the old country after all your adventures and with all best wishes for the New Year and thanking you for all your trouble in lending a helping hand.

Maurice George Bauer worked in partnership with his father Gottlieb Moritz Bauer, a chemical and mineral merchant from Hamburg, in the firm of G.M. Bauer of 17 Mark Lane in the City of London until 9 February 1911 when it was dissolved by mutual consent.[16] In 1904 he married Madeline Speyer, the daughter of Edward Speyer, a wealthy German-Jewish banker who had settled in England in 1859, and singer Antonia Kufferath, who through the Speyer family became friends with the composer Sir Edward Elgar.[17]

Exactly what Bauer's connection was with Stella, or when and where they had met on a train – was it in France or in England? – is unknown. Nor is there any indication that MI5 ever attempted to establish his identity, but he does not appear to be connected with Robert Bauer who was connected with Baroness von Einem.[18] So what information had Stella allegedly given him? Could his letter have been the message from Christian Boulanger sent via Bauer in response to her message of 23 November to 'Phillippe' (Christian), informing her that the situation had changed? It would seem so, otherwise how else would Bauer have known where to contact her? The tone of the message – 'she is still in convalescent stage and intends remaining Nice', and 'things may change very much and very quickly' – suggests the prearranged code about illness if things had gone wrong, and her 'friends in Marseille', a reference to Boulanger and company.

Chapter 12

Major Masterman's Report

John Masterman's incisive report dated 25 December 1941 on Stella's case stressed that MI5's objectives needed to be perfectly clear and what advantages they could derive from them. There was 'an almost overpowering temptation to develop the case for its own sake and to spend an immense amount of time and labour on securing information which has little concern with the main issue'. He felt that the amount of time expended on it by people such as Mills was not necessarily worth the effort. In his opinion MI5 should make no attempt to send her back to France under any circumstances, owing to their lack of trust in her, what she might pass on to the Germans about Knight's Dolphin Square operations, and MI5's general set-up:

> It appears from the file that Mr. Mills entirely agrees with Mrs. Grist that MICHAEL is, "a liar of such convincingness as I would not have believed existed". Mrs. Grist also points out that Stella's sole aim is to "amass as much money as possible", and adds that she would "stick at nothing to achieve this".

Evelyn Grist ran the listeners' room known in MI5 as 'the Gristery': 'Her typists sat in cubicles muttering and occasionally giggling at the conversations they were monitoring through their headphones.'[1]

The only possible use Stella could be to MI5 was as a 'reference book', but the material contained therein would have to be sorted and checked before they could make any use of it. He suggested three options which were open to them:

> 1. On 22.11.41 MICHAEL was told that "we had read some of the reports about her ... and could only admire her for what she had done and gone through since the German occupation of France ... Major Robertson then said that he and I intended to go into the whole question of STELLA's proposed return to France, and with that in view we should no doubt have to spend a lot of time questioning her for we felt that we could only lay on plans for her return when we had every detail of her recent history at our finger tips". Since that date Mr. Mills' policy (see 102a) has been to avoid orthodox interrogation

but "pump her for information at interviews". The reason for this was that Mr. Mills felt that MICHAEL's story was so carefully rehearsed that it was necessary to jump her backwards and forwards throughout her story.

It is open to us now to tell her that the preliminaries have taken a long time as many checks have had to be made, but that we now propose to interrogate her hour by hour and day by day throughout her whole story. We might hope from this to gain a certain amount more information from her, and it is at least probable that if she were interrogated for three or four hours during the day, [*redacted*] would provide some commentary from her later on.

This line of conduct has much to commend it and is indeed the proposal made in November, but we must face the fact that it is probable that at the end of the interrogation we shall be compelled to discharge her and simply tell her that she cannot be employed by us. In other words, she would probably have to be allowed to run free at the finish though of course she would not be allowed to leave the country.

2. It is possible that we might say to her that we had now decided that in no circumstances would she be allowed to return to France. The risks, both to her and to us, were far too great. Had she, in these circumstances, any proposal whereby we might secure the benefit of RENÉ's services? The development of this policy would depend, of course, upon her answer. (2) could be made a preliminary of (1) above, or even of (3) below.

We might put her in Prison and there interrogate her on an unfriendly basis. The difficulty of this proposition is that, so far as I can see from Mr. Mills' report, we have no evidence against her other than the evidence in our possession when we took over the case. It is true that she has revealed herself as a liar, for example with regard to Christian Boulanger's knowledge of René, but she would lose little or nothing by confessing that she had simply lied on that point, hoping to check our efforts to discover René's identity. It seems to me that we should cut rather a poor figure in later proceedings if we showed shut her up now when we had adopted the policy of friendly questioning a month ago since no decisive evidence has appeared against her in the interim. On the other hand, she could be more effectively interrogated in Prison, and the hopes of success would be greater. If she finds herself actually imprisoned and threatened with the possibility of remaining indefinitely in Prison, I am inclined to think, if her character is accurately described on the files, that deprivation of sexual gratification alone will quickly bring her to disclose anything in order to secure her release.

I gather from his report that Mr. Mills himself does not really advocate the plan of trying to trick her (e.g., by sending her anonymous telephone calls in a German voice). I do not think myself we ought to continue this case on a basis of trickery because I think that MICHAEL would be better at it than we should.

In all the circumstances I think that the first step which should be taken is to take legal opinion as to whether we are in a position to shut her up. If the legal section are clear that we could do so, that would, I think, be the best course to adopt. If, however, the legal section considers that our position is questionable, then I do not think that we should risk taking this rather drastic action but should turn to porposal [sic] (1), using (2) as a preliminary if Mr. Mills thinks that this might bring an interesting answer from MICHAEL.

I should add to this that I think it important before the interrogation starts, that we should get hold of Garrow's reports (see 13a). I have not found any report which I thought we were to have from? Superintendent Fabian.[2] I also think that we might make some investigations at the Wellington Club which has been prominent in connection with the Harbottle case.[3]

Masterman added a footnote:

Mr. Mills has a much greater knowledge of the details of this case than I have and may well, therefore, have cogent reasons for rejecting some of these proposals. They represent a view of the case only as it appears from the files, and I hope therefore that he will regard this document rather as a basis for discussion than as a summing up of the present position of the case.[4]

Chapter 13

'Damn the Torpedoes!'

In the New Year Stella received an invitation on 5 January from her sister-in-law Diana Vernon for her to come down to the 'country', which Mills surmised was to the Royal Aircraft Establishment at Farnborough. But Nina's investigations revealed that it was to view a new aerial torpedo being tested by the RAF at the top-secret Aircraft Torpedo Development Unit (TDU) at Gosport and the torpedo dropping zone at nearby Stokes Bay.

The TDU was established by the Air Ministry at Gosport in 1921 to undertake the development of aerial torpedoes and mines, the means of carrying them, and of delivering them from aircraft. It carried out work exclusively for the Air Ministry until 1942 when the Ministry of Aircraft Production (MAP) took control. Thereafter, it carried out work both for the RAF as RAF Gosport and the Royal Naval Air Service (RNAS). Control of the unit passed to the Ministry of Supply in 1946.[1]

Interrogations of Stella and 'Jimmy' Bruce conducted after the event reveal what occurred.[2] When Stella was questioned by Detective Sergeant Rhodes of Special Branch at New Scotland Yard on 14 January 1942 about the trip she told him that on 6 January she and Diana were accompanied by Wing Commander 'Jimmy' Bruce in a car driven by a Major Hatcher. On arriving at Gosport Hatcher dropped Bruce off at a camouflaged house guarded by two policemen, then left her and Diana in the car, as he 'was on private and official business' and set off on foot along a track. Stella was unclear whether Bruce had stayed at the camouflaged house the whole time but the two men were gone for about an hour and a quarter.

In the account she gave Toby Pilcher at New Scotland Yard on 11 January the two officers went off to conduct their business, while she and Diana had stayed in the car for an hour and a half as it was a cold day. The hedges were too high to see any aeroplanes, but someone in the car, she couldn't remember who, had said something to Bruce about experiments with aerial torpedoes. Then they'd driven back to London. She claimed not to have said anything else which was untruthful, but 'refused to admit that she had ever said what was attributed to her and persisted in her assertion that she had never seen and knew nothing about any new aerial torpedo'.[3] She expressed concern that MI5 had not been fully apprised of the advantages of sending her back to France or the repercussions if they did not, but Pilcher refused to discuss the matter with her as it was not his area of concern.

Wing Commander James 'Jimmy' Douglas Ferrier Bruce was born on 1 October 1905. As of May 1940, he was in the RAF's Directorate-General of Research and Development, Joint Directorate of Research and Development.[4] In 1941 he married Mary Augusta Bartlett. Stella's address book shows him living at 155 Gloucester Terrace, London, W2 and his office at the Ministry of Aircraft Production at Thames House, now the modern headquarters of MI5.

Mills, posing as 'Mr Grey', interrogated him in depth at Room 055 of the War Office on 19 January 1942, and began by questioning him about Stella. Bruce said that he'd been introduced to her by Diana Vernon shortly after her return from France, and knew of her 'interpretation of her recent history', taken to mean their trip.[5] Her release from prison in France had been due to a personal friendship she'd had with someone who'd been infatuated with her, but, as he admitted, 'Frankly she has told me such a mass of penny dreadful stories that I don't know.'

When Mills compared Bruce's version of their expedition to Stella's, Bruce first appeared vague but when pressed for details he elaborated on the sequence of events. An experiment had taken place on the beach at Gosport, although not when they were there. Besides, the two women would not have been able to see anything because the car had been parked below a rise. He tried to assure Mills that in spite of Stella's claim, nothing about his work or the aerial torpedo had been discussed in the car going down or coming back, but when pressed about whether Diana knew what he did replied, 'Oh she knows that I am connected with torpedoes, yes.'

At the TDU Bruce and Hatcher were accompanied in the car by a Mr Bowden, possibly Dr Bertram Vivian Bowden, 'a man of unusual ability', later Lord Bowden of Chesterfield, a radar specialist who helped to develop the Identification Friend or Foe (IFF) equipment used on aircraft.

Wing Commander Richard 'Dickie' Griffith Shaw had been stationed at Gosport since 30 August 1937 and was now in the RAF Technical Branch (Engineers) in charge of the TDU.[6] However, on the day of their visit he hadn't been present as he'd been flying. Nina confirmed that he was a new boyfriend of Stella's with whom she'd been out the night before. He'd told Stella he was feeling 'very poorly because he was not entitled to be alive because on that day or the day before he should have flown a new and revolutionary type of aircraft but for some reason it was flown by somebody else and the pilot who flew it crashed and was killed'. He'd told Bruce about the crash, but in Bruce's account it was not a new type of aircraft; nor had the crash occurred on the day when they'd gone to Gosport because he said that they'd been in London that day. Bruce admitted that it was a concocted story.[7]

Mills was taken by surprise when Bruce said he'd heard from Stella that she'd been talking about a new type of torpedo she'd seen at Gosport – a telephone check on 6 January had revealed that Stella had rung Sideroff late that evening and told him about her visit to the TDU. Bruce supposed that she'd been talking indiscreetly but denied that this was the first drop of this new type of electric torpedo that day; it was 'entirely concocted' and 'an absolute figment of her imagination'. Mills warned him that, should Stella be sent back to France, she might be 'extremely dangerous' and any information he may have given her would likely be passed on to the Germans. Bruce later stated that Stella and Diana were left with Bowden the whole time, but their entry to the area was unrecorded in any log. Mills pointed out to him that 'this is leakage of the worst kind'.

When Mills persisted with questions about the nature of testing at the TDU that day Bruce hesitated, but Mills assured him that he had clearance to do so. It turned out that it was a dummy shell that was dropped. The experiments which Bruce and Hatcher were conducting were with electrically driven torpedoes which Mills believed to be inferior and were only being used because the requisite number of diesel-driven torpedoes couldn't be produced, but certain firms were able to produce the former more easily. Bruce admitted that they were 'considerably worse'.

Mills concluded that Stella had not returned to Gosport, nor had there been the opportunity of obtaining any information from Shaw. On 16 June 1942 Shaw was killed together with the test pilot, Flying Officer Michael Orme Davenport, RAFVR, while flying in a Bristol Beaufighter Mk VIC which crashed during torpedo trials over Stokes Bay.[8] Whether Stella ever became aware of this is not mentioned in any of her files.

Throughout the interrogation Bruce was 'extremely nervous, and became defensive when reminded that he had committed a breach of King's Regulations and the Defence Regulations', claiming it was only a 'trivial and technical breach'. 'Most Secret Sources which cannot be disclosed' (telephone checks) had revealed that Stella had discussed all of her affairs with him while Diana Vernon was present. She'd also told Bruce that she'd received money from Bosio, although Bruce denied it. Bosio and Christian Boulanger were unfamiliar to him, although the name Christian was known to him.

Judging from his demeanour, Mills was convinced that 'he was lying throughout'. The same 'Most Secret Sources' had also revealed that Bruce had gone into great detail about financial arrangements which Stella should make between herself and the War Office in connection with her services. He'd suggested to her that she should 'demand £1,000 a year', as well as that 'we should have to pay her 100,000 dollars, later changed to 10,000 dollars, for her proposed mission to France on our behalf'. Given the current exchange rate between the dollar and the franc, it would enable her 'to make herself a large sum of money'.

Major Hatcher was employed by J. Stone & Co. (Deptford) Ltd., a marine and railway manufacturing company based at Charlton, southeast London, primarily producing nails and rivets, and building light aluminium and magnesium casings for the aircraft industry. During the Second World War it produced 22,000 propellers for the Royal Navy, filing a patent for electrically powered torpedoes in May 1942.[9]

Mills told Bruce that if Stella were an agent of the German Secret Service, she was now in a position to go to J. Stone & Co. and ask for Hatcher in order to see what was going on. She could then pass on information to the Germans which would enable them to deduce that Britain was experiencing production difficulties with manufacturing diesel-powered torpedoes and was forced to revert to electrically driven ones. Given what Bruce apparently knew about her, he should have known better than 'to have been the instrument for producing such a state of affairs'. When he asked Bruce why he had exceeded his authority in signing an order for the deputy director for the sum of £4,800 when his power to sign off on requisitions and contracts was limited to £100, his 'evasiveness became quite spectacular' when he tried to claim that it was 'a question of getting on with the job as expeditiously as possible'.

The conversation was steered back to Stella's remark about the new aerial torpedo, giving Bruce the opportunity to deny that Diana had known anything about it. He was then asked to account for Stella's comment that it had been discussed in the car going down to Gosport, giving him the opportunity to blame Hatcher, and whether Hatcher had told Stella anything about it in the car. Bruce admitted that as the car was a closed one, he didn't see how Hatcher could have told Stella about the torpedo without his overhearing it. In fact, on the way back, Bruce and Diana had fallen asleep and Stella and Hatcher had sung Schubert's songs. He laughed. Stella was an imbecile, he said. 'She has got a complex that she must be the centre of attention.'

He scoffed at Stella being truthful, 'Because she tells such fantastic stories to tell you the truth'. But had he ever caught her deliberately lying? 'The principal lie, yes, is the tale of hers about having seen a new aerial torpedo.' Mills took him to task over this, pointing out that, 'Her words were exactly these. "We went to Gosport near Southsea, near Portsmouth, to see a new kind of aerial torpedo". She did not say she had seen it, she said she went there to see it, which is a bit different'. Bruce again admitted that Diana had known of his work with aerial torpedoes, but denied that she'd told Stella about what they were going to see.

Overall, Mills formed an extremely bad opinion of Bruce, recording that there was an element of evasiveness in every answer: 'Whereas MICHAEL's story that she saw the new aerial torpedo may be nothing more than boastfulness, Squadron Leader Arnold informs me that BRUCE is in fact intimately concerned with a very secret new aerial torpedo and it is therefore evident that this device has been discussed by BRUCE in front of MICHAEL.'[10] Arnold was going to make enquiries as to whether Stella or Diana had actually obtained admission to the facility where the aerial torpedo was located, but no action would be taken because Mills did not want to risk blowing the telephone checks that MI5 was carrying out on Stella and her friends. He concluded: 'The seriousness of MICHAEL's conversation with SIDEROFF is emphasized by the fact that she has on more than one occasion ranted at him for his indiscretions in connection with her own affairs and now we see her actually talking over the telephone in this way.'[11]

This was not the end of the matter. Mills was reliably informed that Bruce was paying his ex-wife £60 a month (£30 for her and £30 for the children) and that he had recently remarried. 'Most Secret Sources' on Stella on 22 December 1941 had revealed that Bruce had been living with Diana Vernon while his wife Mary was away in Scotland over Christmas. Stella had remarked at 'how pleased Diana will be'. Indeed, on the night of Stella's party Bruce had left the flat early but sneaked back in again about 2 am, spending the rest of the night there and leaving about 8.30 am, a fact which Stella flatly denied. 'It was pointed out to her that a man had been seen leaving the flat in the morning,' whereupon she remembered Bruce dropping by at 8.30 am. A note at the bottom of the transcript added, 'It is not difficult to gather from this telephone check that "Jimmy" (Wing Commander Bruce) is a thoroughly unpleasant type.'

A telephone check had revealed that Stella's friend 'Peter' may also have been privy to what she'd been up to, although he didn't know Bruce at MAP. First thought to have been Peter Hislop, he was later believed to be George Hicks who Stella frequently telephoned at the Royal Aero Club, 3 Clifford Street, London W1, and a guest at her Boxing Day party. Sideroff later confirmed that 'Pete' was a nickname for George Hicks, who was one of Stella's prewar lovers, and had been the subject of an attempt to marry her off by Sideroff's aunt (see Chapter 28).

From what Mills could see, Bruce was spending far more than his wing commander's salary allowed, and while he conceded that Bruce may have private means, or his wife was supporting him, he recommended that his bank account be examined closely. The whole affair was 'extremely distasteful' and he felt sure that Bruce was 'mixed up with some racket or the payment of illegal commissions'. He wrote to Lakin at SOE on 7 March 1942:

> I am operating a H.O.W. on Wing Commander J.D.F. BRUCE, commonly known as Jimmy Bruce, who is at present stationed at Finningley R.A.F. station, Yorkshire. Until recently he occupied an important position at M.A.P. in connection with a secret device but it was discovered that he had taken two undesirable women into a secret Government establishment, and certain irregularities were also found in connection with his work.
>
> One of the two women he introduced into the Government establishment was Stella LONSDALE, wife of the notorious 'Mayfair Playboy-robber'. She is at present detained, having come back from Occupied France with an entirely unsatisfactory story of her connection with high officials of the German Secret Service.
>
> I believe that, although Bruce was married recently, he is living with Diana LONSDALE, the sister of John LONSDALE, and she was in fact the other woman whom Bruce took into the Government establishment.
>
> I have just seen a letter which may or may not emanate from Diana LONSDALE, which indicates that the writer is probably in the M.T.C. at the present time, and is expecting to be transferred to the I.S.R.B. on Monday next. She says that she has been driving vans and doing loud-speaker work, and that Mrs. Buckley had just telephoned her (presumably on March 5th) to say that she was to start work on Monday at 9 o'clock.
>
> I have had a fairly close look at a number of the people with whom BRUCE associates generally, and would say frankly that I do not think they are usually the type of people whom one would want to see employed in secret establishments.
>
> I should be extremely grateful if you could help me to identify the writer of the letter. All I need to add is that the writer appears to be on the most intimate terms with BRUCE, and although I know you will have had her vetted, and she may in fact be perfectly all right, I feel bound to draw your attention to the facts, as we only got on to the LONSDALE-BRUCE gang quite recently, and it may be that we have records now which we had not at the time she was vetted.[12]

Lakin's enquiries led to the immediate termination of Mary Bruce's employment at SOE. In a letter to Lakin on 13 March Mills replied that 'although we have nothing direct against Mrs. M.A. Bruce, I feel easier now that she is out of your organisation'. Bruce retired from the RAF Technical Branch as a Group

Captain on 1 November 1960.[13] Curiously, neither Hatcher nor Diana appear to have been interviewed about their involvement in this escapade.

Accompanied by Susan Barton and Miss Rowbotham, Mills interviewed Mrs Ina Lonsdale, Stella's mother-in-law, at her flat at 274 King's Road, Chelsea on 12 February 1942. She told him that 'Jimmy' Bruce had never liked Stella and only took her to parties because she was lonely and a friend of Diana's. Stella was the cause of his disgrace and she was furious with her. She emphasized that the two women couldn't have known anything about what was going on at Gosport, and that 'Diana has had several offers to go up in a plane but she has never done it', that Bruce was 'very discreet and never discussed his work' (though she herself seemed to know a great deal about it), and that she 'knew quite well that he never discussed it with Stella'.[14]

Chapter 14

Jean Castelain

Jean Castelain arrived at Whitchurch from Lisbon on 10 April 1942 accompanied by his French mother, Marie Thérèse Antoinette Castelain and sister Marguerite. Jean Joseph Xavier Castelain was born in Nice on 27 June 1925. His late British father, Joseph, had been the headmaster of the Royal College School, Port Louis, Mauritius.[1] When he called in to Room 055 on 16 April Jean provided more information on aviation matters, Stella's activities, and her contacts so Mills made arrangements for Flying Officer H.P. Ferrier of AI1(Z) (Air Intelligence) to meet with him the following day.[2]

Madame Castelain had told Captain Patterson of the SCO's office that she had left London on 2 November 1939 and had been living in Aix-en-Provence until 16 March 1942. Aix was the headquarters of the Aeronautical Section of the Armistice Commission and she had information on their personnel. Furthermore, she had been discovered sheltering British soldiers who were trying to escape, which is why she'd left France. All her information she'd reported to the British Embassy in Lisbon. She intended to join her son Jacques Antonin Maurice Cochemé by her first marriage to Alfred Ernest Cochemé, whom she thought was living in Swansea and working in the Meteorological Department of the Air Ministry.[3] Her other son, Dr Manuel Alfred Xavier Castelain *né* Cochemé, 1913, was working for the British Colonial Medical Service, but since the fall of Singapore had been reported missing and was now officially interned in Malaya.[4]

Jean claimed that he'd been acting as an agent for British Intelligence, assisted by three members of the Deuxième Bureau, and had supplied Stella with maps of aerodromes and French identity documents for which she'd promised to pay him, but never did. This caused his suppliers of the documents to accuse him of pocketing the money.

The SCO at Whitchurch, Major Humphrey, was taken aback when Jean told him that Stella was double-crossing them and had an inkling that MI5 doubted her integrity. Jean also thought she was now in custody in Britain, something hinted at by Robert 'Bobby' Johnstone, a prewar stockbroker in the City, and deputy to Cecil Gledhill, the SIS Head of Station in Lisbon. Johnstone's and his wife Mary's names appear in Stella's address book, with their address as 59 rua Riberro Sanches, Lisboa 63373, along with Mary Johns, wife of Commander Philip Johns, RNVR, who was the SIS Head of Station in Lisbon from 1941 to 1942; her address was 1 Repatriation Dept., British Embassy, Lisboa 29942, rua da Emenda 37.[5]

Castelain also mentioned Raymond Dennis Auxillou who had landed at Whitchurch on 24 March 1942 and was sent to Brixton prison.[6] His accounts reveal that he had all sorts of contacts in France and a lot of information in which AI1(Z) were interested. Humphrey believed that Castelain was 'quite genuine' and had a lot of real information. That information, initially given to Patterson, was reported by a Mr Buckley (VCB) in Room 055 when Castelain paid him a visit on 16 April. His friend in Aix, Raymonde Caubert, whom he had met while staying at 25, rue Roux Alpherons, 'would do anything for England'. Caubert had been demobilized from the French Air Force and had once been an engineer for the Arts et Métiers in Paris. He had also been secretary to the chief of the French Aeronautical Bureau, and known to Squadron Leader Lord Clelon [sic] who had been with the RAF in Nancy in 1940.[7]

According to Castelain the region from Marseille to Nice was pro-Vichy, although 80 per cent of the food arriving from North Africa went straight to Germany, but he had been buying some of it at the docks and selling it on the black market, earning about 500 francs a day. The American Consulate in Marseille had allowed him to draw an allowance of 2,700 francs a month to support his mother and sister. He had also bought gold – 'he does very definitely create the impression of being a man who would, in ordinary commercial life, stick at nothing to attain his ends or make money. In fact, he has all the makings of the typically cunning French business man.'

He said that some in Vichy hoped Britain would win the war, but would be in such a weak position that Vichy France could step in with its unused army and navy and 'demand certain things from Britain and the Empire.' If the Allies were to make a successful landing in France and the Germans retreated, then France would co-operate 100 per cent, but that would depend on 'which way the wind was blowing'. Nearly all Frenchmen respected Pétain, while very few liked Darlan or Laval, but of the two, Laval was the lesser of the two evils because he was a 'shrewd and crooked politician and one more able to cheat the Germans than Darlan who is not versed in diplomacy'.

Copies of the Room 055 report sent to Major J.R. Whyte and Mills revealed that:

> Castelain professes an ardent desire to help in our war effort, and it would appear from his remarks that while in France he spent all the money he could spare in helping Britishers to escape, and in generally furthering

our cause. Although not yet 17, he is very self-assured, but has a pleasing manner. He speaks good English, which he attributes to his period at St. Paul's School in London in 1938. I should say in his general outlook and experience he is more like a boy of 21 than 16½.[8]

Mills described Castelain as 'extremely astute and quick witted and displays more intelligence than a great many men of 25 or 30 … he told the truth throughout and when he was not able to give dates he accurately said so'. Mills told Whyte that he was only interested in information about Stella, but it gave him a better opportunity than Buckley of summing up Castelain's character.

Castelain didn't trust Stella because whenever he gave or sold her information, she made an enormous profit from it when she passed it on to the English, but Mills believed that, in spite of his initial suspicions, Castelain genuinely thought that Stella was a British agent. He confirmed that he'd given her plans and photographs of French aerodromes which he'd obtained through his network of friends, but as Mills observed, he and his friends were not doing this for altruistic reasons but for mercenary ones:

> They were not able to spy against the Germans but they were able to spy against their own country and were willing to do so on behalf of the British if paid enormous sums … it is clear that even if CASTELAIN and his friends disliked the Vichy Government and wanted to help de Gaulle and the English, they still put a heavy price on their help. [F]rom these and other remarks I gather that the whole gang of them were really more interested in personal gain than the allied cause.

Garrow had advised Stella that although Castelain's information was good, she should drop him as he was too indiscreet. Castelain told MI5 that the flow of information stopped because she hadn't paid him, nor supplied a camera which he'd asked for. In fact, he'd thrown one plan away because she'd tried to obtain it from him on loan rather than pay him the 100,000 francs he wanted. Mills summed up:

> I do not think young CASTELAIN has any security interest whatsoever but this note may be useful for his file having regard to the fact that the circumstances under which I interrogated him gave me a very much better chance of finding out what he was up to than I should have had if I had had to interrogate him for his own sake rather than for that of a third party.

Castelain did not know Garrow or Kenny. Nor was he able to give a definite date when he'd first met Stella, but thought that it must have been after

Christmas 1941 when Flight Sergeant Mond had introduced them. Mond had been at the American Consulate in Marseille when Castelain had gone to see 'Grannie' Dodds. He'd last seen her in September 1941 when she was living with an unidentified Russian painter at the Hôtel Scribe, who would visit her every night. He was someone well known to the American Consulate, someone whom Dodds might know, as well as a Mr Wilmot who was a secretary at the consulate and knew about her. Later he heard that she'd left for England and suggested that she may be in prison there, which Mills confirmed but did not elaborate on.

Stella had gone to Paris with Castelain's friend, Raymonde Caubert, the supplier of the plans, crossing the demarcation line near Angers with a French identity card in the name of Simone Lavallière. On her first trip to Paris, 'She crossed the line with many papers and documents concealed next her skin[*sic*]. About 60 pages of documents all around her body.' She did not return by the same crossing as RENÉ had warned her that the crossing was guarded.

Castelain didn't know Vilmorin, only heard of him, but he'd heard that Viner had been imprisoned for wearing false decorations and had been warned to steer clear of him. He'd also heard of Christian Boulanger and had gone to his house with Stella, but had waited outside, so never actually met him. He had, however, met a man named Copie [*sic* – Robert Coppe], one of Stella's many friends in the police. She also had very good friends at the Hôtel de Noailles and the Italian Armistice Commission. Once she'd claimed she was going to Italy with them and was also invited to a lot of their parties. She used to claim that she was in the British Secret Service, and he'd been told that he could trust her, but after he'd given her the plans and still saw them sitting on her table a week later, 'I thought she was just taking them to please us, but she didn't care for them. She had a lot of money in Marseille.'

When he last saw her in Marseille in September 1941, she told him that the French police (most likely 'Leclerc') had given her an identity card and that her 'friend', whoever he was, was being held as a hostage so that she could not leave Marseille. She also said that she didn't want any information about the French. Mills's questioning then focused on others she might have known, such as Marcilly.

Yves François Jean Le Corvaisier @ Yves François Jean de Marcilly @ 'Californien' was born in Marrakesh on 7 July 1916 and later became a W/T operator for SOE, recruited by Selwyn Jepson in early October 1943.[9] In October 1943 he was sent by MASSINGHAM to STS52 at Thame Park for W/T training, then to STS51a, Dunham House, Altrincham, and on 2 January 1944 to Fulshaw Hall, Wilmslow, Cheshire (STS51b), near RAF Ringway for parachute training. MASSINGHAM was the codename for the SOE base (ME38 and ME45) at Guyotville, west of Algiers, established following Operation *Torch*, the invasion of North Africa, 'headed by John Munn from the Training Section, accompanied by (Sir) Douglas Dodds-Parker (from AL), who was to succeed him in January 1943, and two former merchant bankers, David Keswick and (Sir) Francis Glyn'.[10]

There was also René Gournan of the *Mot d'Or* newspaper who was 'chief of the French Press in Vichy'. She had had her photograph taken with some Polish officers at a wedding party, but shortly thereafter all the Poles were arrested by the Deuxième Bureau and shot as spies. It is unknown whether these officers were connected with the Polish TUDOR organization based in Marseille.

The line of questioning now turned to secret writing and whether he knew anything about it. Stella had taught him about a secret ink using bird droppings and a secret code from a page of a book. However, neither of them ever chose a book; consequently, he never used the code.

Chapter 15

A Parting of the Ways

With Stella's gregarious lifestyle and John's own infidelity it was inevitable that a divorce should be in the offing. John, who was now living with his girlfriend, Betty Fuller, at 6 West Halkin Street, Kensington, SW1 (actually Belgravia), wanted to divorce Stella but she was unwilling to be the respondent, so Leslie Crane, his solicitor, was willing to fix it for him in return for an unspecified sum of money, but as their marriage was a Catholic one, it would be illegal to get a divorce before three years of married life had elapsed.

Stella was curious about Betty. She told John that she was still very fond of him and hoped that he was being well looked after and happy and that Betty was a 'good knitter' so that he had plenty of pullovers and socks.[1] In another time, on 17 April 1941, the long and rambling letter he'd written to her from his mother's house in Chelsea reflected his obvious love for her, and probably not untypical of the thoughts of many who were forced to endure long separations during the war. But its very effusive, cloying, overly sentimental, clichéd wording belies just how little he really knew about her and, unbeknown to him, what a cuckold he'd become.[2]

When she called him on 8 December and tried to borrow money from him, he was unable to commit until he'd spoken to Crane about his financial situation. She claimed she'd lost her handbag in the blackout the night before and needed the money to pay her taxi fare home to 199 Cromwell Mansions, Cromwell Road, SW3 – a cover address given to her by MI5 'for the use of John'. Finally, he relented, agreeing to lend her £6 which she would have to collect from Crane. But when she phoned Crane, he was adamant that he would not finance any 'expeditions'. The ensuing argument resulted in her calling him 'a mean little Jew'. The whole thing, according to MI5, was a ruse because she'd invited the Wambachs to lunch at Claridges 'for business reasons … And I am trying to do something and I think it is going to have quite a good result'. In fact, Otto Wanbach had agreed to pay for the dinner, but for appearances' sake the invitation was to come from Stella.[3]

On 3 January 1942 Maxwell Knight received a note from Crane wanting to see him. For reasons best known to Crane, he didn't want Knight coming to his office at 27 Old Bond Street, but wished to meet him outside the post office on Albemarle Street, just round the corner. Knight suggested that it would be best if Mills met him, so posing as 'Mr C. Brooke' he walked up and down Albemarle Street while Crane talked – 'it was evident that CRANE did not want to make a statement which could be overheard or on which he could be pinned down in any way.' Mills went to the meeting somewhat prejudiced against Crane but admitted that,

> I came away with the firm conviction that his one aim is to put MICHAEL on the spot … I formed the opinion that his desire to be of service to Major Knight is little more than a badly concealed attempt to make himself appear an honourable man in Official eyes.[4]

What Crane told him was a garbled, brief version of what Stella had told MI5: before he left France John had told her that if she should fall into German hands, she should pretend to work for them. This was not something which Mills believed because John had left France long before there had been any threat of invasion by the Germans, or French capitulation. There was no reason to suppose that she should fall into German hands 'unless John had made some plot of which we know nothing'. Furthermore, when Mills asked Crane whether Stella had told him that she'd been in a German prison or concentration camp, he said that while nearly all her friends had been in prison, she denied ever being in one. The only thing they agreed upon was that she was a 'polished liar'. Crane claimed to know her very well and said 'one could not attach any veracity to a thing she ever said.' He also told Mills that he was dealing with Knight over some other matters and offered to tell him about them, but Mills rebuffed the offer. What these 'other matters' were is unclear. Mills asked him to look into when she had acquired the scar on her forehead.

On 9 January Knight sent a note to Mills 'from our friend HERON [Crane]', confirming that Stella *had* received the scar on her forehead from Dernbach, and that Stella's mother-in-law had been to see Crane, during which she told him that Stella had only revealed RENÉ's name under duress, but that Gerhardt Gunther du Pöel was not his real name (see Chapter 9). Mrs Lonsdale confirmed that the real RENÉ was anti-Nazi, had a sister living in America, and had other good reasons for being anti-Nazi. Stella had told her that she was in love with him and intended to marry him after the war. Crane was afraid that if MI5 had believed her story about RENÉ being pro-British, they may have sent an emissary to contact du Pöel, thus endangering his life, as du Pöel was known to be pro-Nazi.

Even though Crane was acting for John, Stella still saw him from time to time. They had even been at the same party, during which she had come out with an expression like 'you filthy little Jew', which disturbed Crane. However, it turned out that the man to whom this insult was directed was not Jewish, but Crane suggested that whoever it had been was probably someone from whom Stella had tried to obtain money. From her tone he began to believe that her story wasn't true and that perhaps she *was* 'Nazi-minded' and working for the Germans. Given how she had previously uttered an anti-Jewish slur to him on the phone, it seems likely that this may also have been directed at him and not someone else. On 12 February 1942 Mills, accompanied by Susan Barton and Miss Rowbotham, interviewed Mrs Ina Lonsdale at her flat at 274 King's Road, Chelsea, to examine the story that Crane had just given him. He reported that Stella had discussed the matter of RENÉ's name with her mother-in-law and agreed that if forced to she would give MI5 a name, but not the real one. After being interrogated a second time Stella still hadn't confirmed whether the name she'd given them was true or false. She tried to persuade John to give her an authentic-sounding German name, but he refused to have anything to do with her. Mrs Lonsdale was quite confident that Stella wouldn't give MI5 the right name, and that everything she'd told her was what 'Mr Martin' (Mills) already knew.

According to Mrs Lonsdale Stella had never had any intention of going back to France, and the very thought of it 'utterly and perfectly paralized' her [*sic*]. She'd told her different stories about how long she'd been in prison – three weeks, ten days, two months. One day she'd said, 'you know it was a very wonderful thing to work for the Germans as they have method and they always foresee one, two, three and four contingencies,' but the English weren't methodical and didn't look ahead. Asked whether she meant 'for the Germans', 'for RENÉ' or 'for this German', Mrs Lonsdale replied emphatically, 'for the Germans.' She said that Stella was in love with RENÉ and 'mad about that man', but didn't care a damn about Frank Viner or Christian Boulanger. Stella fully intended to contact RENÉ's sister in America, but was afraid that if she did MI5 would be able to trace who he was.

During the interview, Diana Vernon entered and told Mills that Stella's code was based on a little pink book of French poems. He thought that this was probably the book which MI5 had returned to Stella. Diana also said that the dummy number (1863) Stella had given MI5 for use in the code was false and now she daren't give the right one. Mrs Lonsdale and Diana both denied ever hearing her mention *Les Climats* by André Maurois. Mills noted that the dummy number was something Gladstone had said in that year.

In 1940 Mrs Lonsdale had not wanted Stella to go to France as she wasn't ill and wasn't going to have an operation. Nor had she or Diana provided Stella with a letter to that effect. Stella and John had planned to go to Switzerland to work for the French to double-cross the Germans and give information to the English. Stella told her that John was in contact with the Sûreté and was given 'a pass to run around in private clothes', but this had got him into trouble and he was finally sent home. She confirmed Mills's suggestion that Stella was trying to contact RENÉ through Christian Boulanger, but 'she never told me how she got the letters to René'. Nor did she know the significance of 23 November.

Stella claimed to have given back 40,000 francs of the money the Germans had paid her, but she kept a fur coat they had given her. Bosio had also given her money, 'to give to the English people ... He did not know that he was financing the English but she would ask him for money and then used to give it to the English'. Mrs Lonsdale told Mills that 'She has a perfect genius for getting information out of people. I have seen her getting information out of a person coming over from America (Swenson). After a few minutes she had his wallet out and everything'.

Sideroff hadn't 'the faintest idea' who RENÉ was. After his first interrogation he had gone to see Mrs Lonsdale 'in a great state of nerves' and asked what he should do. She advised him to tell the truth. Stella had confided in Otto Wanbach who, she claimed, worked for Czech Intelligence (unconfirmed).

Stella had told Mrs Lonsdale that before Elisabeth Haden-Guest was imprisoned she had sent in an unfavourable report about her, which will be discussed later. Mrs Lonsdale said that Stella intended to send a message to Christian, for onward transmission to RENÉ, giving her name and address for him to contact if he should arrive in England and couldn't find Stella: 'If the German turns up he will give the number 23–40 Pasadena so that I shall know that it is the genuine article.'

When asked whether she knew that Stella had made trips to occupied France to see RENÉ, Mrs Lonsdale said that after she was released from prison Stella went to Paris to her hotel and saw her maid 'Marie' who gave her a message to transmit to her. RENÉ's quarters were near her old hotel in Paris, i.e. near the Boulevard Raspail (Abwehr headquarters were at the Hôtel Lutetia, 45, Boulevard Raspail), and 'she went to Poitiers and Anglois [*sic* – Angoulême] on a holiday with him'.[5]

* * *

On 30 May 1942 Stella wrote to 'Little Gran' saying that John had asked her to divorce him. She'd come to the conclusion that, even though she'd been waiting for the outcome of the war and still mentally clung to him, she couldn't refuse his request: 'I must admit that I was rather astounded that an englishman [*sic*] could choose a moment like this to come to his wife to ask for a divorce, that it seemed horribly unkind, but there it is, apparently John has rather a thick skin.' She wondered whether John's sudden haste at seeking a divorce was because Betty Fuller was pregnant.

There was still the question of Stella having no money. The previous year she had approached 'Little Gran' for some financial assistance. John had said that he would gladly pay all the costs of the divorce and his solicitor confirmed that he was in a position to do so, 'although he left me no money!' she declared, only a third of his army pay. This left her wondering how he could support another woman. She assumed that he and Crane had now broken up their friendship. John denied ever having told 'Little Gran' anything other than the fact that she'd been interned: '[I]t all hurts me so I can't just reconcile the change in John from the man with whom I was so very, very happy. Surely I was sure that he loved me, weren't you?'

Later, when she met 'Little Gran', Stella felt guilty about not being able to tell her about her first marriage because she'd been 'so wonderfully kind and sweet', but John had made her promise not to discuss it with her and wouldn't release her from it. He'd told 'Little Gran' that he'd not known about Stella's first marriage, which Stella said was untrue because he'd gone to see Sideroff on 2 June 1939. The five of them – Stella, John, Diana, Sideroff and his aunt – had had lunch together at Au Jardin des Gourmets, 5 Greek Street, Soho. After that John had asked his lawyers, Kramer & Co.,[6] to look into the validity of that marriage, which had been declared null and void because there had been no civil ceremony, thus enabling them to marry legally. When they told Sideroff on their wedding day over tea, he was quite naturally 'very much distressed'.

Stella blamed Ina and Diana for not preparing her for 'this Betty business': 'I was broken up over it and cried.' When she stayed at the Waldorf, she saw Sideroff about half a dozen times, but Diana was always with her; at her flat Nina was there, and Diana had also stayed with her. When she saw Sideroff outside it was at the Savoy. She justified her reasons for continuing to see him because they had never quarrelled and because of their baby son. The trouble was he reminded her too much of him and made her so unhappy that she couldn't bear to stay with him; she had to start afresh and forget about the dead child.

Sideroff had always been very fond of her but she emphasized that she hadn't been disloyal to John. She knew that Sideroff would be only too happy to remarry her but she couldn't bring herself to do so. She was sorry that she'd hurt him by leaving him for John when he'd been so loyal to her but remarriage was out of the question, 'simply because I have this ridiculous phsychological [*sic*] obsession about my baby'. She hated writing to 'Little Gran' about her grandson as she knew it must have hurt her, because she had loved John, but now she was hurt too. She hoped that 'Little Gran' would understand that she was forced to divorce John now, even though she'd originally promised to do so at the end of the war.[7]

This apologia was Stella's way of trying to assuage her conscience of her own infidelities and to continue to endear herself to 'Little Gran', who always seemed to be there with ready cash whenever she needed it. But it was a classic example of 'the pot calling the kettle black' – her calling John a 'barefaced liar' being a case in point. Stella was a selfish woman who didn't really care about anyone else's feelings and seems to have been in total denial that she was ever guilty of infidelity to John.

It is unclear when John began his affair with Betty, but most likely when he first got wind of the many affairs Stella had had, both in France and once back in England. Clearly, he was always suspicious of Sideroff's relationship with her – there was a bond between them because of the baby they had created, and that could not be broken. He probably never believed that it was now simply platonic – with Stella nothing was platonic!

As Stella pointed out to 'Little Gran', divorcing John would cause some problems because she was a Roman Catholic, but to say it was ironic that he should eschew the basic tenets of Catholicism to suit his carnal needs was also hypocritical on her part. Having become a Catholic at John's insistence, it didn't seem to trouble her that she too had had many affairs, 'one-night stands', and possibly other raunchier relationships, if Susan Barton's 'farm yard' observation is to be believed.

To say that she felt she could not 'remarry' Sideroff because he reminded her too much of her dead child implies that had he not reminded her of him she might have considered it. Had they decided to 'remarry' and conceive another child together this might have helped bring some closure to their loss. Perhaps Stella was right about not wanting to put the clock back and needing to move forward, 'to start a fresh life and forget about my poor little dead child'. But in reality, what she wanted was to be free to have many more relationships and not be tied to one person, or have the encumbrance of raising a child during wartime. It seems that 'in the privacy of [her] own mind' she may have believed she was a Catholic, but not in practice.

'Little Gran' was relieved to be told about Stella's first marriage but she said that she was not the best person to give advice; she should take guidance from her priest. To a large extent, she was supportive of Stella's situation. John had a mind of his own and was not worthy of her love; he would not stick with any woman. She should wait until after the war before getting a divorce.

Chapter 16

Declarations of Love

Of the many men who openly declared their love for Stella, Christian Boulanger wrote to her regularly, declaring in such effusive, cloying terms that he loved her and wanted her to return to France. The many telegrams and letters they exchanged indicate that he thought she was still in Lisbon. On 3 November 1941 the tone of his letter sent there was fatalistic and an expression of his undying love for her in the same cloying manner as the one John had written to her – the fact that Stella had been unable to stay in Marseille, and the impossibility of being able to marry her: 'In ordinary times it is a mere nothing but now it is a tragedy.' It was also melodramatic: 'I don't know what I'm going to do, whether I shall be able to stay in Marseille; every little thing, every minute, every person, every corner of the street reminds me of you.'

Until he'd met Stella, Hélène de Lonza Dantas, the Brazilian ambassador's niece, had been the only woman he'd ever cared for.[1] He beseeched Stella to stay faithful to him and to 'Look after our child', forbidding her to dance or drink: 'It is frightfully dangerous for you though I know that the attentions of men are agreeable to a woman who has been deprived of them.' The revelation that she may have been pregnant by him is new, and not referred to again by either of them, so was it just wishful thinking on his part, or was it a coded message?

In the letter which followed on 12 November, again sent c/o Mrs Mary Johns in Lisbon, he seems to have realized that it was all for naught. This time the letter was scented with Shocking, an Oriental floral perfume launched by Elsa Schiaparelli in 1937, 'but so slightly … Like our love which is fading because it is doomed'. In an undated reply to a letter Stella had sent him he refers to when she told him she was beginning to be unfaithful to him. He was shivering because it was cold in Marseille 'and my heart also is cold'. The love he declared for her was unrequited, and he seemed resigned to the fact that she was never going to marry him, but he persisted in wearing her ring. He ended by declaring '*É finita la comedia*' [sic] ('So ends the comedy' or 'The game is up').[2]

His letter of Friday 12 December 1941 is again full of melodrama when he talked about the perfume and used the same quote about their love fading.

He bemoaned how desperately sad he still was and had no distractions such as dancing or pretty girls to make love to but then declared, 'in any case I have no wish for such things … I know that if you go to England you are lost to me forever … I have never loved anyone but you and never will.'[3] So much for Hélène de Lonza Dantas!

On 16 December 1941 he mawkishly described himself as 'tender as a schoolboy' when he cuddled her 'nightie' against him, and asked whether she remembered the old castle where he used to sing to her and recite verses by Paul Géraldy (poet Paul Georges Lefèvre-Géraldy). These memories, now in the 'realm of the Past', still sustained him but left him with the 'impression of a break as clean as that of death'. He chided himself for being silly, trying to struggle against destiny, 'and I cling, with the despairing but useless energy of a ship-wrecked man on the open sea to L. Gerschel's exhaltations to patience [*sic*]', a reference to French psychoanalyst Lucien Gerschel. He was eaten up with his love for her, but 'I don't deserve you – you will find a thousand men for one like me' and concluded 'Everything is over – I want you to find here the expression of my overpowering love, the infinite tenderness which I feel for you and also my profound despair.' His mention of Paul Géraldy might have been a reference to his *Toi et moi* (*You and me*), the little pink book of poems referred to earlier, which was used as a code book, and not André Maurois' *Les Climats*. Christian's writing certainly echoes Géraldy's prose.

Paul Holme also wrote passionate letters to her. On 22 January 1942 he said how sorry he was that they had not been able to meet up when he'd been in London two weeks previously. He wanted her to meet a certain Captain Hemsley with whom he was about to enter into business, but was cautious about putting anything into print, 'with John Lonsdale at the trap door waiting for only one thing, for the moment when he can pull the lever, and down I go', an obvious allusion to naming him as a co-respondent. He quoted lines from A.E. Housman's *A Shropshire Lad* as he refreshed 'old memories from bygone days in Shropshire' and pondered on what would become of either of them as he reminisced about their days together before she went off to France, and how futile it would have been to try to dissuade her from going because she was so determined. MI5 does not appear to have taken his musings as some sort of code containing a covert message. Instead, here we see yet another victim of unrequited love, a man with a broken heart mourning a lost relationship, and the realization that time is short and *carpe diem*, one must 'seize the day'.

He wondered when they were going to write a book together, based on her 'unbounded experiences, virtuous and virulent alike'. There had to be a love story in it, perhaps theirs, or was he presuming too much? Then, with a certain irony, compared her to Mary, Queen of Scots 'with whom you seem to have much in common'. Indeed, like Mary, Stella was wont to plot and scheme when it suited her. Once again, he resorted to quoting Housman.

Frank Viner's two identical letters were sent, one c/o the Waldorf, the other c/o the Dorchester. He said that he had been in London 'for a considerable time' (being questioned at the RVPS) and had tried in vain to get in touch with her but hoped they would still be able to see each other. He was going to Leamington Spa to join the Czech Army, where he could be contacted, or through a friend, a Mr Harvey at 46 Townshend Road, London NW8, close to Primrose Hill. By this time Stella had been interned so the letters were forwarded to Inspector Whiting of Special Branch at New Scotland Yard for inspection. A message dated 14 February 1942 from Viner addressed to Stella and handed in at the Waldorf Hotel read: 'Just arrived. Please phone Primrose 3895, Mr. HARVEY, any morning up to 9-30 or late evening; or? BORIS MELIKOFF, Sloane 8738. I am staying until Tuesday, Wes.0087. Frank.' However, the telephone numbers given for John Harvey (Primrose 3895; Mayfair 3483) were traced to Alan E. Hope of 45 Townshend Road, NW8 and Mrs Dorothy Daubeny, 7 Culross Street, W1, respectively.[4]

Chapter 17

'A Person of Hostile Associations'

The day Stella went to Gosport her fate was sealed. MI5 now felt they had sufficient grounds to initiate the process of issuing her with a detention order under Defence Regulation 18B. They discussed her case with Arthur Hutchinson at the Home Office who agreed that the order should be made.[1] Pilcher noted that, 'the whole case against Mrs. LONSDALE rests on hostile associations, and these again are based on her own admissions made to M.I.5 officers on various occasions when she has been interrogated'. She was, he said, habitually untrue, venal, and lacking all moral sense, all of which needed to be taken into account when the Home Secretary made his decision. 'S.I.S. have viewed with the strongest apprehension the idea that she should ever be allowed to return to France.' But even if she were to be locked up, he warned that she might resort to 'some form of subterfuge to get away'.[2]

A Home Office minute dated 22 January 1942, initialed by Hutchinson, Sir Alexander Maxwell, Sir Frank Newsam, and Herbert Morrison, the Home Secretary, stated that 'It is a most remarkable case', and that Stella qualified for detention 'on the grounds of hostile associations'. They recommended that the Advisory Committee be presented with her case for examination.[3]

The following Monday (26 January) after she had been detained Stella wrote to Sideroff saying that it had been 'some dreadful kind of mistake or test or something'. No one must know, especially not her mother whose heart was not strong, nor 'Little Gran', Ina, nor Diana Vernon. It was not until 20 April that she wrote her mother 'a dreadfully long letter for the Censor to wade through', explaining that she had been interned under DR.18B, but she should not worry about her, nor doubt her loyalty to Britain. She misquoted St. Paul's Epistle to Timothy: 'I have fought a good fight, finished my course and I have kept the faith. Hence forth there is laid up for me a crown of righteousness'[4] [*sic*] – and ended by saying that she and 'Little Gran' needn't worry 'about the possibility of this coming out into the newspapers – it won't', words which would later come back to haunt her. She believed it was God's will and that of the Virgin Mary which had led her to her present circumstances and got her out of the sticky situation in France. Once she'd heard from her mother she would write to her sister Norah but asked that she not discuss the matter with her brother Dennis and his wife – 'you know of this stupid antipathy we have for each other'.

True to form, she was hypocritical about how her friends had apparently used her, when she was wont to do the same. Referring to 'Little Gran', she expressed concern that John was 'busily engaged in poisoning her mind against me … I really do find his callousness was beneath contempt'. She compared life in Holloway to being at college or in a convent, 'although naturally there are some Kranks, there is a set of cultured, charming, much travelled and most interesting women with whom I am friends' – an allusion to fellow internees Mathilde Carré, Vera Eriksen, Mathilde Krafft, My Eriksson and the Duchesse de Château-Thierry. Her only request was for a couple of exercise books and her old school Bible, which she needed for study, but Norah was unable to find it.

Tar made arrangements that all mail sent to her c/o the Waldorf and Dorchester hotels would be collected by one of Harry Hunter's men in B6, MI5's 'Watcher' service. Likewise, Dr Matheson, the Governor of Holloway, would forward any mail received there to Box 500, Parliament Street (MI5's postal address). The contents of a scrap of blue paper, which he sent to H.L. Smith in A6, MI5's Scientific Section, for analysis turned out to be common salt from a packet of Smith's crisps, which could be used to make secret ink but had 'certain drawbacks'.[5]

Mills met Sideroff at the Piccadilly Hotel to give him a letter and permit issued by the Governor allowing him to visit Stella in Holloway. He explained to him that her internment was because she had not told the truth and 'for all I knew the duration of her stay in prison would probably depend upon her willingness to tell us everything she knew and at all times the truth'. It came as no surprise to Sideroff that Stella had lied but he was surprised that MI5 had been so patient and had spent so much time on her. He asked whether there was any way he could help as he considered it her duty to tell MI5 everything she knew about RENÉ and anything else which would help them deal with the Germans.

Given that Sideroff still had a certain amount of influence over her, Mills suggested that he 'should try to exert pressure on her to tell the truth. It was time to stop wasting any more of anyone's time on her, only to be fed with small talk and/or lies'. He warned him that it was only a matter of time before they caught up with RENÉ, most likely at the end of the war, when they would finally get at the truth. But if Stella thought that she could now quietly sit out the war thinking that the whole problem would go away she was mistaken. If she had not been honest with them, she would still have to face the consequences. Sideroff resolved to visit her that same day to try and persuade her to realize that by not co-operating with MI5 she was 'running a very risky course'. He had a plan to get her to talk freely and truthfully to MI5, but Mills was less than enthusiastic and didn't attach very much importance to it.

John Lonsdale wrote to Major Rupert Speir at MI5 from the London Clinic, 20 Devonshire Place, London W1, where he was recovering from an appendectomy, stating that Stella was claiming to 'all and sundry' that she worked for MI5 and that Cyril Martin (Mills) was her contact at the War Office, as well as having the power to 'denounce and even have arrested people that she dislikes and that, of course, I am to be arrested at any moment'. Speir would only confirm that she was detained under DR.18B in Holloway prison. John's reply to Speir from his mother's address at 41 Daver Court, Chelsea Manor Street, London, SW3, named Jacques Forrest, who he said had come over from Paris to see Stella, as well as Nicholas Sideroff, alias Prince Megaloff. He alleged that, shortly after his marriage to Stella, Sideroff had intimidated her into leaving him, but when that didn't work Sideroff and Forrest had enlisted some thugs to beat him up, but mistook him for someone else.[6] Under the name Forrest, someone has written 'N.L.T.' ('No Living Trace'), but he was believed to be a wholesale clothing merchant aged 25–30 who had left Newhaven on 16 July 1939. A note in Stella's file states, '<u>Very</u> unlikely trace of a French communist.'[7]

During her interview with Detective Sergeant Rhodes on 14 January 1942 Stella admitted to knowing Forrest and believed him to be a friend of Sideroff's. She had first met him at Bexhill in 1936 where she was living at that time, and on other occasions in France, Monte Carlo, and London when she and John gave notice at Kensington Register Office; but didn't see him again until 1939, then again in Marseilles in July 1941.[8]

Her mother wrote to Katherine Lonsdale ('Little Gran') on 22 April about Stella's internment and her earlier so-called 'marriage' to Sideroff, asking if she could see a letter from the War Office in 'Little Gran's possession. Her reply addressed the 'sad story' of their marriage, saying that 'J's marriage and hers was no marriage at all' and that John was trying to get his marriage to Stella annulled. She couldn't believe that Stella had been passing information to the enemy while allegedly working at the War Office. She gave John's current address as Spr. J. Lonsdale, No. 2181102, BDCHQ, Signal House, Atkins Road, Balham, SW12, but added that he was constantly moving around.[9] A further letter from her to Stella's mother on 5 May asked that she be told about the termination of Stella's first marriage – 'I am not devoted to J. and only tolerated him for Stella's sake when she was so fond of him, all that is passed now.'

Stella asked Norah for copies of Hans Andersen's fairy stories in French and German ('rather a forlorn hope') and any children's books by the Comtesse de Ségur (Sofiya Feodorovna Rostopchina), which 'are very easy French beginning books – little stories that are easy for my pupil to understand'. Clearly, she was teaching French to one of her fellow internees in Holloway. She reminded her not to discuss anything with their brother Dennis: 'I don't want him to interfere thinking that he could help me – I don't need help – things must just ride as they are for the time being ... I know there are things that I am not at liberty to discuss and therefore there is no point in my agitating for an Advisory Committee etc.' In April 1941 her mother had informed Ina Lonsdale that Dennis intended to contact Sir John Mellor, Bt., the MP for Tamworth, to try to get Stella repatriated from France.

Sideroff had been very sweet to her, visiting her frequently and giving her money, food and wine, but now he was suffering from tuberculosis:

> [W]hatever his faults have been towards me in the past, at least he has been exceedingly loyal and has done absolutely everything to make me comfortable and happy – that at least he must be given credit for – and it is entirely without arrière pensée [ulterior motive] because he knows I have not the slightest intention of remarrying – how can I as a Catholic? Of course if John wants to marry his little Betty I shall give him a divorce in the civil courts, but all this talk about Bigamy is bunk since he stayed with Nicholas [sic] and I in 1939, so to pretend that he only learnt of his existence in 1940 is slightly pathetic – it surprises me coming from such an intelligent boy as John. If I had thought of remarriage I should never have come home – I could just have stayed on in France and let John divorce me and married one of the three people who individually urged me to do just that. Poor John, I really am sorry for him because he can't get away with these wild accusations ever – as he thinks at a moment when I am entirely without defense [sic] ... I think that people who behave like that are really more to be pitied than anything else, because they will certainly pay on the Day of Judgement.[10]

Those 'three people' were undoubtedly Christian Boulanger, Frank Viner and RENÉ. She was shocked to find that John 'could be so utterly mean as to try to blacken me with the most filthy lies in the eyes of his grandmother – all of course, because she only accepted him because we were married and he was afraid that if she knew that our marriage was ending, she would cut him out of her will. Really some people's treachery has to be seen to be believed'.[11]

She criticized how John would go off to Mass at Brompton Oratory every Sunday morning from the bed of his girlfriend and 'saying a few Pater Noster's in front of the very alter [*sic*] where we were married', then return for lunch. In her continued castigations of him for his infidelity she seems to have conveniently forgotten how her own behaviour and sexual conduct left much to be desired. She therefore made excuses for herself and set herself up as the pious, wronged woman, when in fact, she was equally guilty.

Her letter to her mother dated Whit Sunday 1942 (24 May) continued to speak of her faith in God, and if 'Little Gran' needed a witness that John *had* met Sideroff in August 1939 she should ask Hugh Leveson-Gower.[12] They had all gone out for aperitifs at the Dorchester – Stella, John, Kolia (Sideroff), Diana (John's sister), and Kolia's aunt.

* * *

The 12th of May heralded the arrival in the UK of Henri Léon Sougne who had travelled on the RMS *Llanstephan Castle* with Count Baudouin de Borchgrave d'Altena[13] and claimed to know Stella. The CX report SIS had received from Gibraltar forwarded to Mills from Frank Foley in section VB4, the SIS section dealing with France, Corsica, Andorra, Belgium, the Netherlands and Luxemburg, noted that Sougne believed she was still in France. When he reached the UK, Sougne was to contact her family and get in touch with John, 'who is in the Foreign Office'. He described Stella's nocturnal habits as coming home to his room at 2 am, tired after writing her reports for the Intelligence Service. 'She was always writing them and worked very hard. SOUNE [*sic*] has the highest opinion of her, possibly because she appears to have pretended to be in love with him.'[14] Mills told Foley that he didn't think there was any point in interrogating Sougne because nothing of any value in Stella's case would emerge – she was resigned to her fate and showed no intention of appealing to the Advisory Committee. However, Sougne *was* interrogated at the RVPS on 28 May and their report sent to MI5.[15]

Shortly after Sougne returned to Marseille on 15 December 1941 preparations were being made for the visit of Admiral Darlan. There was a general round-up of aliens and the police came to the Hôtel Victoria where he and Pavie were staying and arrested them. Pavie had recently been released from prison, having been charged with what Sougne thought was black marketeering, and for having Gaullist sympathies. They were taken to the 'Évêché' (Bishopric) prison near the cathedral in Marseilles, the headquarters of the Sûreté where hundreds of other foreigners were being held. While there they chatted and Pavie noticed a friend of his: 'a girl of about 27 years of age who came up to him, and began saying a few words to him in English.' He learnt that she was a British subject named Stella Lonsdale @ Simone La Valliere who was living at the Hôtel Scribe, 92 rue de Rome.

The report claimed that Stella had got to know Pavie while she was in England, and had recently been working as a nurse at the front (!), but was now working for the Deuxième Bureau. She was also collaborating with the British in helping British and Allied airmen escape. Her contact in the Deuxième Bureau, Brun (Lebrun), arranged to have Sougne and Pavie released. When they met with her at Le Colibris bar, Sougne told her that he was a sergeant pilot in the Belgian Air Force because he assumed that the British would make more of an effort to help a pilot escape than a mere civilian. She told him to stay at his hotel and await further instructions – to take a train to Perpignan and proceed to the Hôtel de la Loge, Place de la Loge, close to the cathedral, where a British agent would contact him. His cover story – where he had been shot down and service number – would be that of Henry Marshall, RCAF, a story he should stick to if arrested by the Spanish police, as his Belgian-French accent could pass for French-Canadian and make things easier for him to be released.[16]

At the hotel he waited until a certain 'Captain Adolf' @ 'Captain John' arrived, who told him that he would be included in an escape party with another British officer, a captain whose name sounded like 'Achis' – probably Francis Paul Blanchain, codenamed 'Achille'[17] – two British sergeants, a Belgian flying officer and a Polish doctor. But when he reached Barcelona, he discovered that the British had not been forewarned about him so he maintained his Belgian identity and sought refuge at the Belgian Consulate.

When he arrived in Gibraltar, he gave a full account of his contact with Stella to an intelligence officer, then boarded the *Llanstephan Castle*. Coincidentally, another passenger on the ship was Janusz Włodarczyk, codenamed MAURICE, who had been part of the Interallié network in France and had escaped arrest by the Germans in Paris on 18 November 1941. The ship arrived in Gourock on the Clyde, Scotland, on 11 May. From there they were taken to the Camberwell Institute, an outstation of the London Reception Centre.[18] The extract of the RVPS report concludes that 'SOUGNE gives the impression of being a very alert and active young man. He tells his story with great wealth of detail, which, subject to checking up his statement regarding the alleged British Agent called Miss LONSDALE, I see no reason to doubt.'

* * *

When Sideroff visited Stella on 6 June, she told him about John's visit the previous Friday, accompanied by his solicitor. She was angry that Sideroff hadn't visited her earlier, but he explained that he'd been ill.

She'd apparently been spotted in Mayfair by Lady Foley, and John had also said the same, so somebody must be impersonating her, she replied. She begged him not to tell 'Valvar' – Princess Vavara Magaloff, mother of pianist Nikita Magaloff – that she was in prison and gave him a list of food to buy, as well as asking him to get her a solicitor.[19] Then she pleaded with him to come and visit again, saying she was dreadfully depressed, but couldn't expect any sympathy from her mother or 'Little Gran' as she wanted them to believe that she was actually happy and comfortable; the reality was, '*au fond* [deep down] I'm very lonely and sad in spite of my studies'.

'Little Gran' was sympathetic about the recent developments regarding her divorce, and suggested that she wait until later rather than making it easy for John. It would test his constancy to Betty Fuller, which she doubted as 'He will <u>never</u> stick to anybody', adding, 'You will always be my beloved and precious Stella.' But she pointed out that she would be unable to pay the costs of her divorce, nor did she know who could, as John had no private means. He was 'so profoundly cowardly and heartless' which left Stella's mother 'hurt and disgusted'.[20]

Stella's solicitor contacted her on 3 July 1942 while she was in Aylesbury Prison. He was ready to instruct counsel to present a petition for dissolution of the marriage and requested the first and last addresses where the couple had lived and the date when they last cohabited, which she clarified the following day in her reply, naming Elisabeth Fuller as the co-respondent:

> I first lived with my husband at Broadwalk Court, W.2. [actually W8] (but I forget the number of our flat) & last was the time we spent his leave in, first Nantes (Loire Inférieur) 29 Bd. Victor Hugo and the last two days at the Hôtel Windsor-Etoile, rue Beaujon, Paris 8me [most likely now the Sofitel Paris Arc de Triomphe]. My husband had to take the train back to England on, if I remember correctly, 2 May, 1940.[21]

On 13 December 1943 she was granted a decree *nisi*, and a decree absolute on 19 June 1944.[22] John married Betty F. Fuller in Chelsea in 1944, but true to 'Little Gran's' prediction it was a short-lived affair; in 1949 he married Dorothy I. Page *née* Walton and lived at 7 Somers Mews, London W2.[23]

Acting on a call from Matheson, Cyril Harvey made enquiries about a missing parcel containing a second-hand copy of Hans Andersen's fairy tales in German and perishable foodstuffs being sent to Stella. But upon reflection he decided to take the matter no further. The parcel finally arrived on 1 June. Stella assumed that various pencilled notes in the margins of the book must have raised MI5's suspicions, but if they did, they are not included in any of her files.

A priest named Canon Brown had suggested that Stella dedicate herself to God one hundred per cent by entering a Carmelite convent, 'but honestly I do not feel that I have the vocation. I feel that to live a good life in the eyes of God one should rather stand up against & overcome the temptations in the world rather than shut oneself away in a Convent'. But so far, Stella had succumbed to too many temptations and committed far too many mortal sins to receive absolution for them.

Matheson held back a letter dated 10 June to Stella's mother mentioning a fellow detainee. He sent it to MI5 seeking their permission for it to be forwarded to her:

> a woman here who was detained, nine months later her detention order was made into a charge. She was <u>tried and acquitted</u> at the Old Bailey & yet brought back here on the <u>original detention order</u> where she has remained ever since! Now she has been here for over two years!! ... The woman in question is the British born wife of a British Admiral by the way![24]

Mills replied that Stella's letter had not been censored and contained 'a certain amount of material which is obviously very undesirable' but was unsure whether it was in his power to censor outgoing letters, so he returned it to Matheson, referring him to certain pages which required his attention, and leaving it up to him to decide the next step. He also sought Pilcher's opinion, who added a handwritten note saying: 'I sent the letter back to the Governor with your covering letter. I think many [*illegible*] letters are allowed to go on.' Jim Hale didn't think MI5 had any legal power to stop her letter without first referring to the Home Office and the regulations for the '100 per cent censorship of mail and visits for special internees'. Edward Blanchard Stamp of MI5's Legal Section (SLA) waded in saying:

> I feel that if we stop this letter we are, in fact, evading the Home Office ruling ... that the special internees at one time detained at Aylesbury should be allowed to have visits. I think for this reason that the letter should not be stopped without reference to the Home Office and I would suggest that the draft letter attached should accordingly be sent to Sir John Moylan with a copy to S.O.E.[25]

In July 1942 MI5 drew up a series of regulations to monitor all communications between detainees at Aylesbury prison and the outside world, but they would not resolve whether they had the power to censor detainees' mail until 18 October 1943 when Mathilde Carré wrote to a friend of hers in the Forces Françaises Libre (FFL). What is surprising is why it should have taken them so long to work out what to do with internees' mail!

Chapter 18

'Well, There is Only One Lie …'

Stella was in a nervous state when she met with Nina Myers on 20 February 1942. She complained that Mills had only been to see her once since she'd been interned 'with Fascists who made every reverse we suffer … a cause for jubilation'. If he didn't come and see her soon, she wouldn't be able to remember anything.[1] She wanted to know what was going to happen to her and didn't want to be left in prison until the end of the war. There were certain things she needed to explain about the people whose names she'd written on a piece of paper and left with Nina when she was arrested. Nina told her that Mills was far too busy and it was a sheer waste of his time seeing her over and over again when all she told were lies. Stella retorted, 'Well there is only one lie that I have told that is important, and anyway what does it matter now? They have put me here and anything I now say will be pinned down to exact dates and it's no good. I can't remember any more.'

She admitted that she hadn't been in prison all the time between the dates she'd told Mills. The Germans had approached her to work for them and she'd agreed; then they'd put her back in prison. But when Nina prompted her for more details and correct dates, she started crying and didn't want to be pinned down to dates and times, then shut up altogether. A few days later she explained to Courtenay Young that the lie was the same one she'd told Garrow so that her story seemed less complicated. She assumed Garrow would report back to MI5; therefore, she dared not alter it in case they compared it with the one she'd given him and the one she'd given MI5 (see below). Before she'd been arrested, she'd told Nina that 'Mr Loftus' had said that her detention was because she knew too much and that MI5 didn't know what else to do with her. Mills commented, 'MICHAEL has repeated this sort of thing when she has been visited in prison by Nina and Nina feels that she may be setting a stage for an appeal based on these lines.'

She recounted to Young how when she'd first met Fullerton, he'd told her about an English captain (Garrow) who, the Commissioner of Police in Marseille had warned him, was about to be arrested so there was no point in putting her in touch with him. Fullerton asked her, 'Are you aware how much Garrow distrusted the people at the American Consulate?' It was true. Garrow didn't trust Fullerton because he couldn't keep his mouth shut, nor Lee D.

Randall, the vice-consul.[2] Fullerton's secretary, Camille de la Pre (or Dupret/Duprez), vetted everyone who wanted to see him. Viner didn't trust her and accused her of spying for the French. Indeed, 'Leclerc' had hinted as much to Stella, as whenever she went to see Fullerton, he always knew about it. Viner was also acquainted with George Truman and knew that he was working for Garrow (see below).

While on a train between Paris and Marseille Stella had met Josef von Lenitz, a German Army major, who RENÉ had told her was going from Aix to Casablanca to take charge of espionage or counter-espionage at the end of July/beginning of August 1941. Von Lenitz offered to give her a nice job there if she would come and visit but she never saw him again. Mills commented on this episode in his report to SIS:

> The story about Josef von LENITZ does, I think, add a good deal of weight to my belief that MICHAEL is a German agent, even if only a dupe, for it is sheer nonsense to ask us to believe that such a tale is the result of a coincidence. It is almost evident that René intended Von LENITZ to meet MICHAEL and that Von LENITZ knew all about it. I feel convinced that otherwise Von LENITZ would have promptly kicked her out of the compartment which was specially reserved for him. He would probably have had her thrown in prison for her impudence, as although she would murder me for saying so, I refuse to regard her as being so attractive that every German Officer should immediately fall for her as she tries to make us believe.

Garrow asked her about 'Vergiers', whose name Stella said she didn't know – actually Marcel Verges, associated with Elisabeth Haden-Guest, whom she had met through Walter Stangroom at the Hôtel Noailles. But when Stella and Viner had ended up at a party in Verges's hotel room (number 110) this got back to Garrow via Viner, causing him to ask her why she'd denied knowing him. He suspected Verges, who was dealing on the black market, of working for the Germans. Later, he left for Lyons.[3]

It seemed that all of a sudden, she was remembering more names: Fernand Le Maire (or Lemaire) from Le Mans, the local leader of Jacques Doriot's PPF (Parti Populaire Français), and a known German agent even before the Germans invaded. RENÉ had once spoken to him on the station at Angoux-la-Moutour. He'd shown Stella his photo and asked whether she recognized him. There was also Joaquín del Campillo, and Yves Delbar, whom she'd met through Viner. Kenny had written to Admiral Darlan in Vichy, although at the time she didn't know his name, nor the nature of the communication.

RENÉ told her that the Germans didn't know anything about Viner, but Viner claimed that they'd approached him about the time when Czechoslovakia had fallen – which would make it sometime between 1 October 1938 when the Germans occupied the Sudetenland and 15 March 1939 when the remainder of the country was annexed. But the story he'd told her was rather vague: the Germans had asked him to find out who in Prague was likely to resist them. He'd also told her that he'd been practically running the Czech Intelligence Service under the cover of being a journalist, as well as working for a while for the Deuxième Bureau.[4] He claimed to have served in the French Army, ostensibly to find out about fifth columnists. When he went down to Marseille, Garrow checked up on him with London.

Dr Stephan Moncek, the Czech representative in Vichy, had come looking for Viner but Stella informed him that he'd gone away. Major Schow, the military attaché at the American Legation in Vichy, had written to him saying that they would be glad to receive any information he was able to provide, but Fullerton said he didn't want anything from him, declaring that he was an 'agent double', which resulted in Stella having a row with him.

American journalist Varian Fry had formed the Emergency Rescue Committee in June 1940, and was known to 'Lieutenant Leigh' (Langley). It was either Gars or 'Leclerc' who'd warned her that Fry was about to be arrested, but Fry had arrogantly proclaimed that he had too much influence. Stella had gone to Fullerton to warn him, but he'd replied, 'I don't think I can do much about it.' Influence or not, Fry was arrested on 29 August 1941 and deported.

The second version of Stella's arrest helps to clarify many of the points raised during this and other interviews with her. She said she'd met de Nayere through René Dazy, but RENÉ had shown her a photograph of him. The first tribunal had been around 12 December and focused on the Sainte-Luce plans, but had not gone into any details about her. A couple of days later she was released and she agreed to work for the Germans, rather than risk being shot or sent to Germany. RENÉ had come to her cell and told her, 'I am going to do everything to help you and the only thing I can do is to persuade them that you would be useful.' She believed that he had lobbied Meissner on her behalf. She couldn't remember when Meissner had come to see her, possibly in between the two tribunals, but when he did, he'd brought her some soap and told her she would be released.

At the second tribunal the Germans had wanted to find out through her personal affairs and relations with John whether she was telling the truth in her letters to RENÉ, 'that I was on the track of an Englishman, and they came to the conclusion that I had good reason … to hate the English Government because of John etc.'.

She had left behind her copy of *Climats* by Maurois and her identity papers in Marseille. There was no one else in England she remembered telling about any other book she was using for her code, but added that if she had, 'it was a deliberate attempt to mislead them'. The number 1863 and *Climats* were 'honestly the right things'.[5] Nor did she remember telling Diana Vernon that she'd given Young the wrong one: 'I did not make a mistake about Mr. Gladstone's number or the book. I don't remember ever discussing the code with her but it is very possible that I told her another book. I would not have told her the real book.' Young queried the fact that she'd told him how Garrow could only send messages verbally, but she denied it. She understood that messages were put into tubes of toothpaste. Stangroom had told her he carried them through in his luggage.

Her reason for applying for permission to go to France in 1940 was based on a lie, she said, because she had wanted to be with John: 'I gave the story about my mother-in-law's illness because I wanted to prevent myself running into extra trouble.'

She admitted that when she reported to Garrow it was simply easier to tell him that she'd been in prison from the middle of November until the middle of February and leave it that way. Not telling Young about Marcilly was 'sheer carelessness on my part'. The only other thing where she'd not told MI5 the truth was when RENÉ used to go swimming in the Loire with Stueppler but she claimed that she'd never gone with him, 'not even to watch', yet admitted to seeing him swimming once at La Baule. Whoever had asked her was trying to establish an intimacy between them.

Susan Barton reported on 26 February 1942:

> I think you will agree with me that the story of MICHAEL's two arrests, typed out, looks even worse than when she told it. She seems to be losing her grip and not have been considering all the possible implications and questions that might arise (provided it is taken seriously at all).
>
> It looks more than ever as if her first story was carefully worked out by somebody pretty clever and she was well rehearsed in it. On the other hand, I think that probably she herself added some of the touches about her thin dress, the hidden revolver and various things like that and immediately took away some of the credibility.
>
> I should say (as you have always said) that she has not been in prison at all and has probably amused herself at 'playing being a spy' and willing to tell both sides anything she saw or heard. It is not always easy to judge women of another country, particularly outside their own country, and RENÉ may quite well have been taken in by her and seen as an ideal tool for his purposes in her.

Considering her present attitude and hope that she may still be allowed to go back to France, it looks very much as if the seriousness of her situation has never dawned on her. She talks glibly about German threats of shooting her, but for all her wild imagination she does not seem to be able to visualise what exactly being shot means.

MICHAEL seems to be incapable of any thought or idea that does not make her the centre. I am more and more convinced that she is not quite normal (although I do not think that that is an excuse in her case), that she has given quite a lot of useful information to the Germans when in France, that if she had gone back to France she would quite happily have given any information that she had picked up in this country to the Germans, that she possibly would have sent us anything she picked up in France plus what the Germans wanted her to send and that, in fact, she would have played along happily with both sides merely to amuse herself.

I think the Germans meant her to be their agent but she probably made one of her famous mental reservations when promising to work for them and decide that she would only do what pleased and amused her.[6]

Mills sent a copy of his report to SIS, explaining that Nina had 'produced a small crack in MICHAEL's story':

3. MICHAEL now has the impression that her imprisonment may have something to do with the fact that we suspect her of being at the bottom of the trouble in which the Garrow organisation is. In fact, I have told her that I should not be at all surprised if this were the case, having regard to the fact that she was running around Marseille telling every other person she met that she was an English spy and that Garrow was her 'chef'.
4. Her earlier explanations are clearly designed to make it appear to us that several others were spying on behalf of Garrow and it is therefore just as probable that they are to blame.
5. [See above]
6. The revised statement to the effect that there were four 2eme Bureau inspectors with whom she was in contact, instead of two, as previously stated, may again be due to the fact that she now realises that even if it takes time, we shall get these small details in the end. The same may be said about all the other new details which she has just decided to give us.
7. The reference to André VILLEMORIN's [sic] address arises out of the fact that he has recently cabled to the Manager of the Waldorf Hotel asking for news of MICHAEL. He gave his address as 42, Rue

Paradis, which we know to be that of Christian BOULANGER. I am not at all sure that we have yet obtained even a fraction of the truth about either of these people and I believe that it is still possible that Christian BOULANGER may have some close connection with René.

8. The reference to DELBAR is interesting in as much as he is supposed to be a refugee from Bolshevism and I was able to pin MICHAEL down to the fact that DELBAR made the statement about working for Garrow as his war effort against the Bolsheviks at a time when the Russians were fighting against Germany.

9. The crack in MICHAEL's original story comes in the new version of the prison story which is only one more proof of the fact that MICHAEL can never be counted on to speak one word of truth unless it suits some specific purpose which she has in mind. You will note that she was not in prison on Christmas day and the whole story of DERNBACH's orgy and his burning her forehead with a cigarette is disintegrated. Of course I did not draw MICHAEL's attention to this fact for had I done so she would immediately have said that the affair with Dernbach took place on some other date, and we should then have had another bunch of lies to puzzle out. I feel that it is better now to keep a few things up our sleeves against the time when she may appeal to the Advisory Committee, who will hardly be able to accept her word for anything if we are able to prove how she has lied to us consistently for weeks on end.

10. I must confess I did not appreciate quite why MICHAEL had decided to change the prison story when Nina told me this was the case. Under interrogation, however, MICHAEL herself gave what is I think most probably the true reason. She has remembered that Mr. Dick, the American Consul in Nantes, will no longer be there and that sooner or later we shall be able to hear his side of the story. I suppose it would not be possible for you to get in touch with Dick through your representative in the U.S. and try to get a brief report from him about MICHAEL?[7] Even if he had to destroy all his papers it may well be that he took home in his head enough details about MICHAEL to enable us to have a pretty good idea as to what, if anything, that she has told us is true for it was to him that the famous St. Luce [sic] plan was offered and from him that MICHAEL used to receive her monthly allowance.

11. You will see that MICHAEL has also confessed to having told a lot of lies about a visit to a bathing place near Nantes when she was

interrogated by six of us at Special Branch. Her only excuse is that she thought that we were trying to establish intimacy between her and René.
12. MICHAEL's refusal to be pinned down about the code book and the dummy number are worth noting, for she always boasts of her excellent memory and it is sheer nonsense for her to pretend she does not remember what [she] told her sister in law Diana.
13. Both Diana and Mrs. Lonsdale (mother in law) have said that there was absolutely no question of the latter having to have an operation in January 1940. MICHAEL concocted this story in order to get a passport, and although both Diana and Mrs. Lonsdale had been asked to co-operate, they had refused. MICHAEL now confesses that the whole story was a lie made up because she wanted to be with her husband.[8]

Major C.J. Howard Foulkes in Room 055 reported that John Wilson, a ship's officer, had returned to England on a destroyer with Viner and Boris Melikoff. During the crossing Viner asked Wilson to deliver a letter addressed to Stella to the Dorchester announcing his arrival and that he could be contacted through the Free French Forces. But when Wilson went to the Dorchester, they told him that she could be found at the Waldorf. The porter at the Waldorf set off a wild-goose chase when he mistakenly wrote down Viner's name as Binder. Mills contacted Mackenzie at SIS trying to track down who Binder was 'who she believes to be in the Free French Forces … The only BINDER I am able to trace at the moment is the one mentioned in the report which accompanied your CX/12678/0 dated 1.10.41'.[9]

Francis Martin Binder @ Jacques Berges @ Marquis Berges @ Rebane was known to SIS, prompting Mills to contact Major C.W. Hordern, the RSLO at Leeds, on 4 February based on information he'd received from Major W.S. Mars in D4d(3) on 26 January: 'I know from very secret sources that the name BINDER does not mean anything to Mrs. LONSDALE, but that she suspected that the man might be the bearer of a message for her from either Occupied or Unoccupied France.'[10] As Mills wrote on 22 January 1942:

MICHAEL says that the only persons aboard who knew the Waldorf Hotel address were Christian BOULANGER and his partner Lucien GERSCHEL and that she thinks that BINDER therefore has a message for her from Christian. As we know Christian is in communication with René it may well be that BINDER has a message from him. Michael has said to me that she does not think this possible – in fact she rejects the

> idea altogether but she has in fact said to Nina on more than one occasion that the man may have brought her a message from RENÉ …
>
> This episode gives me cause for a certain amount of anxiety as it is not beyond the bounds of possibility that BINDER has brought a message from RENÉ or Christian BOULANGER and that finding Michael had left the Waldorf, he has given a dud name and dropped out of the picture. The fact that MICHAEL has told Nina that the man may have a message from RENÉ and that she persists to me that the message could only be from BOULANGER only makes the affair more puzzling.[11]

He wondered who else knew Stella could have passed on such a message since the only people who knew where she was were her French and German friends. Therefore, 'it seems probable that he [Binder] must have obtained her address from France and in that case, he would almost certainly be a German Agent who is being used as a "cut-out"'.

Foulkes wrote to Wilson on 7 February seeking clarification on a couple of points from their meeting the previous day – about when Viner had become aware that he might not be allowed to land immediately on arriving in the UK, and how he had come by this information. Had it been in Gibraltar or on board ship?

MI5 assumed that since Viner had asked Wilson to contact his friends, and could be contacted through the Free French Forces, that he did not expect to be 'detained permanently'. Wilson thought that he must have phoned the Dorchester and Waldorf hotels and left a message about Viner on 16 January when he was in London, having arrived in England on 8 January. But a telephone check on 9 January 1942 revealed that Stella had telephoned the Free French Forces headquarters in London at 4 Carlton Gardens trying to get in touch with 'some Free French man who has arrived in this country and I thought maybe he would be able to help me', suggesting that it must have been 8 or 9 January. They advised her to contact the Bureau de Recherchement in Dolphin Square. She sent a telegram to Binder c/o the Free French Forces requesting an emergency telephone number where he could be contacted, but the Post Office returned it as the Free French Forces knew nothing about him.

Wilson replied that it was common knowledge on board ship that Viner would not be allowed to land immediately, but he couldn't recall discussing it in Gibraltar. Someone, most likely Captain Gubbins, had mentioned the name of the camp to which they expected to go to be 'checked over' and had informed Viner about the disembarkation procedures:

> In my mind he had no doubt at all that he and his friend would be passed through fairly speedily as he mentioned he expected to be in London on

leave in about a fortnight … With reference to Mrs. S.L. – I could not have phoned before the eighth of Jan., as that was the first day I arrived in London. I <u>think</u> I phoned on my first visit to London after that date, & I would have thought that it was on the 16th. I cannot be definite about the exact date.

B. Thompson of the RVPS reported on 12 February that when Viner was questioned about Stella, he confirmed that the only mention he'd made of her between leaving Gibraltar and arriving at the RVPS was to naval officer Lieutenant Thomas aboard the SS *Batory*.[12] He asked him to ring her and tell her that he'd arrived safely in the UK, but hadn't mentioned Wilson.

The request for the police to investigate Binder was cancelled when Mills realized that the porter had made a mistake.

Chapter 19

Aylesbury or Bust!

The Home Office decision to transfer Stella Lonsdale, the Duchesse de Château-Thierry, Mathilde Krafft, and My Eriksson, to Aylesbury prison created a storm of protest to Governor Matheson from three of the women – the Duchesse, Krafft and Stella. Fellow detainee Enid Mary Riddell described the episode:

> On July 1st at 12.30 p.m. three "Detenues", who are detained in our "Wing" were called to the Governor and informed that he had received an order from the Home Office instructing them to pack immediately in order to be transferred to Aylesbury Prison at 3 p.m. Their request for the reason was refused, also permission to telephone their lawyers before departure.1

Krafft and Eriksson made no objection, but Stella enquired whether they were going as 'prisoners', and the Duchesse's request to petition and telephone her solicitor was denied. Matheson explained that once she was at Aylesbury, she would be able to write to him or petition the Secretary of State. He was unable to give the women a reason for their transfer, but the conditions under which they would live would be the same. Accompanying them would be prison officer Baxter who was familiar with all their privileges, etc., but they had to be packed and ready for transfer by 3 pm; anything not packed by then would be forwarded later. That seemed to satisfy everyone.

But by 2 pm they were all refusing to pack or preparing to be transferred, egged on by other detainees in 'E' Wing, in particular Muriel Whinfield, Christabel Nicholson, Mrs Kelly and Olive Burdett, who Matheson blamed for the ensuing disruption, but described in Brett-Perring's file as 'quiet, courteous and not in any way pro-German'.2 Whinfield was the wife of a former commanding officer of the 1st Battalion, The Queen's Royal (West Surrey) Regiment and a friend and neighbour of the leader of the British Union of Fascists, Sir Oswald Mosley and his wife, Lady Diana Mitford. Olive Burdett *née* Hawks was the chief women's organizer of the BUF and her husband Frederick had been the district leader in Peckham. The Duchesse demanded to see the Governor, complaining that they were not going to be herded like cattle, and that she was being moved under protest.

Prison officer Doris Andrews was instructed to inform the four women that if they were not ready by 3 pm they would be forcibly removed and their property packed up and forwarded afterwards, but officers were instructed to use only such force as might be necessary. Stella complained that she was suffering from excessive menstruation, and Krafft complained that she had had a heart attack, both of which were unfounded.[3]

At 3 pm the women were assembled in the common room. Stella was asked if she was ready to go, whereupon she refused to leave. As Riddell's account continues:

> At least 10 prison officers (this is the term used for wardresses and <u>not</u> police officers) returned and carried Mrs. Lonsdale from the room at the same time pulling from her chair and onto the floor another detainee who happened to be in the officers' way. The resistance offered was passive. The 10 officers soon returned for the Duchesse de Chateau-Thierry and we were witness to her announcement that it was only as an alternative to her removal by force she consented to walk away with them. Shortly afterwards they came back for Mrs. Krafft, who had to be helped out of the room, suffering very much from the shock owing to her age and, I believe, a bad heart. We were kept locked in until they had all left … This affair has distressed us all very much and we hope it will be enquired into, so that we may be protected against its happening again.

Stella regarded two and a half hours as insufficient notice, considering that they had been there for over a year, and hadn't been given enough time to pack.

In the common room Deputy Governor Wilson was met by an ugly scene and 'greeted by a storm of abuse from the other occupants – cries of 'British justice! This is England; More will be heard of this', and 'This scandal will never be forgotten'. Only Eriksson was prepared to move, with two of the women lying on the floor in an attempt to hinder the officers and the whole room in an uproar. Stella resisted, protected by Burdett and Nicholson, who sat either side of her refusing to budge, but the officers carried her through the door:

> Mrs Lonsdale hung onto the table and fought and struggled. Burdett had her leg twisted round the table in order to stop Lonsdale from moving – in the struggle the table was pushed across the room, pulling C. Burdett [*sic*] off her chair. I. Ryder stood at the door struggling to bar the way. Mrs Lonsdale was taken from the room, I remained with others in the room. All these women were most abusive in their remarks to us, and about the Home Office and the Government.

At the top of the stairs Stella started to scream. Miss Wilson told her, 'You would be wise to walk down the stairs or you may get hurt,' but she was still struggling violently and replied, 'I will not walk.'

The officers were instructed to carry her down the stairs, but she struggled so hard that it was impossible to lift her off the ground and she was dragged part of the way down. During the course of the struggle the flowing dress she was wearing was trodden on and a large part of it torn off, leaving her naked from the waist down, as she was wearing nothing underneath. At the foot of the stairs Wilson tried to reason with her, telling her to 'stop behaving like a baby and walk on her feet', but Stella refused. Prison officer Dooley attempted to fasten her dress but there was not enough to cover her so she picked a used sheet from a pile of laundry by the door. It wasn't until Stella was wrapped in the sheet and 'carried struggling into the coach [that] … she became quiescent and sat quietly crying'. Krafft and the Duchesse became more cooperative and after being helped down the stairs by two officers, boarded the coach quietly.

Somehow the incident came to the attention of the newspapers and was reported in great detail in the *Daily Express* on 11 July with the headline '18B woman carried to bus in Holloway uproar'.[4] On the same day A.H. Robertson of B1a @ 'Captain Robson' visited Aylesbury to ascertain whether the detainees had learned of the publicity generated by the disturbance. The Deputy Governor assured him that they were told that the normal newspapers they received were not available that day and were given *The Times* instead, which had not reported it. Therefore, it was hoped that they should not learn of the publicity, the enquiries, nor questions in the House of Commons. Afterwards Stella wrote to the Governor complaining about their treatment. Prison officer Andrews reported to the Governor of Holloway, Molly Mellanby, that a letter had been written to the Home Secretary by the DR.18B detainees, including Whinfield, Molly Stanford, Iris Ryder and Fay Taylour.

Known as 'Flying Fay' or 'Fabulous Fay', Fay Taylour was an Irish motorcyclist in the 1920s who was interned under DR.18B as a Fascist;[5] Iris Katherine Ryder was a member of the Bournemouth branch of the BUF; and Mary Agnes Geraldine 'Molly' Stanford, described in Brett-Perring's file as 'mental', who had supported the National Socialists, was a member of the Right Club, and a friend of Anna Wolkoff. On 7 January 1943 she was the first to raise the issue of VICTOIRE (Mathilde Carré) being a 'stool pigeon' at Holloway when she wrote to Sir Archibald Southby, the Conservative MP for Epsom, Surrey, and to Sir Ernest Graham-Little, the National Independent MP for London University. P.M. Burke in F3c2 described Stanford as looking on the war as 'a fight between the Powers of Light (the Nazis) and the Powers of Darkness (the Jew-controlled Bolshevik democracies)'.[6]

On 6 July Mills met with Miss Mellanby about a letter which Stella had addressed to her mother and was being photographed by MI5 (cited in the previous chapter) to tell her about the arrangements MI5 had made to censor outgoing mail 'modelled on the code which was drawn up for Camp WX, but are of course not quite as strict'.[7]

On 14 July Stella petitioned the Home Office to be returned to Holloway, because '(a) it was inconvenient for her to be at Aylesbury where her friends find it difficult to come and visit her, and (b) whether she might be allowed to go and see her mother under escort who is … suffering from a weak heart and is likely to have a heart attack at any moment'. The Home Office intended to ignore her request but Tar commented to Mills that he saw no reason why she shouldn't be allowed to see her mother under escort. He was curious to know whether her mother was really suffering from a weak heart,[8] which was later confirmed when she told Stella that her doctor had advised her to live quietly, free from worry, no stooping and no violent exercise.

Viner, now serving with the Czechoslovak Forces in Yeovil, visited Stella on 31 July. Afterwards she wrote to him, constantly referring to him as 'Darling' and 'darling heart' and saying that mentally she was 'lacerated with lust' and 'weighed down by the utter futility of all our efforts and strain'. She asked whether he still loved her – or was he simply feeling sorry for her? – and gave her love to Bosio.[9] She felt hard done by – about what she'd done in France, all the risks she'd run, and 'some people sitting comfortably at home, at a desk, drawing large salaries I could just scream'. He'd cautioned her about not getting bitter, and not adopting the mindset of the people she would meet in prison who 'really are in for what they have done and are anti-British'. The biggest mistake she'd made was not getting out of France when she'd had the chance. She retorted: 'You don't understand. Elisabeth [Haden-Guest] didn't want me to leave her, and she asked me to bring a letter for a friend the next day, and then it wasn't ready, and I was persuaded to stop.'[10]

The following day she apologized for such a depressing letter, explaining that she was 'appallingly tired and hurt'. Her fear was that if the Germans were to invade, she would 'just be sitting there like a beautiful present from Father Christmas, or rather a mouse in a trap'. She asked that if he were wounded or 'unspeakably hurt' she be given as his next of kin, not so that she could benefit financially from his death, but he was to tell his commanding officer that they were engaged. Here we see an interesting new development as far as their relationship is concerned. Viner had always 'carried a torch' for Stella, but this was all sheer fantasy on her part because, as her mother had already said, his love for her had never been truly reciprocated. Earlier she had expressed a wish to marry RENÉ once the war was over. Stella lived constantly in 'cloud cuckoo land', falling in and out of love with whomever she met, as the mood suited her.

She asked Viner to get in touch with Elisabeth through her father at the House of Commons. This must actually have been her *father-in-law*, Dr Leslie Haden-Guest, the Labour MP for Islington North, because Elisabeth's father's name was Paul Wolpert. When Viner suggested that she should let her mother visit her, she retorted that 'it would kill her to come here and see me in prison. That is my greatest trouble, and then you ask me not to be bitter. It's bloody awful'. Sideroff visited her on 7 August saying that he'd been in a nursing home and indicated that he was still recovering from tuberculosis.

On 9 August the *Sunday Pictorial* published a brief article under the heading 'Playboy's wife in Gaol – 18B' as the result of a visit to Stella's mother in late July enquiring about her and John Lonsdale. The journalist wanted to raise the question of ill treatment of internees, but Mrs Clive told him that her daughter had not been ill-treated, just misunderstood – 'which is almost inevitable in wartime'. The article simply gave a short background of John and his involvement in the Mayfair robbery; how he'd met Sideroff in Wandsworth prison, a friend of the 'beautiful daughter of a Birmingham business man', and that she was now interned under DR.18B. It also mentioned that she was one of the women moved from Holloway.[11] Mrs Clive wrote to the editor afterwards to confirm what she had said, stating that:

1) He must not publish my daughter's name nor make any reference to her without her except with her express permission.
2) He must not publish my name nor make any references to me under any circumstances.[12]

When she next wrote to Stella, she urged her 'to take some steps to justify yourself & put an end to this miserable position. You can have no idea of the anxiety & unhappiness it causes me'. But Stella replied that she couldn't afford to, citing the case of Muriel Whinfield who had spent £1,026 on her case, but was still interned 'so what on earth's the good? I can only trust in God to help me and pray!' She wished her mother could have warned her about the *Sunday Pictorial*'s visit so that her solicitor could have stopped it:

> I saw it afterwards and cringe still with humiliation – my God it seems as if there is to be no end to the indignity & mental crucifixion that is heaped on my shoulders & all because last year I risked my life many times, ruined my nervous system, lived a precarious and hideous nightmare to do my infinitesimal "bit" towards helping my country!

She also expressed her 'deepest regret at being an unsatisfactory daughter'.

Stella Lonsdale. (*TNA KV2/740*, © *Crown copyright*)

John Lonsdale. (*Keystone/Hulton Archive/Getty Images*)

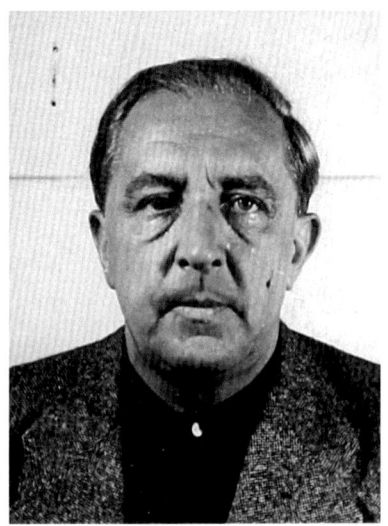

Hans Meissner. (*TNA KV2/282, © Crown copyright*)

Olgierd Około-Kułak, front row, far right. (*National Digital Archive, Poland*)

Cyril Mills. (*Royal Aero Club Trust*)

Ian Grant Garrow. (*Christopher Long*)

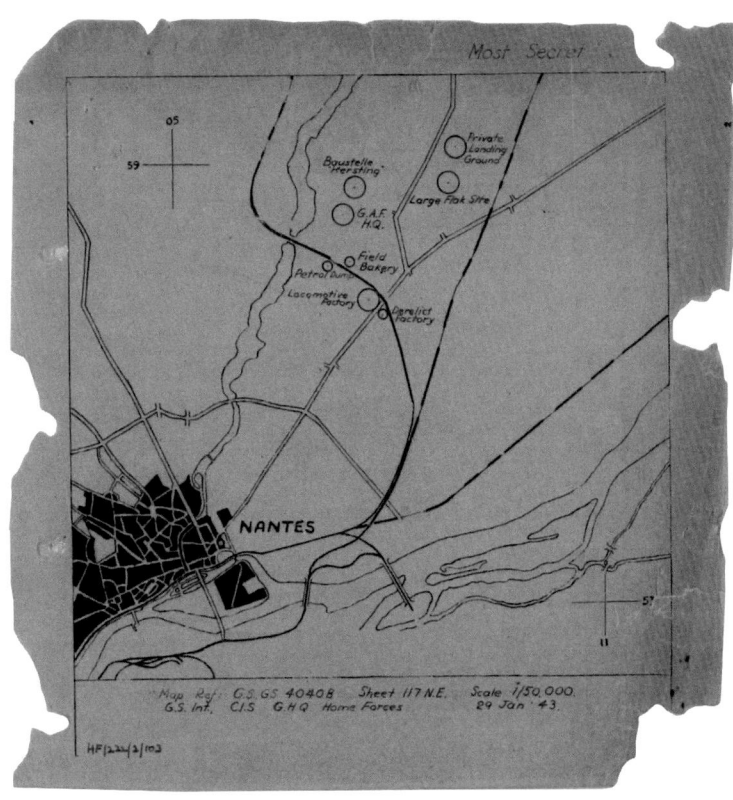
Nantes petrol dump. (*TNA KV2/456, © Crown copyright*)

Waldorf Hotel Co., Ltd. Telephone: Temple Bar 2400

Room 519 Mrs Stella Lonsdale

THE WALDORF HOTEL,
LONDON, W.C.2.

Bills are presented Daily or Weekly for settlement.

V.C.S.

The Management respectfully give notice that they reserve to themselves the right to make an Extra Charge for Apartments when Meals are not habitually taken in the Hotel. An Official Printed Receipt is given for all payments made; no others can be recognised.

Nov 1941

	£ s. d.	£ s. d.	£ s. d.	£ s. d.
Brought Forward		2 4 2		
Apartments	1 7 6			
...				
...				
...				
...				
...	2 9	5		
...				
..., Milk	2			
..., etc.				
...				
Servants' Board				
Wines		1 2		
Liqueurs				
Spirits	1 1 2	4 8		
Ales and Stout				
Minerals	6 6	- 10		
Cigars and Cigarettes	3	4 6		
Disbursements				
Newspapers				
Pressing				
Laundry				
Flowers				
Cabs and Carriages				
Postage				
Telegrams and Cables				
Telephone	1 3	2 6		
Service Charge	2 4 2	3 3 8		
TOTAL		7 -		
Less Paid		4 - 8		
Carried Forward				

Expenses for Stella. (*TNA KV2/732, © Crown copyright*)

Waldorf Hotel Co., Ltd.　　　　　　　　　　　Telephone: Temple Bar 2400

Room 519　　*Mrs Stella Lonsdale*

THE WALDORF HOTEL, LONDON, W.C.2

Bills are presented Daily or Weekly for settlement.

V.C.S. The Management respectfully give notice that they reserve to themselves the right to make an Extra Charge for Apartments when Meals are not habitually taken in the Hotel.

An Official Printed Receipt is given for all payments made: no other can be recognised.

Nov 1941	17 £ s. d.	18 £ s. d.	19 £ s. d.	20 £ s. d.	21 £ s. d.	22 £ s. d.	23 £ s. d.
Brought Forward		2 11 1	5 - 10	8 12 -	10 9 10	16 11 6	21 18 7
Apartments	1 7 6	1 7 6	1 7 6	1 7 6	1 7 6	1 7 6	1 7 6
Fires	1 -	2 -	2 -	2 -	2 -	2 -	
Breakfast	2 9	2 9		2 3	6 6	3 9	
Luncheon	5 9		1 -		19 3		15 9
Dinner	10 6	8 -	16 -	9 3	11 -	19 6	1 1 -
Teas and Coffee Milks							
Sandwiches, etc.	2 3	1 9	6 -			8 -	2 -
Supper							
Servants' Board							
Wines					13 8		
Liqueurs							
Spirits	7 -	2 4	3 -	2 4	17 6	22 8	
Beers and Stout		- 10				1 2	
Minerals	2 4	1 6	- 10	1 6	5 10	5 -	2 8
Cigars and Cigarettes		1 6		1 6	8 4	3 -	2 3
Disbursements							
Newspapers							
Dressing						3 -	
Laundry							
Flowers							
Cabs and Carriages							
Postage							
Telegrams and Cables							
Telephone	2 -	11 7	1 4 10	2 -	10 1	1 6	1 8 8
Service Charge 10%	2 11 1	5 - 10	8 12 -	10 9 10	16 11 6	21 18 7	26 9 2
							2 13 -
TOTAL							29 2 2
Less Paid							
Carried Forward							

Expenses for Stella. (*TNA KV2/732*, © *Crown copyright*)

Christian Boulanger. (*TNA KV2/741,* © *Crown copyright*)

Frank Viner, third from left. (*Source: TNA KV2/741,* © *Crown copyright*)

Two men and a girl. (*TNA KV2/736, © Crown copyright*)

Top Row—G. Haimbaugh, J. Martin, T. Cochran, L. Sutton, R. Thomas, N. Grieser, G. Heil.
Row Two—C. Cox, S. Horowitz, R. Baldwin, S. Rauch, Prof. E. M. Mueller, Prof. G. H. Grueninger, J. Showalter.
Row One—I. Wössner, E. Ivey, C. Heimerdinger, C. Donnohue, R. Brandenburg.

Siegfried Rauch. (*DePauw University Archives*)

Siegfried Rauch. (*TNA KV2/739, © Crown copyright*)

Siegfried Rauch. (*TNA KV2/736*, © *Crown copyright*)

Siegfried Rauch with Charlotte Rieth. (*TNA KV2/736*, © *Crown copyright*)

Airey Neave and Albert Guérisse. (*Ted West/Central Press/Hulton Archives/Getty Images*)

SECRET AGENT
British traitor betrays three of my best men

by .... Lieut.-Com.
PATRICK O'LEARY, G.C., D.S.O., R.N.

WHEN I took control of "Pat" the first great problem was money. Without money we could not pay the Spanish guards who led our escaped prisoners across the Pyrenees; we could not bribe when bribes were essential; and we could not buy the vital food we needed.

I set out to solve the money problem—and had an amazing stroke of luck.

I discovered, by accident, that J. and P. Coats, the spinners, had a representative in France. He had been in charge of their French factories, and when I contacted him I found that he was holding millions of francs on behalf of his company — and hadn't the faintest hope of getting the money out.

I arranged that he should hand the francs over to me while the British Government, in London, paid his firm the equivalent in sterling.

On an average it cost about £300 to get each prisoner out of Occupied Europe.

Ideal hide-out

The money problem solved, I set about dealing with the suspected traitor "X" — an Englishman who, as I said last week, was ultimately shot in Paris while resisting arrest after the war when we caught up with him. I ordered "X" to come to Marseilles.

We were then working from a doctor's flat. This made an ideal hide-out, for patients were passing in and out at all hours, and no suspicions were aroused.

"X" duly arrived.

And here let me give the devil his due. He had brought a number of men safely south, and when these men returned to Britain they spoke so well of him that I was later to find it very difficult to convince the authorities in Britain that he was a traitor at all.

Stormy meeting

MY three chief lieutenants were Bruce Dowding, a young Australian; Prassinos, a Greek, and Dupree, from Lille.

They were with me when "X" arrived.

It was a stormy meeting. I lost my temper and hit "X" so hard that I broke the knuckles in my right hand and will carry the disfigurement to my grave.

"Pat," declared Dowding, "there's only one thing to do

In England, the war over, three men talk over their adventures. Lieut.-Commander O'Leary is in the centre, on the left is M. Maurice Dufour, former French officer and member of the organisation known as "Pat." On the right is Squadron-Leader Jimmy Higginson, who escaped from the Germans disguised as a priest.

with him. Kill him or he'll betray us all."

"But we haven't proved he's a traitor yet," put in the Greek.

I hesitated—and in doing so made an error of judgment that was to cost Dowding, Duprez and Prassinos their lives.

"Look here," I said to "X," who was slumped in a chair with blood pouring from his face and tears streaming from his eyes, "you'd better go back to England.

"I won't tell the authorities there anything about this, and I'll even recommend you for a decoration. After all, you have done some good work. Will you go?"

"X" nodded.

"Then I'll meet you today week, at the corner of the Boulevard, at seven in the evening," I said, "and you can go back to England by the Spanish route."

"X" did not keep that rendezvous.

With his removal from our ranks, we had to reconstruct the organisation in the north—and Dowding volunteered to be the key man.

We met in Lille, and I took Bruce around to meet our various workers.

One of the most active was the Abbé Carpentier, at Abbeville, a priest with a secret printing press and all the facilities for forging identity cards, demobilisation papers and ration books.

* * *

WHEN I reached the outskirts of Lille on a return visit shortly afterwards, bad news began to pour in on me.

One of our workers told me to keep out of the town. He reported that Postelviney, one of our best men in Paris, had been arrested by the Gestapo, and added that he suspected there was something seriously wrong.

I found Postelviney's sister, and had my worst fears confirmed.

"X," whom she knew well, had been with the Gestapo when the house was raided.

I learned that Dowding, Duprez and the Abbé Carpentier had all been rounded up.

I was never to see them again. The Abbé was in the Prison de Locs, near Lille, and several of our sympathisers were prison guards. I contacted one of them, and got him to smuggle a message to the Abbé in which I asked about his arrest.

I had a reply within a few days—a pencilled letter of six pages which told the whole grim story and incriminated "X."

Betrayed

The Abbé was in his office one morning when "X"—whom the Abbé knew—arrived with three strangers, and introduced them as escaping R.A.F. pilots in urgent need of false papers.

The Abbé took them into his study, opened his large desk, and from secret drawers proceeded to take out false identity papers, ration books and demobilisation cards.

"X" then produced passport photographs of the men, and the Abbé bent over his desk to complete the work.

Suddenly he looked up and found himself gazing into the muzzles of three revolvers. The alleged escapees were from the Gestapo.

The Abbé, along with Bruce Dowding, was later beheaded. Prassinos was shot.

Duprez died in a concentration camp.

I returned to Marseilles feeling suicidally depressed.

Our organisation in the north had been broken up again, every key man was in prison along with 25 other workers, and dozens of R.A.F. men were in hiding on the scantiest rations, in farmsteads and cottages throughout the northern area.

Had I laid hands on "X" then I would have torn him limb

from limb. The authorities in London were so surprised at my news about "X" that they ordered me to report to Gibraltar to discuss the whole set-up with an agent who was flown from London to meet me.

I travelled, taking with me the Abbé Carpentier's letter and other incriminating evidence.

From the day I produced them at Gibraltar "X" was a wanted man.

A new route

MY stay in Gibraltar lasted six weeks, and resulted in the opening up of another escape route.

It was arranged that men would be picked up off the Mediterranean coast and taken straight to Gibraltar.

In this grim battle of wits there were amusing incidents.

On one occasion we had a flatter pilot, Squadron-Leader J. Higginson, in hiding in Monte Carlo.

The Monte Carlo to Marseilles route was full of dangers. It was controlled by the Doriot police, who were every bit as vicious as the Gestapo, and we had to be certain that the "parcel" was well disguised.

Fortunately, we also had a Polish priest in hiding and he had two suits of clerical black.

So we dressed Higginson in one of these, complete with Roman collar, and boarded the train.

There was only one seat in the compartment, which Higginson took.

The Polish priest and I stood in the corridor nearby, but I soon had to intervene.

On edge

An elderly woman, anxious to be on the friendliest terms with the clergy, started jabbering away in French to Higginson—and he didn't speak a word of the language.

I explained to the good lady that shell-fire had made him somewhat deaf and he was very tired. That silenced her for the time being and I rejoined the Polish priest.

But Higginson was very much on edge and suddenly his hand came out round the compartment door to grab the Polish priest by the coat.

He leaned down and I heard Higginson in a hoarse whisper say : "For God's sake lend me your Bible."

Higginson, who was neither a priest nor a Catholic, grabbed the breviary with obvious gratitude and started to read the Latin as though his life depended on it.

We got him home all right.

Love letters

We also sent home an attractive young Englishwoman who contacted me in Marseilles, admitted that she had been working as a Gestapo agent but was now anxious to serve in our organisation.

Her husband was a Mayfair "playboy."

As soon as she left I came across two trunks she had left behind.

I searched them and found bundles of love letters written to her by the Chief of the Gestapo at Nantes, along with a number of pictures showing the "happy couple" together.

I sent these back to London, and when the former woman Gestapo agent landed in her native country she found Scotland Yard waiting for her.

THE problem of traitors, spies and Gestapo agents grew as time went by. Whenever we lost a worker—through capture, ill-health or pressing domestic cares—we had to replace him.

But it was the hardest job on earth, when investigating the credentials of a newcomer, to know whether the man was genuine or not—especially as Gestapo agents always had the best references!

Man in a café

One day, in January 1943, following the arrest of one of my best workers, I was approached by a man—a native of Alsace—who wanted to meet me in a Marseilles café.

I had to be cautious, but I did see him, and he opened the conversation by asking me if I would pay him two million francs for a copy of the German naval code.

I leaned across the rickety café table.

"What proof have you that your copy is the real code?" I asked.

"You'll have to take my word for it," he replied.

"We don't take anyone's word nowadays," I replied. "If you want to work for any organisation, then you have to prove your worth.

"Could you, for example, get the names and full descriptions of any German agents recently landed in Britain by parachute or U boat?"

The stranger replied that he could, so I gave him enough money for the return trip to Paris, and told him to contact me on his return.

And sure enough he did return —but I could not meet him. I had an urgent escape job on hand, so had to send one of my men.

The stranger brought back with him the names and descriptions of three German spies who had been landed in England.

Suspicious

But my man was suspicious because he had noticed certain documents in the stranger's possession, and all the facts were reported to me.

There and then we decided that the stranger would make a trip to the Pyrenees—from which, for Gestapo agents, there was no return.

He set off with four "parcels"—our name for escaping prisoners—and instructions to lead them into the mountains to a certain rendezvous, where he was to hand them over to one Vidal, a Spaniard who worked for us.

Vidal later fell into the hands of the Germans and was burned alive. But even when faced with this terrible death he refused to give a scrap of information about us.

The great heroes of the war were not entirely confined to the belligerents.

What the man from Alsace did not know was that men from "Pat" were following, men acting on strict instructions from me.

Cornered

Up in the mountains they watched the "parcels" being handed over, and then cornered the stranger.

They searched him and found all they needed to find in the way of incriminating evidence.

This Gestapo spy was taken to a deserted crevice, stripped of all his clothes, and his mouth was forced open.

A small pill of cyanide of potassium was slipped between his jaws, and within five seconds he was dead.

The upper part of the corpse was then saturated with petrol and set alight. In less time than it takes to tell the body was unrecognisable.

It seems grim—and it was grim. But we were all living under the shadow of the Gestapo, and we either had to eliminate or be eliminated.

If the rocks of the Pyrenees could speak they would tell one of the grimmest stories in history.

Hundreds of people, listed as "missing," are actually rotting heaps of bones hidden, perhaps for ever, in crevices and crannies among those desolate heights.

And even if the remains are ever discovered they will never be recognised.

NEXT WEEK
44 men snatched from the enemy

Abwehrstelle
Südwestfrankreich
Tgb.Nr. 2674/1.41 g.III F Az.3a1

Geheim

O.U., den 1o.1.41
Bp.Nr. 22 414

Bezug: dort.Vorg.12356/40 g.III f
Betr.: Englische St.A. L o n s d a l e
Anlg.: 1 Akte

An die
Abwehrleitstelle Frankreich)III F)

P a r i s.

    Die Angelegenheit Lonsdale wurde von III f Angers durch V-Mann Emile bearbeitet. V-Mann Emile hatte sich bisher als zuverlässig erwiesen. Im Laufe der Erhebungen wurde jedoch festgestellt, dass er in ein sexuelles Abhängigkeitsverhältnis zu der L.gekommen war und er daher nur noch beschränkt für die ihm übertragene Aufgabe verwendbar war.
    Da durch die vom Militärbefehlshaber Frankreich für Anfang Dezember vorgesehene Internierung sämtlicher feindlicher Ausländer die Fortführung der Ermittlungen in der begonnenen Weise unmöglich wurde, musste zur sofortigen Festnahme sämtlicher bis dahin in die Angelegenheit hineinspielenden Personen geschritten werden, obwohl das bis dahin gesammelte Material noch nicht zu einer einwandfreien Beweisführung ausreichte.
    Am 24. und 24.11.40 wurden daher im Falle Lonsdale 11 Personen verhaftet (siehe Aufstellung)
    Im Verlauf der durch Ast Angers durchgeführten vorläufigen Vernehmungen bot sich die Lonsdale zur Arbeit für den deutschen Nachrichtendienst an. Da durch eine sorgfältige Prüfung des vorhandenen Beweismaterial und der noch nachträglich in der Sache anfallenden Nachrichten festgestellt worden war, dass der L. ein Zusammenhang mit dem feindlichen N.D. in jüngster Zeit nicht eindeutig nachzuweisen war, wurde dem Angebot vorläufig nähergetreten. Die L. wird bis auf weiteres in Angers zur Verfügung gehalten.

Stella's Abwehr statement. (*TNA KV2/739*, © *Crown copyright*)

– 2 –

Von den restlichen 10 in Haft genommenen Personen sind 5 inzwischen wieder freigelassen worden, da ein dringender Tatverdacht gegen sie einstweilen nicht mehr besteht.

Im Zusammenhang mit dieser Angelegenheit hat es sich erwiesen, dass V-Mann Emile mehrfach unwahre oder übertriebene Nachrichten geliefert hatte, die der Nachprüfung nicht standhielten. Er ist deswegen wegen Nachrichtenschwindels dem Kriegsgericht überstellt worden.

In den übrigen 5 Fällen, und zwar hinsichtlich der bulgarisch französischen Staatsangehörigen Besedinoff, Fougeron, Delattre Delrue und Marchesseau wurden die Akten dem Kriegsgericht bei der Feldkommandantur 588 übergeben.

Über die weitere Entwicklung der Angelegenheit wird jeweils Bericht erstattet.

Vernehmungen liegen an.

I.V.

Nachrichtlich:
Abw.III F 3 x

Major.

Stella's Abwehr statement. (*TNA KV2/739*, © *Crown copyright*)

George Pitt-Rivers. (*Churchill Archives Centre, Churchill College Cambridge; the papers of George Pitt-Rivers, PIRI 10/2/4*)

Torpedo Development Unit. (*Imperial War Museum, © Crown copyright*)

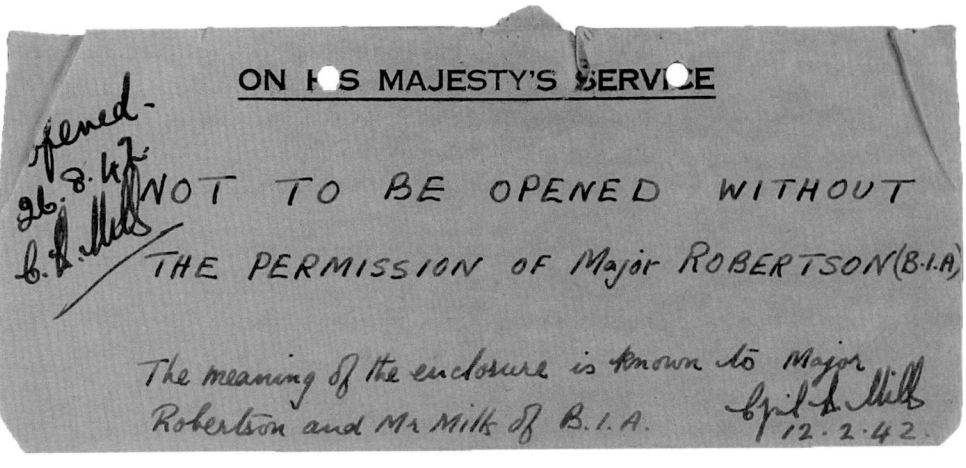

ON HIS MAJESTY'S SERVICE

Opened –
26.8.47
C.? Mills

NOT TO BE OPENED WITHOUT THE PERMISSION OF Major ROBERTSON (B.1.A)

The meaning of the enclosure is known to Major Robertson and Mr Mills of B.1.A.

Cyril B. Mills
12.2.42.

.... GERHARDT GUNTHER du PÖEL

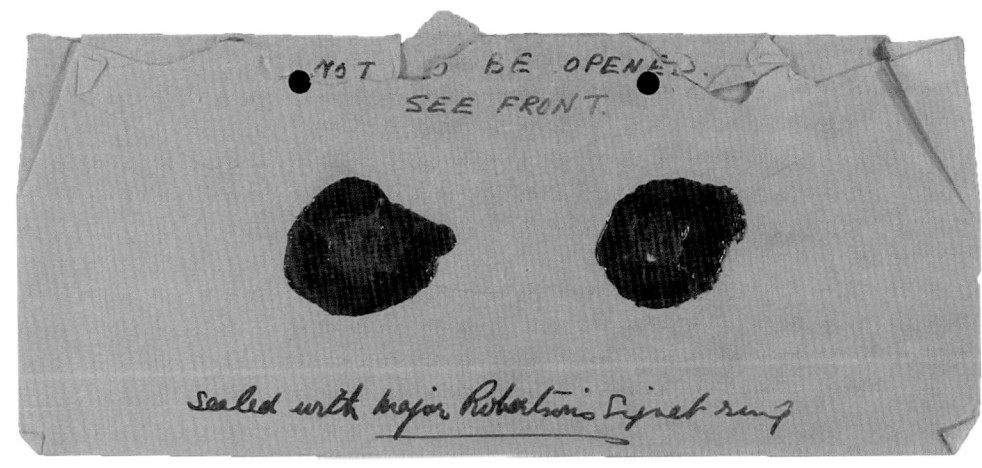

NOT TO BE OPENED. SEE FRONT.

sealed with Major Robertson's Signet ring

Notes on RENÉ. (*TNA KV2/740*, © *Crown copyright*)

Mills sent some of Stella's letters and a photograph to H.L. Smith in the Scientific Section (A6) for examination, to look for any secret writing done with B.S. (baking soda),[13] as well as 'duff' – the MI5 codename for a microdot, because their distribution was random, rather like the raisins in a 'plum duff' pudding. No traces of B.S. or other secret ink, nor any 'duff' were found on the three letters, which will reappear later in our story. He wrote to Miss Mellanby at Aylesbury on 19 August informing her that it was unnecessary to submit incoming telegrams to MI5 unless there was anything incriminating in them. The purpose of the censorship was to ensure that Mathilde Carré and others didn't communicate with the outside world.[14]

During Norah's visit on 22 August Stella told her that the only way she could clear herself was with the help of a certain Scotsman (Ian Garrow) who, the last she had heard of, was interned in France. Otherwise she would have to give away RENÉ, without whose help she would not be alive, something she refused to do. Norah kept repeating that surely all the things she'd done in France could be proved if only she were to ask for an Advisory Committee hearing, but Stella retorted:

> Surely you don't think I'm enjoying this. You don't understand, if I went before the Advisory Committee I couldn't tell them the facts, the War Office wouldn't allow me, but one day, it will all come out, and then I shall get the honours I earned. The position at the moment is absolutely damnable, but don't worry, it will all come right.[15]

An unnamed French girl interned with her was unable to speak much English, so she had to interpret for her. This was clearly Mathilde Carré (VICTOIRE) interned under an Article 12(5a) Detention Order on 1 July, and largely responsible for the betrayal and break-up of the Interallié network in France.[16] In his report on Viner of 17 October Mills commented:

> The Germans are undoubtedly anxious to know what has happened to the French woman, and the coincidence of dates would undoubtedly lead them to assume that she is in Aylesbury with LONSDALE.
>
> The French woman was connected with certain S.O.E. and S.I.S. agents, and for this and other reasons we are most anxious that the Germans should not get any information as to where she is or what she is doing now.[17]

Stanford would later report to Colonel Hinchley Cooke, MI5's senior legal advisor, that although VICTOIRE claimed not to know any English, when excited 'it became so obvious that she knew English quite well that she finally gave up the pretence, and used, or openly understood it, whenever it suited her'.[18]

When Mills wrote to Tar on 25 August, he referred to Stella's remark about giving away a German officer:

> If the RENÉ story is true and there is nothing more in it than MICHAEL would have us believe there is no question of giving him away. Unless he sent her here as an agent the more truth she tells about him and herself the better it will be for both of them.
>
> It would not be going too far to say that the whole of MICHAEL's present trouble arises out of her determination to protect him from something. What that something is can only be the truth for that alone is what she persistently refuses to tell.
>
> Are we still entitled to conceal what we think <u>may be</u> RENÉ's name? Or do you think I ought to see MICHAEL the next time I have half a day to spare and tell her that I am one of the four people to whom 'MR LOFTUS' made the disclosure and get her to discuss RENÉ with me on this basis?
>
> I think S.I.S. ought to be told that we have got 'a name' out of MICHAEL but that we doubt whether it is a genuine one.
>
> SOE and M.I.14d between them probably have the name of most important officials and I should very much like to submit the name to both of them but this cannot be done as long as S.I.S. are ignorant of the fact that we have got 'a name'. If I go down to see MICHAEL again I have a feeling that she might say more than she has ever said about RENÉ before for she gave the impression of being on the verge of opening up when Louise [Green] and I went down with the photos of RENÉ a month ago. Even if she cannot be persuaded to talk I could at least come back with a name of some kind which could be passed on to S.I.S.[19]

Tar thought it would be worth enquiring of SOE, MI14d and SIS to see whether RENÉ really did exist: 'With regard to disclosing the fact to MICHAEL that you are one of the four people to whom "MR LOFTUS" made the disclosure about RENÉ's name, I think you ought to have a word with him about this before taking any action. I am personally inclined to agree.'[20] He also requested that Pilcher look over the exchange between them and provide an opinion on the second paragraph of his reply. Pilcher appended a handwritten note saying: 'I see no reason why you should not tell Stella that you are one of the four (or was it three) present to whom Mr Loftus disclosed the name. I was under the impression that we already knew that the name "rang no bell" with SOE, SIS etc!!'[21]

Stella's mother finally paid her a visit on 2 September. She had written to Elisabeth Haden-Guest, reminding her that the two women had met in France and that Stella was now in Aylesbury Prison; however, there was no reply. 'Surely she will do something to help, considering what I did for her when she was imprisoned in France. I had an S.O.S. for some clothes, and I took her up four new dresses and Heaven knows what,' Stella declared peevishly. She told her mother how she had risked her life in France, and referred to RENÉ only as a German officer who had helped her to escape; how she feared that if she told MI5 everything about him he would be shot – 'I couldn't possibly do this after him saving my life.'

In spite of Stella's exhortations her mother was less than enthusiastic about seeing Viner, saying that she didn't see any point in it. But Stella responded that he was largely responsible for her activities in France and for her being in prison and was doing everything he could to help her. He had given her the courage to continue when she'd told him she daren't go on. The English had treated her unfairly, she complained, and how she had not been put on trial – 'The Germans do at least give you that.' The upside was now that her mother had seen her at last, she wouldn't worry so much. John's solicitors, Bentley, Stokes & Lowless of 32 Bishopsgate, London EC2, wrote to her on 4 September informing her that he had been discharged from the army on account of stomach trouble.

An undated note in what appears to be Mills's handwriting states that

> Frank Viner, one of Stella's men, has written a letter in which he asks her to tell him about ? "Milton" who I think is Victoire – he also asks for a photo. He also intimates that he has understood some "double sense" in a letter he has had from Stella. I don't think I saw this letter as I was on leave. Will you please be sure to let me see all Viner-Lonsdale correspondence going both ways as I suspect they are up to something. I have let Viner's letter go on in order to see how Stella replies to it.

This was probably a typo for 'Mitou' as it is the only time that the name 'Milton' has been used as a codename for Carré and never appears in any of her files. The letter to which Mills was referring was probably the one sent on 15 October in which a sentence has been underlined in red ink: 'the wool is pure Indian Cashmere, the same as that little dark blue pullover you had sent down to Marseille from Paris, le souviens tu? [do you remember it?]' Whatever this was supposed to mean was not elaborated on in the file, but may have been a code for an agent or airman sent from Paris to Marseille, possibly by Garrow.

Chapter 20

'A Very Cheap Specimen of a Human Being'

Captain C.A.W. Beaumont of E1a/F, the French sub-section of MI5's E Division, Alien Control, wrote to Mills enclosing Elisabeth Haden-Guest's letter, dated 28 October 1942, written to him from 16 Bray House, Duke of York Street, London SW1, calling it an 'effusion', and someone 'whom I had the misfortune to interrogate recently'. Her letter revealed why Stella and Mrs Clive had not heard from her:

> If I felt any sympathy with Stella Lonsdale I would do all in my power to help her. But I disliked her entirely always and felt most awful when she thrust food on me whilst I was in prison. I know it was not because she liked me but because she desperately wanted to be in contact with Captain G. [Garrow] and our organisation. I accuse her for having got Captain G. to communicate with the French S. [Secret] Service, when after 9 days of interrogation, I finally achieved to convince them that Captain G. had left France. But that isn't to the point. Hypocrisy is not one of my caracteristics [sic], and I don't want to have any more to do with St. [Stella] who in my eyes is not a spy, but a very cheap specimen of a human being. But she <u>did</u> bring me food when I was starving to an extent which can only been known [sic] to those who have gone through that experience themselves and food meant a lot. And that is what I owe Stella Lonsdale: I was not hungry for a few hours several times, because she brought food to the Court Martial in M [Marseille]. I will gladly send her a parcel in order to repay my debt, but I cannot write her encouraging letters, because I feel that it is justice that she should pay for all the harm and dishonourable things she has done. This is hard coming from me, knowing that prison is a million times worse than death ... but I am sure that our prisons are very good, and they are not going without food, without books. They don't live with rats, lice and bugs as we did.[1]

She asked whether Beaumont would agree to her sending Stella a parcel – 'I cannot write a letter. I would not know what to say' – and expressed concern about the fate of Henry and Nancy Fiocca who worked for SOE.

Elisabeth had nursed Garrow through a *'fièvre d'Orient'* contracted in Fort St. Jean, which had made him prone to fits of high temperature, sickness, bile, liver and stomach trouble, heart attacks and eczema; she had been afraid that he wouldn't survive. The French, she said, had had tremendous respect for him. In a postscript she added: 'Frank Viner unfortunately called on me, asked by Stella Lonsdale to do so.' When Sideroff next visited Stella on or about 13 November she complained about Elisabeth's letter and the

> very condescending reply, saying she would get in touch with anyone she could, but "it was a pity Stella ever went to France." Bloody bitch, using my experience of crossing the frontier to make a sensational story for the papers. She never saw a German in uniform, and telling that tale, a pity she hadn't the good manners to pay me back for all I gave her when she was in Prison.[2]

In a long and rambling account which SIS had passed on to MI5 Elisabeth described how she, Garrow, O'Leary and Viner had been arrested at the Hôtel Noailles in Marseilles. On Monday 14 July she had been due to meet O'Leary in Kenny's room. While she was with him the telephonist summoned her downstairs saying that there were two men who wanted to see her. She was arrested by two Sûreté inspectors and taken to the 'Évêché' (Bishopric), near the cathedral. When she didn't return, O'Leary, who'd been waiting for her upstairs, went down and left a letter saying, 'My dear Lise, I can't wait any longer. It's absolutely necessary that I see you when I return at 2.30. Regards, Adolphe.' (His false papers from the north were in the name Adolphe Lecomte.) That afternoon he was also arrested.

The Sûreté asked her about Garrow. Elisabeth thought he was probably at Saint-Hippolyte-du-Fort, his intended destination after he'd left Marseille, and admitted to meeting O'Leary at the Café Gaulois about a week earlier. He'd told her he'd come down from the north looking for work, a story he maintained when the Sûreté interrogated him.

That evening Blanchain, codenamed 'Achille', whom they didn't know, was brought in.[3] He'd been sent by a friend named Dickinson to the Hôtel Noailles to ask Kenny for a way out of France, and already had his passage to America booked and all his identity papers. The hotel told him that Kenny wasn't there so he left a letter saying that he was a friend of 'Marcel' and wanted to meet him, and would return the following day. That letter, and the fact that he'd wanted to cross the border, were enough for the Sûreté to keep him in prison with the others for four months before releasing him. Blanchain's sparse SOE file only reveals that he was a commercial traveller in France, but hinted that he had been considered for SOE but rejected by 'FG' (Selwyn Jepson).[4] He was 'one of the line's most gallant couriers' who became O'Leary's secretary when they were repatriated to London, having escaped from Canet-Plage in September 1942 as part of Operation *Titania*.[5]

The following day Elisabeth was cross-examined again about Garrow's whereabouts, much of which she made up to satisfy the Sûreté. Around midday Mario Prassinos was brought in, having returned from Perpignan with many papers (which Elisabeth had been able to destroy), and over 20,000 francs. He explained nervously that he had called on Kenny to congratulate him on his marriage, but denied knowing any of them. On the newspaper in his possession the inspectors found a few lines of a message from Garrow to him written in pencil, so they kept him in the prison hospital for four days because he wouldn't tell them who the message was to or who it was from. Elisabeth didn't know whose handwriting it was and refused to tell them anything, so the cross-examination was abandoned. The inspectors told her: 'You will talk when we get Kenny and Garrow.' But the newspaper was enough to keep her separated for two days in another part of the building.

Viner had been warned a long time ago not to call at the hotel but Elisabeth said that he was one of those people who was hard to get rid of. When he was arrested, he'd tried to hide some papers, one of which contained an Italian Armistice Commission (Anti-American activities) report. The Sûreté removed all his identity papers when he was taken away, but returned them later, and behaved very friendly towards him.

That day three others were arrested: Jean Fourcade,[6] Elisabeth's son's guardian, who was going on holiday and wondered why she hadn't turned up to take her son; Nadia de Pastré,[7] who had called on Elisabeth at the hotel an hour before she was due to go to Antibes with her mother, Countess Lily Pastré (Marie-Louise Hélène Double de Saint Lambert), but was released four hours later. The countess used her home, the Château Pastré in Montredon south of Marseille, to hide Jewish artists, musicians and performers from the Germans, including Edith Piaf's lover, composer Norbert Glanzberg. The third was Paul Dubart, who had just arrived from Lille. He'd been asked by some English people in the north to go and see the padre (Rev. Caskie) at the Seamen's Mission, but it was shut. The Mission told him to call on Kenny at the Hôtel Noailles, but denied knowing him or Elisabeth.

When the Sûreté searched Elisabeth's hotel room, looking for secret codes and transmitters, they thought they'd hit the jackpot when they found in her suitcase some old papers with a list of technical terms in English and French which they assumed must be her secret code. Six years earlier she'd done some technical film work in London and had kept a few things as souvenirs. She also had a snapshot of herself with Garrow and Kenny, taken by Pierre d'Harcourt.

While at the hotel a Polish captain, whose name she didn't remember, called on her but Jean Fourcade recalled that this was Jan Jankowski.[8] He'd been hunting for her and her colleagues for the past two months wanting her to get him and his friend out of France. She'd told him to keep quiet and wait until she could arrange a meeting between them and a Polish flying officer who would contact their staff officer, then 'our people'. Once the order was received, they would arrange the escape. However, Jankowski and his friend were both arrested.

Elisabeth and the other prisoners were kept together in one room so they were able to corroborate each other's stories, thus avoiding any contradictions. The Sûreté questioned her frequently about Garrow, whether the Americans had ever provided the group with false papers, and the location of the transmitter which had been in Kenny's room. How many Frenchmen had she got out? From whom did they receive their orders, and their money? They threatened her and told that she would never see her son Anthony again.

The day after Prassinos and Viner were released she was taken to a bistro with Viner. Stella appeared and admitted that she and Viner had had dinner with Gars and Brun, the two Sûreté inspectors, and had offered to work for them. Before Prassinos left, Elisabeth told him how to get hold of Garrow to warn him. After lunch Lieutenant Esway, a Hungarian-born film director, writer and producer whom Elisabeth had known in London before the war, turned up and offered them a room in his flat in St. Luc where Garrow was staying.[9] When she was taken down to a bistro for some coffee, suddenly she saw Kenny sitting there. Even though she was being watched she managed to tell him that she hadn't said anything.

Over dinner the inspectors told Kenny that Elisabeth had refused to talk, that she was suspicious of them, and that she thought they were German agents. They tried to reassure him that he could have complete confidence in them – they were only trying to clarify a few points. If Garrow had been there he could have clarified everything and they'd both be released. He was asked if Garrow had left France. Kenny replied that before his marriage he'd seen him in Marseille but couldn't find him there because he didn't know where he stayed. Elisabeth's account added that Kenny knew only one of their hiding places but no important ones. The next day when she saw Kenny again, he told her that she shouldn't have refused to talk, as the Sûreté appeared to know everything so it was no use denying anything. They only wanted to know what they'd been doing; by not talking she'd complicated things and made them suspicious. He told her they would be released that evening.

Kenny told the Sûreté that Garrow had been in charge of a 'soldier's escape scheme', which he, Garrow and Elisabeth had been working on; that Elisabeth was a sort of '*main droite*' (right hand) and liaison officer; and that he had been responsible for the 600,000 francs Murchie had brought to Marseille, as well as 45,000 francs from Perpignan a fortnight earlier from Thomas Parker[10] when taking down Flight Lieutenant Frederick William 'Taffy' Higginson.[11] He'd handed the money over to Garrow but also told Madame Digard, his mother-in-law, about it.

'Darling ... [was] a man who lets us know when our men arrived over the other side,' and the Padre (Caskie) 'sent off wires to England telling the families over there of the safe arrival of men,' he said. He claimed not to have had anything to do with the escapes from Saint-Hippolyte-du-Fort, but the number of people brought down from the north was between 300 and 400. He also spoke about 'Paul' (Harold Cole @ Paul Delobel) and attempted to impress them with how much 'pull' they had in Vichy by mentioning Dehillotte, a journalist,[12] Pierre d'Harcourt and Captain Agier of the Deuxième Bureau in Marseille.

He confirmed that the American Consulate *had* supplied them with false papers, but Elisabeth thought that the inspectors had added that, so when Kenny was taken to the *Juge d'Instruction*, he asked that it be removed from his statement. The next day Elisabeth was called in and told that Kenny had decided to co-operate and it wasn't worth her playing dumb. Like everyone else she had to sign a *Procès Verbal*, then everyone except her, Kenny and Blanchain was released.

She struggled to decide what to do: 'I had something like an internal fight in myself. I did not want to make a statement but by than [*sic*] I knew that everybody was free, none of our lodgings, papers nor the transmitter discovered,' so she agreed. The night before she had informed O'Leary of the work, addresses, papers, etc. so that he could carry on in the hope that Garrow had cleared out. In order to get Kenny discharged, Madame Digard claimed to the Commissaire Général de la Sûreté in Marseille that he had been strongly influenced by Elisabeth, his mistress, and now that Garrow had gone away she was left in charge of the organization. Kenny had never done much for it, latterly nothing at all, but all of this got them into more trouble.

Elisabeth didn't trust Prassinos as an intermediary, so while still in prison she managed to send messages to Garrow via Maître Ginette Kahn (secretary to Maître Gaston Deferre, one of her lawyers) warning him about Stella, Viner and Madame Cathala.[13] At the *Tribunal Militaire* on 18 August Stella gave an account to Dutour and Elisabeth 'all about lovers and sex and all in an argot too much put on. It was embarrassing ... Dutour gave me some funny looks'.

Sometime in May, Stangroom had come up to Kenny's room while Elisabeth was there with Garrow. In a departure from what Stella had claimed about meeting him at the American Consulate, he told Kenny how he'd met her in a bar. She'd supposedly escaped from a German prison having been charged with espionage, and was looking for intelligence service people and had heard of Garrow. Garrow was in hiding and didn't want to get mixed up with her, but because it involved British soldiers hidden in the occupied zone, he'd agreed to see her and asked Stangroom to bring her to the Fiocca's flat at 5, rue Eduard Stéphan the following day.

When Stella met Garrow she told him that Castelain had told her about thirty-five British soldiers hidden somewhere in the occupied zone who wanted to escape and wondered whether she could arrange to have them brought down to Marseille and through to Spain. Garrow told her he could arrange to take them over to Spain in groups of four or five and would pay 1,000 francs per head. Castelain asked whether she could get fifty francs and share the balance. Stella told her interviewer that Viner could confirm that she had given Castelain money several times, but she never did find out whether these soldiers really existed. Stangroom told Garrow that it was a garbled version of the truth:

> You know she is rather fast and has many affairs. She said she came over to France in the month of May 1940 [*sic*] because her husband came over with the BEF and she said that she had a special permit from the Foreign Office [*sic*] to come over to France as usually wives of men or Officers are not allowed to join their husbands abroad. But she said that she had a special pull and got a brand new passport for her stay in France. She was in Brittanny [*sic*] (Angers) and could not get away when the Germans arrived. She is a converted catholic and very religious etc. You ought to see her – she may be of some help to you.

Parts of that statement are incorrect. Firstly, it was January 1940 when Stella went over to France, *not* May 1940; second, it was from the War Office, *not* the Foreign Office from where she'd obtained special permission; and third, Angers is in the Pays de la Loire region.

Stella told Garrow she'd met a German intelligence officer whom she'd previously met in England (not Paris as she'd claimed earlier) and who was very much in love with her. She'd offered to go up to the occupied zone and return with information from an officer of the Italian Commission (Bosio) who was also very much in love with her. In exchange for payment she claimed she could extract a lot of information out of him. But Garrow wanted nothing to do with it; he was only interested in 'our men in the North', telling her that he would inform her of his decision the following day. After meeting her, he told Elisabeth: 'I talked to that girl and don't like her much – I would even go as far as suspecting her. She used the sort of terms which are not used by young well bred women etc.' He sent her down to the bar at the Hôtel Noailles to keep an eye on Stella. Elisabeth decided that she was 'not the type of girl I would trust or like' and told him that their resources didn't extend to keeping an eye on her; other people should employ her who were able to do so. Nevertheless, he decided he would pay for Stella's journey to the occupied zone, but only if she came back with definite information concerning the hidden soldiers.

That was the last Elisabeth heard of her until a fortnight later when she asked Garrow what had happened. He'd seen Stella but the men had disappeared and she'd had no way of contacting them or the people who'd been looking after them. Then Paul Dubart turned up at the Mission and told Stella about the men. But Elisabeth collected all Garrow's messages for him and as far as she knew, he hadn't had any further contact with Stella. Garrow told Elisabeth: 'Big detour around that girl. I heard from [Lee] Randall and other people [at] the Consulate and our own people that she was leading a very fast life in Marseille but that was not our business.'

Viner provided Garrow with information from time to time but Elisabeth repeated what she'd said earlier about how difficult he was to get rid of, always hanging around asking for money and suggesting that they employ him as one of their agents because of all the languages he could speak. Garrow strongly denied Viner's suggestion that he'd promised to employ Stella. As Viner had been seen with Stella on a number of occasions, Elisabeth bluntly asked him about his relations with her. They were friends, he said, and persisted with his suggestion that they employ her. Then Garrow sent Stella a message telling her to clear out.

Stella returned from the occupied zone with important papers which Viner claimed to have and for which Garrow had promised to pay her. Elisabeth's patience was wearing thin. She told Garrow that she'd had enough of Stella and asked him point blank, had he employed her, and had he promised her money. 'No,' came the reply, 'But I'll have a last interview with both of them and tell Lonsdale to clear out.' Somewhere outside Marseille Elisabeth, Viner and Stella met with Gars, who told them that they were mistaken and made it clear there was no question of the Deuxième Bureau employing or paying Stella.

Viner approached Kenny with a photograph of Stella, asking for a false identity card but his request was refused. Another time he came up with a report from the occupied zone saying that Pierre d'Harcourt was keeping in contact with a German intelligence officer and that he should be told not to trust him: 'This was most amazing but we could not check up on that because shortly afterwards we were all arrested,' Elisabeth remarked. Four days later d'Harcourt was arrested (see next chapter).

At the meeting between Elisabeth, Stella and Garrow, Garrow had waited until she'd left Capitaine Dutour's office before requesting that he be allowed to meet with Elisabeth again, but this time alone. A few days later Elisabeth received a letter from him via her lawyer saying that she shouldn't make any plans to escape as 'things were going alright [*sic*]'. The only dangerous person was Kenny's mother-in-law, Madame Digard, who was the reason she was in prison. He also warned her never to reveal his address to Stella. Elisabeth retorted that she didn't know his address, and would certainly not give it to Stella anyway: 'I do not want St. L. to help me but I must trust her as you trust her. But you do know that I don't like her. There was no reply to that letter for some time.'

At the second *Tribunal Militaire* on 6 September Elisabeth encountered Garrow and Stella. Gars and Brun asked Dutour, the examining magistrate, whether he would allow Stella, alias Simone Lavalliere, to accompany Garrow to see her and bring her some food and to see to her personal needs. Elisabeth tried to warn Garrow, saying, 'For heaven's sake clear out, St.L. is there,' but he replied, 'She is perfectly alright [*sic*] and has been very good. Don't you worry.'

Stella told Dutour that she was Elisabeth's friend and had brought her some food, soap and a towel. She made light of their conversation and pretended to be on very good terms with her. As Elisabeth described it, 'Stella L. played the part of a tender friend and I tried the best to make believe the same.' At the same time, she wondered what had brought all this about. Why was Garrow allowed to walk about, talk to her and Stella, and why were they together? Little by little, she started to understand something of what had happened. The remainder of the SIS report concerns 'all I know concerning Stella Lonsdale and her sudden appearance and interference in and with our case and people'.

When Garrow and Stella arrived to meet with Elisabeth on 22 September Dutour asked him to find the four who had disappeared. While they were alone Elisabeth asked Garrow why he hadn't left yet. He explained that he was simply waiting for her to get out. But when they started to discuss Kenny, he became angry. She told him:

Th.K. is <u>not</u> a traitor but he had the wrong political ideas and he did not realise our position that we were in between the two camps – the Darlan and Pétain camp – that means the anglophile and anglophobe and we were alright [*sic*] until and as long as the anglophile people in Vichy protected us but that situation changes every day and depended on so many events etc. G. said "Kenny is a saligaud [dirty or filthy pig] – you don't know all he has said and done."

Dutour said that Kenny had behaved himself and was the best-treated prisoner at the Fort.

When Stella came to visit Elisabeth on 3 October, Dutour took Elisabeth to one side and asked her whether Stella was really a good friend of hers, as he didn't think she came from a good family and had seen her in restaurants with lots of Poles, spending a lot of money. 'He told me to tell her to be careful when talking and to frequent less the Bars in Marseille,' as well as asking her whether she had ever suspected that Stella might be working for the Germans. Elisabeth told him that Stella was not her friend, but she'd been kind enough to help Garrow get some food for her. 'Well, Garrow must know what he's doing,' Dutour replied.

As if on cue, Stella entered and became hysterical. She was meant to go to the occupied zone but half an hour before leaving she'd received a postcard from RENÉ in Paris warning her not to come: 'Your latest photograph (follows description) with details (glasses) dyed hair is known to the people here. Wait for a while and lie low.' She told Elisabeth about working for 'Leclerc', with whom Gars and Brun had been in contact, but her boss was really Garrow. How was it then, Elisabeth wondered, that the Germans knew of her photograph, etc.? Dutour had advised Stella that she should return home to England if she was afraid, but she told him that she had a friend in the occupied zone. Elisabeth recounted, 'St.L. behaved in a rather lunatic way. I got frightened and felt instinctively that things were going wrong and that something must be done about it.'

Downstairs in a waiting taxi Stella confided to her that she'd agreed to work for the Deuxième Bureau, but was then transferred to 'Leclerc'. He was a 'very hard and tough fellow' who told her 'from now on you will work for us alone. You'll be my first spy. Neither Garrow nor the inspectors will be up-to-date on your activities.' She said that she didn't want to be a real spy but wanted to go off on her own and gather intelligence. Elisabeth reported that Stella was 'frightened and getting nervy' and told her she should leave the country before it was too late. It frightened her that Stella had told her that Garrow had already offered to go to the occupied zone to get the information from her friend, and to take her over the Swiss border. She suggested to Stella that if she didn't want to return to England she should go to Lisbon and then decide what to do.

They arranged to see each other again on 7 October but only Garrow showed up, saying that Stella was ill in bed. Elisabeth had already told him that she thought nothing good would come of Stella's relations with the Deuxième Bureau:

I am under the impression that the French hold you responsible for her as she told them that you are her Chief and you will have to stand up for anything she does. Please do come along and explain Dutour regardless of my personal interests. Explain Dutour that St.L. has not worked for us … Please come and explain before it is too late.

Elisabeth was finally freed on 27 November. Neither she nor Garrow completely trusted Stella, mainly because of her cosy relationship with the Deuxième Bureau. Nevertheless, in spite of his misgivings about her, Garrow was prepared to stick his neck out for her.

Chapter 21

The 'Pot Calling the Kettle Black'

Mills admitted to Tar that he'd never had the time to go and see Stella about RENÉ and tell her that he knew his true name. MI5 had never passed on that snippet of information to SIS, but he refused to accept the fact that the name they had been given was the right one.

During Sideroff's next visit Stella told him that he must get hold of Mills as she had something important to tell him about the 'Scotch Captain' (Garrow) and 'Pierre de H.' (Pierre d'Harcourt) that she had just learned from Mathilde Carré. However, during the first week of December Mills was sent to Canada to deal with the RCMP's first double agent, Werner von Janowski, codenamed WATCHDOG, so Tar asked Susan Barton to see her instead. Mrs Barton asked Christopher Harmer, Mathilde Carré's case officer, if he could provide her with any information on Garrow and d'Harcourt before her visit, particularly whether she had any information on d'Harcourt's arrest which would help them assess 'the guilt or otherwise of VICTOIRE'.

Garrow and Pierre d'Harcourt had planned to meet in Nice, but the latter had failed to show up. Shortly after he'd dined with his friend Alfred 'Freddy' Kraus and his wife-to-be, Princess Jacqueline de Broglie, on 8 July 1941 at the Pavillon d'Armenonville restaurant in the Bois de Boulogne in Paris, he'd been arrested at the Métro station. Kraus worked for the Abwehr's Abt III F (counter-espionage) in Paris and had betrayed him, according to Capitaine Danielle, Mathilde Carré's (VICTOIRE) contact at the Deuxième Bureau.[1]

During this period, while Eddie Chapman (double agent ZIGZAG) was being interrogated at Camp 020, Major Bernard Sampson and Captain Eric Goodacre asked him about the visit of the head of the Angers Dienststelle to Nantes. Whoever he was, Chapman said, he must have been important because his case officer, Dr Graumann (real name Stephan Albert Heinrich von Gröning) treated him with respect.[2] Chapman thought that the 'ugly major' (Dernbach) had come to see him in September and had asked him about 'Lord and Lady LONSDALE [sic]'. He was shown a photograph of a woman, about 28, good-looking, dark, wearing an evening dress who he thought Dernbach had told him was the wife of the Lonsdale who he knew had been involved in the Hyde Park jewellery robbery, and that she'd been in Nantes since the war.[3] The 'ugly major' told him that Stella had been working for British Intelligence in Nantes, but was not more forthcoming; he seemed more interested in John than her.[4] Chapman was also shown a photograph of a British soldier wearing a tam o'shanter (most likely Garrow) with a group of French soldiers, but he didn't know his name.

Mathilde Carré had told Stella that d'Harcourt was loyal and enthusiastic, but very gossipy. When he was arrested, he had a list of names on him which included Garrow's, which she'd seen in d'Harcourt's dossier (which must have been when she was at Maisons-Lafitte with Hugo Bleicher). As Mrs Barton reported:

> Michael remembered vaguely that Victoire had told her that D'HARCOURT had an Austrian friend who had given him away to the Germans. Michael then said that she remembered that RENÉ had told her that D'HARCOURT was arrested because he had a friend whom he trusted but that this friend was in reality working for the Germans. (I cannot remember whether Michael ever mentioned this before. If not, it may still be true or it may be just something she has now made up.)[5]

Stella was unable to contribute anything else on the matter and suggested that Mrs Barton see Carré herself to corroborate the facts. But 'because Victoire and Michael had asked Miss Baxter whether they were correct in assuming that Miss Green and Mrs. Barton was one and the same person', she decided not to see her.

When Stella had met Phillip Mond in Marseille at the Café Pélican, he'd never mentioned Garrow, nor having any connection with his escape organization; however, he'd introduced her to Walter Stangroom, who then introduced her to Garrow. A copy of the report on Mond was sent to Captain Derbyshire in E2a, the MI5 section monitoring aliens from Finland, Poland and the Baltic States.[6] In a separate report on Castelain Stella said that she'd hoped he would be able to give her information to take to England from his friend in the French Air Force, Raymond Clauber, who could get aerial photographs of the aerodromes of unoccupied France and its colonies. Tar noted, 'I do not think that it adds very much to the information which you already have on the subject of Phillip MOND.'

* * *

Stella asked Frank Viner whether he'd seen Elisabeth Haden-Guest when he visited on 18 March 1943. He said that he had and that she had written to her, but 'It is not a nice letter and you will not like it', the reason being that Elisabeth was comparing herself and her lifestyle to that of Stella's – Elisabeth was a one-man woman and didn't approve of Stella's racy lifestyle; in fact, she'd never liked her. Stella hadn't received the letter but declared, 'My God, and the way I helped her when she came out of prison. I gave her food and helped her in every way.'

He tried to reassure her that she would soon be out of Aylesbury as he'd made several representations, which had actually cost him a promotion. She grabbed his arm. 'My God, Frank, you believe me, don't you!' she exclaimed. He reassured her that he did, otherwise he wouldn't have visited her. The problem was, even though *he* believed her, MI5 didn't and they wanted to know what she'd been doing after leaving Marseille and before arriving in England. That unaccounted-for time was the reason why she'd been interned, not to mention that they were entitled to be suspicious of an English girl associating with a German officer.

Viner pointed out that Castelain and also Eamon de … had both suffered as a result of her, implying that she had been in some way responsible for their arrests.[7] He then told her that his mother and sister had been shot in Prague but offered no further details. Their deaths may have been part of the reprisals for Operation *Anthropoid*, the assassination of SS-Obergruppenführer Reinhard Heydrich in Prague on 27 May 1942 by Jozef Gabčik and Jan Kubiš of SOE, after which 13,000 randomly selected Czechs were arrested and possibly up to 5,000 executed, as well as the subsequent Lidice massacre. Stella kept asking him about what work he was now doing but he refused to divulge anything, saying that he'd been sworn to secrecy.

She still couldn't understand why Elisabeth should have written such a nasty letter. 'Well, she has a grievance about something which happened at a Court Martial in France at which you were both present, and you either did someone she cared for a great harm or it was someone she cared for and you took from her,' he explained. That prompted a denial that they had ever been at a court martial, but she and Elisabeth had visited Garrow at Fort St. Jean and had attended the *Tribunal Militaire*.

He agreed to give her his London address so that when she was finally released, she could come to him. She kept harping on Elisabeth's letter, but he advised her not to reply if she ever received it. After they had parted fondly, she mused, 'To think that he is free, and I am here, and if he had not told me to stay another day in France I would not be here and then someone else asked me to stay a day or two.'

Susan Barton's visit on 27 May 1943 attempted to find out about a certain 'Sonderfuehrer Wrede', a name Mills had given her to check, but Stella was unable to help. Sonderführer Dr (also listed as Kapitänleutnant) Joachim Wrede @ Wiegand @ Winter was the Alst Paris representative of the Abwehr in Brussels attached to the Hôtel Lutetia in Paris and *Leiter* MK Paris[8] working out of 30, Avenue Kléber. He was involved with TRICYCLE (Duško Popov) as well as WATCHDOG (Jankowski), and later executed for his part in the July Plot to kill Hitler in 1944.

It may be that Walter Simon, about whom My Eriksson and Stella had spoken,[9] was being confused with Louis Simon, because there is nothing in his MI5 file to connect him to Stella's case, or the same person she'd mentioned earlier to Milmo. She was still proclaiming her innocence and wanting to do war work, preferably as an interpreter, otherwise she was likely to become bitter against Britain. Paul Holme's visits bored her stiff but Mathilde had begged her to keep them up because of the food parcels he brought. When Sideroff visited her again on 23 June 1943, she was very happy to see him.

Early in July 1943 Mathilde, the Duchesse de Chateau-Thierry, Krafft, Stella and Eriksson had been moved out of Aylesbury and back into Holloway, this time without incident. Tar had informed Frank Foley of SIS on 15 July 1943 that the move had taken place a few days earlier because 'the particular reason for which the Aylesbury special wing was instituted no longer applied'. MI5 considered that Mathilde no longer posed a particular threat so she didn't need to be kept in the special wing at Aylesbury.

However, the move had not sat well with Air Commodore Archie Boyle, SOE's director of security, intelligence and personnel, who expressed to Guy Liddell their dissatisfaction and disagreement with Tar's comments: 'the Home Office will not unnaturally have assumed that enquiries had been made before this advice was given.' He reminded Tar that VICTOIRE's (Carré's) internment had been agreed upon in June 1942. Tar was forced to adopt a conciliatory tone when he and Harmer met with Boyle on 5 August 1943 and apologized for having had VICTOIRE transferred without SOE's input. He undertook to visit the Governor of Holloway to ascertain whether conditions there were the same as at Aylesbury.

On 19 August Harmer interviewed Mathilde at Holloway, trying to find out more about Stella and her contacts. VICTOIRE thought that Stella might have been turned, but since she'd returned to Holloway, she'd become completely anti-British and pro-German again. He reported that after talking about Mrs Nicholson VICTOIRE told him that in her opinion MI5 would never get to the bottom of Stella's story by interrogation, because she was incapable of telling the truth – a case of the 'pot calling the kettle black'. In her time, VICTOIRE had been called 'a superb liar' by Patricia McCallum of MI5's Registry, and also one who was untrustworthy when telling her story which, like Stella's, often changed, depending on when it was told, and to whom.

Other titbits about Stella were that during the war John had wanted to send her to Zurich to work for the Germans. VICTOIRE was certain that she had not been in prison for three and a half months as she'd claimed, but while there had met Campillo. Stella also claimed to know Dr Hans Thomsen, the well-known Nazi diplomat who was now German ambassador to Sweden (1943–5) and previously chargé d'affaires in America (1938–41). She'd told VICTOIRE that she knew Beirut and Syria well, causing her to think that she may have gone there during the time she was working for the Germans, although this seems unlikely.[10] There was also a suggestion that Stella would be sent to Rome during that period, but it never came about.

VICTOIRE claimed that Stella had been getting messages out of Aylesbury by enclosing small notes in cakes sent to her mother. Stella had asked her whether she knew a method of writing messages in secret ink. VICTOIRE informed her that when she worked for the Deuxième Bureau she had been given alum as a means of writing and had somehow managed to keep some with her in the prison. When Viner came to see her Stella gave him some cakes to eat on the train on the way back, one of which contained a message. Viner had actually put a message in *The Times*, headed 'STELLA' and signed 'F.V.', referring to 'an old family custom' or 'an old custom'. Harmer told VICTOIRE not to take any action without instructions; MI5 would see her again after they had considered her information.[11] He was going to discuss with Tar her suggestions of trying to steal Mrs Nicholson's box with some notes in it and supplying Stella with secret writing material, or that she should become a stool pigeon.

Whether Stella had actually been smuggling notes out of prison is highly questionable, but not impossible. While it is true that she had sent home a couple of cakes to her mother which VICTOIRE @ 'Mitou' had baked, this may have been another example of VICTOIRE making mischief and setting Stella up, something she was wont to do when she was in France, by shifting the blame away from herself. Certainly, Viner and Stella's family had made sure that nothing was mentioned in any letters, or within earshot of a prison officer if this had been the case.

In his note of 23 August Mills offered his thoughts to Tar and Harmer on the points raised about Stella saying that some of VICTOIRE's statements appeared to be accurate. He disliked Viner and had always considered him highly suspect, 'even though we could pin nothing on him and he is almost certainly inactive at present'. He thought 'Prince Schwartzenberg' was probably an alias and should be looked up. Nor did he believe that Viner was a prince, 'but he is just the type of man who would call himself one if he thought he could get away with it'.

Regarding RENÉ's identity, while Stella had said it was du Poel, VICTOIRE had said it was Von P., 'which if she knows the full name, is probably nearer the truth'. It was worth looking him up in case ISOS had revealed anything, as his name hadn't been carded, but should be in the B1 Registry. He also thought that it was worth looking up Campillo's name. If Stella was sending messages out of prison, she was only doing it to be mischievous and to show others how clever she was. If VICTOIRE was to be used as a stool pigeon, then Stella should be given access to VICTOIRE's alum, in the hope that she 'might do something really foolish … which would earn for her the punishment she so richly deserves, but which we have had no chance of inflicting'. He rejected Stella's claim to know Dr Hans Thomsen as typical Stella bragging: 'She has a mania for "knowing" important people.'

There was nothing which indicated that John had wanted her to go to Zurich to work for the Germans or that he was in contact with the Germans at that time. Stella 'has told a better story about what is probably the same affair … that she and John had ideas about working for the British in Switzerland at about this time'. Mills felt that the story was a 'plant' 'in order to try to compromise her unfaithful and hated husband'.[12] No information on Campillo would become available until 12 January 1945 when Major Malcolm Muggeridge, the SIS British Liaison Officer to DSDOC in Paris, received a report from Capitaine Devauges, chief of the BSM (Bureau de Sécurité militaire) at BDOC in Nantes, which shed more light on Stella and her circle.[13]

Muriel Whinfield, now an ex-detainee, and Katherine Lonsdale had exchanged letters and discussed how they had contacted 'the powers that be with no result'. Tar instructed Mrs Barton to find out who Katherine Lonsdale was, as she was unknown to them; she was, of course, 'Little Gran'. According to Stella's mother, she had complained about the conditions at Holloway – 'the cold and damp (no heating) and … in consequence, she is now suffering from rheumatism in addition to her other troubles', prompting Susan Barton to remark drily that Stella's 'touching description of the conditions under which she has to live in prison is in keeping with her usual dramatic instincts. She has always suffered from rheumatism and used to blame the German prison for it'.

On 4 November 1943 the *Evening Standard* published an article on conditions in Holloway, resulting in Eleanor Rathbone, an Independent MP for the Combined Universities, raising a question in the House of Commons about an 'insufficiency of soap, articles of clothing nominally supplied unavailable or supplied dirty, new prisoners put into dirty cells, prisoners with minor complaints unable to see the medical officer except by sacrificing a day's work and exercise' and asked what was the Home Secretary doing about it? Morrison replied that 'war conditions have affected the standards of efficiency' and that some of these complaints had been addressed, but cited staff shortages, rationing and the nature of the buildings. He was working with Ernest Bevin, the Minister of Labour and National Service, to recruit more staff.[14]

Chapter 22

Stella's Circle

Isabel Maria del Pilar de Catalan, a teacher of Spanish at the Berlitz School, and her brother, Manuel (Manulo), had been introduced to Stella at Le Grand Café in the Place Graslin in Nantes at the end of September 1940, according to G. Brisson, a café proprietor in Pont-Saint-Martin (Loire Inférieur), a commune outside of Nantes. Brisson had been friendly with Stella until she disappeared, but had begun to suspect her of being a German agent, a suspicion shared by Salvador Campillo, brother of Joaquín Campillo-Mercader, a republican refugee and ex-secretary to the last Minister General of War of the Spanish Republic, Carlos Masquelet Lacaci, who Brisson said was Stella's lover. Salvador and his brother Joaquín lived in a hotel on the rue de Gorges which Brisson said had an exit into the rue de la Poste, near the Restaurant Pujol, but a study of a map of Nantes shows that the two streets are on either side of the Loire. More likely the name of the street was misheard and was actually rue de la Fosse, which runs close to the rue de Gorges.

Stella had 'feigned a lustful passion' for Joaquín – 'a handsome Andalusian, intelligent and passionate who was really in love with Stella' – born on 17 November 1909 at Molina de Segura in the province of Murcia, Spain. A naturalized Spaniard, and married with a child, he had been living in Nantes since 1939 where, until February 1943, he delivered vegetables.

The Campillo brothers were arrested on 30 September 1940 and taken to Angers and charged with espionage, but released a month later on 31 October. As Brisson put it, Stella was also 'arrested'. In the prison courtyard while he was exercising Joaquín heard Stella singing a tango in Spanish that he'd taught her, 'no doubt in the hope of making Joaquín give himself away by this means … She only sang the first phrase of this tango and Joaquín continued it at the top of his voice'. He told Brisson after his release that the Germans knew the names of everyone with whom he had been associated, including his.

The brothers' return to Nantes coincided with Stella's. She told everyone 'in her usual fashion, the most fantastic stories: that she had broken everything in her cell; boxed the ears of the Germans; insulted them, defied them all etc.'. After her release, she'd gone to the Spanish Consulate and presented Mercedes de Silvera of the chancellery of the Franco faction with a bouquet of red roses as a thank-you for everything she'd done for her. Brisson observed that in Nantes Stella was always well dressed, 'like a princess, fashionable and elegant'.

Stella's affair with Joaquín came to an end when he was visited by an officer of the Kriegsmarine (German Navy) from the *Kommandatur* of the German Admiralty billeted opposite the offices of the Marinerpolizei on the Quai de la Fosse, and ordered him not have anything to do with the 'English girl'. The officer occasionally dined '*chez Pujol*' and his name (Otto) would have been known to Joaquín. He was 'about 50 years old, small, dark, cleanshaven [*sic*], grey-blue eyes, and disarmingly stupid ... a dolt with neither breeding nor education', who had made love to his teacher, Isabel Maria del Pilar Catalan.

Brisson told Capitaine Devauges that Monsieur Martineau and his brother were arrested twice, immediately after Stella and the Campillo brothers were released. Since then Martineau had died. He asserted that when Stella arrived in Nantes and took a position at the Berlitz School, she had kept an eye on Martineau, who was a well-known Anglophile, as well as any foreigners such as the Campillo brothers, who were likely to indulge in espionage. She became Joaquín's mistress, but then had him and his brother arrested. He also alleged that she was sleeping with one of her pupils, the young Platiau, whom she made join the German '*service de surveillance*'. But as we shall see, Stella despised Platiau and always denied sleeping with him. He did very little work, but he and Stella were implicated in the arrest of Hubert Caldecott, which Brisson claimed was a 'put up job by the Germans'.

Hubert George William Caldecott was a '*médecin-pharmacien*' (doctor-pharmacist) living at 66, rue du Maréchal Joffre, born on 9 June 1913 in Saint-Nazaire, and the son of English painter Frederic Caldecott and Julienne Protin. In June 1940 he was living in Paris where he helped French and English soldiers to escape. Someone claiming to be an Englishman went from house to house seeking a hiding place until eventually Max Veper (Caldecott's friend and deputy) took him in.[1] Brisson was going to hide him at Pont St. Martin, but when Joaquín told him that Stella knew about it, he tried to warn Caldecott. But it was too late. On 10 April 1941 Caldecott was arrested by the Abwehr in Paris, together with Veper, Marcel Hévin, Philippe Labrousse (Veper's cousin) and Labrousse's fiancée, Jeanne Gelabert, having been denounced by André Barrault, a collaborator agent of the Abwehr.

Caldecott was first taken to the notorious Cherche-Midi prison in Paris, where he remained until he was transferred to the Lafayette prison in Nantes. On 1 October 1941 he was tried by the *Feldkommandantur* 518 military court at the Romainville camp (Seine, Seine-Saint-Denis) for providing 'help to the enemy and helping escaped prisoners of war' and became another of the forty-eight hostages executed at the Fort de Mont-Valérien on 22 October

1941 in retaliation for the assassination of the *Feldkommandant* of Nantes, Oberstleutnant Karl Hotz, by the resisters two days earlier.

Veper, a lawyer, was born in Saint-Nazaire and had studied there and in Nantes. By a sheer fluke, and partly German incompetence, he managed to escape from a car near the Palais de Justice in Nantes where he was to be tried, and laid low for several days, also believing that he had been denounced by André Barrault.[2] While trying to escape in Saint Émilien-de-Bain he was shot in the head by the Germans. For his part in their betrayal Barrault was sentenced to death and executed on 18 December 1945. Labrousse was another of the hostages shot at the Fort de Mont-Valérien.[3]

The Home Office was pressing for a decision on Stella Lonsdale and a report on René Dazy was outstanding. Replies from Paris on 26 February and 8 March 1944 suggested that the information had already been sent to Young and may have been overlooked. A report about Stella, dated 23 February 1945, received from the Préfet de la Loire-Inférieure via the French Ministry of Foreign Affairs and the MI5 Liaison Section at the British Embassy in Paris confirmed much of what MI5 already knew – Campillo and his lover Stella had regularly eaten their meals at the Maire restaurant on the rue La Pérouse, which was also frequented by Caldecott; however, the Préfet had been unable to establish exactly what her relationship with Caldecott had been. The report shed new light on where Stella had lived in Nantes:

- 24 January–29 May 1940: Hôtel Moreau, 29, Boulevard Victor Hugo;
- 29 May–19 June 1940: Marcel Dugast, 1, rue St. Julien. There she was frequently visited by an unnamed English colonel who she called her godfather, and English aircrew who stayed with her but never ventured out during the day;
- 19 June–27 November 1940: Berlitz School, 11, Place Royale. Maud Martineau had now taken over running the school.

Stella had claimed that she hated the Germans, but at the same time had been seen regularly in their company and received gifts from them.

Stella's contacts in the police had been Louis Simon, the Commissaire de Police in the rue des Olivettes in Nantes who had often boasted about working for the Deuxième Bureau during the First World War, and was very close to Stella's husband John. Now he was a captain in the FFI (Forces Françaises de l'Intérieur) in Libourne, a commune in the Gironde *département* of Nouvelle-Aquitaine. Another was Charles Henri Martin, Commissaire de Police and Chef de la Sûreté au Commissariat Central in Nantes, and also intimate with the Lonsdales. According to Capitaine E. Rochat of the FFI,[4] she and John would frequently come to the police station to see Simon, who would often have them over to his house, and went out with them in the town. Later Rochat saw her with another man on the Quai de la Fosse who was definitely not John because he was shorter, and must have been René Dazy.

While Léon de Naeyer was in custody in Nantes, he told the police that he had been in contact with Stella through René Dazy. He'd first met her at the end of January 1941 at the Café du Cycle in the Place de la Bourse. Stella told him that she worked for the intelligence service and could put him in touch with an American for the purpose of creating an arms dump. He met the unnamed American at least two or three times, but mistrusted him because he boasted that he could provide them with $200,000 or $300,000. He finally managed to prise out of him that he was working for the Abwehr, based at the Boulevard Delorme (Cercle Nautique). After that de Naeyer never spoke to him again, but if he saw him on the street the American pretended not to recognize him.

On the two occasions de Naeyer saw Stella she was accompanied by René Dazy. He was supposed to meet with them on 28 January 1941 but they never showed up. Henceforth, he ceased trying to meet with Dazy as he didn't trust him either and became convinced that Stella worked for the German Secret Service. Moreover, he said she was always armed with a 6.35mm pistol up the sleeve of her pullover. He told the police that Stella had tried to insinuate herself into the Resistance organization and get to know all about their activities. His friend, Aimé Poirier, thought the same and warned him not to get involved with her. Later de Naeyer said that she'd often told him that her husband was an officer of the British Intelligence Service, but she hadn't seen him for four or five months and was afraid that he'd been captured by the Germans as he'd been sent on a mission into the Ruhr in Germany. This, of course, is pure nonsense as John Lonsdale was in England at the time.

Young informed Malcolm Muggeridge that de Naeyer, who was living at 1, Place de la Bourse in Nantes, had been detained by the French at one time, which had already been given verbally to the BSM (Bureau de Sécurité militaire) in Nantes. He cautioned that, 'It is, of course, necessary to point out that Stella LONSDALE is one of the biggest liars ever born, and no statement by her can be accepted as gospel, unless it is corroborated by other evidence'. He also confirmed that de Naeyer was destined to go to Tangier.

De Naeyer would collect arms, recruit students and incite them to rise against the Germans. He would convene a meeting to which they would all come, while informing the police who would arrive and arrest them all, including himself. Shortly afterwards he would be released and start the process all over again. Stella alleged that she was working with RENÉ to double-cross the Germans and didn't trust de Naeyer, who'd asked her for money to set up an arms dump. When she told RENÉ about him, he'd called him a swine and a local *agent provocateur*. She'd tried to warn Dazy about him but he hadn't believed her and was arrested. She described de Naeyer as aged 38, of medium build, rather thin-looking, with a centimetre of hair missing from his right eyebrow.

Writing to her friend Odette Châtenet on 30 March 1941, Stella said it was a great pity that René Dazy had ever spoken about all his girlfriends and never thought for a second that he would make trouble for her. On the contrary, he'd served her well as a true comrade; it was simply that he lacked confidence in her and preferred '*à croire cette salaud, Leon!*' ('to believe that bastard Leon!') Madame Dazy's deposition, made on 22 October 1944, referring to her son René's arrest, stated that Marcel Corgnet was a friend of Léon de Naeyer, who in turn was a friend of Stella's.⁵

In his report, Special Inspector Cousinier of the Brigade Régionale de la Surveillance du Territoire confirmed Campillo's address as 20, rue de la Petite Bilange in Saumur and that he had never been convicted by the Germans but had been arrested four times:

1. 3 September–31 October 1940, suspected of being a spy;
2. 10–25 February 1941, because he knew Stella whom he had met through Pilar de Catalan;
3. 13 March–2 June 1941;
4. 25 June 1941–24 May 1943, in Rouillé concentration camp in the Vienne *département* of Nouvelle-Aquitaine.

He admitted to being Stella's lover and had stayed with her until his first arrest. He'd never suspected her of being pro-German because, much to his embarrassment, she always proclaimed her anti-German feelings everywhere, such as in cafés where she spoke quite vocally to all and sundry and risked being arrested, or those arrested who were with her: 'I frequently had to tell her to shut up.' He recalled that at her flat he'd seen a German officer in civilian clothes who'd made the first arrest, someone who'd come for lessons and might be another of her lovers. His description of the officer tallies with that of Bendemann, mentioned earlier. Stella told Campillo that she couldn't possibly refuse to give the man lessons simply because he was German.

The Germans quizzed Campillo about whether he knew Stella, whether he was Jewish or a communist, whether he had ever spied for the British, and whether he regularly went to Saint-Nazaire. He said he found it strange that he'd been arrested during this period along with Stella's other friends, including his brother Salvador, Martineau (who'd been tortured), Caldecott and René Dazy. He said that Platiau had been working for the Germans from an early age. When Stella had introduced them, she'd asked them to work together, but they never did.

Just by chance, about fifteen days before Campillo's arrest, he happened to see Platiau as he was passing the Gestapo building at the Hôtel de Pyrénées in Nantes. He didn't recall speaking about it to any of his friends, only Stella, who told him that he should be suspicious because various people had accused Platiau of cosying up to the Gestapo. This then begs the question: if Stella was suspicious of Platiau's affiliations, why did she suggest that Campillo work with him? The report on Campillo stated that if further information was required about 'this woman [Stella] you should get to know the young René Darcy [*sic*] who lived in Nantes at 1, rue Marceau, who had been her lover before me, as well as Madame Martinon [*sic*] who was the wife of the Director of the Berlitz School'.

Albert Jolivet, Secretary of the Aliens Department of the Central Police Station in Nantes, told Campillo that Stella's husband was an officer in the British intelligence service. He said that they had both boasted of working for British Intelligence, as well as Stella claiming to be related to a previous Viceroy of India (the same claim she'd made to Walter Speck), and to Leslie Hore-Belisha, who had been Minister of War under Neville Chamberlain from 1937–40, neither of which can be confirmed, but are unlikely to be true.

Chapter 23

The Advisory Committee

On 3 July 1944 MI5 submitted Stella's case to the Advisory Committee considering appeals against DR.18B, stating that it was 'one of some complexity, and it is not therefore easy to frame Reasons for Order'. J.L.S. Hale suggested that the chairman should consider that between 1940 and 1941 she 'associated in France with members of the German secret service, and on her return to the United Kingdom misrepresented the nature of that association'. Specifically, that she had:

1. secured a permit to travel to France in 1940, by falsely stating the object of her journey;
2. remained in Nantes when the town was to her knowledge about to be occupied by the German armed forces, and when it would have been possible to return to the United Kingdom;
3. in 1940 agreed to enter the employment of the German Secret Service;
4. on her return to the United Kingdom, misrepresented the nature of her connection with the German Secret Service.[1]

She was 'completely shameless' in sexual matters; in money matters she was 'shamelessly predatory', and 'above all an egoist, ruthlessly selfish in material matters and inordinately vain about her own intelligence and charm'. He cited 'a lady of good judgement who was familiar with the whole case' (most likely Susan Barton) as saying,

> I believe she hardly knows herself when she is telling the truth or lying. Although I do not think she is certifiable, I should say she has a mental kink [and] a persistent history of nervous instability in the family, instancing Mrs. LONSDALE's brother John and one of her aunts … Whatever the ultimate causes of her behaviour, M.I.5 are satisfied that Mrs. LONSDALE is an exceptionally dangerous woman, and have no hesitation in recommending her continued detention.

Her case was heard before the Advisory Committee at the Royal Courts of Justice in the Strand on 8 September and 21 September 1944. The committee was composed of John W. Morris, KC, a Judge of Appeal on the Isle of Man (chairman);[2] George Harold Stuart-Bunning, JP, a trade unionist who had been president of the Trades Union Congress (TUC) 1919–20; and Mrs Jacqueline T. Cockburn, JP, wife of Archibald W. Cockburn, KC.[3]

At first Stella had not taken the charges seriously, thinking that it must have been some kind of test or misunderstanding which would soon be cleared up. But as time wore on, she grew more apathetic, her health deteriorated, and she became increasingly aware that MI5 had no intention of releasing her, a decision that was entirely up to the Home Secretary based on the committee's recommendations. One of the reasons why she wanted to be released was so that she could help her 70-year-old mother take care of her brother John, who suffered from dementia praecox.

Apart from confirming that she was now divorced from John Lonsdale, Stella declined to discuss other personal matters, or that her case had anything whatsoever to do with Sideroff. The committee expressed considerable interest in why she had stayed in France, but she maintained that John had asked her to join him because he was worried about his mother being ill and alone in Paris and might need an operation. But when she arrived, he'd asked her to go home, saying he was going away, possibly to Marseille. Exactly when this was, she was unable to say, perhaps the beginning of March, but 'I am rather hazy on dates', as if such details were unimportant.

The collapse of France had come as a shock to her. Just beforehand she had had tea with Major Gordon and was due to have tea with the priest, Captain Murray, on 17 June. A number of people advised her to go home, including Gordon, but she couldn't recall him saying anything about the British Army leaving France, which seems extraordinary as orders had been issued for Operation *Aerial* (*Ariel*), the evacuation from Nantes and Saint-Nazaire of the remaining 140,000 troops of the BEF, to take place between 15 and 25 June, and unofficially until 14 August. In fact, the last 4,000 troops left for Plymouth on 18 June, the day before the German Army marched into Nantes. Besides, John had written telling her to stay put; he was coming to get her, so she hung on. Like many of her friends, she knew nothing of political or military matters, nor the gravity of the situation. However, the committee remained unconvinced. As if to try to throw them off the scent, she digressed by further justifying why she'd been right not to have gone with the Polish seaman.

It was later determined that Gordon was her godfather – Lieutenant Colonel Edward Anthony Gordon, later of 58th Group Pioneer Corps, MEF (Middle East Forces) – always known to her as 'Sammy'.[4] She'd sent him a telegram on 20 December 1941 expressing her sadness that Father Murray was dead and informing him that she was back in England. Her file states that Murray was 'killed at the Quay of Calais or Dunkirk', although this is incorrect as only a month before on 19 November Milmo had interviewed him at Room 055 of the War Office![5]

The half-truths, contradictions, obfuscation and lies just kept coming: how the Dugasts had offered to help her escape from Nantes; how she had come to be detained in prison; and how she had been recruited by the Germans. She had told MI5 how Marcel Dugast had gone out to fill up the car with petrol for the road trip but found that the Pont de Pirmil across the Loire was closed, 'otherwise on Tuesday the 18th I should have gone with them to Biarritz. When I left Nantes, they were still there … they had not been able to go … it was not deliberately waiting to encounter the Germans. That was just bad luck in the circumstances'.

But the story she now told of the Dugast's offer of escape was different: on the morning of the Germans' arrival, Claire Dugast had burst into her room and told her, 'It is true, the Germans are coming, you must go at once very quickly.' She was afraid that she and her husband would be accused of hiding her and was most insistent that she move out. Stella protested that if she moved into a hotel it would only draw the Germans' attention to her – her address was registered with the police and it was all out in the open – but Claire would not be dissuaded. The Dugasts' change of heart will be explained when the Advisory Committee delivered its report (Chapter 26), and the story Marcel Dugast told Courtenay Young would differ again.

Stella didn't leave Nantes then. Monsieur and Madame Martineau arrived at the Dugasts' flat and asked her again if she would teach English at the Berlitz School, which she agreed to do. Monsieur Martineau wouldn't tell the Germans how long she'd been at the school and all would be fine. But a short while later she was questioned by the Commandant of Nantes about her situation and required to report every morning to the *Kommandatur*.

The story of how she had come to be detained in prison and then placed under house arrest in a hotel room, as well as her recruitment by the Germans, had also changed. Instead of being arrested after leaving the US Consulate, she now claimed that it was sometime in November as a result of Jean Platiau, 'a rather odd sort of young man' of 19 or 20 who had arrived at the school asking for English lessons. He was very nervous and jumpy and wanted to talk, but she reprimanded him for not paying attention. He wanted to escape to England and join the Gaullists, but she refused to help him, and dismissed him as a silly young man in whom she was not interested. Resorting to subterfuge, he'd asked Martineau if he could borrow her for an hour if she wasn't teaching. Without realizing he was being played, Martineau agreed and Platiau ended up having lunch with her. She later learned from the Germans that he'd been acting on their instructions, but at that time hadn't suspected him of being a fifth columnist.

One evening while she was in a café with some friends Platiau had approached her, very excited, saying he had something terribly urgent to tell her. She dismissed him, telling him he must go home, but he followed her back to her flat at curfew time around ten o'clock and rang the doorbell continuously until she came down. She tried to shoo him away but he pushed past her and entered the building, very upset and crying – 'which is an unusual thing for a man to do' – and told her he had to talk to her. Upstairs in her flat he confessed to being a German agent and that he'd fallen in love with her. He'd been watching her for months and told the Germans that she was a Gaullist who'd been helping people to join de Gaulle. Now he wanted to undo whatever damage he'd done, but it was too late.

He warned her that there were two Gestapo agents outside watching the building, so she told him to get rid of them. They went away, but he insisted on staying the night. Reluctantly, she allowed him to sleep on the divan while she retired to her bedroom and locked the door. In the morning he told her that she would be arrested. Shortly afterwards a German military car arrived to take them to Angers. During the journey he tried to convince her to work for the Germans and to say that she was in love with him; that way, she would be unharmed. 'I was very frightened and did not think it was very convincing to say I was in love with this boy.' It was not until the following day that she was taken to a house where she first encountered the man she referred to as 'Danbach'.

Dernbach asked her lots of questions through an interpreter and 'was a very unpleasant man altogether'. She told him she was in love with Platiau and would be prepared to work for the Germans so that she could be with him. Not convinced, he sent her downstairs to Hans Meissner, who was much nicer, courteous and quietly spoken, and dressed in naval uniform. 'Surely you cannot expect us to believe you are in love with this young man. Is it not rather that you have found yourself in a corner and are trying to get out of it?' he asked.

Meissner apologized that she would be going to prison and would have to appear before a military tribunal, but if she were to agree to work for them, they would release her; otherwise, he couldn't guarantee what would happen, which frightened her. She told the committee,

> I did what I think most people would have done, I said "Yes, I will," with the mental reservation it was a means to get out and to be free and escape. As far as agreeing to enter the employment of the German Secret Service, yes, I did, if one must reply yes or no, but you see my motives and as far as associated [*sic*], I only associated with one man and that for the service of my country, as I will afterwards tell you of the information he

gave me which was true, and I never at any time did any work or gave any information to the German Intelligence section whatsoever, important or unimportant.

That remark left the committee puzzled. They thought it strange that the Germans had never questioned why she had done nothing for them. She explained that this was because they were trying to decide where to send her. It was much easier for her to escape from Madrid or Lisbon, so Meissner had proposed sending her to Yugoslavia or Turkey, but she'd disagreed with him.

RENÉ's identity was to become a *leitmotif* throughout her two appearances before the committee. He had been present during her encounter with Meissner and had offered to help her when he came to visit her in prison. But she simply repeated to the committee what he'd told her, that she should never disclose his identity unless it was to one person only, and then only verbally. If it were to get back to Germany it would cost him his life. He told her he was anti-Nazi and had been educated in the USA. During her time in custody she claimed that there had been no social association with him, nor with any of the other Germans, except having dinner with him, or going to his flat to listen to the BBC on the radio. But she emphasized that he was not her lover. Indeed, Susan Barton, relating to a comment Sideroff had made about Stella sleeping with RENÉ, stated,

> she maintained that she had never said that as she certainly had not done it nor could she have as RENÉ was "circo". (This was a French phrase and may be French slang for something perverted.) She added that she knew this because they had been bathing together. She later told Nina and me, who were present when she telephoned Sideroff, that she thought Rene was a pervert, that he was in love with her, had kissed her, it seems rather perfunctorily, that she was glad she had never slept with him as she felt sure she would not have enjoyed it or even been able to pretend that she had enjoyed it.

A note linked to 'circo' adds, 'this is not quite what she said!!'[6] Earlier, she had told MI5 that when RENÉ had gone swimming in the Loire with Stueppler, she'd never gone with him (see Chapter 18).

Stella had trusted him implicitly, largely because of the information he'd given her – 'he appeared to me to be utterly sincere, to this day I believe in his sincerity' and was 'absolutely convinced' that he was still working against the Germans. She'd even taken him to meet Abbé Jean-Baptiste Luneau, who counselled her that she should have confidence in RENÉ and continue to deceive the Germans. But now that France had been liberated, she tried to rationalize that it released her from her obligation of revealing his identity.

The chairman suggested that there might be someone in British Intelligence to whom she could confide the name, but she was still afraid that if his true identity were to leak out as a result of a fifth column in France the French would punish him. He had also been very nervous at giving her any information in case it should get back to the Germans, warning her that when people were arrested and put in prison, they often gave away a lot of information out of fright: 'When you go and when you speak about these matters remember you carry my head under your arm.'

Could it be, the committee suggested, that perhaps RENÉ didn't actually exist, or that he was a composite of several people she'd met? It was something upon which the War Office (i.e. MI5) needed to check. It was in her best interests to tell the committee of his identity, but it was entirely up to her, since the name she *had* given to MI5 had proved to be a red herring. Stella insisted that he did exist but wouldn't be swayed into revealing his real name, claiming that to do so might compromise his sister in America who was married to an American. But who could she trust? 'When you are suddenly detained by people in whom you have had confidence it makes you frightened.' But if she were to reveal his name would it do him harm, and would it help her release? That was something which Morris was not in a position to answer.

Hermann Hyman [*sic*] was someone she'd met in the café of the hotel where she was staying who was trying to escape and needed her help. He was a Jew and his wife had been 'terribly hurt' by the Nazis. Stella was sympathetic, but regretfully told him that she couldn't help. RENÉ later told her that 'Harry' was 'a cheap agent of ours, an agent provocateur, and he has been making a lot of reports about you when I was away, how anti-Nazi you were and you were trying to find a way to help him'. A friend and colleague of Meissner's in Oslo, Heinemann had been brought to France in 1941 to work as Dernbach's personal agent.[7] RENÉ told her she'd better leave and gave her false papers enabling her to make her way to Marseille.

She denied having at that time any information in her possession which would have been useful to the Germans, or ever working for the Deuxième Bureau – John had been the only one involved with them before the war through Louis Simon – but she admitted that later on she *did* have information which could have been useful, namely, the identities of the various people she'd met in Marseille. But since she'd arrived back in England, she hadn't had any contact with anyone who might provide her with information, either politically or militarily, that she could have passed to the Germans. Conveniently, she appears to have forgotten the trip down to Gosport to the Torpedo Development Unit, Wing Commander Bruce, and the possibility of obtaining information related to the TDU which could have been passed on to the Germans.

As the hearing concluded she tried again to resurrect the events of the summer of 1941 in Marseille, but the committee had obviously heard enough of her obfuscations. They re-emphasized that they were not trying to make her reveal anything she didn't want to, nor were they saying that if she should do so her situation would be improved by it.

Morris agreed with Hale's suggestion that during Stella's next appearance before the committee he should advise her that enquiries were likely to be made in France which would affect her case. To that end, Young arranged to travel to France to make on-the-spot enquiries in Nantes and Angers, and if necessary, Paris, after which the case could be reconsidered and a decision made as to whether he needed to travel to the South of France to make further enquiries. Therefore, he should make two proposals to her:

(a) that she should put forward on her own account a little list of matters, the investigation of which she herself invited, in the belief that they would establish her innocence. In effect, she would be being asked to give references, for verification in France.
(b) that she should give an intelligence officer who would come to see her certain further details in amplification of the story which she has already told, in order to facilitate enquiries abroad.

When the second hearing convened on 21 September 1944 the committee requested clarification on the various other points Stella had tried to raise at the first hearing,[8] namely, whether the entire Deuxième Bureau was working for the Vichy government. She explained that it was actually divided into various factions – some were pro-Vichy, some were pro-de Gaulle, some were pro-England. Dutour had told her that 'Leclerc' was absolutely trustworthy as he was anti-German.

Contrary to popular misconception, according to Simon Kitson, *all* the French intelligence organizations worked against both Axis *and* Allied forces.[9] He has pointed out that the Deuxième Bureau was only one part of the service which operated from 1870 until 1940 when it was dissolved. It was 'an organisation attached to the Staff Headquarters of the armed forces … both at the national level as well as the local level … an essentially office-bound service whose role was to centralize and analyze intelligence derived from other sources'.[10] The real intelligence-gathering organization was the Cinquième Bureau established in 1940, divided into the Service de Renseignements (SR) collecting intelligence, and the Section de Centralisation du Renseignement (SCR), centralizing the intelligence. In June 1940 Travaux Ruraux (TR) was established as part of the SR, the other part being the Bureau de Menées Antinationals (Bureau for Anti-National Affairs).

As the hearing concluded the committee suggested that the Germans considered her 'an infernal nuisance' and were glad to get rid of her as she had done nothing for or against them. But Stella saw it differently: 'they must have thought they could not trust me very far. They had not any reason to trust me in anything very vital … I had not said I wished to see Germany victorious and occupying England, and now you say that it is a definite possibility.'

There were enquiries to be made. Mr Morris suggested that someone from the intelligence services, i.e. 'Cyril Martin' (Mills), should go and see her in Holloway in the not-too-distant future to sort out the points she'd raised during the hearings, but cautioned that she need not tell him anything she did not want to.

Chapter 24

'If I Had Been a Nasty Piece of Work …'

Before Young interviewed Stella on 23 September 1944 he established the following terms of reference:

1. He will say that he is a colleague of Mr. Cyril Martin's and that he regrets that Mr. Martin is abroad and is not available, but that he himself is fully apprised of her case.
2. He will explain that he does not in any sense represent the Advisory Committee, and that his interview with her is in no respect a continuation of her hearing before the Advisory Committee.
3. He will say that he understands that Mrs. LONSDALE has appeared before the Advisory Committee, and has expressed a desire that her story should be checked by enquiry in France.
4. He will then ask Mrs. LONSDALE to state in her own way the things which she thinks could most usefully be looked into, in order to establish her bona fides.
5. He will then go over the story in his own way, getting such further details (addresses, occupations, personal descriptions, etc.) as he wants, irrespective of whether Mrs. LONSDALE suggests that these are the matters that she wants looked into.
6. Any questions which he addresses to Mrs. LONSDALE will be factual not controversial. He will not interrogate her, in the sense of taxing her with inconsistencies, challenging her statements, or trying, generally speaking, to "break her down", but will stick to questions and answers as to what it is she is saying.
7. He will not let it become obvious that we have seen the shorthand notes of the Committee hearing.
8. If Mrs. LONSDALE says that she does not wish to answer a particular question, he will not press it, and he will break off the interview if at any stage she says that she does not want to go on with it.

His aim was to verify her story by retracing her steps – the places she'd stayed and obtain descriptions of the people with whom she'd been associated.

She asked that he not tell them that she was in prison in case they thought she was a collaborator. Much of what she told him had already been stated to the Advisory Committee, but some of it was new. After that the flood of names just kept on coming. This sudden brain storm was a classic case of 'post-usefulness syndrome' when a spy no longer has any operational value, 'which may be interpreted as a manifestation of underlying narcissism or attention-seeking. The syndrome is associated with claims that the individual has further, hitherto undisclosed information, or is in a position to re-establish their lost status' or 'The implication is that some defectors are pathological attention-seekers who succumb to embroidery to retain contact with their new professional colleagues.'[1]

Any letters from her husband John would be collected at the Café Mouillard in the Place Royale where she would have a drink with Clémence, the cashier, 'a kind girl', who gave her a bunch of roses on her wedding anniversary. Odette Châtenet, aged about 19, and René Dazy were students at Berlitz. Odette worked as a secretary for a firm called Brunner (L. Brunner et Cie which made tools and drill parts). When Stella returned to Angers after her release, she lived at L'Hôtel des Voyageurs on the corner of the Quai d'Anjou, what is now the rue du Général Leclerc.

She confirmed what Harry Heinemann had said about her being anti-German and unreliable, and how RENÉ had told her that she must leave, so she'd travelled back to Marseille via Tours and Vierzon. Someone who could vouch for her being pro-English was Sister Marie Cuthbert, a 30- or 40-year-old nun, one of only a handful of English people left after the German occupation of Nantes, who stayed at a nursing home-cum-hospital in Nantes with a name like Surgilles.[2] Unfortunately, there is no record of Young ever tracing her during his visit to France.

When Stella returned to Nantes to collect her clothes, she met up with René Dazy, Odette and Joaquín. Dazy and some student friends were organizing the collection of arms to fight the Germans, led by Léon de Naeyer. As noted in Chapter 22, she'd tried to warn René about de Naeyer, sending him messages via Odette, even going to Nantes, but several weeks later he was caught with a revolver and spent twelve months in prison. Dazy had given her the information about the petrol installation, now said to have been an underground aerodrome, but the information about anti-aircraft guns had come from a friend of his named Alexandre, known by the diminutive Sacha.[3]

Monsieur Martineau had been imprisoned as a result of Platiau's treachery, and accused her of having German friends if they'd let her out of prison. She'd wanted to tell him what had happened, but Abbé Luneau cautioned her to do nothing and to trust nobody. In Nantes and Marseille, she'd stayed mainly in hotels; in Tours at the Logie d'Autrefois. Each time she met RENÉ she'd posed as his secretary, so they stayed in separate rooms. She couldn't remember the address of his Paris flat as she'd written to him *poste restante*, but knew she could find it if she went to the street.

Now that France had been liberated, Young thought it might be possible to discover in Angers RENÉ's identity; if he were available, he could corroborate her story. But what if he'd been taken prisoner? she asked. If so, MI5 didn't know about it, he told her. So, based on his impending trip to France, and the fact that France had been liberated, she revealed his parents' address in Wiesbaden and his sister's in California, which she hadn't told the Advisory Committee, as well as his real name – Siegfried Rauch. But she still harboured the fear that he might be betrayed to the Germans – already, his sister in Germany had drowned and his brother had been killed in Russia in 1941. She asked for Young's unofficial advice, but he said that he could only speak officially.

In Angers RENÉ had used the name Serge Robin, so Young asked whether she was sure that the name she'd now given him was the correct one. She assured him that it was because she'd seen letters from his mother and father, as well as from a girl outside of New York whose name was Elsa, who was very fond of him, and must have been the fiancée referred to earlier. As far as she knew, Siegfried Rauch had 'perfectly clean hands' because he'd always given her plenty of warning about people so that she could warn them.

She cautioned that Louis Simon of the Deuxième Bureau, who could be found at a police station in the rue des Olivettes in Nantes, was someone whose identity must be treated with discretion. She was unsure what he might say about her as they'd had a row when he'd tried to kiss her. Fradet was the owner of a typewriter shop[4] and 'a nasty piece of work' whose son's name was Raymond. Fradet's wife Berthe had been the mistress of Trensche, the head of the SRA in Nantes as well as several German officers: 'She is waiting for you to come to speak to her because she is in prison ... It would not surprise me if he was in trouble somewhere or other.'

Jean Castelain may have been the young man from Aix whom Elisabeth Haden-Guest had referred to, but could equally have been Paul Dubart. Clauber, Castelain's friend, was able to obtain false identity cards on a couple of occasions. Young was careful not to mention that Castelain was now in England.

She said she was very fond of Christian Boulanger and hoped to see him again after the war was over. His father Lucien's address was 42, rue Paradis, Château de Houree, Auch-Gers [*sic* – Hourre]. Both he and Christian would be able to vouch for her political views, as could Charles/Henry Cohen, 25,

Quai de Belges, a businessman in Marseille who occasionally sent letters across the border. Rafael Gars, whom she knew as André Gars, at 15, rue Clovis Hugo, Marseille, had tried to transfer to the Garde Mobile to get more pay. He would be able to provide a testimony about her story and how he'd persuaded Garrow to see Capitaine Dutour. As noted earlier, when Garrow was arrested he'd asked to see Dutour. A police friend of Dutour's was Pierre le Brun (referred to earlier as Brun or Lebrun). What is curious about this, as noted in Chapter 7, is that she had earlier suspected Gars of betraying her.

She now said that Garrow and Elisabeth had been betrayed by the reception clerk at the Hôtel Noailles, which bears out what Elisabeth had told SIS. But RENÉ had said that if Garrow were to be arrested he couldn't help him, nor did he wish to meet him since he couldn't speak good French. When she asked Young whether he thought there was another side to that he replied, 'René might have been playing you for a sucker. It was more important for him to keep up his friendship with you than it was to give help to get someone away from the South of France.' She suggested that '[T]hat nasty little piece of work, MARCILLY' might be able to provide 'Leclerc''s true identity.

Others she had known were André and Roger Vilmorin; a Madame Rose who ran a café in the old port in Marseille and was also known to Viner and Garrow; Lucien Gerschel, a friend of Christian, and his wife Marcelle Vérité, who wrote children's stories. 'If I had been a nasty piece of work they would have been arrested too,' she added, meaning Patrick O'Leary, Nancy Fiocca (Wake), and Pierre Landeau. Elisabeth didn't trust Prassinos, Garrow's right-hand man, but Stella thought he was 'perfectly wonderful' and could also attest to her loyalty, but by the time Young went to France Prassinos had died of typhus in a concentration camp at Schwerin, Germany, on 4 March 1945.[5]

Finally, Young managed to prise out of her a description of RENÉ. She now claimed that the girl with the two men in a car in the photograph she'd shown 'Cyril Martin' (Mills), was *not* her, but one of the men *was* RENÉ. Mills wrote:

> The officer standing in front of the motor car is RENÉ. MICHAEL says she does not know who the woman is and that the photograph was probably [taken] in Germany some time ago as RENÉ's uniform shows that he was then of much lower rank than he is now. At some time in the p[ast] she said that RENÉ is now a Hauptmann [captain] but it is impossible to see from the photo what rank he held at the time it was taken.[6]

She'd lied about it to Mills because she was trying to protect RENÉ from any harm.

At the conclusion of Young's interview Stella's head was spinning and her hands were shaking. Trying to give him all the particulars had spooked her. By Monday she was still in the same condition, but after being given some medication she recovered enough to see 'Mr Willis'.

That same day, Young informed Milmo of his forthcoming trip to France, and asked if photographs of RENÉ, including the one with the girl in the car, could be shown to anyone who'd passed through, or had had contact with, Ast Angers. But when they were shown to detainees in Camp 020 in 1942 there had been no reaction. He wondered whether Charles Olivier Boyd, who had been sent by the Meldekopf in Paris, and was now in Dartmoor prison, might recognize him, or if the name Siegfried Rauch rang a bell since he was alleged to have been Meissner's assistant in Ast Angers.[7]

In his inimitable way Stephens, the Commandant of Camp 020, described Boyd as 'a precious creature of half-baked ideals'.[8] Robert Charrier and Comte Gabriel Billebault de Chaffault thought the car picture was taken in the Angers district, possibly near Saumur, and that the uniforms were those of a Sonderführer (left) and a private (right).[9] Charrier had trained under Bergeret at the Abwehr's headquarters at 10 ter, rue des Dervallières in Nantes, but he was not at that address until August 1943 so could not have come across Stella.

Young wrote to Captain Noakes in B1b on 7 October to ask whether Paulsen could be interrogated and

a) Whether the name Stella LONSDALE or Mrs. CARR-GLYNN means anything to him.
b) Whether, when he was at Ast. Angers, he had any knowledge of an Englishwoman who had been used by the Ast. as an agent in 1940–41.
c) Any information he may have about MEISSNER.
d) Whether the name Siegfried RAUCH conveys anything to him; or whether he could give the name of MEISSNER's assistant who was with MEISSNER at Angers and later at Paris. The assistant is alleged to be about 30 years old, speaking fluent English and also possibly the Scandinavian languages, Russian and Japanese. He is also supposed to be a Doctor of International Law, who had studied in America and possibly in England.
e) I should be grateful if he could also be shown the attached three photographs, and asked if he recognises anybody in them.[10]

But neither Lonsdale nor Carr-Glynn meant anything to him, nor an Englishwoman who'd been used by Ast Angers in 1940–1. Paulsen knew of Meissner, but he'd never met him as he'd joined Ast Angers in July 1942, by which time Meissner had left for Paris, and a Sonderführer Rauch who had been attached to Angers III-F for a short while, but didn't recognize him from the photographs.

Another name Stella had remembered was Janetz Salowski, to whom she'd been introduced by his friend, Captain Robert. Robert had been sent to France from Malta by Colonel Bertram Montague Ede and Captain Hill, but was caught working for the Gaullists and had appeared before a tribunal. Ede had been MI5's DSO in Malta from 1930–42, and now headed MI5's F Division, Overseas Control, to whom all DSOs reported.[11] In Marseille Stella would go with Robert to the Café Suzanne in the Place de Rome, where she occasionally met Garrow but neither the owners, Monsieur and Madame Suzanne, nor Salowski knew her as Lonsdale. What might jog Madame Suzanne's memory was that she and RENÉ used to drink green Chartreuse which she would get from the back of the café. There might also be some letters for her there. Robert had told her that she could also have letters addressed to him c/o Nelle Heinen, a friend of his wife's, at 55, rue St. James, Gannat, Allier. Salowski told her he'd been a Polish consul in Africa before the war. Most of his time was spent between Avignon and Marseille, where he would spend the night in 'a nice brothel, off the Place de Rome'.

Young had forgotten about how Gars had persuaded Garrow to see Dutour and asked her whether she knew anything about a letter Kenny had written to Vichy claiming that he and Garrow could give information to a friend of his in the office of Admiral Darlan. But she *had* told him in 1942, and it *was* documented in the transcript of her interrogation at the time. He also claimed that she hadn't told him about Maurice Duclos[12] and his head clerk Viseau (or Viseaut/Visot) at 8, Place Vendôme, Paris (the Hôtel Delpeche de Chaunot) whom RENÉ had warned her about, but again, she *had* told him about it.

As if that wasn't enough, she dropped another name, Mumet (also written as Maumen),[13] who had been mixed up with the Gaullists and escaped from prison just before Garrow had been arrested. Garrow didn't trust him and thought he might be a German agent. Mumet was not the same person as Raoul Maumen, who will appear later in Stella's story.

Stella further elaborated on Pavie's activities with the black market when Young asked for clarification that she meant the unoccupied zone. There was also more on Yves Delbar: when he knew she was going home, he'd approached her and asked her to inform the British authorities that he had a way of getting information to them on a strictly financial basis. When Garrow disappeared, Delbar had asked Fullerton to get in touch with him, but Fullerton denied knowing anything about him.

'Leclerc' had told her about someone called de Hillotte [*sic*] who lived in the Gulfe-Juan on the Côte d'Azur whom she'd met through Henri Muntzi.

Young asked whether he was an official, but Stella didn't know.[14] Muntzi and Garrow had had some financial dealings with him, whereby Muntzi would pay money to Garrow in Marseille which would be credited to him in Barcelona. At the beginning of August Garrow asked her if she would ask Dehillotte to meet him in the Café Suzanne, so she took him there and left them as she was going north.

'Leclerc' and Dutour had offered to help Elisabeth if Stella would help them, so she gave them an address at 23, Quai Joliette, given to her by RENÉ, where German agents met. The proprietor was a wholesale fruit and vegetable dealer named François Fayyang (see the end of Chapter 7). But 'Leclerc' said that Elisabeth and Garrow were making things difficult for themselves, because Elisabeth was making reports on her co-prisoners to Dutour and therefore was useful to him. That was when Darlan visited Marseille on 3 and 4 December 1941.

RENÉ once told Stella that an agent of theirs was in very well with the American Consulate and was getting information from the American consul, so she warned Fullerton to be careful of George Truman. Young was growing tired of her ramblings and told her to stick to the facts.

Others who could vouch for her being 'far from pro-German' were Robert Coppe – Young would be able to check whether he'd been attached to New Scotland Yard – and Marcelle Norman in Nantes who was in love with an English soldier, but was married with children; and Lucien Hareng, a businessman in Nantes who'd been liaison officer for the English military when they were in Nantes, who had taken German lessons and his wife English lessons. Young could get their addresses from the Berlitz School. Then there was Samson in Nantes who used to call her '*l'Ange Gabrielle*' (Angel Gabrielle) because she stopped his car once and persuaded him to take three British soldiers to Sainte-Nazaire (referred to earlier). She now thought it was he who'd given her the paper about the aerodrome at Sainte-Luce. RENÉ would be able to confirm when she'd received the other plan about the anti-aircraft guns, which she thought was after her arrest.

Before she'd stayed with the Dugasts she'd stayed at the Hôtel Moreau, 29, Boulevard Victor Hugo (mentioned in Chapter 22), near where John was stationed, run by a Monsieur and Madame Klein from Strasbourg, but she didn't like them very much. She and John then went to Paris from where he'd returned to England. When she returned to Nantes, she found that the hotel had been requisitioned, so she went to the Café Mouillard in the Place de Commerce and asked where she could stay. Clémence at the café told her about the Dugasts who took in paying guests, but Stella appears to have confused their address at 1, rue St. Julien with the Hôtel Moreau, where she had stayed earlier.

Stella thought she might have shown the piece of paper found in her handbag to the American consul, Hassell H. Dick, but it had had nothing to do with her arrest – that had been Platiau's doing. The Germans had then rounded up anyone to whom he had spoken.

Young established that RENÉ spoke fifteen languages: very good English, with a slight American accent, excellent French, as well as Japanese, Russian, Polish, the Scandinavian languages, and Spanish, although not well. Stella didn't think he'd been in Spain during the Civil War, and had never seen him in uniform: 'No, luckily. He went to America to see his married sister, and when he came home he had to go into the army. I gathered that was around 1939. He had written a book about International Law, published in Germany,' which was under his own name, Siegfried Rauch. 'That is why I know that was his name, because I saw the book.'[15] If she was telling the truth about not seeing RENÉ in uniform, then the girl in the car with the two soldiers in the aforementioned photograph cannot have been Stella.

Chapter 25

'A Fog of Falsehood and Misrepresentation'

Young compiled an aide-mémoir of the questions he would ask the various people on his list (see Appendix 3) when he went to France. He wrote to Lieutenant Colonel Dick Brooman-White of SIS (formerly of MI5's B1g), currently serving in north-western Europe attached to SHAEF, to warn Malcolm Muggeridge of his forthcoming visit and asked if he could put him up. He also asked that Brooman-White warn Dick Goldsmith White[1] that he was 'coming out to report to him in case he has forgotten – as he almost certainly has ... This investigation will necessitate the co-operation of the French and especially the French Police in Nantes and Angers'.

The testimonies Young obtained from these people form the appendices of his 3 November 1944 report and summarize his investigations. Space does not allow those appendices to be included here in their entirety but they can be consulted in full in Stella's MI5 file.[2] Not surprisingly he noted that, 'The evidence available in Nantes regarding Mrs. LONSDALE's life there before and during the German occupation, and after her arrest is contradictory'.[3] This he attributed to the 'present rather disorganized state of the local French authorities, and also by the lapse of time which had occurred since Mrs. LONSDALE left France ... the evidence now available makes it even more confused'. That, and the fact that the witnesses were not trained observers and unable to remember dates. But what was clear was that Stella had lied and was still not telling the whole truth.

Monsieur Dugast confirmed that what Stella had told the Advisory Committee about her intentions to accompany him to Biarritz was untrue. While he was unable to remember other dates, he remembered the trip to Biarritz, which he supported with telegrams, giving the date of his meeting. Unbeknown to Stella, the Madame Dugast she knew was not his wife but his mistress, and Michel was her son. Furthermore, there had never been any intention of taking Stella or his mistress to Biarritz, and certainly not when the Germans were about to occupy Nantes. Instead, he went to La Baule on the evening of 17 June to pick up his wife and returned the following day. The French police were re-interrogating him about the date (1 April) which Stella claimed was when she'd left him, as this contradicted the testimonies given by Mesdames Dazy and Martineau.[4]

Jenny Dazy stated that when she arrived in Nantes from Rennes at the end of May 1940 Stella was already at the Berlitz School and living at the Dugasts' apartment and didn't leave until the Germans arrived, or just after, when Stella moved from the school to a flat. Due to Allied bombing that district was heavily damaged, but the French police were making enquiries as to whether anybody remembered Stella's residence in the Impasse La Fontaine (rue Jean-de-La-Fontaine), or the circumstances of her arrest.[5] But Madame Dazy, Madame Mouillard of the Café Mouillard, and Odette Châtenet all confirmed that Stella's arrest was about the middle of October 1940. When she returned to Nantes later, she had to report daily to the *Kommandatur*, also confirmed by Madame Martineau who believed that Stella was living with the Dugasts until the Germans occupied Nantes.[6]

Abbé Luneau was guarded in his conversation and also suspicious of Stella when Young interviewed him, but he was able to support Stella's story by referring to rough notes made for his diary. The complete diaries were hidden in a safe place in the country, but when he gained access to them, he promised to pass on any relevant extracts to MI5. He'd had tea with Stella and John Lonsdale at their hotel in the Boulevard Victor Hugo (possibly the Hôtel Trianon) and seen them socially a few times; he was also present at her baptism on 27 April 1940. He'd learned of her arrest when he was visited by a plainclothes officer.

The next time he saw her was on 12 December 1940 when she'd telephoned him for a meeting later that evening. She informed him of the Germans' plan to have her work for them in France, then later send her back to England and shown him a plan of German positions at the mouth of the Loire which she'd hidden in the heel of her stocking. He'd told her that, while she was playing a dangerous game, she should take this opportunity to serve her country and use it as a means to escape. When he saw her again on 16 December, she told him she was due to go to Germany, but the Germans had allowed her to prolong her stay in France.

She'd also taken RENÉ to see him. He was very circumspect in front of RENÉ when she told him that they intended to double-cross the Germans, only uttering 'God bless you', which she inferred as his approval of the plan she'd previously discussed with him. Later, RENÉ visited him and said that she'd left France, that she was safe in England, and 'doing good work', which the Abbé inferred as meaning for the Allies. Young noted, 'His statement is important as it gives definite dates for Mrs. LONSDALE's visits to Nantes, namely 12th. and 16th. December, by which time she must have been released for the first time.'[7]

The French police were attempting to interview Joaquín Castillo and would pass on the results to MI5. Odette Châtenet and Maud Martineau agreed that Monsieur Martineau was only interrogated about what he knew about Stella. In May 1944 he'd died so it was impossible to confirm this with him. Likewise, Jean Platiau, a 'vital witness', had been shot as a hostage, but his twin brother was being interviewed to see what he knew about Jean's activities. One thing became clear, 'no one in Nantes with the exception of Madame MOUILLARD has any affection for Mrs. LONSDALE'. Maud Martineau's hostility towards Stella was understandable. As MI5's report of 10 November 1944 sent to the Advisory Committee stated, she blamed her for her father's two arrests and subsequent death, to her activities. Nor did Madame Dazy have any time for her and attributed her son René's arrest to her. Marcel Dugast regarded her as an immoral woman and a nuisance in his flat.

The authorities in Nantes stated that there had never been an aerodrome at Sainte-Luce, either above or below ground, nor a petrol dump, nor anything of remotely military importance. But contrary to this claim, one of Eddie Chapman's (ZIGZAG) files shows a petrol dump on a map just north-west of Nantes, close to the Luftwaffe HQ, and also a private landing ground and flak site: 'Fuel and Ammunition: a refueling loop was in the North dispersal area, another refueling point near the hangars at the center of the W boundary and underground tanks for bulk storage were off the E boundary.' The airport near Sainte-Luce is most likely now Nantes Atlantique airport, eight kilometres south-west of Nantes in Bouguenais, used by the Luftwaffe during the war for anti-shipping, long-range reconnaissance, weather reconnaissance, and a rest and refit stop for bomber units.[8]

Fradet was in detention at Cholet and being interrogated about what he knew of Stella or RENÉ. Leon de Nyeres, denounced by her as an *agent provocateur*, was still alive but had left Nantes. There was no trace in any bureau in Nantes of Loshensky nor of Stella's stay in Angers – the Bureau des Étrangers had no trace of her under her real name or Carr-Glynn, and the Commission Spécial de Surveillance de Territoire had no record of an Englishwoman having been in the prison at Angers. But if the Germans had imprisoned her and billeted her at the Hôtel des Voyageurs, all their prison records had been burnt before they left, and hotel proprietors did not record in the Livre de Police the names of persons billeted on them.

The Bureau de Securité Militaire had a trace in their records of a Serge Robin, who had been denounced as a German agent. Stella had given RENÉ @ Serge Robin's address as 43 or 34, Boulevard Maréchal Foch. However, number 43 was the Intendence de Police requisitioned by the French police in September 1940 and had been used by them ever since, but no German had ever stayed there. She also stated that the flat was near a 'clinique' but the only 'clinique' was some distance away from the Boulevard Maréchal Foch, and occupied the entire street on one side with a military establishment on the other.

The proprietor of the Hôtel des Voyageurs when she stayed there was now dead so enquiries were being made of his widow and a former chambermaid to see if they could recall her. However, her stay there was borne out by letters she'd written to Odette Châtenet, now in MI5's possession. From what Odette had told Young in her statement, she'd received a number of letters from Stella, some of which she handed over to him. She didn't fully understand their content, and only knew about her plan to double-cross the Germans. Young noted that 'From internal evidence it is clear that the one dated "Vendredi matin" [Friday morning] was written after 25.12.40 and before 22.1.41. The one dated "Dimanche soir" [Sunday evening] is obviously written on Sunday 30.3.41. and the third is dated'. There was also a Christmas card from Stella and RENÉ, which Odette thought she must have received in the middle of January, as by that time she already knew who 'Serge' was, even though she'd never met him. René Dazy was fighting with the Maquis but he could be contacted by the French authorities c/o Georges Tardy, Villa Rose, Vauclaix, Nièvre.[9]

In Paris, the Direction de Securité Militaire were investigating the Marseille end of Stella's story to see if they had any traces of those mentioned by her, as well as the *poste restante* address for RENÉ in the rue Balzac. However, Young did not travel to Marseille to follow up on 'Leclerc' or the other members of the Deuxième Bureau, such as Gars, with whom she had been associated, otherwise several more issues relating to her case might have been resolved. Nor is there anything in Stella's files to suggest that the French authorities ever supplied him with a report.

Young was mostly able to confirm the facts surrounding Stella's stay in Angers and Nantes – the places where she'd stayed, her relations with various acquaintances, and certain aspects of her dealings with RENÉ – especially from the Abbé Luneau. However, the reason why she had remained in Nantes when the Germans were about to occupy it had proved to be a lie according to Monsieur Dugast's statement. What she tended to do was to take a true incident, but change facts and dates to her own advantage. He reported:

> It is striking that all the facts that Mrs. LONSDALE has recently given us regarding "RENÉ" have so far been proved to be untrue. She gave us his name and also the facts regarding his residence in the University in America. Investigations in America have shown that no man of the name

as given by Mrs. LONSDALE was a student there. She also has given the address of "RENÉ's" apartment in Angers and this address has equally proved to be incorrect ... Mrs. LONSDALE has deliberately surrounded the vital facts regarding her relations with "RENÉ" in a fog of falsehood and misrepresentation.[10]

Of course, as confirmed in Chapter 9, we now know that RENÉ *was* a student in America.

He noted that some of the timing of Monsieur Dugast's account of his trip to Biarritz was confusing as it had been for business and not prompted by the Germans' arrival in Nantes. Dugast had left on the morning of Tuesday 11 June 1940 (a week before the Germans' arrival on 19 June) and returned on Saturday 15 June, but he had gone there alone. The encounter with the Polish seaman and his offer to take Stella back to England was prompted by his coming to look for her, which suggests that this was not simply a chance encounter at the café and adds credence to the possibility that a Polish intelligence network in France, either TUDOR or Interallié, was trying to help repatriate her.

Jenny Dazy only saw Stella once in Nantes after her arrest when she returned to make a deposition in favour of her son, René, who had been denounced by Marcel Corgnet, a friend of Léon de Nyeres, and arrested on 21 January 1941. René's trial took place on 1 April and he was sentenced to a year's hard labour; he was released on 15 August 1941 (see also Chapters 22 and 24).

Stella had used the Café Mouillard as a *poste restante* for her mail. Any Germans who came in or who tried to approach her were given the cold shoulder, but Madame Mouillard warned her not to be too stand-offish lest it should cause the café any problems. She was genuinely fond of Stella, so Young though it prudent not to mention that she had been arrested and was now in prison. He was informed that Monsieur Mouillard had died on 1 January 1941. Jenny Dazy said that while in Nantes Stella was practically penniless and earned extra money by knitting.

Monsieur Martineau's daughter Maud confirmed that Stella had been friendly with René Dazy and Campillo, and was also seen in the company of members of the Gestapo. Martineau had been arrested again in May 1943 and was released on 13 January 1944, but later died as a result of his experience in prison. Stella's reason for being on friendly terms with the Germans was so she could obtain information which might be useful to the Allies. Maud only saw her a couple of times after her release, so she was unable to say what Stella's relationship was with the Germans at that time.

Odette Châtenet confirmed that Stella's arrest had come after being denounced by Jean Platiau, who had personally made the arrest. In January

1941 Stella had told her about how she planned to double-cross the Germans with RENÉ's help, whom Odette knew only as 'Serge'. She also confirmed Jenny Dazy's account that Stella had returned to Nantes once to give evidence at René's hearing. Stella had told her that both she and her husband worked for British Intelligence.

* * *

Young noted that a message from Most Secret Sources (ISOS) sent by Meissner in Paris from Marseille and to Berlin on 5 November 1941 'is perhaps not without significance': 'Arrival of V man – Simone's report confirmed,'[11] the day when Stella arrived at Bristol (Whitchurch) airport from Lisbon. Simone Lavallière was one of her aliases known to the Germans – others were Simone de Vallière, Madame Carr-Glynn, Solange Léprevier, Suzanne de la Roche, Eugenie Landais and Mademoiselle Landeur. The use of the term 'V-Man' (actually *V-Mann*, *Vertrauensmänn* – confidential person) suggests that this was Stella. Young concluded: 'It is possible that once again she is using her favourite device of taking an actual fact, namely, contact by a member of the German I.S. in Lisbon, who may have taken a report from her, and has twisted this fact into a story to her own advantage which she told the authorities here.'[12] The question remains, how did the Germans know that she had arrived, and who told them?

A revealing paragraph in Stella's letter to Odette Châtenet, a former pupil of hers at the Berlitz School, dated 1 April 1941, gave a clue as to RENÉ's identity:

> About S, dear, when we write in the future, it's better for us to call him, for example, Raoul – that way, if ever one of our letters was read by somebody else it would not get him into trouble – isn't that much wiser? Don't forget, and above all, if anyone asks you who is this "Raoul" you must say that you don't know him, but that he's a Frenchman I am in love with … whom I knew some years back when I was at Monte Carlo and that I met him here by coincidence.[13]

The René whom she had not seen for a fortnight was René Dazy not RENÉ: 'I thought a lot of René this morning and I am so impatient to know the result of the Tribunal – be sure to tell me. I even hope that when you get this letter he will be freed – poor kid!' She added that if she could arrange a meeting with Odette and introduce her to 'Raoul': 'I am sure you would fall in love with him. In that case – look out, I put poison in your coffee !!!!!!' Another letter written from Angers dated only 'Friday morning' (4 April) asks Odette to:

Find René [Dazy] and tell him that I have written to him, that I am so worried – that I wrote to him as arranged and he has <u>never</u> answered. Say I'm almost crazy. Tell him to write to me by express letter, as I shall be sending this letter to you. Tell him that I want to come to Nantes on Tuesday next [8 April] – that I shall catch the train which arrives in the afternoon, and that I'm going straight to the Maison du Café in the Rue d'Orléans near St. Croix – and that he <u>must</u> come and meet me there – tell him to write to me immediately to say whether or not he can keep the appointment there – tell him that he <u>must</u>, Odette. Things will be bad for us if he does not.

Besides, it's too long a journey to make for nothing, and anyway it is difficult for me to come to Nantes at the present time.

She then asked that Odette come to the Maison du Café when she finished work and to confirm by sending a note *poste restante*, but not to put her address: 'I am sure you are full of curiosity, but I'll explain when I see you on Tuesday.' She was most insistent that René Dazy write to her '<u>most urgently</u>' to confirm their meeting and that Odette should see to it: 'Tell him, it must be Tuesday, afterwards will be too late for me – I am sure, certain really, that you will do as I ask, with <u>complete discretion</u> and absolutely <u>urgently</u>.'[14] As Young noted, 'It will be remembered that Mrs. LONSDALE left Marseille in October, arriving Lisbon on 28.10.41, and that one of her many aliases known to the Germans was Simone LAVALLIÈRE.'[15]

Chapter 26

The Advisory Committee's Report

The Advisory Committee delivered its long-winded, eight-page, twenty-eight-point report on their findings on the Lonsdale case on 6 December 1944.[1] A week later Jim Hale discussed the case extensively with Courtenay Young, and also with Mrs D. Spring. They all agreed that they could not advise the Home Secretary that Stella would be likely to do anything actually 'prejudicial to national interests' if she were released, subject to certain restrictions. He also spoke to Sir Ernest Holderness, Bt., Assistant Secretary in charge of the Home Office Aliens Department indicating that whatever decision the Home Office arrived at it was important that MI5 should have another opportunity to interrogate her before she was released. The report gave the following 'particulars' of the case:

The said Stella Edith Howson LONSDALE:

(i) remained in Nantes when the town was to her knowledge about to be occupied by the German Armed Forces, and when it would have been possible to return to the United Kingdom;
(ii) in 1940 agreed to enter the employment of the German Secret Service;
(iii) in the years 1940 and 1941 associated in France with members of the German Secret Service;
(iv) on her return to the United Kingdom misrepresented the nature of that association.

It stated that she had claimed to be working for the Germans because she had had no other choice if she were to save her own life after her arrest; however, it had always been her intention to double-cross them, and she had sent some important information to Britain. The committee accepted the part of her story where she appeared to incriminate herself, while rejecting the part where 'she sought satisfactorily to explain the conduct which, without explanation, was incriminating'. They expressed their appreciation of how thoroughly and skilfully MI5 had prepared their case, in assembling all the facts, and their further investigations. They then summarized the basic facts, but rejected her proposal to work for British Intelligence by returning to France. Given that her account of events was not in all respects true, she was detained on 22 January 1942.

The committee acknowledged that her suggestion that enquiries could be made relating to the people with whom she was in contact in Nantes, or indeed anywhere else, was a good idea. It was their opinion that her case be considered as it appeared from available evidence, and not to infer too much from the fact that she had delayed her appeal until 1944, even though they remained unconvinced by her explanation of why she had left it so long. Since 'she had been colloguing[2] with the Germans,' she was no doubt apprehensive as to how this conduct would be perceived. As they pointed out, 'the real issue in the case concerns the question whether her liaison with the Germans was actuated by treacherous and blame-worthy motives, or whether it was the result of duress, and whether it was throughout undertaken with a real desire to give assistance to the Allied cause'. Had she appealed in 1942, the committee's task would have been to determine whether or not she should be interned, but now in 1944 their job would be to decide whether she should remain in custody.

In their opinion, since MI5's 'Statement of Case' was twenty-four pages long and contained 'a very full and interesting account of the facts and theories relating to the case', it was not necessary to summarize all her explanations. That, and the three interviews MI5 had carried out after her second hearing, as well as obtaining information from France, all of which needed to be considered 'before any views or conclusions or findings, or recommendations can be formed or made'. To assist the Home Secretary, the committee would 'attempt to submit new views and conclusions in the hope that these may assist the Secretary of State in forming a view in regard to this somewhat unique and bewildering case'.

They recorded that there was 'nothing very remarkable in her early upbringing and ... no suggestion of political interest or attachment' while noting that she had a brother in the RAF, and that her other brother was 'to some extent mentally affected', which they regarded as possibly significant. They acknowledged that 'There is nothing to suggest that Mrs. LONSDALE would be predisposed to be antagonistic to her own country, and beyond a possible love of excitement and intrigue, there is nothing in the history of the case to show any reason why Mrs. LONSDALE should have any traitorous intent'. Nor did they think that when she first went to France, she had had any intention of working for the Germans, or afterwards when she had stayed in France after March 1940. The Lonsdales had been attracted to intelligence work 'and doubtless would have been glad to assist either the French or the British Intelligence Services'.

The committee did not question that she had been arrested by the Germans at some date, but dates given when she was detained, and then before the committee, did not tally, but 'no adverse inference' should be drawn from it. As to the circumstances of her possession of the plan of the Sainte-Luce oil installation, it appeared that she had been betrayed by Platiau. They wondered why she hadn't destroyed such incriminating evidence, but noted, 'the Committee are told that there was, in fact, no underground petrol installation at Sainte-Luce' (see previous chapter). The 'competing theories and deductions [were] extremely baffling', but they should not reflect adversely on Stella Lonsdale; it was only the facts of her arrest by the Germans which required attention.

They assumed that there were circumstances in which she was arrested and subsequently agreed to work for the Germans, but 'a very great deal seems to depend in this case upon what those circumstances were'. What they found remarkable was that, while she had appeared before Dernbach and Meissner, RENÉ had helped her with her appearance before the tribunal, resulting in her release and recruitment by the Germans. She had asserted that he was really anti-Nazi, and 'well-disposed to help her'. She had been reluctant to reveal his true identity – that it might jeopardize his sister in America, as well as possibly costing his life – but they found it perplexing 'that the suggestion should be made that the revelation to the British authorities of somebody who, in the German organization, was anti-Nazi, might possibly result to his detriment'. Furthermore, they failed to grasp that the Germans 'should have in their organisation someone who was anti-Nazi, and who was deliberately willing to assist a British girl in the circumstances disclosed in this case [or] who was deliberately willing to have the secrets of the German organisation made known to the British'. Exactly when she had first met RENÉ was uncertain.

It was to her credit that she had attempted to communicate knowledge of Gaessler's treachery and his betrayal of British agents to British Intelligence and succeeded in getting a message back to England about it. But as the committee noted:

> This service might have been a very considerable one to this country. It is, however, suggested by M.I.5 that the mischief done by Gaessler had all been effected before the time that Mrs. LONSDALE got her message back, and that therefore it was a deliberate piece of strategy on the part of the Germans to cause an Englishwoman to send back to England what ... would appear to be most extremely valuable information.

In so doing she would establish her *bona fides* for any future services she may offer British Intelligence, while actually serving German Intelligence, something the committee fully accepted and understood. They recognized that in the spheres where double-crossing has to become the stock-in-trade or art of those engaged, infinite subtlety is required in assessing and diagnosing the motives of every action of every person concerned. Recognising all these things the Committee yet feel most disinclined to the view that Mrs. LONSDALE was ever lending herself to a course of contemplated treachery to this country, involving deep cunning and deliberate and measured calculation.

The possibility that she had been willing to work for the Germans in Nantes was also considered, although her reason for doing so had not been revealed. On the whole, after considering all the facts, they did not accept that she had been willing to be sent to England by the Germans in order to be employed by British Intelligence, then return to France with valuable information which the Germans could use against Britain: 'Whatever view is the true view of this case, the Committee do not think that Mrs. LONSDALE was ever willing, or ever contemplated, going to such lengths.'

While her activities in Marseille suggest 'that they were thoroughly mischievous ... she did render certain services to some English sympathizers who never had cause to regret the connection.' Those views were based upon the opinions of Bingham, the American vice-consul, and Fullerton, the American consul-general. But their statements 'rather record opinions formed, and do not set out any very striking statements of fact'. The British authorities did not think that their statements were 'deserving of careful consideration as indicating that Mrs. LONSDALE's activities and methods did provoke suspicion', while bearing in mind that supposing she was innocent, her activities might still have aroused suspicion.

It was extremely difficult to come to any clear conclusion about RENÉ. As they pointed out, 'So much of the case depends upon a consideration of the story told by Mrs. LONSDALE herself.' Even though MI5 had obtained statements from people in France, the case was built upon little outside evidence. Weighing up the various theories and possibilities, the committee was trying to decide how much of her story was credible and how much of it was not. She was not considered 'a wholely [sic] reliable witness', as she had misstated some of the facts about RENÉ: 'Since to a considerable extent the case against Mrs. LONSDALE depends upon what she herself has stated, it becomes perplexing in the extreme to decide how much of her story which is damaging to her ought to be accepted, while refusing to accept other parts of the same story by which she explains her conduct.'

It was also difficult to accept that RENÉ had been willing to assist the British, 'but in that sphere, where everybody seemed to be double-crossing everybody else, it may well be that "René" was double-crossing Mrs. LONSDALE'. They speculated that perhaps he'd fooled her into thinking that she was actually helping the British while using her to serve the Germans, but ensuring that he never gave her any really valuable information. And though she was not consciously seeking to help the Germans 'they thought that in fact they could get assistance from her without her knowing that she really was serving them and not England' when she returned to England, then to France as an agent of the British. However, the committee felt that this theory held certain difficulties. [Author's note: If this were true, this suggests that the Germans may have been instrumental in engineering her escape.]

The committee further suggested that RENÉ's friendship with Stella may have been designed to deceive her into working for the Germans and that 'she would really not be damaging, but assisting, her own country'. However, it was also possible that there had been a mutual attraction and that she agreed to work for them, 'though possibly not proposing to do any harm to this country'. But she realized later that, if she hadn't actually been under duress, her action would be indefensible so she embellished her story to excuse her conduct. That being the case, and if her life hadn't actually been in jeopardy had she not worked for the Germans, then her actions must be considered more seriously.

They 'rejected the extreme view that Mrs. LONSDALE lent herself from the start and throughout to a deliberate course of calculated and calculating assistance to the Germans'. They also rejected the view that RENÉ actually *wanted* to help the Allies. Recent evidence obtained from France suggested that he was in love with her, but she claimed not to be his mistress. They drew attention to the original letters written by Stella and Odette Châtenet as 'striking evidence' that she and RENÉ were on 'most affectionate terms'. Therefore, in the spirit of adventure and her affection for him, when Stella was arrested, in order to avoid internment, 'she compromised herself by accepting employment with the Germans, and that possibly in her own mind resolved to use her position to do what she could for England [and]… the main-spring of her later action'.

Evidence obtained from France had confirmed much of what Stella had said, such as her stay with the Dugasts, although they had never had any intention of her accompanying them to Biarritz; the meeting with Olgierd Około-Kulak was mainly true. Abbé Luneau's testimony about meeting with her and RENÉ was on the whole considered favourable to Stella as was Madame Mouillard's testimony, whereas other statements were not. That she had a plan of an underground petrol installation at Sainte-Luce was not supported by the witnesses interviewed because they said that there was no such underground installation (contrary to what we now know).

It was 'almost impossible' to 'come to any clear view that gives full weight to all the considerations, some of which are strongly in favour of Mrs. LONSDALE, and some of which are strongly against her'. There were so many 'maybes' – that 'she was an adventuress without scruple', or that she was confused and did try to help Britain – but if there were any suspicions of her story 'she had only herself to blame'. Even though she claimed to have been ostensibly working for the Germans it was something the committee had to regard very seriously, unless a satisfactory and acceptable explanation could be offered. 'The case has undoubtedly been one of considerable suspicion,' but had a criminal charge been brought against her they felt that there was insufficient evidence to support a serious charge in a court of law.

It was a 'tantalising and bewildering case' involving 'a woman without principles and obviously very immoral', but they rejected the view that her conduct was motivated by deliberate disloyalty and treachery: 'Nothing in the history of the case suggests that she would be anxious to do harm to Britain as of set purpose.' Bearing all that in mind, would she still present a dangerous threat, 'even though the doubts as to the precise nature of her past actions may remain unresolved' and remain in custody? In summary, overall, she could do no harm; neither would she be a dangerous person, nor 'wish to take part in any sinister enterprise'. They acknowledged that her current good conduct might be a means to secure her release because her mother was ill, but they remained uninfluenced by any personal considerations. It was their opinion that

> whatever the processes of thought of Mrs. LONSDALE in 1940 and 1941 may have been, she would not be, today, in the least willing to do anything harmful to the war effort or to the Nation's cause, and that, quite apart from these considerations, she would be much too frightened ever to think of such things … [O]n the whole that, in present circumstances, it would be appropriate to discontinue the detention, though possibly certain restrictions might, if this course were adopted, be imposed.

As to the question of whether Stella should continue to be detained for the foreseeable future, at the end of December Sir Ernest Holderness minuted: 'This is a very curious case and I am sure we have not got to the bottom of it yet.' He noted MI5's view that she hadn't told the whole story and since she had admitted to agreeing to work for the Germans, 'her detention should be continued for a further period in the hope that some further light may be shed upon it as a result of the enquiries which are still being pursued by the French'. However, MI5 did not consider that enquiries in France would produce further evidence which might justify a charge of treachery against Stella:

They recognise that it wd. be virtually impossible to proceed with a charge against a person who has been under detention for about 3 years [but] that some further attempt should be made to unravel the mystery of her story which has baffled the Committee, now that there is an opportunity for testing, whatever she may be willing to disclose further, through enquiries in France.

The material obtained in France, 'while it is largely negative … casts considerable doubt upon the various versions which Mrs. Lonsdale has given to explain her relations with the Germans'. In Holderness's opinion Herbert Morrison should accept MI5's recommendation 'that detention should be maintained for a further period, for the purpose of further examination of any material which may be obtained from France, in the hope that the facts may become clearer.'

On 8 January 1945, Sir Frank Newsam, Under-Secretary of State at the Home Office, wrote to the chairman of the Advisory Committee about the report sent to Morrison about Stella's case, and thanked the committee 'for the great case and patience which they have tkane [*sic*] in examining this very complicated and difficult case and trying to sort out its tangled skeins'.

Until the French had completed their enquiries Morrison considered that Stella remain in detention 'for a further short period in the hope that the facts may become a bit clearer'. After two or three months he would review the case again. 'In the meantime, subject to any view you may care to express, he does not propose to treat this as a "disagreement case".' Morris replied to Newsam on 19 January 1945 that he and his colleagues 'fully recognise and appreciate the reasons which have led to the course which the Home Secretary is proposing to follow'. On 31 January 1945 Stella was informed of the Home Office's decision that, based on 'the report of the Advisory Committee about her case … [the Home Secretary] has decided not to release her from detention'.

Chapter 27

'The Woman Who Laughs Like a Horse'

Henry L. Platiau, the brother of Jean Platiau, confirmed to the Sécurité Militaire (SM) that Stella had been a teacher at the Berlitz School, and very closely linked with Campillo and three friends of Mademoiselle Silvera at the Spanish Consulate. Jean's denouncer, he said, was someone in the Gestapo who occupied several high administrative positions in Berlin, corroborated by a declaration Jean had made: '*Ils (la Gestapo) ne savent rien. C'est la haute police (Berlin) qui m'a fait arrêté.*' ('The Gestapo knew nothing. It was the headquarters police in Berlin who arrested me.') Henry suggested that Stella's photograph be shown to Madame Mahe, Caserne Cambronne,[1] Madame Hevin, 46, Boulevard Gabriel Lauriol,[2] at the Hôtel de France in Angers, and the Hôtel des Pyrénées in Nantes, the old Gestapo headquarters.

It has been suggested that Jean Platiau and Victor Marie François Saunier 'provided false information as informers and were strongly suspected of working for the opposing SR [Service de Renseignements]'. Furthermore, that Dernbach manipulated Stella and when he no longer needed Platiau he got rid of him 'by including him on the list of hostages under the pretext of being a Gaullist agent'.[3]

Monsieur Brisson's statement and other documents from Capitaine Devauges of BDOC (Bureau de Sécurité) in Nantes (referred to in Chapter 22) were passed to Malcolm Muggeridge stationed with DSDOC (Direction des Services de Documentation) in Paris, and forwarded to Courtenay Young. But in December 1944 Young was posted to SIFE (Security Intelligence Far East) in Kandy, Ceylon (modern-day Sri Lanka) as their only Japanese-speaking officer, so on 3 February 1945 Major J.F.E. Stephenson, MI5 Liaison Section at SHAEF, asked Edward Cussen in MI5's SLB3 that these documents and a report on '*la dame au rire de cheval*' ('the woman who laughs like a horse') be forwarded to whoever was now handling Stella's case. The report materialized more than a month later via the French Ministry of Foreign Affairs and the British Embassy:

> She is intelligent, attractive, exuberant and has none of the good breeding or reserved manner of the English "aristocracy" to which she claims to belong by virtue of her marriage with a LONSDALE, of the great family

of old English nobility. Her language is coarse extravagant and affected – a trait rare among the English and especially in the society to which she says she belongs; the first thing I took a dislike to was her loud laugh; no Englishman of the aristocracy, however debauched, however destitute, however low he had sunk, would dream of laughing as she does. The English would call it a horse's laugh – rire de cheval. It is an unforgivable sin amongst those of good breeding.[4]

* * *

While in prison Stella enlisted the help of the left-wing writer, Quaker and anti-colonial activist Reginald Arthur Reynolds, who had collaborated with Mahatma Gandhi and writer, pacifist and Quaker Horace Alexander. From 1933–7 Reynolds was General Secretary of the 'No More War Movement'; in 1938 he married prolific left-wing novelist and travel writer Ethel Edith Mannin. In spite of an allegation that she was bisexual,[5] Mannin had married Alexander Porteous in 1919 and had been the lover of Irish poet W.B. Yeats from 1934–5; she also had an affair with philosopher Betrand Russell, and corresponded with playwright, writer and illustrator Laurence Houseman, and Maud Gonne, the Irish nationalist, Suffragette, and friend of Yeats. During the war Reynolds was a conscientious objector and served in Air Raid Precautions (ARP) and a mobile hospital unit. In 1948, together with George Orwell, he edited *British Pamphleteers* and a second volume with historian A.J.P. Taylor in 1951.[6] He also wrote weekly satirical poetry for the *New Statesman*.

Stella wrote to 'Reg Dear' on 13 March 1945 at his address at 20 Jubilee Place, Chelsea, SW3, about her case, enclosing letters from her mother and 'Little Gran' concerning her ex-husband John.[7] John's claim not to have known of 'Kolin's' existence (a pet name for Sideroff) was 'a deliberate lie intended naturally to make Little Gran detest me,' she told Reynolds. He *had* known 'Kolin' very well and had actually stayed with them before she left him, but she stressed that she had never stayed with or made love to 'Kolin' when she returned from France in November 1941.[8]

Her mother claimed that 'Stella had gained a good deal of valuable information when working at the W.O. [War Office] which she could have put into enemy hands', but had been interned for disclosing information to the enemy – something which John had confirmed. She disputed that Stella could have made such a disclosure and requested to see the letter, but since it had never materialized, Stella didn't believe that it actually existed. She said that the War Office might have used the phrase 'gained a great deal of valuable information' to justify interning her.

John had allegedly been involved in a gun-running incident supplying arms to Franco, as well as the so-called 'accountants deal' involving Edward Chichester, 6th Marquess of Donegall. John and Victor Hervey, Lord Bristol's nephew and heir, had gone to Helsinki as guests of the Finnish government where they 'got uproarously dru[nk] and fired shots out of their cars'. In Helsinki, he and Hervey, who was a pro-Franco columnist for the *Sunday Dispatch*, 'assembled a vast collection of arms', intending to make '$250,000 from the sale of $10 million worth of munitions'.[9] That incident provoked a question in the House of Commons on 31 March 1937 from Captain Victor Cazalet, the Conservative MP for Chippenham.[10]

Anthony Eden, the Foreign Secretary, confirmed that Hervey, the Marquess of Donegall and John Lonsdale had visited Finland at the beginning of March and established connections with Finnish army officers and officials of the Finnish arms and munitions factories, declaring that they were buying arms for Brazil. But Eden was

> satisfied, as a result of inquiries ... that, contrary to reports which have appeared in the Press, there is no evidence that Finnish officers gave any assistance to these gentlemen in obtaining arms for Spain under false pretences. When they were unable to produce any authorisation from the Brazilian Government for the purchase of arms in Finland, all negotiations with them were broken off. I regret that allegations against Finnish officials should have received publicity in this country.[11]

Both *Vapaa Sana*, a Finnish newspaper published in Canada, and the *Winnipeg Free Press* reported the incident – 'Plot to Ship Arms to Spain to Be Probed'. *Vapaa Sana* described how after Lonsdale and Hervey had met with Finnish officials they had partied 'with no lack of liquor'. Then they absconded without paying their hotel bill of 15,000 Finnish marks and boarded a ship bound for Hull, but were returned to Finland. The Finnish government announced that they would conduct an investigation into the matter, especially given Donegall's claim that 'Finland was being used as a storage location for a weapons cache worth 10,000 dollars, destined for delivery into Spain',[12] an allegation also reported in the *Winnipeg Free Press*.[13]

During the Spanish Civil War Hervey, later 6th Marquess of Bristol, had sold arms to both sides and was Franco's principal agent for many years.[14] He'd also been the ringleader of the so-called 'Mayfair playboys' involved in the jewellery robbery for which Lonsdale was convicted, although the Metropolitan Police failed to prove that he had taken part in the actual robbery. He was later convicted of a similar offence in Mayfair in June 1939.[15]

Reynolds had been warned not to have anything to do with Lonsdale whose name stinks among his friends in Chelsea and all over ... He boasts about putting you here, and if you only allow me to make fuller enquiries I will bring the whole thing to light ... he snoops on people and informs the Police and if he dislikes a person for any reason, he just makes a frame up, informs the Police and they are out of his wa[y] for the time.

Stella begged him not to take any action or print anything without consulting her first because she was afraid the publicity would kill her mother. 'For myself I don't care, for my mother, yes.' He responded, 'In that case I can only appeal to the [prison] officer that nothing is said about this conversation, but I tell you straight you are shielding John Lonsdale, the rat.'

Leslie Crane, the crooked lawyer, had been in prison, but was now working for 'the biggest crook lawyers in London'. If she would provide Reynolds with notes of introduction to people in France, he could make discreet enquiries. She told him how John had consoled her about her dying son Felix and had taken her to Brompton Oratory to 'talk to her of his soul and what was happening to him', but it was hard for her to understand how someone could be so different. Reynolds thought that John was suffering from a split personality. Their meeting left Stella in a state of considerable stress that evening and needed to see the prison doctor about it.

Lydia Lewińska @ Lydia Link advised her that she should see a Mr Lane, who was the only person who could get her out of prison; had it not been for him Mitzi Schreier would still have been there. Ethel visited Stella on 26 March 1945 after she and Albert Lynden @ Albeert Lewinski, a Polish Jew, had gone to Petersfield to visit Muriel Whinfield. Lynden was a member of Oswald Mosley's British Union of Fascists, Ealing Branch, who had written for the BUF's *Blackshirt* newsletter,[16] and fallen in love with Ethel. Stella told Ethel that she'd written to Mr Lane and the Advisory Committee hoping for good results, but if they had already made up their minds, then it was hopeless. RENÉ had written her a letter in French which, when the word *'femme'* was translated, meant 'darling little woman' or 'wife', leading MI5 to thinking that Stella had been living with him.

Reynolds's enquiries revealed that John Lonsdale was 'near the edge of a crook' and had got into trouble before Stella returned from France but had used her to worm his way out of it. Loshensky, whom she'd met while hailing a taxi to take her back to the hotel, had offered her money to work for the Germans, but she'd refused.[17] Viner had since married a well-known (unnamed) clergyman's daughter. She supposed that had she not helped him escape from France he would not be alive today.

Reynolds apologized for having rushed Stella into seeing Mr Lane as he didn't know him and had very little faith in him. He suspected that Lane might also be a crooked lawyer if he was mixed up with Mosley and all the other DR.18B cases. Nor did he agree with DR.18B or have any sympathy for Mosley and the BM (British Movement). So far, he had been unable to find out what sort of trouble John had been in with the police, but Stella suddenly remembered an unpleasant experience, which she reluctantly shared with Reynolds in great confidence.

She and John had arranged to meet Sidoroff at Guildford, but were unable to when John had gone to France. While Sidoroff was waiting he'd met and gone home with a girl and caught a sexually transmitted disease from her, which Stella stressed was not syphilis. Greatly distressed, he came to her wanting to know what he should do. She advised him to see a doctor, but when she discovered that he wasn't bothering with the treatment she brought him to stay at her flat so that she could keep an eye on him and ensure he was taking the medication. Shortly after writing to John about it a note arrived from a police officer whom she'd met before but whose name she'd forgotten, inviting her for a cup of tea that afternoon at New Scotland Yard. When she arrived, another officer present asked if she was having any trouble now that her husband was away, because they'd heard that John was blackmailing her and she couldn't get Sidoroff out of her flat. They told her, 'First give us the facts and we will dispense with him all right,' which shocked her. When she'd recovered her composure, she told them that Sidoroff was there at her invitation. Reynolds enquired whether this was John's pal Detective Chief Inspector William Salisbury, but she couldn't remember.[18]

She also told Reynolds about Major 'Sammy' Gordon, although she couldn't remember his real name or which regiment he was in, which seems surprising since she claimed he was her godfather. Major (later Lieutenant Colonel) Edward Anthony Gordon, Pioneer Corps, who had been in Nantes, later served in Egypt and Libya as Deputy Director of Pioneer and Labour (DDPL). He couldn't understand why such a charming woman as Stella had married such an awful man as John, whom he detested, but was amused when she told him that John could also be charming. Reynolds was anxious to meet him, as well as Viner and Sidoroff. She was happy for him to meet Viner, but not Sidoroff because he was a White Russian and might easily get into trouble, which he had almost done with her. Nor did she want Reynolds to get into trouble making so many enquiries and would never forgive herself or be able to face Ethel Mannin.

John Lonsdale was now director of The South Counties Linen Co., [sic] on the King's Road, Chelsea.[19] Reynolds was convinced that it was a 'front' for stolen goods and blackmarket items since whenever he'd passed by there had never been anyone coming or going. Someone had also suggested to him that maybe Stella could sue Herbert Morrison for wrongful detention and its effects on her health, to which she replied:

> Oh yes I fully intend going into this matter just to give my mother a little comfort for that is my greatest worry, the misery and sorrow they have brought on her by putting me here, I have lost confidence in people and I find my nerves are shattered, although I don't intend to go round like the Links and get bitter with everyone and embitter myself as they are doing.[20]

That was music to his ears. There was nothing he liked better than a good fight! He wrote to Resi Weltlinger[21] at Camp WY on the Isle of Man about it, but there are no documents in any of Stella's MI5 files to indicate that she pursued the matter any further.

At this point Stella was feeling buoyant that she would soon be released as the war was coming to an end, but worried about what she might do when she was released. After three and a half years' detention she felt her brain was getting rusty, but she still wanted to do something constructive. Reynolds offered to employ her as honourary secretary, which she thought would be 'delightful'. On 2 May 1945 Jim Hale informed Mrs D. Spring of B1b that 'unless we had a strong case for wishing to continue the internment of Stella LONSDALE under Regulation 18B for a further period', Holderness proposed releasing her immediately. Hale suggested that

> We could not really object to the Home Office releasing Mrs. Lonsdale, since the enquiries which were now proceeding were largely academic and could not produce information which would justify holding [her] other than under 18B of the Defence Regulations. It was therefore agreed that we should not object to her release.[22]

On 4 May 1945 the Home Office issued a 'Direction Suspending Operation of Detention Order' requiring her to provide an address to which she would be going within twenty-four hours, and not to change it unless she notified the police station of any changes; should this involve moving to another police district, she should notify the nearest police station in that area.

The direction specified that her national registration identity card was not endorsed, nor was she registered under the National Service Acts. Dr Matheson, Governor of Holloway, informed MI5 that she was released from his custody on 7 May 1945, and the Home Office sent a notice to Graham Mitchell in F3, the MI5 section dealing with Fascists and other right-wing organizations.[23]

Stella gave Ethel Mannin's address for the night of 7 May: 'Oak Cottage', Burleigh Road, Wimbledon, SW19 [sic]. The following day she went to stay with her mother at 44, Reservoir Road, Olton, Warwickshire, where she would remain for a time. The Chief Constable of Warwickshire, E.K.H. Kemble, and Major Gerald Glover, the MI5 RSLO in Birmingham, were also informed.

* * *

From 27–31 May Major Peter Hope of SCI 106 Unit made enquiries about Stella during his visits to Rennes, Angers and Nantes. In Rennes he contacted Capitaine Meyer of the TF [sic – possibly meant to be TR – Travaux Ruraux] at 31, rue Edmond Rostand on 28 May. In Angers he met with Capitaine Nicollet, chief of BDOC at the 'Villa Fleuri', after having gone to the BST at 18, rue des Écoles. Nicollet was extremely co-operative, but Hope discovered that the BST had not been informed that Stella had been in prison in England and had therefore washed their hands of her case. With so many others to investigate, it was not exactly a priority for them, and since BDOC were trying to locate her in France, they would wait until she was arrested there.

Nicollet took him to Nantes and La Baule where he made several phone calls on Hope's behalf. However, Hope was somewhat unprepared as he had not been in France with Young and, surprisingly, had not read MI5's papers on the case. He reported on 1 June 1945 that Stella had fallen in love with 'a G.I.S. informer (D'Arzy)' [sic], who passed her on to Rauch, whose informer she became, although in Angers and Nantes she was regarded as pro-British. 'Captain Nicollet has recently completed an investigation into French traitors in the area and he has come across no trace of LONSDALE in this connection. He is, in fact, satisfied that if she was an informer for the G.I.S. it was in a low grade capacity and of no particular importance.'[24] Dazy was currently serving as a sergeant in the French Army, but was wanted by BDOC as Rauch's informer (see below), so Hope made arrangements to have him interrogated. Hope reported that Stella was a woman

> of low morals to whom the truth is a complete stranger ... of no morals whatever, who frequently changed her lover and cared little as to his nationality ... of no morals who has played for both sides depending on her lover of the moment. If this view is confirmed there seems little risk in releasing LONSDALE subject possibly to a restriction preventing her from obtaining a British passport for some time to come.[25]

Lucette Souchard, a 33-year-old divorcee who lived at 66(?) rue des Jardins in Angers, told him that 'Lonsdale lodged in a hotel requisitioned by the

Germans for about 1 month. I suggest this may have immoral rather than security implications'. Towards the end of 1940 she knew '*l'Anglaise*' (the Englishwoman) and also Serge ROBIN whom she identified from photographs shown to her by Inspector Georges Cousinie of the BST. L'Hôtel des Voyageurs had been requisitioned by the Germans and ROBIN had a requisition order for Stella's room, which Lucette found surprising, given Stella's nationality. She told Cousinie that Stella was highly thought of by management and staff alike, and that ROBIN spoke very good French. He'd told her that he worked as an interpreter in the German office at the town hall. One day she'd been taken for interrogation at 43, boulevard Maréchal Foch about Stella's activities but was released two hours later.

Stella spoke good German but Lucette never saw her in the company of any Germans in uniform since she only saw her for meals so she didn't know anything about her activities. As far as she knew Stella's husband worked for the Intelligence Service and was an officer in the RAF. She referred to HARRY as HARRIS who was also staying at the hotel but made weekly trips to Paris. She got the impression that while Stella was staying there, she was ROBIN's mistress, and confirmed that he had paid her bill when she left.

After Stella left, ROBIN went to Nantes, then to Tours where he worked as an interpreter in the *Feldkommandatur*. Lucette described him as 1.74 metres tall, healthy, with blond hair, and good-looking, who answered to the name MULLER. Her description pretty much concurs with other descriptions of RENÉ, apart from Moglia's claim that he had brown hair. She described his 'fiancée' as about 1.56 metres tall, very thin, with brown hair, who always wore sombre clothes, but very fashionable, aged about [25], very well made-up and wore very high-heeled shoes. Hope showed her the photograph of the two men with the girl in front of the car, whom she said was ROBIN's 'fiancée', but couldn't be certain. Therefore, it is debatable whether it was Stella, or whether either of the two men was RENÉ. The remainder of the report sheds no further light on what has already been determined elsewhere, and some of the information is inaccurate.

News of Stella's arrest travelled through Angers after she'd left the hotel. HARRIS reported seeing her in Paris at the Brasserie Kepler in the Place Clichy [*sic* – actually Wepler], very well dressed, with two silver fox furs draped on her shoulders, thus destroying the theory of her arrest. He'd also run into her at La Rotonde restaurant (La Rotonde, 105, Boulevard Montparnasse, or La Rotonde de la Muette, 12, Chaussée de la Muette).

Madeleine Levacher, the 25-year-old manageress of a cocktail bar at 23, Quai Ligny in Angers, also worked as a waitress at Le Colibri restaurant at l'Hôtel des Voyageurs and was familiar with ROBIN (Rauch @ RENÉ) and

HARRIS, as well as *l'Anglaise* (Stella), whose photograph she was shown. Stella never took her into her confidence so she knew nothing of her activities nor had any kind of relationship with her, apart from serving her meals at the restaurant. ROBIN had been a client of the bar before Stella's arrival and had an office on the Boulevard Maréchal Foch. He came to Le Colibri several times with people who appeared to be Gestapo so Madeleine believed he was German. At the end of 1940/beginning of 1941 Stella was only ever accompanied by him, the first time just after she'd been released from prison. One day when he saw Madeleine serving some Germans, he asked her, '*Qu'avez vous a dire à ses sales Boches?*' (What did you say to the filthy Boches?), but she didn't answer him. She also believed that he had paid Stella's bill when she left.

At first Madeleine claimed never to have seen HARRIS and ROBIN together, but then later contradicted herself by claiming that whenever HARRIS was with Stella and ROBIN he was always full of himself and she often served him at the same table. He always wore civilian clothes and always had German cigars and cigarettes, which made her think he too was German. Stella was with him the last time she saw her. After Stella's departure he'd told Madeleine that she'd been arrested. She confirmed that Stella would often come to the café accompanied by Serge ROBIN and another person called HARRY, who could have been Hermann/Harry Hyman/Heinemann referred to earlier, and not HARRIS.

Hope's report mentioned Stella being Joachín Campillo's mistress; her arrest on 27 November 1940; that six of her friends were arrested at the beginning of 1941, one of whom was René Dazy, who had been denounced a number of times to BDOC as a sub-agent of Rauch; and her contact with de Naeyer. As noted before, Dazy had been denounced by Marcel Corgnet who was now said to be the one who'd given Stella the information about the petrol dumps and anti-aircraft sites. The French believed that Dazy had been turned by the Germans while in prison in 1942 and subsequently worked with his friend de Naeyer. They planned to reinterrogate Campillo on certain specifics, which Young hadn't done when he interviewed him, 'to discover just how far LONSDALE was responsible for informing the G.I.S. about resistance activities'. It was Hope's opinion that while Stella had been

> in touch with a number of petty informers employed by the Ast at Nantes in the years 1940, 1941 ... [t]here have ... been no indications in the wave of denunciations from the civil population to the B.DOC in the past nine months that LONSDALE was notorious as an informer or that, in fact, she was particularly successful, and the French are certainly not anxious to try her as a war criminal.[26]

He saw no point in pursuing the matter any further 'Unless … some really damaging information is forthcoming from RAUCH or D'ARZY [*sic*]'.

On 1 January 1946 Stella wrote to Cyril Mills from the Seymour Tyre and Motor Co. Ltd, 2 Coal Wharf Road, Shepherd's Bush, London W12, where she was listed as a co-director,[27] in the hope that he would keep in touch with her, saying that she had divorced John, 'as I believe you know'. Mills wrote to Liddell saying that he had no intention of replying to her. Liddell agreed that 'the lady would only be a nuisance, and I do not think there is anything she could tell us that we do not know already'. However, he would be proved wrong on that score!

Chapter 28

Stella's Statement to the Abwehr

Late in 1945, months after MI5's investigations into Stella's case had been completed and she had been released from custody, 'an incomplete copy' of her interrogation carried out by Ast Angers III F after her arrest, dated 10 January 1941 and prepared by Sonderführer Wachter, came to light. Some points of interest not previously discussed elsewhere, or which add new information, are summarized here. The statement contained a confession that she *had* volunteered to work for the Germans, but the Sainte-Luce documents had been an entrapment engineered by the Germans to force her to work for them. John Gwyer of MI5's B1b wrote to Billy Luke of B1a on 27 November 1945 enclosing the original document saying that

> They do not carry the case much further except that they show that Stella LONSDALE represented to the Germans that her husband was a member of S.I.S. This may explain the continued interest which they took in her.
>
> I think it can be assumed that the Renate von GELNHORN, referred to … is the mysterious René who figured so largely in Stella LONSDALE's later interrogations here. As this name yields no trace in the Registry I do not think we are much further forward.[1]

Stella had tried to impress the Abwehr with her illustrious connections by mentioning that in John Lonsdale's family was the youngest major general during the First World War,[2] and his grandfather was a bishop and president of Eton College.[3] Among the other lies she told were that both her brothers were flyers 'and fell in this war'. Her brother Dennis was in the RAF, but as noted earlier, only with the rank of leading aircraftman, and not aircrew; her other brother, John, suffered from dementia praecox.

The report stated that:

> The affair Lonsdale was handled by III f Angers through V-Man Emile [Jean Émile Platiau]. V-Man Emile had hitherto proved himself reliable. In the course of the investigation, however, it was ascertained that he had established a sexual relationship with the Lonsdale [*sic*] and he was therefore of only limited use for the mission given him.

But the Abwehr's investigations failed to establish a firm connection between her and British Intelligence, so she was held in custody in Angers. It continued: 'In connection with this matter it has been shown that V-Man Emile has several times delivered untrue or exaggerated information which did not stand investigation. He has therefore been charged before a military court with *Nachrichtenschwindel* [in modern jargon, 'fake news'].'

The report contained a series of episodes and spurious claims highlighting Stella's dysfunctional family: that her sister Norah had fallen in love with her cousin, the suicide of her uncle Harry Gardener, and her aunt Winifred's marriage to a student at university and transfer of her entire estate to him. When she became pregnant, they mutually agreed to separate. Eight months later, she learned he had committed suicide, having spent her entire fortune, resulting in her going mad. Their child was brought up by Stella's father and later went to a cadet school and joined the Royal Navy.

Nickolas Magaloff's (Sideroff's) uncle in New York was a wealthy stockbroker and allegedly business partner of actor Gary Cooper's father Charles. Sideroff's mother's name was Baschkiroff [*sic*], from a well-known family who owned large cornfields and a house in the Crimea. His father may have been Vladimir Bashkiroff who had immigrated to America in 1919 to live in New York, having been director of the Volga Kamsky bank in Nizhny Novgorod (known as Gorky from 1932–90). He was 'a close friend and major supporter of numerous writers, artists and composers ... instrumental in the preservation of Russian culture in the United States and ... an important collector of Modern Russian art'.[4] Stella's mother had always thought that he had a hypnotic effect on her. Stella continually refers to Sideroff as her husband, whom she loved very much, except that he was 'the laziest man I have ever known in my life'. It was while she was staying in the hospital with her dying son that she learned of John Lonsdale, which contradicts what she would later tell MI5 about meeting him while she was visiting Sideroff in prison.

John's alleged career in the 'I.S.' (Secret Intelligence Service) after leaving university is extremely doubtful. He supposedly carried out a variety of missions, such as taking a letter from Tangiers through Gibraltar to London, supplying reports on morale. But in 1932 when he was 18, he had been working for a firm of accountants, and in 1933 served briefly in the King's Royal Rifle Corps. Before the Spanish Civil War, he was supplying detailed reports on the situation in Spain. Possibly another embellishment, but as noted in the previous chapter there was evidence that he had been there, which may account for why during his trial following the Mayfair jewellery robbery he had been unable to provide an alibi for what he had been doing for the past three months. While in prison he was apparently not treated like an ordinary prisoner and was visited by Lord Munster of the War Office and Colonel Davidson 'who played an important role in the English Secret Service (He has only one eye)'.

Major General Francis Henry Norman Davidson was Director of Military Intelligence (DMI) during the Second World War (1940–44),[5] succeeding Major General Frederick 'Paddy' Beaumont-Nesbitt, who had been DMI from 4 September 1939 until 16 December 1940, but there is no mention of his having only one eye. He *was* a colonel in 1938, but *not* at the War Office, and the Military Intelligence Museum at Chicksands has been unable to confirm that this is the same person.[6] The 5th Earl of Munster became Under-Secretary of State for War from January to September 1939. When John was released, he was apparently again approached by SIS to work for them.

Sideroff's aunt, Barbara Lithgow-Smith, had played matchmaker trying to find Stella a suitable spouse. She first selected Evan Frederic Morgan, 2nd Viscount Tredegar, a widower who owned extensive property and coal mines in Wales, an intelligence officer working for MI8 and MI14d, and an associate of fellow occultist Aleister Crowley. As Stella remarked, 'Morgan was looking for a woman of standing as mother to his heir [but] I myself had a great aversion to him. He was known in London as homosexual and in London he bore the epithet of "Queen of the Queens".' In 1939 he married the impoverished Princess Olga Sergeievna Dolgorouky, but their marriage was annulled in 1943 owing to his homosexuality.

After the death of her son Felix, Stella had no further time for Sideroff and 'couldn't stand him anymore'. He was aware of Barbara's matchmaking games and had agreed to her machinations but 'wanted to know nothing of it officially':

> B. once spoke very loudly of it while John was in the next room. She also said that it would be all right with my husband, and she played on my religious feelings by arguing that it would be right with my dead child. John heard everything and was upset.
>
> My first marriage was dissolved. I married John. Kolja however remained with us, as he was financially dependent on me. Also I could not leave the father of my child, which I had very much loved, in money difficulties.

If true, this *ménage à trois* lends credence to Stella's earlier claim of three-in-a-bed on her wedding night. Nevertheless, Barbara 'tried repeatedly to sell me to Peter' (actually George Hicks, a wealthy RAF Wing Commander).[7] Stella's description of their strange first meeting at a hotel was reminiscent of a Feydeau farce.

She and John both depended on their respective families for financial support – she from her mother, who had refused to give her any more money after she'd married John, and he on his grandmother, 'Little Gran', who had denounced him while he was in prison, but gave him more money once he was released. Sideroff, whom Stella continually refers to as 'Kolja', had gambled away all her money. Once the Germans occupied France, she stopped supporting him and believed that he'd left London to avoid the air raids.

She claimed that John's service in France was in the 'Pioneers' (Pioneer Corps), but was in fact the Royal Engineers, and a cover for observing the troops for the intelligence service. Her idea to accompany him to France had been said in jest, then carried out 'with the help of the War Minister'. But as noted in Chapter 2, Lord Cobham was Under-Secretary of State for War in 1939, a senior civil servant, but *not* the minister. When she arrived in France she'd brought with her a letter from him for the local commandant, Brevet Lieutenant Colonel William Turner Murray-Bisset, who she claimed was a distant relative of hers, saying: 'I am sending you the daughter of a good friend and ask you to look after her.'[8]

In Nantes Stella enjoyed being surrounded by the officers in spite of their being lower class. They in turn 'were flattered to be able to talk with a woman from the best circles and to flirt with her'. However, when she was investigated by the intelligence service in Nantes, she reported them to the War Office, resulting in their recall once they found out her pass had come from the 'War Minister'. She denied working for the intelligence service but sent reports directly to 'Lord C[obham]' as she did not get on well with Murray-Bisset.

In July 1940, while teaching at the Berlitz School, she met Harry Clifton,[9] who claimed to be from the intelligence service who London had sent to find her. However, she was suspicious that he was not quite above board. He told her that there were two other British officers in the town. But when she suggested that he hadn't given her any password or name from her circle, he scoffed at her, saying that she had a very romantic concept of intelligence work.

There is no further explanation about a German doctor named Brommert who came for lessons at the Berlitz School and knew a friend of hers, Renate von Gelnhorn [*sic*] from Düsseldorf, but as noted earlier, Billy Luke thought von Gelnhorn was a pseudonym for RENÉ. In their spare time they would chat, amongst other things, about espionage. Brommert told her that he'd heard rumours of a number of Englishmen in town. After the German occupation she decided to stay – 'I cannot say why. I simply had the feeling that I must stay; that it was the right thing to do.'

When the Abwehr interrogation resumed on 3 December she told how Platiau had asked her for the name of an Englishman in Nantes (Clifton), and whether she knew Desimiroff who he thought was an English agent in Saint-Nazaire. Platiau wanted to take her there to meet him, but if he wasn't genuine, he would have him arrested. She intended to ask Clifton about Desimiroff but after she told him about Platiau he disappeared, so the question remained unanswered. At this point, Rauch interjected to explain that when Platiau was working for the GFP (Geheime Feldpolizei) in Nantes he became acquainted with Desimiroff in the Café de la Baule: 'Desimiroff had confided to him that he worked for the Germans and had particularly good connections in officer circles in the port, so that he was constantly informed over the proceedings there.' Desimiroff didn't take Platiau's offer to collaborate with him seriously as he regarded him as a young fool and made fun of him, but he still wanted to use him to forward papers to England in a U-boat. If he could travel in the unoccupied zone, he would have Platiau deliver a report to friends.

The local Dienststelle issued Platiau with a permit to cross the frontier of the unoccupied zone, but when he showed it to Desimiroff he was sent home with a flea in his ear, leaving him with the impression that they were playing a joke on him and demanded that Desimiroff be punished. Rauch concluded that he'd come to the same opinion. Platiau also claimed that because Desimiroff had a building contractor's office in Saint-Nazaire he must be in a good position to pass on information to England and be working for them. A note adds that nothing is known of Platiau as a *V-Mann*.

All the English nuns had to report to the *Kommandatur* every morning, the only exception being an Englishwoman dressed as a nun whom Clifton had told Stella about. She concluded that since she couldn't be a real nun but someone posing as one, she would ask Sister Marie Cuthbert – 'a very timid simple woman' – at the clinic in the Place Anatole France, who'd been living in Nantes for nineteen years. Platiau wanted to meet her but she managed to talk him out of it by telling him that the only thing the nun could do was to pass on his name to whoever made the decisions. But he persisted, pressing her to take him with her to meet her when she visited the Hôtel-Dieu hospital in Nantes, but Stella insisted that the nun was not there, nor at any hospital.

Rauch again interjected to offer further clarification: 'After the visit to the hospital Platio [*sic*] had to report ... that the nun in question was not always there but only occasionally and to-day was not to be met. She worked apparently only from time to time. Later, on my orders, he made further investigations in the hospital, but they were however unsuccessful.' Stella stated that she had been to the Hôtel-Dieu hospital only twice, and then only spoken with Sister Marie Cuthbert on the second occasion when Platiau accompanied her.

Platiau's good command of English at the Berlitz School had given him away as a German agent. He was convinced that Stella must be a German agent and not a genuine Englishwoman, otherwise how could she roam around so freely? He was only satisfied when Monsieur Martineau had intervened and confirmed her nationality. Later Platiau told her that he didn't regard her as an English spy because she never paid him anything, whereas Desimiroff had offered him large sums of money.

His feeble attempts to seduce her and entice her into taking him on as an agent have already been addressed. When he offered to introduce her to a U-boat commander he knew, she refused. Stella was never romantically interested in him – he was forever bursting into crocodile tears whenever he professed to love her, and she declared that his love for her was only platonic – 'the boy was too stupid for me' – what might be called a 'schoolboy crush' for an older, more experienced woman. He claimed he could arrange for her to stay as a foreigner in Nantes as he knew several people in the OKW (Oberkommando der Wehrmacht) in Paris. It was not until 23 November that he confessed to being a German spy earning 2,000 francs per month – 'He offers himself to the Germans just as to the English in order to earn money. I personally could never imagine that the Germans could take on an agent as unsteady, nervous and mentally not normal young man.'

The story of how she was betrayed by Platiau was now different: one evening while she was dining with him and Campillo his tiresome behaviour annoyed her so she boxed his ears. He began to cry again: 'You don't understand me. If I go away now it is death for me; I am ruined. I would sooner kill myself by driving my car against a tree.' He continued to make a scene and told her he was a German spy sent to betray her and would be shot if he didn't. After spending the night at her lodgings, he'd collected a military car from the headquarters of the GFP at l'Hôtel des Pyrénées and taken her to Angers. During the journey she decided to accept his offer of working for the Germans:

> The fact that as an Englishwoman I decide to work for Germany is difficult to explain. It concerns my upbringing, the impressions of my childhood and the influence of my husband. My father had become strongly pro-German. He also spoke German. For me also music played a great part and that brought me nearer to the German character, as the Germans are very music-loving people. My second husband in particular had many friends in Germany and spoke fluent German. The war between England and Germany shook him badly and he joined the Army only out of family considerations.
>
> If I now place myself at the disposal of Germany, I mean it sincerely. I would like to make thereby a contribution to ending the war sooner and bringing everything back to a normal life. I believe that through my brilliant connections with English Society I could be of great use. I know that my family will condemn my step. But I believe that my husband will approve it.

This again contradicts her claims that she'd only volunteered to work for the Germans *after* meeting Dernbach, Meissner and RENÉ.

Stella's admission of accepting to work for the Germans now becomes much clearer as Rauch elucidates:

> Concerning her reasons for working for Germany Mrs. L. declared further: I believe that the present war situation shows a slight advantage on the German side, but I should like to emphasize that this is not the decisive reason for me. I emphasize once again that I have no kind of financial interest and would not like to work for money. Unfortunately I am compelled to accept money for my necessary expenditure. I will submit an account concerning this. In the course of the German occupation I have been impressed by the good bearing of the German officers. I also had personal relationships with German officers (Herr Bendemann and Dr. Brummert) and thought that if such intelligent people follow an idea it must have value. Then my intimate knowledge of English Society and of its rottenness and depravity played a part.
>
> In judging my offer one must not leave out of consideration that I have a very practical side indeed, as I have proved through my success in business life, but principally I am motivated through the idealistic side.
>
> I cannot yet imagine the type of work for me; I leave it to you. I simply think that I would have the best success in my homeland, on account of my good connections. It is all the same to me where I go. I do not insist on going to London; if I had wanted to go there I could already have gone last June.
>
> I imagine that I should have the money at my disposal in advance for financing my work, and then submit the account, or that I should pay the money out and receive it back afterwards from you. I regret that I am not in a position to finance the work out of my own means. What assignment I should carry out I have no idea. I simply have the wish to make use of my brilliant connections in England for the German cause. If I have spoken of working in London that is merely by chance, and arises because it was discussed at my first interrogation.
>
> At my first encounter with the German officer I stated, through lack of confidence, that I must decline to give any kind of information over my connections with English circles in Nantes. I did this because I did not know the interrogators and had to mistrust them. Now through my conversation with the Captain on Thursday I have decided to speak with all frankness.

After Stella separated from John, many men had pursued her but she had the impression that Campillo was respectable and she could trust him; Platiau by comparison was socially and intellectually beneath her. He asserted that she should admit that Campillo was an English officer, which he wasn't. She claimed that Monsieur Martineau had not treated her well and had taken advantage of her status as an Englishwoman by only paying her ten francs an hour instead of twelve. Platiau alleged that:

> Doubtless she works for the English Government, not for de Gaulle. I know that Mrs. L. reported to English officers, and if she worked for France it would have been unthinkable that she should give these reports to an Englishman, as this would go against the national *amour propre* [pride, self esteem].
>
> I do not believe that Mrs. L. has transmitted military intelligence, but merely established the connection between England and the people who want to go to England. If she however received military information, she also passed this on. She told me that she had received and transmitted information about the coast defences in Ciberon [*sic* – Quiberon] and Lorient. She also speaks good German, by the way. Of course, I have not seen that she handed over information. I have seen her with several people who could be English, but I have never followed these in order not to compromise myself. It would now be very difficult to meet these again, especially as they will certainly have learned in the meantime that Mrs. L. is arrested and they would not return to the same place.

Rauch summed up Platiau's career and character:

> Platiau had worked for a long time as a V-Man [*sic*] for III F S.W. France. He was taken over by GFP in September 1940, in the course of a unification of the V-Man administration. He received the assignment to carry on with the current inquiries. It concerned inquiries of a III F type, principally respecting the Bulgarian national Dessimiroff [*sic*] and Frau Balnc-Coquard [*sic* – Blanc-Coquard]. He withdrew from D. [Desimiroff] on our instructions, as he was believed to have played with him too rashly.
>
> Of his own accord and without instruction Platiau made the acquaintance of Mrs. L. and produced immediately such important information about her that from then on (about the middle of October) he was set exclusively to the observation of Mrs. L.
>
> With Platiau we have the case of a 19-year old young man with French nationality who claims that he does not feel himself French. During the time of his activity for the German office he always gave an impression of

loyalty and reliability. From the beginning one was struck by his peculiarly unsteady demeanour and his confused state. In the discussion he was very difficult, as it was scarcely possible to keep him to a particular subject. Besides, it had to be constantly ascertained that he paid no attention to the assignments and instructions he had received. The present interrogation revealed that he as good as never followed the instructions given but perpetually, following his own idea, shot fantastically off the target. Concerning his reports it can be said that he has, by and large, told the truth but in a kind of fantastic cloak that left nothing definite on close investigation. It also appears that he has combined in a wild fantasy facts which have nothing to do with each other. I have concerned myself closely with the man and after scrupulous investigation of what he has done must come to the conclusion that he cannot fulfil the requirements which the systematic III F work demands.

Sonderführer Wachter concluded that, when Stella and Platiau confronted each other, the latter came across as uncertain and confused:

He is rather depressed over the arrest. His fits of linking matters up which have no basic connection point to a fantasy amounting to disease. Platiau is not capable of clear reasoning, as he has not the capacity to recognize the basic essentials of a case. This realization was come to again and again during his questioning. He is obviously not guilty of malice. There are, however, signs which point to a psychotic. He was in no way the intellectual equal of Mrs. Lonsdale. She quickly saw through him and consequently could easily pump him. The persons arrested in the same case are being dealt with according to the detailed discussion of this hearing with the G.F.P. and also the necessary investigations.

The investigations so far have not produced evidence that Mrs. Lonsdale was active for the English intelligence service after the occupation of France. There simply remains the supposition that as an Englishwoman she would take advantage of every opportunity to do something for her country. Even if the suspicion crops up again that she remained in France in order to work for the I.S., there are just as many grounds for arguing to the contrary. Her statements over the moral depravity of English Society and the impression she has gained of German officers and soldiers as a means of understanding the German Movement, are enlightening.

Mrs. Lonsdale give in any case the impression of a very intelligent woman with enough strength to ~~follow~~ pursue a particular objective.

A final judgement on whether the statements which she has made during the interrogation correspond with the facts cannot, of course, be given.

Chapter 29

The *Sunday Express* Affair

More trouble was brewing for MI5. Sylvia Cooper-Smith contacted Tar Robertson seeking guidance regarding letters she'd received on 9 May 1947 addressed to her fiancé Lieutenant Commander Patrick O'Leary @ Albert Guérisse. She was leaving SIS and going to Brussels to see him. One of the letters from James H. Critchley, the Legal Manager at the *Daily Express*, stated:

> A lady named (Mrs) Stella Lonsdale is making a claim against the Sunday Express on the ground that she is the young Englishwoman referred to in the paragraph which I have marked in blue pencil and that the statements about her are untrue. She says that she never worked as a Gestapo agent, but on the contrary was in an internment camp; that there were no love letters written to her by the chief of the Gestapo at Nantes or anywhere else, and no pictures showing the "happy couple" together. She says she was not met by Scotland Yard on arrival.
>
> It will be necessary for us to prove that she admitted to you that she had been working as a Gestapo agent and that she was then anxious to serve in your organisation; also that there were bundles of love letters written to her by the chief of the Gestapo at Nantes and a number of pictures of her and him in her trunks which she left behind.
>
> We shall be obliged to you if you will send an account with as much detail as possible of this lady's call upon you in Marseilles (which she admits) and of what she told you as to her activities and what she wanted to do. Also of the two trunks that she left behind and what you found in them when you opened them. Did you arrange for her passage to England? Assume that you informed the authorities in England of her probable arrival and her history so far as you knew it. Perhaps you will be good enough to indicate what you told the authorities here.
>
> This matter is rather urgent in point of time and we should be obliged if you could write us direct and also tell us where we can communicate with you, or if necessary come over to see you. The only address I have is c/o Miss Cooper-Smith in London.[1]

Critchley enclosed a photograph of Stella Lonsdale to jog O'Leary's memory. In the meantime, she could be contacted c/o Vivian at SIS. O'Leary had obtained approval for publication of an article in the *Sunday Express* from the Admiralty, and the *Daily Express* had first raised the matter with him. Bernard Hill was trying to ascertain his exact position in SIS or MI9 from Vivian.

Tar advised her that the best course of action would be to do nothing, but he would seek a legal opinion, noting, 'She is of the opinion, and I must say I share her opinion, that the visit of PITT-RIVERS to the "Daily Express" was a try-on in an attempt to extract money from the paper on behalf of Mrs. LONSDALE.' We will meet Pitt-Rivers in the next chapter.

MI5 now faced the prospect of a court case for libel where they would be required to produce certain documents considered secret. This was before the days of the UK Freedom of Information Act (2000), but possibly the earliest cited mention of public interest immunity (PII).[2] A series of exchanges between MI5, the War Office and the *Sunday Express* set out to establish the veracity of the allegations made in O'Leary's article published in the newspaper on 20 April 1947, and MI5's position vis-à-vis what, if anything, they could reveal.[3]

Hill noted that the standard defences to libel actions which the *Sunday Express* would have to compromise or defend were: (a) Truth, or justification, (b) Privilege, (c) Fair comment. Of these, only (a) would provide a watertight defence. A plea of justification would require that the newspaper produce witnesses and/or documents to prove that Stella had worked as a Gestapo agent, had received love letters from the 'chief of the Gestapo', and was met by Scotland Yard when she arrived in England. In his opinion it would be

> necessary to show not only that she was in touch with the Gestapo at Nantes, but that she intended to assist the enemy; otherwise it is not fair comment to call her a Gestapo agent. The innuendo from the paragraph clearly implies that her motive was an improper one; from all our enquiries into her case as disclosed by this file, we were unable to prove any treacherous intent … The libel action which is in its essence a civil dispute between a citizen and a newspaper tried in a civil Court, would thus result in highly secret matters being freely disclosed in open Court. There could be no question of the trial being in camera.

But he asserted that 'All our very extensive enquiries into her case failed to substantiate treacherous intent, or rather failed to establish in a legal sense any treacherous intent'. If the case went ahead 'I am afraid it will raise highly complex and difficult legal questions, so complex in fact that I would strongly advise Counsel's opinion being taken … through the Treasury Solicitor'.

Regardless of who O'Leary had worked for, his information was covered by Section 2 of the Official Secrets Act (1911), and while he had obtained permission from the Admiralty to publish the article, that permission only extended to protecting him from prosecution under the Act, but *not* the accuracy of the statements he made. Nor did it give him *carte blanche* to disclose further information. Therefore,

> Without the express approval of the head of his department ... the letters now in the possession of his fiancée cannot be produced in the Court of the Kings Bench Division, nor can he make any amplifying statement disclosing confidential information without the like approval.

Conversely, if the libel action were to proceed, he would become a co-defendant to the action or 'most certainly be subpoenaed by the "Express" solicitors and ... legally bound to attend Court and to testify under pain of imprisonment for contempt if he refuses'. Hill suggested that Vivian consult with 'C' (Sir Stewart Menzies) to determine what information O'Leary could disclose, 'bearing in mind ... that production of State documents cannot be compelled and that a witness cannot be compelled to answer any questions which would incriminate himself or which would be contrary to the national interest or public safety'. An extract from O'Leary's article reads:

> We also sent home an attractive young Englishwoman who contacted me in Marseille, admitted that she had been working as a Gestapo agent, but was now anxious to serve in our organisation. Her husband was a Mayfair "playboy". As soon as she left I came across two trunks she had left behind. I searched them and found bundles of love letters written to her by the Chief of the Gestapo at Nantes, along with a number of pictures showing the happy couple together. I sent these back to London and when the former woman Gestapo agent landed in her native country she found Scotland Yard waiting for her.[4]

But Stella had *not* been a Gestapo agent. The term 'Gestapo' is often given as a generic name for any German intelligence service, unless the organization is specified. If the so-called 'Chief of the Gestapo at Nantes' was meant to be RENÉ, then this was also incorrect – he was *not* the head of the Gestapo in Nantes, as it was the Abwehr for whom he worked, *not* the Gestapo. And as she correctly stated, she had *not* been met by New Scotland Yard when she arrived from Lisbon, but by MI5.

Two documents, originally missing from her file[5] but now included, are a letter (serial 546a) where the date has been redacted (but included in the minute sheet as 10 May 1947) from Vivian at SIS to Dick White at MI5:

> The attached report was written for me by [*redacted*]⁶ a secretary in this office, who, as you will see from the report itself, [*one and a half lines redacted*]
>
> The latter [Guérisse], who is in fact a Belgian by nationality is no doubt well known to you, as are most certainly Stella LONSDALE and Captain PITT RIVERS.
>
> You will be interested to see this last oddity turning up again as the champion of the notorious Stella.⁷

And one from Vivian (serial 547a) [*date redacted*] to White:

> In continuation of my [*redacted*] 9.5.47 on the subject of Stella LONSDALE, etc., I now enclose a letter addressed by the Daily Express to Lieutenant-Comdr. Patrick O'Leary. [*two lines redacted*]
>
>> I feel that you would wish to know that Mrs. LONSDALE is proceeding with her action against the Daily Express, especially as some of the questions which the Daily Express ask O'Leary to answer seem to come into your purview.
>>
>> Another rather interesting letter which is passing through [*three-quarters of a line redacted*] a copy of which I am enclosing, is from a certain Col. E.N. WILLYAMS of St. Columb Minor, Cornwall [*sic*].
>>
>> I am returning both letters to [*redacted*] for forwarding.⁸

Colonel E.B. Willyams's (Royal Engineers) letter dated 20 April 1947 sent to O'Leary said that his former adjutant had drawn his attention to the article. He referred to John Lonsdale being involved in the Mayfair robbery and added:

> The husband was a Sapper in the Unit I commanded in Nantes in 1939/40 and as wives were not allowed there, I did my d---dest to get rid of her without the slightest success. I did manage to part them by sending him on a draft for Norway. I often used to see the lady in one of the hotels in Nantes but, having read the case of Uriah the Hittite⁹ had to be very careful never to be introduced to her.¹⁰

Hill advised that SIS should not assist O'Leary any more than was legally necessary. If they agreed to the *Sunday Express*'s requests they would be creating a harmful precedent by 'virtually ... assisting that paper to defend a civil action, i.e. as a Government Department they would be taking sides in a civil dispute ... [and] they will be morally bound to assist other of their employees in similar cases', as well as incurring strong criticism of SIS from members of the press not sharing the same political views as the *Express*:

[I]f a member of an Intelligence organisation writes a story, then he must accept full responsibility for any libel action which may result, and that it should be made abundantly clear in each case that he can obtain no official assistance for defending any such action ... This case, if it proceeds, will ultimately raise highly complex and difficult legal questions, and I think it will almost certainly necessitate Counsel's opinion being taken.

Tar preferred that Hill communicate with Vivian directly to elaborate on the legal position, and inform him that he had seen Miss Cooper-Smith and told her to take no action.

On 27 June John Gordon, Editor of the *Sunday Express*, sent the Under-Secretary of State for War a page from an instalment of a series of articles written by O'Leary which he said had been passed by the Admiralty 'so far as security reasons went':

Since this article appeared we are being pressed by a Mrs. Stella Lonsdale who says that these paragraphs refer to her and that her friends have identified her with the Englishwoman referred to in the paragraphs. We have had a visit from a solicitor on her behalf, and all that she is demanding is money, and they are apparently relying upon the assumption that we shall be unable to prove that what was said about her was true.

In order for us to resist this claim it would be necessary for us to prove that there were love-letters written to her by the Chief of the Gestapo in Nantes or that there were pictures showing the "happy couple" together.

We may say that she admits that she contacted Lieutenant Commander O'Leary in Marseille and that she came home through his intermediation. It is also a fact that she was interned immediately she arrived in England and was kept in internment until after the war had ended. She is the wife of a "Mayfair playboy" – that is to say, of a man named Lonsdale who, just prior to the war, was sent to gaol for an affair at the Dorchester Hotel in which a lady was robbed of some jewellery.

We have enquired at Scotland Yard and are informed by them that this lady's possessions would not be with them, but would probably be with M.I.5 at the War Office. It is frequently done by the Chief Commissioner of Scotland Yard to permit a newspaper to see any such papers as they may have under a pledge of confidence, and if necessary the papers are produced in Court under a subpoena.

In order to meet this lady's claim it is necessary for us to know whether any such letters are or have been in the possession of the authorities in this country, and the nature of the contents of such letters, as if they are of an affectionate or friendly nature this would be, in our opinion, sufficient proof of this lady's relationship with the Gestapo agent in question. We should be very much indebted to you if permission could be given to the officers [in] charge of any such documents to give us the information which we desire. No use whatever would be made of any such information, but if there are letters of such a nature it would enable us to take a stand against this woman's claims.

Gordon had his facts wrong about the jewellery robbery – it was *not* the Dorchester Hotel but the Hyde Park Hotel; it was *not* a lady, but a man (Étienne Bellenger) who had been robbed; and Stella was *not* immediately interned the moment she arrived in England on 5 November 1941, but on 23 January 1942.

John McCulloch, the War Office's Chief Press Officer, met with Hinchley Cooke and Hill in Room 055 of the War Office to discuss the *Sunday Express*'s letter and their request to know the contents of the documents and letters which Gordon alleged were in MI5's possession. While MI5 admitted to having the letters, they would only produce them if they were subpoenaed, but would 'claim privilege of production on the grounds that the documents were State documents'. But even if the documents were produced, they would merely show that Stella was the Gestapo chief's mistress, but *not* that she was a Gestapo agent. If O'Leary were subpoenaed, he would need his department's permission to expand on his report, thereby committing a breach of the Official Secrets Act (1911). For the *Sunday Express* to succeed in a plea of justification they would have to prove beyond doubt that Stella was a Gestapo agent, which could only be done by bringing all the evidence presented to the Advisory Committee before the King's Bench Court, something the Home Office would prohibit because of an undertaking they had given in Parliament. But this would still only prove that she had 'hostile associations', *not* that she had been a Gestapo agent.

There was also the likelihood of the *Sunday Express* having to pay and make a claim under their libel policy. Hill hoped that as a result of their negotiations the newspaper would settle the claim. But if the libel action went ahead and MI5 were forced to produce the documents he proposed – subject to Sir Percy Sillitoe's approval – to offer Hinchley Cooke as a witness, who would 'first claim privilege for the documents and, if this is overruled, produce them; he will merely say that M.I.5 have no evidence to show that Stella LONSDALE was a Gestapo agent'. (Sillitoe had succeeded Sir David Petrie as Director General of MI5 in the spring of 1946.)

It was pointed out to Gordon that even if they could get the court to order the papers to be produced, 'there was no proof that the woman had, as the article alleged, been an enemy agent. Had she been she would have already been put on trial'. Critchley was more concerned in getting an 'admission that letters of an amorous nature were in your possession … [which] could be used as an argument in favour of mitigation of damages'.

After Stella's escape from France O'Leary had gone through her apartment in Marseille and found photographs, one of which depicted her with four German officers who were toasting her with champagne,[11] which he had couriered to Spain. Those photographs, if they exist, are not included in any of her MI5 files.

A complication arose when the newspaper threatened to obtain a court order for MI5 to produce the letters, and would 'subpoena a responsible body to attend Court and produce the same', in an attempt to mitigate damages. Hill pointed out that while the letters contained no information which might reveal how MI5 or SIS had analysed them, there were concerns that the chemicals used to detect a fairly high-grade German secret ink might be revealed, as well as a high-grade test used as a 'general counter measure' widely used by German censorship, which Hedger suspected would be 'known to other Powers'. Since the tests had disfigured the letters, they were hardly in a fit state to be produced in court, so Hill sought Sillitoe's advice.

With a civil dispute pending in the King's Bench Division between two private citizens Hill thought that MI5 would be 'called to comment if they assist one such private person to the disadvantage of the other, unless it were compelled by the Court so to do':

> [T]his Department has never hithertofore appeared in any Court of law, being an advisory department; any action taken by another department on our advice is the administrative act of that other department and as such we are not responsible in law. In this case, however, there is no other department to whom we can pass the letters … the only major department which can be compelled in any Court of law to produce the documents … no Judge would compel this Department to produce the documents, and I feel that the action of the Express is in the nature of a first-class bluff.

However, Hinchley Cooke, who was their primary public face in court cases, *had* represented MI5 in various spy cases brought to trial up to this time, but the term 'MI5' was never used, since the agency was not on a statutory footing, and therefore technically didn't exist.[12]

If MI5 were to maintain their refusal to produce the documents, they would need to involve the Treasury Solicitor 'to watch our interests and to brief Treasury Counsel in resisting any such application for the production of the documents'. Vivian also needed to be kept informed, 'being the responsible department which recovered the letters'. Before doing so, Hill sought Sillitoe's advice on MI5's policy towards maintaining that refusal to produce the letters, or whether he was 'satisfied that, from the point of view of public policy, we can comply with the request of the Sunday Express'. Sillitoe appended a handwritten note underneath:

SLB.
1. Maintain refusal to produce the letters.
2. Consult with the Treasury Solicitor in case the Sunday Express press for production. As this my own view (?)
3. We could not expect to get protection from a Minister (of War!) by way of an affidavit nor do I see … the newspaper can fail in obtaining a Court order.
4. If they succeed I should personally favour sending them with the "office boy" i.e. somebody who knows absolutely nothing about the case and therefore can give no answers except namely (?) formal ones.

The Treasury Solicitor, Sir Thomas Barnes, was informed that the *Sunday Express* had been advised of Sillitoe's decision to 'maintain refusal to produce the letters'. Therefore, the newspaper would have to make an application to the Court for an Order directing the Security Service to appear for the Director General and to oppose any such Order on the grounds: 'a) that the documents are State documents, or, in the alternative, b) that it would be contrary to public policy so to produce them.' Sir Thomas cited *Asiatic Petroleum Company v. the Anglo Persian Oil Company, 1916 (1 K.B. 822)*[13] as an example where 'privilege from production of documents for disclosure is not limited to public official documents of a political character but relates to all documents which cannot be disclosed in the public interest.' The facts were:

a) that the said letters came into the possession of the Security Service in the course of its official duties as a counter-espionage organisation,
b) that mere production of the letters themselves would not, without other expert evidence, establish that they were addressed to Mrs. LONSDALE or that they were written to her by the chief of the Gestapo at Nantes,
c) that the letters came into the possession of the Security Service through secret channels, they having been seized by another Intelligence organisation operating in enemy-occupied territory in war-time,
d) that the letters have been by the Security Service submitted to certain tests for secret writing and bear the marks of such testing on their face.
   Privilege from production cannot be claimed in respect of the said documents.

Sir Percy was confident that Sir Thomas could be relied upon to protect MI5's interests. Hill added that should the case come to trial, other intelligence organizations, as well as the Home Office and the Admiralty, would become involved if the DR.18B proceedings became an issue. Therefore, Treasury counsel would need to be briefed to oversee those organizations' interests.

The *Sunday Express* was proving difficult but Sillitoe dug in his heels and referred all future communications to the Treasury Solicitor. Hill told Vivian that SIS needed to establish O'Leary's 'exact position … within your organisation' and 'precisely how the letters in question came into your possession.' The records showed that MI5 had received them in 1942 from SIS who had subsequently passed them to MI5 as the lead department in Stella's case (see Appendix 2). He stressed that he would do everything to protect SIS's interests, and had been deliberately vague when explaining their involvement to the Treasury Solicitor. Before further steps could be taken it was important to establish whether O'Leary had in fact obtained permission from the Admiralty or SIS, if he had worked for them.

The Treasury Solicitor's judgement that the letters 'could form the subject of a claim for privilege on the ground that their production would be prejudicial to the public interest', was probably not what MI5 was expecting. Sir Thomas cited the recent case of *Duncan v. Cammell Laird* as an example where a judgement in the House of Lords had been made on withholding documents from production by the Crown.[14] That case in 1942 arose from the sinking of the submarine HMS *Thetis* on 1 June 1939 during sea trials off the coast of Llandudno, Wales, resulting in the loss of ninety-nine lives. Families of those lost claimed damages from Cammell Laird, the shipbuilders in Birkenhead, but the Ministry of Defence instructed the defendants 'not to disclose any details of the ship's construction, on the ground that it would be contrary to the public interest to produce them'.[15] In that case, Lord Simon, the Lord Chancellor, had stated that 'it is not a sufficient ground to justify objection to production that the documents are "State documents".'

If the documents were to be handed back to Stella, they would be subject to disclosure. It was not strictly one of law, but a 'matter for the Minister concerned … whether the public interest would be prejudiced by the production of any particular document.' Sir Thomas suggested that paragraphs (b) or (d) of Hill's letter (above) might be reasons for withholding production, but thought it difficult to adopt that approach considering how much time had elapsed since obtaining the letters and 'the change of circumstances'. It remained an issue of whether the Admiralty had given O'Leary permission to publish the articles, which revealed certain aspects of how the security services operate. He concluded that

If and when a subpoena is served, either the letters will have to be produced at the trial or the subpoena must be answered by a certificate of the Minister that, having seen the letters, he is of the opinion that their production would be contrary to the public interest.

He cautioned that further communications with Gordon would be unwise, and 'a little unfortunate having regard to the attitude which the department wish to adopt that discussions with him have already taken place which seem to have disclosed not only the existence, but also the general purport, of the letters'.[16] Clearly, in its response to the *Sunday Express* MI5 had partially shown their hand prematurely.

Vivian informed Hill that O'Leary had worked for 'a sub-section of M.I.9 whose functions were carried out by personnel seconded to S.I.S. and carrying the title P.15 for S.I.S. purposes', the heads of which were Langley and Neave. MI9's Western European escape line section IS9g was designated P15, one of the production sections of SIS, and a notional branch of MI9's school tasked with recruiting, organizing and supporting escape and evasion circuits. However, another source states that Langley was designated P15, replacing someone known only as IVz or 4Z (whose designation he adopted), and became the point of contact between SIS and MI9, nominally on Brigadier Norman Crockatt's staff, although SIS actually paid his salary.[17]

Vivian recalled hearing about the incident involving Stella in 1942 when Langley was in charge of P15. O'Leary's article *was* submitted to the Admiralty and subsequently SIS, who raised no objection from the security point of view, but no one had considered the question of libel. He was trying to ascertain how the letters reached SIS and who had passed them on to MI5, who he assumed must have been Langley or Neave. Hill concluded that it seemed likely that MI5 had received them from MI9 since 'The representatives of M.I.9 in London, through working at Broadway, were in fact paid and directed by M.I.9 and not by M.I.6; M.I.9 was a department of the War Office, which has now been liquidated'. Except Foot and Langley's account contradicts this. As noted above, Langley was actually paid by SIS *not* MI9, therefore, since Neave also worked for P15, ergo he must have been paid by them too. Nor did they work out of SIS's headquarters at 54 Broadway, but out of Room 900, an office in the Metropole building, and a safe house above Overton's restaurant at 5 St. James's Street, London SW1. It was subsequently established that after Stella had left France O'Leary had broken open her cases and found letters and photographs of her and RENÉ, which he'd sent to London via Donald Darling in Lisbon although he couldn't remember who carried them out of France.

Hill suggested to Vivian that the best solution might be for MI5 to return the letters to Stella and inform the *Sunday Express*:

> Whilst this course would get us out of the present difficulty of production I do not think it would permanently solve the problem; if the action proceeds to trial, it seems certain that not only may Lt. Cmdr. O'LEARY be subpoenaed but a subpoena may well also be received by my Director-General.

Now that the Treasury Solicitor had said that the letters were *not* State documents and had disagreed with the four reasons for withholding them the situation had become more complex. Therefore, whether they could be 'claimed to be privileged from production on the grounds that it would be contrary to the public interest for disclosure on that account' was still open to question in light of the Crown Proceedings Bill becoming law before the libel action could be tried. It would be difficult for the 'appropriate Minister' to intervene and issue a certificate since there was in the article 'material information as to the way in which your Department operated in war-time ... The only way we can be protected adequately is by the issue of the Minister's certificate. There are, of course, practical difficulties in this connection, quite apart from the point mentioned previously'.

The Crown Proceedings Bill became law on 31 July 1947, but did not fully come into force until 1 January 1948. For the first time it enabled civil proceedings to be brought against the Crown, and reasserted the common law doctrine of 'Crown privilege', but by making it for the first time justiciable – the limits upon legal issues over which a court can exercise its judicial authority – it paved the way for the development of the modern law of public interest immunity. Section 28 of the Act gave the courts for the first time the power to order disclosure of documents by the Crown and to require the Crown to answer requests for further information, but with the proviso that the Crown could resist disclosure where this could be 'injurious to the public interest'.[18]

O'Leary sought Wilfred 'Biffy' Dunderdale's advice on how he should respond to requests from the *Sunday Express* that he produce the letters proving that Stella was a Gestapo agent. Dunderdale advised him to inform the *Sunday Express* that he no longer had them in his possession but that they had been forwarded to the authorities in London. When Hill met with Vivian and Dunderdale of SIS to advise them of the latest developments in the case, they decided that SIS would arrange for Collinson[19] in the British Embassy's visa section in Paris to interrogate O'Leary to try to establish exactly what had happened, which would then enable Vivian to decide how much O'Leary would be able to tell the *Sunday Express*. But while Dunderdale suggested that Stella may have admitted to O'Leary that she had been working as an agent for the Germans, Vivian pointed out that:

- SIS was not in any way responsible for O'Leary, and statements made in the field did not necessarily reach the appropriate people in London;
- O'Leary had been solely responsible within MI9 in organizing escape routes;
- Brigadier Crockatt, who had been in charge of MI9, had decreed that the organisation should not become involved in intelligence matters; and
- MI9 personnel were not trained in intelligence work, which was why SIS had a liaison with them in order to extract intelligence from their records.

Once Vivian had received Collinson's report, he would contact Hill. In the meantime, O'Leary was told not to do anything until instructed otherwise, and definitely not to get in touch with the *Sunday Express*.

Vivian also passed on to Hill a minute dated 5 June 1942 addressed to Section VB4 (Mackenzie) and signed by Langley, which read as follows:

1. In the attached envelope are Stella Clive Lonsdale's personal papers despatched by O'LEARY from Marseille.
2. Would you forward them to the proper authorities in M.I.5 after you have extracted any information which might be of use to you?

A pencilled note in [*redacted*] handwriting dated 6 June 1942 reads, 'Given to Mills of B.1.a on 5.6.42.' Hill informed Vivian that they would let him know what MI5 proposed to do. He explained to Sillitoe the Treasury Solicitor's doubts based on the Crown Proceedings Bill coming into law before the libel action was tried in court, and that because of the recent House of Lords' judgement on *Duncan v. Cammell Laird*, the letters could not be claimed as privileged from production as State documents. But if MI5 did, on the grounds of public interest, they would be required to obtain a certificate from 'the Minister' stating that production of the letters would in some way or other prejudice the work of the Security Service.

Hill's note to Sillitoe is significant since it explains exactly to whom at that time the Security Service was answerable, there being no legal Statute until the Security Service Act (1989) – apart from the Maxwell Fyfe Directive of 1952, which became the de facto constitution of MI5 – and MI5's position vis-à-vis their response to the request for the letters.[20] They needed to decide whether (a) they should try to obtain the necessary certificate; (b) obey the subpoena and produce the letters in court; or (c) return them to Stella and advise the *Sunday Express*:

As to a):
The Treasury Solicitor seems to be under a misapprehension as to the Minister accountable for the Security Service. He seems to think that the Under Secretary of War is the accountable Minister whereas, under the Prime Minister's Directive, the Director General of the Security Service is accountable only to the Prime Minister. If any attempt is to be made, therefore, to obtain the necessary certificate, the original approach would presumably be made by the Director General to Sir Edward Bridges [Cabinet Secretary, 1938–46 and Permanent Secretary to the Treasury and Head of the Home Civil Service, 1946–56].

The question the Director General has to decide is whether the work of the Security Service would be hampered by the disclosure of the said letters. To assist in coming to a decision on this point, I would place before you my own views and the result of certain enquiries I have made, namely:-

i) In my view, the question of whether the work of the Security Service could be impeded by the production of the letters in Court is a question solely for the decision of the Director General of the Security Service. The Director General alone can advise the Prime Minister on this point, he alone possessing the necessary qualifications; I do not think it is a matter for the Law Officers of the Crown, as the Treasury Solicitor seems to think.

ii) As will be seen, the Treasury Solicitor is of the opinion that the fact that the letters have been submitted to certain tests for secret writing is no reason to refuse to produce them in open Court. The Director General may here care to consider Mr. Hedger's report at serial 574a [mentioned above] from which it will be seen that certain secret tests were applied and that Mr. Hedger is of the opinion that the work of the Security Service, both offensively and defensively, would be rendered more difficult if foreign Powers were to become aware of our use of these tests. Mr. Hedger's report would not be strictly relevant to the issue as to whether or not the letters should be produced, but would seem to be a bar to the Security Service voluntarily returning the letters to Stella LONSDALE; in view of the unprincipled character of this lady, the chances of her selling the letters to the Russian Embassy cannot be discounted. It may well be that, if claim be made to the letters, we shall be forced to return them, but I think we should wait until such a claim be made and then consider whether application cannot be made to the Court for their destruction under the Defence Regulations.

iv) Enquiries made by Colonel Vivian show that Lt. Cmdr. O'LEARY was not employed at any material time by M.I.6 but by M.I.9, a department of the War Office responsible for organising escapes by prisoners-of-war, which department is now defunct and its remaining functions are carried out by M.I.1(a). My interview with Colonel Vivian and the substance of what I agreed with him is reported in Minute 573. If the Prime Minister, on the advice of the Director General and possibly also in consultation with the Lord Chancellor [Lord Jowitt], thought fit to issue such certificate, not only would it be a complete answer to the difficulties of the Security Service in this particular case as, the letters not being before the Court, no verbal evidence amplifying or explaining them would be relevant, but it would also have a wide salutary effect throughout the Press world; the Press would realise that they could in future expect no help from the Security Service, thus having them more careful in publishing stories which would embarrass the Security Service.

v) To sum up, the difficulty as I see it is that no reason alone is sufficient for the necessary advice to be tendered to the Prime Minister, and the matter is more complicated by the fact that both M.I.6 and the Admiralty took no security objection to the publication of the original article. Nevertheless, the Director General may well feel that the cumulative effect of the whole of the circumstances of this case, when combined with the resulting publicity, might harm the work of the Security Service and would thus justify his consulting Sir Edward Bridges on the matter and obtaining his views. I would advise against a direct approach at this stage to the Prime Minister himself, as it is difficult to particularise the grounds on which it can be said that the work of the Security Service would be impeded by the production of the letters.

As to b) and c):

In view of Mr. Hedger's report, it would not seem practicable at this stage to adopt recommendation c). If, therefore, the Director General is of opinion that no approach can be made to obtain privilege from production of the letters, I advise that we await the subpoena and then send an officer to the Court to produce the letters, hoping that the matter will end there and meeting any further difficulty as it may arise.

Sillitoe met with Gordon over a convivial lunch on 15 August. Gordon was receptive, and confident that 'we shall suffer no embarrassment over this case' when Sillitoe explained MI5's position to him. Sillitoe was confident that the case would be settled out of court and nothing more would come of it. Gordon gave his word that the matter would go no further, and that MI5 would neither be required to testify in court nor to produce the documents. As a quid pro quo, Sillitoe promised Critchley that MI5 would give him as much assistance as he needed to bluff Stella in order to avoid damages but, he emphasized, this was all on an unofficial basis.

Nothing was heard by the *Express* for two months since a visit from Stella's solicitors, so it was thought unlikely that she would proceed with the case. Hill concluded that when O'Leary had written his article, 'he had no real grounds for thinking that Stella was a Gestapo agent – certainly not in my opinion sufficient grounds to justify the paragraph in question in any libel action, where in a plea of justification strict proof is required'. That conclusion was borne out when Collinson interviewed O'Leary.

O'Leary explained to him that he'd known through Garrow and Prassinos that Stella was one of Garrow's agents, and had contacted her when Garrow was arrested in October 1941. He'd been warned about her reliability and the many lovers she had had but when he first met her he hadn't interrogated her, so Collinson asked him whether she'd admitted to being a Gestapo agent: 'If the answer is in the affirmative, testimony of witnesses will be important, but it is almost certain that she did not make this admission, judging by the evidence on the files at present.' 'No,' O'Leary replied, confirming that there was no hard evidence, merely his own intuition. Collinson warned him that his allegation was pretty weak and would not stand up to in-depth scrutiny or cross-examination, 'and we shall all, as an intelligence organisation, look pretty foolish in a court of law'.

O'Leary emphasized that Stella had had no desire to return to England, but after interviewing her, even though he had no proof, he felt that she would prove dangerous to him in France and wanted her to leave as soon as possible. She was sent to England by plane from Marseille to Lisbon via Madrid, travelling on her own passport. He told her that

> if she returned to England, she would be sent back to France with a most important mission and that I felt I myself was too small in the Intelligence world to handle a woman of her calibre. LONSDALE was so convinced that she would return to France with a mission that she left behind, with me, the heaviest items of her luggage.

There was no doubt who had written the letters, although 'I am not now able to give my reasons in detail, as they are no longer clear in my memory, but I think that I noticed that the writing on the photos and that of the letters was the same'. His inability to identify RENÉ after only a few years had elapsed since he'd found the photographs may be explained by his torture at the hands of the SS at Natzweiler and Dachau.

When asked what evidence he had for assuming that the letters were between the local head of Gestapo and Stella Lonsdale, since they were signed only with a single initial, he replied:

> I have never interrogated Stella LONSDALE, and if I had ever adopted the attitude of an 'interrogator', I would never have known anything from her and she would never have left France. Instead, I let her think that she was completely in my confidence, and I just let her talk. In this way, I learnt from her herself that a German officer whom she herself named as the chief of the Gestapo at Nantes, was very much in love with her, and that in order to see her he obtained for her the necessary laissez-passer to cross the demarcation line. She also said that this German officer had gone so far as to tell her of the German plans to attack Gibraltar. After LONSDALE's departure from France, I broke open her cases and found a packet of letters tied together with photographs of her and this German officer, whom I recognised, owing to LONSDALE having previously shown me photographs of him. I would like to point out that I have never had any doubt in mymind as to the writer of the letters in question. I am not now able to give my reasons in detail, as they are no longer clear in my memory, but I think that I noticed that the writing on the photos and that of the letters was the same.

Stella liked to to impress people about who she knew; by promoting RENÉ to the rank of 'Chief of the Gestapo at Nantes', and not Meissner's assistant, she had elevated his status to make herself appear more important. Given the warnings from Garrow and Prassinos of her unreliability, it seems strange that O'Leary hadn't questioned or interrogated her more closely about her relationship with the Germans and RENÉ. Nor had any witnesses been present during that interview, so anything she said was simply his word against hers. Yet the fact that he'd learned from her that she'd been intimately acquainted with this so-called 'Chief of the Gestapo at Nantes' and received important information from him was not an admission of guilt, nor incontrovertible proof that she'd actually been working for the Germans. It was simply a case of 'hostile association'.

Hill wrote to Vivian on 4 September that:

I hope this point will now prove to be academic, as I am confident that by reason of the steps taken by my Director-General we shall suffer no embarrassment over the case. I think it now extremely unlikely that either your department or mine will be called upon to testify, or my Department called upon to produce the letters.

There seems also some doubt as to whether Stella will proceed with her threatened action, as my Director-General was informed by the Editor of the Express only last month that the Express had not heard anything about this matter for some two months.

This seemed to be the end of the matter, as no further documentation exists to suggest that Stella pursued her libel case.

Chapter 30

'A Champagne-loving Brunette'

After her release Stella lived at 3 Seymour Place, London W1 close to Marble Arch, from 22 August 1945 but continued to remain on both the P&PO and MPO (Military Permit Office) Stop Lists until well into 1949, 'in view of this woman's unsatisfactory background'. During this time Sidoroff lived at 27 Sherwood Court, Seymour Place, W1 from 14 August to 3 November 1945, then at 157 Holland Park, NW10, employed as barman at West End Lane Club, 86 West End Lane, NW6.[1]

The 'champagne-loving brunette with a past that the term "checkered" could hardly begin to describe', met Captain George Henry Lane-Fox Pitt-Rivers over cocktails at the Ritz where she was 'initially the one serving them rather than partaking'.[2] Anthony Pitt-Rivers, George's son added, 'It was the imprisonment that formed an initial bond between Stella and my father (not ignoring the fact that she was on the lookout for financial security) when, rather incongruously, they met having tea at the Ritz.'[3]

The twice-divorced Pitt-Rivers, described by Graham Mitchell of MI5's F3 as 'a man of depraved character', was an anthropologist and eugenics expert, a cousin of Clementine Churchill, as well as second cousin to Lady Diana Mitford. He was also a member of The Link, the Fascist January Club, a known Mosley-ite and Nazi supporter, although 'not known to be openly a member of the B.U.F.'.[4] This had led to his being interned under DR.18B (1a), spending 1940–42 in Brixton and Liverpool prisons, and at No. 7 Winter Quarter Camp on Ascot racecourse, formerly used by Bertram Mills's circus.[5]

Stella began working for Pitt-Rivers as his secretary at his home at Hinton St. Mary, Dorset, but according to Bradley Hart 'it was obvious it was more'; their relationship was 'tempestuous but enduring', and 'Her own libertine sexual attitudes were much in line with his, and among the services she provided was the management of his casual love affairs on the condition that none of them would become permanent and threaten her status in the household'.[6] According to Hart and F. Landis MacKellar:

> Pitt-Rivers took up with Stella, a young woman whose past marriages included Christopher Mainwaring Lonsdale [sic], one of the upper-class perpetrators of the brutal February 1937 [sic] Hyde Park Hotel jewel

robbery. She had enjoyed a good war in Occupied France, working for both German and English intelligence and exercising her charms with equal success on German officers and French resistance fighters before being arrested and imprisoned in England. Her MI5 interrogation officer uncharitably dismissed her as "a sewer."[7]

She merits only a brief mention in Pitt-Rivers' heavily weeded MI5 file in a note dated 17 September 1947 referring to his visit to the *Daily Express* regarding the O'Leary libel case:

> I see that PITT RIVERS' name has been coupled with Stella LONSDALE's by S.I.S. in the report at 546a in PF.63191 [Stella's file, KV2/739]. If you have no objection I should like to take an extract from this report for PITT RIVERS' P.F. (an open file), and should also be grateful if you would give me an indication of what information from the Lonsdale case may be suitably passed to the Chief Constable.[8]

Bernard Hill expressed no objection to a summary of the SIS report being forwarded to the Chief Constable of Dorset, but cautioned that 'It would not be advisable … to mention the libel case save in the barest outline, more particularly as it seems more than probable that no proceedings have yet been instituted'.[9]

In 1949 Pitt-Rivers went to bat over the case of Mathilde Carré who had been tried in a Paris court, found guilty of treason for her part in the betrayal of the Interallié network, and sentenced to death, later commuted to life imprisonment in 1950, but released in 1954.[10] Matthew Sweet suggests that it was Stella who had asked him to plea for clemency in Mathilde's case, both having been in Aylesbury and Holloway prisons together. Writing to Lord Selborne, the wartime minister at the Ministry of Economic Warfare, Pitt-Rivers's diatribe or rant in defence of Carré purported to 'clear the air', urging the War Office to stop what he represented as a miscarriage of justice.

While they never married, Stella took Pitt-Rivers's name by deed poll and stayed with him until he died on 17 June 1966, although she is often referred to incorrectly as his third wife or common-law wife.[11] By 1958 she was living at 64 Berkeley Mansions, Seymour Street, London, W1, and from 1960–8 in Flat 14 (owned by him), 77 Cadogan Gardens, Chelsea, London, SW3 (he kept his car at nearby 16 Clabon Mews).[12]

In 1963 she married Raoul R.F. Maumen,[13] referred to as 'a conman from Marseille', and 'a Frenchman with a questionable past that she claimed to have known from the French Resistance but in reality had been a racketeer during the war … with a scurrilous reputation and questionable connections'.[14] The couple later moved to 'Stelladoux', a house on a vineyard in Provence. In the early 1970s, Maumen showed up on Michael Pitt-Rivers's doorstep – George's eldest son – with a piece of family silver as proof of his connection with Stella:

> He claimed that Stella was threatening him and asked for whatever protection could be offered. When he was told that nothing could be done, he returned to France and was found dead in his bathtub soon after. It turned out that the bottle of whiskey he had been drinking that evening contained a strong dose of household disinfectant. Whether or not Maumen took his own life was never fully established, but there were rumours that he might have been assisted in the process by his less-than-savoury acquaintances. Either way, no one ever faced criminal charges in his death.[15]

Anthony Pitt-Rivers added cryptically, 'He might have done it on his own. But equally, he might have had help.' Could that help have come from Stella? Indeed, Sweet suggests that

> there's a strong chance that she killed her last husband by injecting him with floor polish. Certainly getting too close to her could be hazardous … But as one of her friends said to me, "If you were asking her the questions that you're asking now, you'd probably be dead … She'd poison that coffee." He was joking … but not really![16]

Was this perhaps an allusion to the joke she'd made to Odette Châtenet about poisoning her coffee if she were to fall in love with RENÉ when she met him?

Even after her death in London on 9 January 1994 aged 81,[17] controversy still haunted her, and continues to this day. It emerged that she may have been responsible for the disposal and dispersal of the Pitt-Rivers collection of ethnographic artifacts from the museum in Farnham, Dorset, established in 1891 by George's grandfather, Lieutenant General Augustus Henry Lane-Fox Pitt-Rivers, the eminent Victorian ethnologist, archaeologist and antiquarian, to finance her expenses. Exactly when this is alleged to have occurred is still open to debate as opinions and evidence differ – but that's another story!

Afterword

When Stella went to France in January 1940, it was not thought that the Germans would invade, but if they did, the Maginot Line would hold them back. As history has proved, this was not the case. But once the Germans had invaded, was it out of sheer ignorance that she thought she would not come to any harm, or a vicarious thrill for danger and espionage which made her stay on? Or was there an ulterior motive? Was she at any time working for British Intelligence?

An unsubstantiated claim that she had been 'persuaded to "work for England" by acting as a link between SIS and German intelligence'[1] was vehemently denied by SIS and SOE who emphasized that she had never worked for them, not even unofficially, apart from supplying them with intelligence about the 'Channel dash' incident (which was ignored), and agents such as Gaessler. Since SIS has declared that their files will never be made public (except those which have already been seen by their official historian, the late Keith Jeffrey), we may never know the truth. So how then did her address book come to contain the names and addresses in Lisbon of Mary Johnstone and Mary Johns, both wives of SIS officers? Even though the Germans charged her with espionage they found no evidence that she had been actively working for British Intelligence. As with many spies, 'The hallmarks of a narcissistic personality are unwarranted feelings of self importance or self-esteem (grandiosity), a sense of entitlement, and a lack of empathy for others.'[2]

When John Lonsdale was arrested for his part in the Hyde Park Hotel jewellery robbery he claimed to be 'linked to the Secret Service', but Chief Inspector Leonard Burt was unconvinced.[3] Without access to his own MI5 file (PF.46035), if it still exists, Stella's suggestion that he was recruited by the 'I.S.' (Intelligence Service) and carried out a variety of missions, such as supplying detailed reports on the situation in Spain before the Civil War, cannot be corroborated. She told the Abwehr that his service in France was a cover for observing the troops for British Intelligence. Of course, all of this could have simply been her bragging again to impress her captors.

In January 2019 I enquired of MI5 whether they still had Lonsdale's file and if so, whether they would release it to the National Archives. In order for them to proceed, they replied, a death certificate or some other proof of his death was required, suggesting that possibly his file may still exist in the MI5 Registry, and should this proof materialize, they could process my application. So far, I have been unable to find any record of his death, so the trail has gone cold.

How was it then, with John's less-than-stellar career in the RAF and the various army regiments in which he served briefly, that he was able to come and go willy-nilly without anyone clueing in to his being so unreliable and not receiving a court martial and/or dishonourable discharge? Unless this was covered up by the War Office. An examination of his service record may reveal more, but not being a relative of the Lonsdale family, it is harder to obtain, and the information often restricted. Most likely, John Lonsdale was never any more a spy than Stella, but a fantasist and a petty criminal.

Whether Stella ever worked for the Abwehr was a nagging doubt in MI5's collective mind which failed to go away. The fact remains that she *had* admitted to agreeing to work for the Germans, as witness her statements to the Abwehr and the Advisory Committee, 'with the mental reservation it was a means to get out and to be free and escape'. Exactly when she agreed is open to debate – was it (a) in the car going to Angers with Platiau? (b) before being confronted by Dernbach, Meissner and RENÉ? Or (c) before or after either of the tribunals when she met with Meissner? The Advisory Committee suggested that her offer was made under duress,[4] but that duress was lifted when the second tribunal released her. Whenever it was, she was motivated for idealistic reasons – that she detested English Society, a society of which she was an intrinsic part and upon which she fed like a parasite and continued to enjoy.

The allegations that she had betrayed various members of the escape network are for the most part unfounded. Elisabeth Haden-Guest's allegation that Garrow's arrest was partly due to Stella's interference was based on her fundamental dislike of her, so her remarks must be treated with caution, and the late Jean Fourcade, a member of the 'Pat Line', found some of Elisabeth's claims in her memoir to be unreliable.[5] Garrow's betrayal was largely due to Harold Cole. Mesdames Martineau and Dazy alleged that Stella was responsible for the betrayal and arrest of their father and son respectively, but no concrete evidence exists. Albert Guérisse's (Patrick O'Leary) allegation that Stella had been a 'Gestapo agent' was largely based on instinct and an inadequate interview with her, and would not have held up to cross-examination in a court of law.

The testimonies obtained by Courtenay Young from the French authorities in 1945 mostly serve to corroborate some of the facts of her story as they were told to MI5 at various times, but do not incriminate her as a spy, only as a pathological liar. Those statements were obtained at the end of the war, long after MI5 and the Home Office had made the decision to intern her under DR.18B in 1942. She was a female Walter Mitty, a narcissist and egotist, who derived vicarious pleasure out of presenting herself and her husband John as spies for German, British and French Intelligence. However, MI5 officers failed to establish beyond a reasonable doubt that she had committed any act of espionage, treason or treachery, yet they incarcerated her until the end of the war as a person of 'hostile associations'. If there is evidence to the contrary, this either no longer exists, or has yet to come to light.

Prior to obtaining the Abwehr interrogation document, MI5, the Home Office and the Advisory Committee had all agreed that there was insufficient evidence to prove that she had been a spy for the Germans. Now that they had this very admission of her agreeing to work for them, they still had to prove *mens rea* – a guilty mind or criminal intent; the knowledge that the act to be committed was a criminal one.

Under the Treachery Act (1940) it was not necessary to prove treason, nor did someone need to be caught red-handed spying but only, as in Clause 1 of the Act, that the accused had either *committed or intended to commit* [author's emphasis] an act which would endanger life or endanger the forces of the Crown, or *conspire with any other person … with intent to help the enemy* [author's emphasis]. But Stella's confession still does not prove that the *mens rea* had existed and cause for MI5 to have her rearrested and charged under the Act, as she has claimed her offer to work for the Germans was in self-defence, to save herself from being shot. Ironically, the flimsiest of facts did not prevent MI5 from bringing charges against other spies who had come to Britain.[6] Yet in Stella's case no charge was ever brought against her, even though the Act was not suspended until 1946, repealed in 1967 in England, and for the rest of the United Kingdom in 1973. Given that MI5 did not have a strong enough case to get a conviction, it was simply a question of not wanting to waste everyone's time on an expensive trial and an unsatisfactory outcome. The trial would have been held *in camera*, so whatever incriminating facts may have emerged would have remained hidden until her files were released into the public domain in 2002.

Stella's relatively easy escape from France suggests that it may have been officially sanctioned by the Abwehr in order to send her back to Britain as a double agent, possibly with RENÉ's assistance. The ISOS decrypt dated the same day as her arrival from Lisbon: 'Arrival of V man – Simone's report confirmed' revealed that the Germans knew she had arrived in England, and appears to support this. But who had tipped them off? She did not write to Gars until 20 November, so he could not have passed on her arrival to the

Germans, and Frank Viner and Christian Boulanger thought she was still in Lisbon. Therefore, the Germans could have only known of her arrival in Britain if they had been complicit in her escape.

Once back in Britain, there is no evidence that she ever became operational and actively spied for the Germans as a double agent, even though her trip to the Torpedo Development Unit showed that she had the *potential* to obtain top-secret information which could have been passed on to them. And if any of the so-called 'love letters' between her and RENÉ or Christian Boulanger contained coded messages there are no comments in her files, nor any explanation as to whether any attempt was made to decipher their meaning. Therefore, she must be given the benefit of the doubt. However, that doubt still lingered, and that incident was the clincher as far as MI5 was concerned. It was far better to lock her up where she could do no harm, rather than to risk her betraying any information she may have obtained.

Stella was an inveterate name-dropper who liked to brag about her 'brilliant connections with English Society', a society she appeared to also despise and decry. That she should have told the Abwehr how disgusted she was with 'its rottenness and depravity', when her own sexual behaviour must be considered equally degenerate and on a par with those whom she sought to denigrate, is an indication of how she applied a double standard to others' behaviour when the occasion suited her. The many dubious characters who drifted in and out of her life also caused MI5 to regard her with suspicion. They disapproved of her behaviour, and it was a reflection of the social mores of the time that they preferred to keep any explicit details out of their files, even though at that time there was never any intention of making them public. Susan Barton alleged, 'Although I do not think she is certifiable, I should say she has a mental kink.' She was certainly delusional.

How much of her story had she actually embellished, and to what end? Both the Abwehr and MI5 found it very difficult to differentiate between what was fact and what was fiction or fantasy. Above all, Stella Lonsdale still remains a mystery. My feeling is that she was neither a spy for the Germans nor the British, but a fantasist and a nuisance to everyone, who led MI5 such a merry dance that they preferred to err on the side of caution and lock her up.

'É finita la comedia'

Appendix I

Mrs Lonsdale's Secret Ink & Code*

Ink

Procure some white bird droppings. Place in the bottom of a glass container add water and stir up. Leave standing when the dirt will sink to the bottom leaving an opaque liquid on top. This liquid is poured off and ammoniac added. The substance should then turn a clear chrome yellow. With this substance the messages should be written with a steel nib of a type which will not scratch on thick note-paper. The secret writing is only placed on one side of the paper. After writing the paper is steamed before a kettle and is then rubbed lengthwise and crosswise with another piece of the same paper. It is then pressed and dried and an open letter written in ordinary ink on top and across the secret writing.

Developer

Pour some ammoniac into a glass container add nitrate crystals. Take a wad of cotton wool and wash the letter with this substance. This will remove the visible ink. Then develop before the steam from a kettle and the secret writing will come up brown.

There were various methods of indicating whether a particular letter did or did not contain secret writing e.g. a letter containing secret writing was written on a folded double sheet.

Code

RENÉ instructed Mrs. LONSDALE to write her secret messages in code, the code being that which the Germans had obtained from GESSLER. It was of the familiar kind being based on a book and number of four figures. In this case the book selected was André Maurois "CLIMATS" and the number arranged by RENÉ was 1863.

One selected at random a particular page of the book – say page 45 and selected at random a particular line of that page – say 9. One then took the first 10 letters appearing on the selected line and used them as the basis of the code.

---

* From TNA KV2/728

Let it be assumed that the first ten letters of the line 9 on page 45 were G-R-A-N-D-M-O-T-H-E-R. One then writes out G-R-A-N-D-M-O-T-H-E on a squared sheet of paper and on the square beneath each letter one places a numeral indicating the order in which the letters appear in the alphabet. Thus in the example given the result would be as follows:

G	R	A	N	D	M	O	T	H	E
4	9	1	7	2	6	8	10	5	3

One then writes one's complete message into the vacant squares underneath the numerals and then proceeds to re-write it in groups of five letters beginning with column 1 and proceeding vertically down the column then going on to column 2 and etc. This process is duplicated and the message will then appear in code in something like the following form:

MEHMP ELEHA MASTT HJKLM FAIKF

At the commencement of the message one gives the four figure numeral which indicates the selected page and line of the book and which is arrived at as follows:

One takes 4509 (representing page 45 and line 9). To this one adds the selected number in this case 1863 but does not carry forward. The result will be

4509
1863
5362

This number one places at the head of one's message and follows it with another number having the number of letters in the message. Then follows the message itself.

Appendix II

The 'Siegfried' Letters

1. Undated

Dearest, my dearly beloved!
Already you have been gone for a long time. I have again received your two letters this morning, and now there will be no more news for a long time!

I got up this morning feeling very sad and, knowing that I had lost you, not for ever, but nevertheless for long enough. It was very annoying that our last moments together were so unhappy, but it was predestined, and as I explained in my earlier letter, which I sent to the Hotel S., I completely succeeded in getting myself out of the difficulty. My explanation was entirely believed, and I had no difficulties; on the contrary, I was well received, they were happy to see me again and to learn that I had, in order to save time, spoken to the wife of one of my men who had come to see me, in the train, instead of asking her to come to Poitiers for the whole of a day.

I am very well, better than ever, except that I am worried about you; did you arrive safely, are you very tired, did you find everything as you left it, and lastly, do you love me and will you continue to love me in spite of all my faults and in spite of all the obstacles which life has placed in our way.

With regard to my personal feelings, I am very happy in the certainty of your love and of mine, in the idea and the hope of a future, perhaps not very distant, which will reunite us for ever this time, and of a whole life spent together, during which we shall know all those sweetnesses of which, up to the present, we have only been given a small taste.

The moment that I know that you love me, and that you will wait and fight for me as I wait and fight for you, against all the vicissitudes of life, I shall be happy and able to hope and work. We must win as we are on the right road, a love like ours can never die. By brave [*sic*] and of good hope. I can understand that for you, being a woman, many things are harder to bear than for me, and that your intentions and thoughts are weaker and more prone to sudden emotions. But believe me, we live in a life and a world governed by logic and its rules, and those who follow these rules, hard as they may be, must in the long run become victorious. Perhaps it is true that every sorrow is counter-balanced by a pleasure, even during our life on earth and, if this is the case, we are by our present sorrows preparing a glorious future for ourselves.

I think sometimes, faint-heartedly, of the days and weeks and months of separation in front of me, but at the same time I know that one word from your lips, the touch of your hands, will recompense me a thousand times for every second of agony and all trace of these sorrows will vanish. If one is truly in love, bodily separation looses [*sic*] its importance because there exists a spiritual proximity. You are with me, every second of the day and I can talk to you when I wish. Only in appearance are you gone, in reality you have never left me and you can never leave me. Dear, I am waiting for news from you by any means at all. Be careful and good and think of me as I think of you always.

All my love,
S.

2. 21 August 1941 (obviously written from Poitiers):

Write to me before leaving, and also on the way.

Dearest,
I have received your two letters from the Brasserie de l'Univers, and I will act according to your wishes.

There is not the least reason to be worried about the meeting which took place at the Station here. I was able to explain your presence perfectly and not even the least doubt remained in the mind of the little lady who so kindly came to meet me. You know, there is nothing more believing than a jealous woman. If I were philosophic I would say: it is easy to believe what one wants to.

Though on that point: I am feeling better than ever, except for your absence and the misery caused by our separation. And I have the feeling that it was the same for you and that your return journey went off peacefully and without the least interruption. All that remains of that annoying incident at the station at Poitiers is the memory of a few embarrassing moments and of a spoiled leave-taking. I continue to lead quietly my simple life of gardener and bookworm.

I have seen Mr. Marcilly who will, from now on, come up often and visit regularly. You may, if you wish to, entrust him with anything for me, I have asked him to drop in on you.

But once more I beg you not to send me anything. You haven't enough money to go spending it on me, and I can get hold of anything I want here. You know that the nicest present I can have is always a letter or a post-card from you, and that costs nothing. As, however, you won't follow my advice, please let me know the cost of anything you send me, so that I have a chance of paying it back. And as you are leaving, let me know at the same time an address to which I can send the money in question. But once more I beg you not to go to the trouble of sending me anything; there is no need to. Moreover, Mr. Marcilly has promised to send me sweets regularly from Nice – you see, I should do very well in future.

From now on I will not write to you until I hear from you again. If I am forced to write before to communicate some urgent news to you, I will address a letter to the Café Suzanne, Place de Rome, Marseille. Also I am sending a letter there (Café Suzanne) at the same time as this one leaves. In it I have put the two photographs that I have. Unfortunately it was impossible for me to have the others developed because Mr. Marcilly has to leave right away. I will have them done soon at Angers, and they will be waiting for you! Let me know if you were able to pay for the ring. Dear, here I am at the end of the page and I must end. All my love to you and 1,000 kisses.

from S.

The 'annoying incident at the station at Poitiers' refers to when RENÉ and Stella were seen together by his secretary, the 'little lady' who came to see him. Given his phrase about having to communicate urgent news to that address, what might the letter contain that is urgent? It also implies that Marcilly was acting as an agent for him, with its mention of his promise to send him 'sweets' (information) regularly from Nice. That 'Siegfried' should mention a ring is interesting as one was also mentioned by Christian Boulanger in his telegram to Stella of 6 December 1941 where he referred to a ring being sent over to her and that 'RENÉ has been advised of the return of Solange in January confirm date'.

3. Addressed to 'Mademoiselle / Eugenie Landais / Café "Suzanne" / Place de Rome / Marseille / Bouches du Rhone' and dated '*le 20 septembre 1941*':

My dearly beloved!
Our friend had brought me your letter, but unfortunately it was not until yesterday that he arrived at my house, and therefore you must not be surprised that I am so late in replying.

I have written you another letter to the hotel by the same courier. Did you receive the long letter I sent you last week by another of my friends? It was very important.

You know, I am very worried about you, moreover, I don't think that you are very safe there, sometimes I have the feeling that you are completely surrounded by enemies. In these times one cannot trust anyone. I have often advised you to leave, and I repeat that advice today, and I do so more particularly because I am convinced that you will not have any more success in your work there; you are too well known by the opposition. Of course you are free and can decide for yourself what you want to do, isn't it true that you don't want any of my advice. My dearest, through all the misery I have had my love for you has only become greater. I love you today more than I ever believed myself capable of loving anyone. I am practically always thinking of you, in spite of my work, the these [sic] beautiful memories become more and more alive as time passes. And I am cheerful, I know that we shall see each other again, and that soon. Many thanks for all the good things that you have sent me, and especially for the shoes for my mother, which are very very pretty. Unfortunately I cannot tell you whether they fit, for I must first sent [sic] them home. But don't buy any more, my poor mother will have enough with those two beautiful pairs. Thank you as well for all the other things, really you are too good, it is annoying to be overwhelmed with goodness and love without, for the moment, being able to pay it back. My best wishes to Jean. Don't forget to let me have an address when you leave, or should I simply write to Gannat (?). However, I think it would be just as well to restrict our correspondence slightly for the moment; I shall not write any more except for most important events in the family and at home. Keep me advised of everything you do and of your decisions, you know that everything interest [sic] me because I only live for you. Goodbye for now my beloved little wife, love me always and I love you.

Raoul[1]

The author of the letters had signed the first and second ones 'S' for Siegfried, but the third 'Raoul', the name Stella sometimes used for RENÉ, an indicator that perhaps something had changed. And was this friend of theirs Marcilly? A B1a report dated 24 July 1942 refers to 'Gannat', the address given to Stella by Captain Robert (c/o Nelle Heinen, 55, rue St. James, Gannat, Allier) which she'd given RENÉ to write to. 'Keep me advised of everything you do and of your decisions', which could be inferred as an indication that she *was* working for him as an agent of the Abwehr, but in itself is not conclusive proof. The use of the term '*ma petite femme adorée*' ('my beloved little wife') may be a mistranslation simply for 'woman' and not 'wife'. The same report states that '*mes amitiés à Jean*' (my regards to John) meaning that everything was all right, adding, 'This was rather a feeble explanation.' Although the report does not mention it, the quote could be deciphered as:

> Many thanks for all the good things that you have sent me, and especially for the shoes [information she had supplied to him] for my mother [possibly Meissner or Canaris], which are very very pretty [the information was extremely interesting]. Unfortunately, I cannot tell you whether they fit [whether the information was useful], for I must first sent [*sic*] them home [to Abwehr HQ in Paris or Berlin]. But don't buy any more, my poor mother will have enough with those two beautiful pairs.

The term 'our friend' suggests that Christian Boulanger or Marcilly might have been acting as his courier.

Christian Boulanger's undated letter, in which he refers to Stella as 'my dear love', also suggests an intimate relationship with her, as the English translation reveals:

> I telephoned you from the Berlitz my dear love as you would expect me to – whereby in doing so I commited [*sic*] a faux pas in asking for Miss Stella Lonsdale. As of course no one knew of you I bullied everyone, directors, professors, and so on.
>
> I then telephoned a hotel, but you were not there either. I was so upset, I love you very much wanted to tell you once more that I love you.
>
> This evening my aunt (?) is arriving – without my having asked her, so that I will have to fetch (her?) from the station at 8.30.
>
> I have a rendezvous with a client at 8 o'clock. I will pass through Marseille Noailles and deposit this letter at about a quarter to eight, and will be back there again at about 9 o'clock. If, by chance, it will take longer, I will telephone you – all day long I have had a great desire to see you – to hold you in my arms, to kiss you, and to see close again, so very close again the eyes which I love.
>
> So lovingly,
CHRISTIAN[2]

Are these letters – full of pathos, sometimes verging on the poetic, sometimes philosophical, often fatalistic, always affectionate, and constantly harping on about what went before and what might have been – those of desperate men clutching at straws, yearning for their lost love? Or are they written in code disguised as love letters? The language of the love-lorn RENÉ @ Siegfried is syrupy and cloying, verging on the maudlin, indicating he is clearly besotted with Stella. Christian Boulanger's letters are reminiscent of the same style and tone as RENÉ's. So much so, that one might be forgiven for thinking that the two men *were* one and the same, but of course, that was not the case. Their delusion that Stella loved them was simply a sham. In reality, as she had readily admitted, she hadn't loved either of them any more than any other man who came into her life; she had simply been stringing them along. But who was the 'aunt', and why the emphasis on the various times? Are they perhaps a code, or are they simply just an attempt to connect with her?

Appendix III

Notes for Purposes of Investigation in France[*]

A. STELLA's life in Nantes till 19.5.40.
B. STELLA's life in Nantes till arrest.
C. STELLA's life in Nantes after arrest.
D. STELLA's life in Nantes on her one/two visits from Angers.

(a) i. <u>M. SIMON</u>. Police station in rue des Olivettes (2ième Bureau)
  ii. <u>Mme SIMON</u> in close touch with STELLA. Lived by river near Salle des Fêtes in same road as R.E. Mess.
  iii. <u>Abbé Jean LUNEAU</u>, Church of S. Croix (character).
  iv. <u>Sister CUTHBERT</u> of ?Surgilles (character)
  v. <u>HOTEL MOREAU</u> in Bvd Victor Hugo run by KLEINS (check up)
  vi. <u>Taxi driver.</u> White Russian LOSHENSKI [sic]. ?German agent. Asked STELLA to work.
      Check up.
  vii. <u>MARTIN</u> of Commissariat Centrale. Connected with Police. Character.

(b) i. <u>JOLIVET</u> of Prefecture (re Aliens card)
  ii. <u>DUGAST</u> 1 rue St. Julien.
      a) re Poles
      b) re offer to go to Biarritz
      c) life in Nantes
  iii. <u>MARTINEAU</u> 1 rue St. Julien
      a) re Berlitz and employment and stay
      b) whereabouts of René DAZY
      c) whereabouts and description of Jean PLATIAU
      d) his arrest. When and for what reason
  iv. <u>STELLA's address</u> after leaving Berlitz (behind rue Crebillon) (ask MARTINEAU and DAZY)
  v. <u>Abbé Jean LUNEAU</u> (character etc)
  vi. <u>Café MOUILLARD</u> in Place Royale
      a) character and acquaintances there. ?Any letters for her.
      b) did they recommend DUGASTS

---

[*] From KV2/738

vii. Joachim and Salvador CAMPILLO (through MANOLO in Spanish Consulate)
   a) whereabouts of Jean PLATIAU
   b) details of Joachim's arrest and imprisonment
   c) whereabouts of René DAZY
   d) did they know of "René Scheme"
viii. Odette CHATENAY [sic] (through Berlitz where learnt English)
   a) STELLA's life in Nantes
   b) address of René DAZY
ix. René DAZY
   a) STELLA's life in Nantes
   b) whereabouts of Jean PLATIAU
x. Lucien HARENG (through Berlitz (character)
xi. What was there at St. Luce [sic]
xii. Ask concierge and neighbours of STELLA's flat re arrest, life etc

(c) i. Jean PLATIAU
   a) details of STELLA's arrest and interrogation
   b) was there a St. Luce plan
   c) in general thorough grilling
ii. SAMSON
   a) did he give STELLA the St. Luce plan
iii. ANGERS
   a) check stay of one night in Hotel de France – date
   b) records at 1 Ave. Maréchal Pétain
   c) prison at Angers. Cell on ground floor. Nazi eagle on wall. Ask if one wing was taken by Germans. ?any records
iv. Is Heinrich HERMAN known.
v. Joachim CASTILLO
   a) was he arrested
   b) did he know of "René Scheme"
   c) did he know of Leon de Nyeres
vi. René DAZY and Odette CHATENAY [sic]
   a) did he and Odette know of "René Scheme"
   b) whereabouts of Leon de Nyeres
   c) was he arrested as result of action by de Nyeres
   d) did he give her plan of A.A. installations given him by "Alexandre alias Sacha". What did she do with them.
vii. Abbé LUNEAU
   a) did René come and see him. Name, description, etc of René
   b) did René and/or STELLA tell him of "Scheme"
   c) his impression of René and the story

viii. René's address at <u>43 Boulevard Maréchal Foche</u>, General enquiries:
   a) was he known as Serge Robin or ? René Siber
   b) did STELLA visit there often. Was she his mistress
   c) is name Siegfried Rauch known
   d) MEISSNER known there
ix. <u>FRADET</u> 10 or 12 rue Haute Casserie, Nantes. Father owned typewriter shop in Place Royale
   a) what did he know of STELLA and René. General grilling

<u>PARIS.</u> René's cover address: René Siber, Poste Restante, rue Balzac, Paris. Have D.S.M. captured any records to help identify René and MEISSNER.

Notes

TNA = The National Archives, Kew

Introduction
1. TNA KV2/731.
2. TNA KV2/731.
3. Sweet, Matthew, *The West End Front* (Faber & Faber, London, 2011); paperback edition, 2012.
4. Curry, John Court, *The Security Service 1908–1945. The Official History* (Public Record Office, London, 1999); Andrew, Christopher, *Defence of the Realm* (Viking Canada, Toronto, 2009).

Chapter 1. The Beginnings of a Covert Life
1. 'The right to enjoy the use and advantages of another's property short of the destruction or waste of its substance.' (OED)
2. TNA KV2/732.
3. Brooks, Collin, N.J. Crowson (ed), *Fleet Street, Press Barons and Politics: The Journals of Collin Brooks, 1932–1940* (Cambridge University Press, for the Royal Historical Society, 1998), p.53: 'Hubert A. Meredith (1884–1965), Anglo-International Bank 1924–9; City Ed. *Saturday Review*, 1924–31; City Ed. *Daily Mail* Group, 1931 - ; Wg.-Cmd, World War Two.'; Meredith, Richard, *Lords of Fleet Street: The Harmsworth Dynasty* (Routledge/Taylor & Francis, London; New York, 2016), p.192; Wing Commander Hubert Angelo Meredith, OBE, RAF Volunteer Reserve, *Second Supplement to The London Gazette*, 19 November 1946, p.1; also listed as a Second Lieutenant in 1914, *Supplement to The London Gazette*, 18 November 1914, p.9512.
4. TNA KV2/732.
5. Viscount Cobham: personal communication to the author, 1 April 2019.
6. Helen Fisher, University Archivist, Cadbury Research Library, University of Birmingham: personal communication to the author, 24 January 2020.
7. Naturalization certificate, TNA HO334/218/46444.
8. This allows a magistrate or judge to enforce a judgment or order against a person or corporation that has refused or neglected to comply with a known court ruling or order within a known fixed period of time.
9. TNA KV2/732.
10. Linda Pietronigro, Wellington Shields & Co. LLC: personal communication to the author, 15 February 2018: 'There was another Shields & Company prior to this, but it was merged into Bache Halsey in the 70s and ultimately became part of Prudential. The prior Shields & Co. never had any affiliation with our firm.' I am grateful to Ms. Pietronigro for clarifying this.
11. Although unnamed, this may have been Dominique Castellan (1856–1936) who was Archbishop of Chambéry from 26 May 1915 to his death on 12 May 1936.
12. https://en.geneanet.org/fonds/bibliotheque/?go=1&nom=magaloff&prenom=&prenom_operateur=&size=30&with_variantes_nom=&with_variantes_prenom=

13. Gillam, Major John Graham, DSO, *Gallipoli Diary* (George Allen and Unwin, London, 1918). A check by the House of Commons Enquiries of Stenton and Lees' *Who's Who of British Members of Parliament 1919–1945*, *DODs People*, *Who's Who*, and *Who Was Who*, revealed nothing to indicate that he was ever an MP.
14. Smith, Douglas, *Rasputin* (Pan Books, London, 2017), paperback edition, pp.184-5.
15. http://theesotericcuriosa.blogspot.ca/2012/06/dandy-with-mistakes-ingrammar-inthe.html; www.dailymail.co.uk/home/you/article-2340226/Irf--Russian-fashion-label-murderous-past-.html; http://la-saga-des-derniers-romanovs.over-blog.com/article-3112 5600.html. See also: Smith, op.cit.
16. Smith, *op.cit.*
17. In Paris they lived at: 1920–39: 37, rue Gutenberg then 19, Rue de La Tourelle in Boulogne-sur-Seine; 1939–40: they rented a mansion in Sarcelles, rue Victor-Hugo; 1940–43: they moved to rue Agar and 65, rue Lafontaine, in the 16th arrondissement; From 1943 until their death: at 38, rue Pierre-Guérin (Neuilly-Auteuil-Passy). https://en.wikipedia.org/wiki/Felix_Yusupov; www.perfumeintelligence.co.uk/library/perfume/h/h6/h6p7.htm
18. The notorious Carbone gang was founded by Paul Bonnaventure Carbone (1894–1943), a Corsican criminal known as the 'Godfather of Marseille' involved in the Marseille underworld. He and François Spirito (1900–67) joined the French Gestapo, known as the Carlingue, which worked for the German Gestapo, Sicherheitsdienst (SD) and Geheime Feldpolizei (GFP).
19. TNA KV2/737.

Chapter 2. The Mayfair Playboy
1. TNA KV2/734.
2. McLaren, Angus, *Playboys and Mayfair Men: Crime, Class, Masculinity and Fascism in 1930s* (Johns Hopkins University Press, Baltimore, 2017), p.70.
3. TNA WO 339/39840. John Lonsdale's MI5 file (PF.48035) is not available from the National Archives, Kew. No record in the Provincial Archives of Alberta database, HeRMIS, exists for a John Christopher Mainwaring Lonsdale, nor in the General Register Office, London. A 1916 Census for Manitoba, Saskatchewan and Alberta shows 2-year-old John living with his parents in Macleod, Alberta.
4. The *London Gazette*, 20 February 1934, p.1158; TNA KV2/730.
5. Not connected to the current Lonsdale and Churchill, producing leather wallets.
6. Slavik was the inventor of the Leviathan cocktail and first vice-president of the International Bartenders Association. www.cbanet.cz/cba_clanek&pg=119&id=2077; www.radio.cz/fr/rubrique/literature/un-barman-promu-chevalier-de-la-legion-dhonneur
7. McLaren, *op.cit.*, p.41.
8. For more information on the robbery and the four accused see: McLaren, *op.cit.*; TNA MEPO3/902.
9. *Winnipeg Free Press*, Wednesday March 2, 1938, p.5, quoted in McLaren, *op.cit.*, p.96. Shaw's use of the term 'flagellomaniacs' first appeared in an essay, 'Flogging in our Industrial Schools' in the *Daily Chronicle*, 24 February 1895, and later in 'The Unprotected Child and the Law', in *From Time and Tide*, 23 February 1923, and: Shaw, George Bernard, *Doctor's Delusions Crude Criminology and Sham Education* (Constable & Company, London, 1931), pp.234-40 and pp.282-84, respectively.
10. McLaren, *op.cit.*, p.79.
11. TNA KV4/469; West, Nigel (ed), *Guy Liddell's Cold War Diaries, May 1945–December 1947* (Amazon, 2019), vol.1, pp.587, 595. Wilmer is referred to as Hilary Wilmer.
12. For more on Jenkins see: Jenkins, Peter Martin, *Mayfair Boy (Confessions of Peter Jenkins)* (London, W.H. Allen, 1952).
13. TNA KV2/732.

14. TNA KV2/728.
15. John Lyttleton, 9th Viscount Cobham, was Under-Secretary of State for War in 1939, appointed by Prime Minister Neville Chamberlain, a position he held until Chamberlain's resignation on 10 May 1940.
16. TNA KV2/732.
17. TNA KV2/728.
18. TNA KV2/728.
19. A photograph of the crew of the SS *Cieszyn*, dated 1932, shows him as being the senior mechanic: https://audiovis.nac.gov.pl/obraz/93970/; https://jbc.bj.uj.edu.pl/Content/353495/PDF/NDIGCZAS015834_1939_002.pdf
20. TNA KV2/737.
21. TNA KV2/741.
22. TNA KV2/741.

Chapter 3. 'Some Interesting Work'
1. TNA KV2/732.
2. Given his relationship with the Resistance and his residency in Marseille, it is possible that he was related to Henry Simon (1896–1987) who had served in the 31e Bataillon de Chasseurs à pied (31st Fighter Battalion of Foot) during the First World War: www.ordredelaliberation.fr/fr/compagnons/henry-simon
3. TNA KV2/733.
4. TNA KV2/732.
5. TNA KV2/733.
6. TNA KV2/733.
7. TNA KV2/732. The 4th Battalion, The Border Regiment, known as the Westmoreland & Cumberland Battalion, was the last to leave France for Southampton on 18 June 1940. In October 1940 they were still at Kington Camp, Hereford, a base used to house troops returning from Dunkirk; in March 1941 they were sent to Suez and Sidi Barrani in Egypt. A Mr Hutchinson also gives the month as March when the 4th Battalion was posted to North Africa. However, another source states that they went to North Africa in May 1941: www.wartimememoriesproject.com/ww2/allied/battalion.php?pid=837. Bellis, Malcolm, *British Armoured and Infantry Regiments 1939–45* (Privately published by Bellis, Crewe, 1988), p.34; www.bbc.co.uk/history/ww2peopleswar/stories/88/a8714388.shtml
8. TNA KV2/733. Speir (1910-98) is listed in *Wikipedia* and in his obituary in the *Independent* as serving in the Intelligence Corps from 1939–45, ending up as a lieutenant colonel. He later became the Conservative MP for Hexham: www.independent.co.uk/arts-entertainment/ obituary-sir-rupert-speir-1200173.html; www.bbc.co.uk/history/ww2peopleswar/stories/65/a1968465.shtml
9. TNA KV2/733. The hospital was evacuated to Kent during the Second World War: http://ezitis.myzen.co.uk/cheyne.html
10. Hermann Zollinger, according to McLaren, ran an arms company at Limmatquai 94, Zurich; TNA KV2/728; E. Phillips Oppenheim (1866–1946) the prolific pulp-fiction author who had written a number of popular spy and mystery novels.
11. TNA KV2/728.

Chapter 4. Capture and Recruitment
1. TNA KV2/733.
2. This may have been Dr Theodor Gottfried Oswald Bendemann, a private scholar and philosopher (she said he had a PhD from Heidelberg University), born in Charlottenburg in November 1903, who married Goethe and Weimar literature expert Effi Kaiser née Biedrzynski in 1934, although this would make him a few years older than she

claimed. He died on 13 February 1945 in Thorn and is buried in the German War Cemetery at Stare Czarnowo in West Pomerania: https://gw.geneanet.org/pmlhennings?lang=en&pz=peter&nz=hennings&ocz=0&p=theodor+gottfried+oswald&n=bendemann; www.geni.com/people/Theodor-Gottfried-Oswald-BENDEMANN/6000000027529015690; www.heimatfreundebali.de/heimatgeschichte/villen/haus-immertreu/

3. TNA KV2/732.
4. TNA KV2/281.
5. www.cia.gov/library/readingroom/docs/OSS%20-%20SSU%20-%20CIG%20EARLY%20CIA%20DOCUMENTS%20%20%20VOL.%201_0007.pdf, http://numbers-stations.com/cia/German%20Intelligence%20Service%20%28wwii%29%2C%20%20Vol.%201/GERMAN%20INTELLIGENCE%20SERVICE%20%28WWII%29%2C%20%20VOL.%201_0004.pdf. The report says March, which must be incorrect as the Germans had not occupied the area until June.
6. CI Intermediate Interrogation Report (CI-IIR) No.57, 11 December 1946. He was included in those tried at Nuremberg on 11 December 1947: Records of the United States Nuernberg War Crimes Trials Interrogations, 1946–1949: www.archives.gov/files/research/captured-german-records/microfilm/m1019.pdf; www.academia.edu/2019168/The_List_of_857_war_criminals_interrogated_by_CCPAC_Chief_of_Counsel_for_the_Prosecution_of_Axis_Criminality_
7. TNA KV2/732.
8. http://numbers-stations.com/cia/German%20Intelligence%20Service%20%28wwii%29%2C%20%20Vol.%203/GERMAN%20INTELLIGENCE%20SERVICE%20%28WWII%29%2C%20%20VOL.%203_0001.pdf. TNA KV2/2136.
9. TNA KV2/281; and OSS/X2 decrypt. 'Code-named ISOS or PAIR, this was a steady stream of deciphered German intelligence messages, mostly but not exclusively sent by members of the Abwehr, the German military intelligence service', Rafalko, Frank J. (ed), *Counterintelligence in World War II*, (National Counterintelligence Center), vol.2, Ch.3: https://fas.org/irp/ops/ci/docs/ci2/index.htm (accessed 15 September 2016).
10. www.cia.gov/library/readingroom/docs/OSS%20-%20SSU%20-%20CIG%20EARLY%20CIA%20DOCUMENTS%20%20%20VOL.%201_0007.pdf
11. TNA KV2/281 – 'Monthly Summary of Cases at Camp 020 and 020R', 1 July 1945; and KV2/282.
12. Listed as head Abwehr official in Switzerland in: Petersen, Neal H. (ed), *From Hitler's Doorstep: The Wartime Intelligence Reports of Allen Dulles 1942–45* (Pennsylvania State University Press, Pennsylvania, 1996), p.558.
13. TNA KV2/282.
14. Davies, Philip H.J., 'Organizational Politics and the Development of Britain's Intelligence Producer/Consumer Interface' in: Charters, David, Stuart Farson and Glenn P. Hastedt (eds), *Intelligence Analysis and Assessment* (Frank Cass, London; Portland, 1996; 2004), note 30, p.130: IVz was the MI9 liaison with SIS 'before transfer to the operational Production side as P15', who was actually 'Jimmy' Langley.
15. TNA KV2/732.
16. CI Intermediate Interrogation Report (CI-IIR) No.57, Obst/Lt Dernbach, Friederich: www.cia.gov/library/readingroom/docs/OSS%20-%20SSU%20-%20CIG%20EARLY%20CIA%20DOCUMENTS%20%20%20VOL.%201_0007.pdf
17. TNA KV2/738.
18. TNA KV2/734.
19. TNA KV2/158. He is not mentioned in Meissner's description of the organizational breakdown of *Ast* Angers and the Paris *Leitstelle* to MI5 while he was under interrogation at Camp 020 at the end of the war, nor in any of the declassified CIA files currently available.

20. Rennie, David, 'Liechtenstein royalty hired death camp inmates for slave labour': *Daily Telegraph*, 15 April 2005: www.telegraph.co.uk/news/worldnews/europe/liechtenstein/1487906/Liechtenstein-royalty-hired-death-camp-inmates-for-slave-labour.html
21. Dr Peter Geiger: personal communication to the author, 11 July 2018.
22. Geiger, Peter, *Kriegzeit. Liechtenstein 1939 bis 1945* (Chronos Verlag, Zurich, 2010), pp.364-6.
23. *Ibid.*, p.365;
24. TNA KV2/2748.
25. Geiger, *op.cit.*, pp.364-6.
26. TNA KV2/2748.

Chapter 5. 'Pat O'Leary'
1. Neave, Airey, *Saturday at M.I.9.* (Hodder & Stoughton, London, 1969), p.75.
2. West, Nigel, *MI6. British Secret Intelligence Operations, 1909–45* (Weidenfeld & Nicolson, London, 1983), p.109; republished by Pen & Sword, Barnsley, 2019, p.115.
3. Cited in: Clutton-Brock, Oliver, *RAF Evaders* (Bounty Books, London, 2012), p.55; see also TNA FO371/28281 Z5516. Those activities, according to Clutton-Brock, were never made clear.
4. Darling, Donald, *Secret Sunday* (William Kimber, London, 1975), p.14.
5. *Ibid.*, pp.15, 21; also cited in: Clutton-Brock, *op.cit.*, p.55.
6. Read, Anthony & David Fisher, *Colonel Z* (Hodder & Stoughton, London, 1984), p.12, cited in: Keene, Tom, *Cloak of Enemies* (Spellmount/The History Press, Stroud, 2012), p.22.
7. As of 29 October 1939 he was acting captain in the Highland Light Infantry, according to the *Army List* for April 1940 (p.811). The recommendation for the Distinguished Service Order (DSO) listed in the *London Gazette* for 4 May 1943 gives his unit as The Highland Light Infantry (City of Glasgow Regiment), while the file in the National Archives gives it as '1 Glasgow Highlanders, Highland Light Infantry, 52 Division'. Neave said that Garrow was with the Seaforths (as did Read & Fisher). *Supplement to The London Gazette*, 4 May 1943, p.1997: www.thegazette.co.uk/London/issue/36000/supplement/1997/data.pdf & TNA WO373/62/355
8. Neave, *op.cit.*, p.78.
9. Darling, *op.cit.*, p.98.
10. Meyerowitz, Seth & Peter F. Stevens, *The Lost Airman: A True Story of Escape from Nazi Occupied France* (Berkley Caliber/Random House, New York, 2016), pp.189-91.
11. Long, Helen, *Safe Houses are Dangerous* (William Kimber, London, 1985), p.31: It appears as Oflag 124 in Besançon on this page, but the two camps there were Frontstalag 142 (October 1940 - April 1941) and Frontstalag 154 (? – March 1941), so it may have been a typo. '*Frontstalag*' means 'forward prisoner of war camp'; the term 'Oflag' is used for officers' prisoner of war camp.
12. www.myheritage.com/names/thomas_kenny. Captain Patrick William Kenny, TNA WO339/10067; TNA KV1/59, *Chronological List of Staff taken to 31 December, 1919*; Alan 'Fred' Judge, Military Intelligence Museum, Chicksands: personal communication to the author, 6 December 2018, via specialoperationsexecutive@yahoogroups.co.uk; Phil Tomaselli: personal communication to the author, 6 December 2018, via specialoperationsexecutive@yahoogroups.co.uk
13. Long, *op.cit.*, p.75.
14. Conscript Heroes: www.conscript-heroes.com/Art20-Tom-Kenny-960.html
15. Braddon, Russell, *Nancy Wake* (Cassell & Co, London, 1956); republished by The History Press, Stroud, 2010; see also, Fitzsimons, Peter, *Nancy Wake* (Harper Collins, London, 2002), paperback edition.
16. Testimony of M.L.H. Nouveau, Hôtel de Malte, 63, rue de Richelieu, Paris, 10 April 1947, see: FRAN_0866_028440_L: www.siv.archives-nationales.culture.gouv.fr/siv/

rechercheconsultation/consultation/ir/consultationIR.action?udId=root&consIr=&irId=FRAN_IR_053870&frontIr=&auSeinIR=false
17. *The Air Force List*: November, 1943, p.530; October, 1944, p.690; July 1945, p.797. *The Air Force List* for November 1943 shows him as a probationary pilot officer in the Administrative and Miscellaneous Duties Branch as of 11 August 1943, but no mention of the Intelligence Branch.
18. Neave, *op.cit.*, p.54, cited in: Grehan, John & Martin Mace, *Unearthing Churchill's Secret Army* (Pen & Sword, Barnsley, 2012), pp.142-3; O'Leary's description is cited in Grehan & Mace, *op.cit.*
19. TNA KV2/728; His wireless operation known as 'Antsbruder' betrayed between sixteen and eighteen British agents: CIA: CI Intermediate Interrogation Report (CI-IIR) No 57 on Oberstleutnant Friederich Dernbach: www.cia.gov/library/readingroom/docs/OSS%20-%20SSU%20-%20CIG%20EARLY%20CIA%20DOCUMENTS%20%20%20VOL.%201_0007.pdf, https://en.wikipedia.org/wiki/Henri_Honor%C3%A9_d%27Estienne_d%27Orves
20. TNA KV2/728;www.cheminsdememoire.gouv.fr/en/honore-destienne-dorves-1901–1941; http://en.wikipedia.org/wiki/Henri_Honor%C3%A9_d%27Estienne_d%27Orves, Wievorka, Olivier, *The French Resistance* (Harvard University Press, Cambridge, MA, 2016), p.17.
21. Ethel Sephton, 22 Macauley Street, Liverpool, born on 19 April 1897 in Halsall, West Lancashire to William Sephton, aged 45, and Elisabeth Ann Sephton, aged 44. In 1939 she is shown as an 'unpaid domestic', a euphemism for housewife, married, and living in Coventry.
22. TNA KV2/729.
23. West, Nigel (ed), *The Guy Liddell Diaries Vol.1, 1939–1942* (Routledge, London; New York, 2005), p.202.
24. Lochery, Neill, *Lisbon. War in the Shadows of the City of Light, 1939–1945* (Public Affairs™, New York, 2012), paperback edition, p.22; Simmons, Mark, *Ian Fleming and Operation Golden Eye* (Casemate, Oxford & Philadelphia, 2018).
25. Ottis, Sherri Greene, *Silent Heroes: Downed Airmen and the French Underground* (University Press of Kentucky, Lexington, 2001), no pagination in online version accessed.
26. TNA KV2/728. Dodds's own file is not available from the National Archives at Kew. MI1x was part of the Directorate of Military Intelligence at the War Office.
27. Stella was granted a Portuguese visa on 25 June valid for one month, a Spanish transit visa valid for one year on 27 June and a French exit visa valid for one month on 18 September.
28. TNA KV2/729.
29. For more information see: Taylor, Melissa Jane, 'American Consuls and the Politics of Rescue in Marseille, 1936–1941', in: *Holocaust and Genocide Studies*, 30, no.2 (Fall 2016), pp. 247-75.
30. TNA KV2/728.
31. TNA KV2/728.
32. See: Murphy, David, *What Stalin Knew. The Enigma of Barbarossa* (Yale University Press, Yale, 2005).
33. CI Intermediate Interrogation Report (CI-IIR) No.57, Obst/Lt Dernbach, Friederich: www.cia.gov/library/readingroom/docs/OSS%20-%20SSU%20-%20CIG%20EARLY%20CIA%20DOCUMENTS%20%20%20VOL.%201_0007.pdf, pp.12-15.
34. https://ia801607.us.archive.org/12/items/THEFACTUALLISTOFNAZISPROTECTEDBYSPAIN/THE%20FACTUAL%20LIST%20OF%20NAZIS%20PROTECTED%20BY%20SPAIN.pdf, 'Hastuf. Chef de l'Abteilung VI C du BdS Paris': www.cegesoma.be/docs/Invent/AA_1312_ListeAllemandsRecherches.pdf

35. TNA KV2/728-9. Pavie's MI5 personnel file (PF.457970) is not available from the National Archives at Kew. A Jean Jacques Pavie is listed as having been born in 1911 to Jean-Fernand Pavie and Anaïs Camille Joséphine Désirée Pavie *née* Tiranty, and died in 1989. There is also a Jacques Pavie, born in 1901 to André Pavie and Geneviève Drevet. Whether either of these is the same Pavie cannot be confirmed; in the first case the birth year is right, except that his estimated age of 35 does not fit. Pavie died in 1989.
36. See: TNA KV2/2850 and TNA KV2/2848 respectively.
37. TNA KV2/731.
38. http://conscript-heroes.com/Art20-Tom-Kenny-960.html
39. Referred to by Josh Ireland *et al* as Henri Duprez. See: Ireland, Josh, *The Traitors* (John Murray, London, 2017), pp.85, 87, 95-7; websites refer to him as François.
40. Lepers escaped to Spain in January 1942 and joined the Free French Air Force in June, although two websites state he left France on 10 March 1942 and travelled to Gibraltar via Spain: www.39-45.org/viewtopic.php?f=52&t=47504; www.ouest-france.fr/bretagne/vannes-56000/roland-lepers-un-des-derniers-francais-libres-invite-de-la-ville-698030
41. Neave, *op.cit.*, pp.83-4.
42. Full accounts of the life and career of Harold Cole can be found in: Ireland, *op.cit.*; Murphy, Brendan, *Turncoat* (Harcourt, London, 1987); see also: https://en.wikipedia.org/wiki/Harold_Cole; TNA KV2/415-7.

Chapter 6. The Gifted Liar
1. Capt. Patrick William Stanislaw Gubbins (1918–2012), AM/213, AM/7, AM/LT of the 'Massingham' organization: *Lists of SOE Appointment Symbols and Incumbents*, compiled by Alan 'Fred' Judge, Military Intelligence Museum, Chicksands, based on information supplied by Duncan Stuart, the former SOE Adviser to the Foreign Office, the late Lieutenant Colonel Tony Williams's research notes, and SOE administrative files dealing with symbols. He was not related to Major General Sir Colin Gubbins. See also his SOE file: TNA HS 9/630/7.
2. TNA KV2/728. www.conscript-heroes.com/Art09-Murchie-Clayton-960.html
3. TNA KV2/734.
4. From 15 May 1940 to 22 February 1942 the Minister of Economic Warfare responsible for ISRB, the Inter-Services Research Bureau (cover name for SOE), was Hugh Dalton. Conversely, it could have been the head of F Section, Lieutenant Colonel Maurice Buckmaster, or Colin Gubbins, head of Operations.
5. TNA KV2/728.
6. TNA KV2/730.
7. TNA KV2/728. Eigen Fiehl, Press Attaché at the German Embassy in Paris in 1938 in: Orlow, Dietrich, *The Lure of Fascism in Western Europe: German Nazis, Dutch and French Fascists, 1933–1939* (Palgrave Macmillan, New York & Basingstoke, 2009), p.204, n.47; p.205, n.51,n.60; p.206, n.72, n.75; p.209, n.101; p.215, n.29, n.33, n.34; p.217, n.49.
8. Chisholm, Anne, 'The Dangerous Edge of Things', reviewing *Wild Mary* by Patrick Marnham, *The Spectator*, 7 June 2006; Marnham, Patrick, *Wild Mary* (Vintage Books, London 2007), p.44.
9. Commander Giovanni 'Jack' Bosio was consul-general of the Italian Armistice Commission in Marseille, born in Florence in 1893. From 1932–39 he had also been secretary to the Fascist politician and member of Mussolini's Blackshirts Count Dino Grandi, Italian ambassador in London.
10. TNA KV2/733.
11. www.conscript-heroes.com/Art09-Murchie-Clayton-960.html
12. TNA KV2/734.

13. TNA KV2/734. Lieutenant Colonel Robert Horace Christian Drummond-Wolff (1901–83) was the Assistant British military attaché in Madrid as of 20 October 1940 and British military attaché in Lisbon until 4 August 1945. The British military attaché in Madrid was Colonel O.C.B. Smith-Bingham.
14. TNA KV2/734. An MI5 file number, PF.413642 is written next to his name. That file is not available from the National Archives at Kew.
15. MI5 files on Mond and Castelain, PF.413,542 and PF.304,750 respectively, are not available from the National Archives at Kew.

Chapter 7. The Man in Grey

1. Paillole, Paul, *Fighting the Nazis: French Intelligence and Counterintelligence 1935–1945* (Enigma Books, New York, 2003).
2. www.christopherlong.co.uk/pri/secpap.html
3. TNA KV2/737.
4. Kitson, Simon, *The Hunt for Nazi Spies: Fighting Espionage in Vichy France* (University of Chicago Press, Chicago; London 2008); and, *New York Review of Books*: www.nybooks.com/articles/2008/04/03/a-patriot-for-peacutetain/; www.aassdn.org/TR.pdf
5. Marie-Noël Challan-Belval: personal communication to the author, 16 September 2018.
6. TNA KV2/729.
7. TNA KV2/729.
8. TNA KV2/737.
9. TNA KV2/737.
10. TNA KV2/730.
11. Paillole, *op.cit.*, p.171. Captain André Bonnefous served under Paillole in the German section along with Captain Jacques Abtey and Challan-Belval. From 1937–40 he headed the German section of counter-espionage section of the SCR; in 1956 he headed the SSM, Service de sécurité militaire, created by General de Lattre de Tassigny.
12. *Ibid*, p.367.

Chapter 8. Flight from France

1. The only person who appears to fit the time frame is José María de Chávarri y Poveda (1916–2013), shown as a director of Sefanitro SA (Sociedad Española de Fabricaciones Nitrogenadas) of Bilbao, a company manufacturing industrial chemicals such as nitrogenous fertilisers, who seems more likely, but cannot be confirmed. See: Whiteside, R. M., et al, *Medium Companies of Europe 1991/92, Vol.1, Medium Companies of the Continental European Economic Community* (Graham & Trotman, London), p.676; Whiteside, R. M., *et al, Medium Companies of Europe 1992/93, Vol.1, Medium Companies of the Continental European Economic Community* (London: Graham & Trotman), p.686.
2. TNA KV2/729.
3. TNA KV2/728
4. In 1942 his address was still listed as the Avenida Palace Hotel, Lisbon and also Madrid: *US Federal Register*, Saturday May 16, 1942, pp.3642, 3648: www.govinfo.gov/content/pkg/FR-1942-05-16/pdf/FR-1942-05-16.pdf. The Banco Espírito Santo Y Commerciale Lisboa collapsed in a banking scandal in Portugal in 2014: www.cbc.ca/news/business/portugal-s-banco-espirito-santo-collapse-and-rescue-raises-questions-1.2726933
5. Simmons, *op.cit.*, p.45.
6. TNA KV2/728; Weber, Ronald, *The Lisbon Route. Entry and Escape in Nazi Europe* (Ivan R. Dee/Rowman & Littlefield, Lanham, 2011), p.184; www.jewishvirtuallibrary.org/mayer-saly
7. *The Proclaimed List of Certain Blocked Nationals*, Supplement No.7, January 14, 1942 to the *Proclaimed List* issued July 17, 1941, p.13 (Lisbon), p.30 (Madrid) by the Federal Reserve

Bank of New York: January 14, 1942: https://fraser.stlouisfed.org/title/466/item/17093; https://fraser.stlouisfed.org/files/docs/historical/ny%20circulars/1942_02433.pdf;
8. www.gebrpoehner.de/2_Company.htm; http://poehner-hamburg.com/
9. TNA KV2/728.
10. TNA KV2/729.
11. Lochery, *op.cit.*, p.4.
12. https://en.wikipedia.org/wiki/Bristol (Whitchurch) Airport; www.revolvy.com/main/index.php?s=Bristol%20(Whitchurch)%20Airport&item_type=topic; Neil Lochery *op.cit.*, pp.3-4, states flights were three times a week. On the Form for Interrogation, the aircraft was a Douglas DC-3 (G-AGBD) owned by BOAC but operated by KLM. (TNA KV2/728)

Chapter 9. The RENÉ Enigma
1. TNA KV2/728.
2. TNA KV2/729.
3. TNA HW19/17: ISOS decrypts, 12317-14045, 1 November 1941–15 November 1941; TNA KV2/738. 'Should in fact be 13217-14045, but with the same date range "1941 Nov 01–1941 Nov 15" as portrayed on Discovery. The number range 12317-12372 would be found in HW 19/15 but for the period 1–15 October 1941' – TNA email to author, 13 February 2020.
4. Judith Curthoys, Archivist, Christ Church College, Oxford University: personal communication to the author, 27 March 2019.
5. TNA KV2/737. For details of Mrs Marie Anne Teresa de Styczinska Brett-Perring see: TNA KV2/1094-7; HO45/25765.
6. TNA KV2/1097.
7. Sweet, *op.cit.*, p.336, n.23; TNA KV2/740.
8. TNA KV2/738.
9. TNA KV2/738.
10. TNA KV2/2103 (Meiler) quoted in KV2/739 (Lonsdale), referring to a memo from the FBI's Legal Attaché in London (Arthur Thurston) dated 22 December 1943, missing from Meiler's file. His career as a spy is documented in West, Nigel, *Codeword Overlord: Axis Espionage and the D-Day Landings* (The History Press, Stroud, 2019), pp.75-81.
11. http://maitron-fusilles-40-44.univ-paris1.fr/spip.php?article167965; https://stevemorse.org/dachau/details.php?lastname=PIEDBOUT&firstname=Gaston&title=&birthday=07&birthmonth=Jun&birthyear=1901&birthplace=Vitro&from=&town=Angers&street=Maine%20et%20Loire&number=77652&DateOfArrival=zug.%2005%20Jul%201944&disposition=befr.%20Allach&comments=Col.%20E?&category=Sch.%20Frz.&ID=169375&page=4502&Bg.%20Fa&disc=4&image=251; http://memoiredeguerre.free.fr/ccmr/dep35-jo-m-p.htm
12. TNA KV2/729.
13. TNA KV2/737.
14. TNA KV2/737.
15. TNA KV2/728.
16. TNA KV2/729.
17. TNA KV2/728.
18. TNA KV2/729.
19. TNA KV2/728.
20. TNA KV2/728.
21. TNA KV2/728.
22. TNA KV2/728.
23. TNA KV2/728.
24. TNA KV2/729.

Notes   261

25. TNA KV2/728.
26. https://translate.google.ca/translate?hl=en&sl=nl&u=http://www.bel-memorial.org/tribute/tribute_1.php%3FINDIVIDUALS_ID%3D40105%26RECOUP%3D40105&prev=search and www.bel-memorial.org/names_on_memorials/display_names_on_mon.php?MON_ID=1802
27. https://beforetempsford.org.uk/1941/05/page/2/; Clark, Freddie, *Agents by Moonlight* (Tempus Publishing, Stroud, 1999), p.12.
28. TNA KV2/738.
29. TNA KV2/738.
30. TNA KV2/2748; TNA KV2/739.
31. The US Federal Census for 1940: www.ancestry.com/1940-census/usa/California/Hilde-E-Bernard_2j5qx1
32. https://search.ancestry.com/cgi-bin/sse.dll?db=3693&h=4450414&indiv=try&o_vc=Record:OtherRecord&rhSource=2442
33. TNA KV2/2748.
34. TNA KV2/2748.
35. TNA KV2/739.
36. TNA KV2/2748.
37. TNA KV2/2748.
38. TNA KV2/739.
39. CIA: www.cia.gov/library/readingroom/docs/OSS%20-%20SSU%20-%20CIG%20EARLY%20CIA%20DOCUMENTS%20%20%20VOL.%201_0007.pdf. She is also listed as being in Abt III (counterintelligence) by the Sûreté de l'État: www.cegesoma.be/docs/Invent/AA_1312_ListeAllemandsRecherches.pdf
40. TNA KV2/282.
41. TNA KV2/2748.
42. TNA KV2/2748; KV2/739.
43. Charles Platiau: personal communications to the author, 6 & 8 June 2019.
44. TNA KV2/737.
45. TNA KV2/2748
46. TNA KV2/2748: (1) A War Room Incoming Telegram from CRUSADE to ZEBRA dated 12 April 1945 sent via OSS X-2 (OSS counterintelligence): 'SPECK stated Sonderfuehrer Dr. S. RAUCH cover name RICHARD in EVIAN probably working for OSS in SWITZERLAND or south of FRANCE.' (2) An incoming telegram from SPEARHEAD, 12th Rear in Paris to BLISS, Paris and the MI5 War Room, London (WRC4a) suggests that he may have become an OSS agent after his disappearance in Évian-les-Bains; and Fraulein Schneider was thought to have been seen in Sigmaringen in the state of Baden-Württemberg in early 1945. It also mentions that his 'fiancée', Elfie Schneider, had been with him in Évian-les-Bains, the first city in Haute-Savoie to be liberated by the FFI on 16 August 1944, and was a relative of Generalfeldmarshall Job Wilhelm Georg Erdmann Erwin von Witzleben who was hanged for his part in the July Plot of 1944 to kill Hitler. (3) TNA KV2/739: A report from SCI Detachment CIB with the 12th Army Group, dated 12 March 1945 mentions Rauch as probably being in the OSS in Switzerland or southern France.
47. TNA KV2/739. For information on Moglia see: TNA KV2/2284.
48. Manhart, George Born, *DePauw Through the Years*, (DePauw University, Indianapolis, 1962), Vol.II, World War II, Ch.XXI, p.357: https://digital.palni.edu/digital/collection/dpupub/id/85011
49. *The DePauw Alumnus*, March 1948, p.5.

Chapter 10. 'Keeping the Lady on Tap'
1. TNA KV2/728.
2. TNA KV2/729; Detentions under defence regulations: Arrival from Enemy of Foreign Territory Order 1940, TNA CO968/64/16.
3. All quotes, unless otherwise specified, are from KV2/728.
4. TNA KV2/728; KV2/408.
5. TNA KV2/268; KV2/275-77 (HARLEQUIN); KV2/408 (Garthe).
6. Mentioned in Speck's MI5 file: TNA KV2/2748.
7. Admiral Darlan was commander of the French Navy and also deputy leader of the Vichy regime until his assassination at his headquarters in Algiers, North Africa on 24 December 1942 by Fernand Bonnier de La Chapelle.
8. TNA KV2/732; *Unternehmen Seeadler*, often referred to as *Unternehmen Taube II* (Operation Dove II), was actually a German Foreign Ministry plan conceived in May 1941 to land a seaplane off the coast of Ireland around 15 or 25 September to deliver supplies to the IRA. The operation was eventually postponed, then abandoned by Hitler; see: Adams, Jefferson, *Historical Dictionary of German Intelligence* (The Scarecrow Press, Lanham, MD, 2009) p.414; https://en.wikipedia.org/wiki/Operation_Sea_Eagle; http://codenames.info/operation/seeadler-i/
9. TNA KV282.
10. TNA KV282.
11. TNA KV282.
12. 2nd Marquess of Reading, Gerald Rufus Isaacs (1889–1960), who had succeeded to the title in 1935.
13. TNA KV2/728.
14. TNA KV2/733.
15. West, *Liddell Diaries, op.cit.*, pp.195-6.
16. TNA KV4/344. Georges Friederich Vincent Kraft @ Georges André was introduced in Brest to Breton journalist Jean Abel Louis Poumeau de Laforrest in May 1942 by Henri Le Polotec. Two others named Kraft were known to SOE – Henrik Kraft (b.1904), and Gustave Kravtzoff @ Gustave Kraft (b.1897), HS9/861/3 and HS9/862/3 respectively.
17. TNA KV2/729.
18. TNA KV2/729.
19. TNA KV2/3778. As Yves Delbar he was the author of *The Real Stalin* (George Allen & Unwin, London, 1953).
20. Operation *Pastorius*: https://en.wikipedia.org/wiki/Operation_Pastorius. See also: www.nsa.gov/Portals/70/documents/news-features/declassified-documents/cryptologic-histories/german_clandestine_activities.pdf
21. Possibly the Tripartite Pact between Germany, Italy and Japan, signed on 27 September 1940, to which Hungary became a party on 20 November 1940, which later led to Hungarian forces joining the Germans in invading Russia.
22. Grams, Grant, 'Enemies within our bosom: Nazi Sabotage in Canada', in: *Journal of Military & Strategic Studies* (Centre for Military, Security & Strategic Studies, University of Calgary, Calgary, 2012), Volume 14, Issues 3 & 4, pp.1-20.
23. TNA KV2/729.
24. TNA KV2/741. 'Colonel Britton' was Douglas Ritchie, in charge of the BBC's wartime 'V-For Victory' campaign, and later director of European broadcasting for the BBC. Becker was most likely the Franconian pastor and Wehrmacht chaplain, Karl-Heinz Becker, who was later stationed in Vienna in 1944 and court-martialled for speaking out against Hitler.
25. TNA KV2/729.
26. TNA KV2/729.

27. *Navy List*, April 1945, vol.II, p.1360: https://deriv.nls.uk/dcn23/9343/93437585.23.pdf. The *London Gazette*, 1 November 1929, p.7052: www.thegazette.co.uk/London/issue/33548/supplement/7052/data.pdf. The *London Gazette*, 7 July 1933, p.4634: www.thegazette.co.uk/London/issue/33958/page/4634/data.pdf
28. www.fieldtrial.info/familytree/HTML/hans-mark-john-barnard-hankey.html
29. Nigel West: personal communication to the author, 15 April 2018.
30. Margaret Barnard Hankey: personal communication to the author, 10 April 2018; Barnard-Hankey, H. M. J., 'British Junior Training', *D.H.O. Journal* (Downhill Only), November 1954, vol.3, no.12, p.16: www.downhillonly.com/wp-content/uploads/Journal/1954.pdf
31. TNA J77/2788/6395.
32. 1929, 1932, 1933 and 1936; the *London Gazette*, 28 October 1932, p.6896: www.thegazette.co.uk/London/issue/33877/page/6896/data.pdf. The *London Gazette*, 10 January 1936, p.301: www.thegazette.co.uk/London/issue/34241/page/301/data.pdf
33. Author Hermann Friederich Armand 'Pitz' Broch de Rotherman @ Hermann de Rothermann @ Hermann Broch emigrated to the United States in September 1941 and worked for the OSS. His good friend Karl Heinz Ludwig was serving in the French Army. www.psywarrior.com/PSYOPOrgWW2.html
34. TNA KV2/733.
35. West, *Liddell Diaries, op.cit.*, p.199.
36. TNA KV2/729.
37. TNA KV2/731.
38. TNA KV2/728.
39. There had been communications from Brest in 1941 from Gabrielle Cecile Martinez Picabia @ GLORIA, regarding U-boats, but her information was not trusted by Roman Garby-Czerniawski (WALENTY), as well as from 'Colonel Remy' (Lieutenant Colonel Gilbert Renault-Roulier), reporting on the *Scharnhorst* and *Gneisenau*. See: Tremain, David, *Double Agent Victoire*, pp.156, 174.
40. TNA KV2/728.
41. TNA KV2/728.
42. TNA KV2/730. Paragraph 6 is badly damaged and most words are missing.
43. TNA KV2/731.
44. TNA KV2/731.
45. TNA KV2/717 (Hirsch), states: Ernst Alisch was a former member of Siemens and now an important and active member of the Sonderdienst (s.28a); Alisch is listed in the Paris section of the SS-Sonderkommando as an Obersturmbannführer (lt. col.), Political Liaison, (s.25a): 'Former Siemens employee. Brutal type of North Germany. Clever, fanatical Nazi. Shrewd political intriguer, but appears not over-certain of a German victory. Takes presents.' His MI5 file (PF.600, 844) is not available from Kew.
46. TNA KV2/717; KV2/718. Parts of the actual document in KV2/718, a Camp 020 report by Capt. Sampson, dated 11.1.42 (serial 135a), are severely damaged and portions missing. That vice-consul was Bradford who had been appointed to the Marseille Consulate on 19 September 1940, and the girlfriend, first thought to be Stella, was more likely his Italian mistress, but she had nothing to do with the SS. There is no one in Hirsch's file in the SS-Sonderkommando's list of *V-Männer* who fits the bill.
47. TNA KV2/732. Possibly Robert Le Guyon (1899–1974), (Commandant, 2rd Bureau FFI Region 5).
48. Gourvish, Terry, *Dolphin Square: The History of a Unique Building* (Bloomsbury Information, London, 2014), pp.100-101.
49. Amanda Ingram, Archivist, Pembroke College, Oxford University: personal communication to the author, 30 January 2019; *Pembroke College Record*, 1947, p.8.

50. Alan 'Fred' Judge, researcher, Military Intelligence Museum, Chicksands: personal communication to the author, 30 January 2019; Joyce Hutton, Archivist, Military Intelligence Museum: personal communication to the author, 31 January 2019; Van der Bijl, Nick, *Sharing the Secret. The History of the Intelligence Corps 1940–2010* (Pen & Sword, Barnsley, 2013), p.24.

Chapter 11. Telegrams and Telephone Checks

1. Otto Israel Wambach was born in Žatec, Czechoslovakia (now the Czech Republic) on 14 March 1904; married to Olga Wambach @ Wambachova *née* Stahler, born in Bratislava (now the capital of the Slovak Republic) on 22 December 1901. See: TNA MEPO 35/57/6; WO 344/331/2; HO 334/174/24225; MEPO 35/57/5 (on Olga); HO 405/59137. This latter is sealed by Lord Chancellor's Instrument (LCI177) until 2077. Otto Wambach is also mentioned in the Holocaust Survivors and Victims database of the US Holocaust Museum as having property confiscated by the Nazis: www.ushmm.org/online/hsv/person_advance_search.php?SourceId=42389&MaxPageDocs=25&start_doc=51.   He arrived at Croydon on 15 March 1939 and gave his address as 36 Netherhall Gardens, London NW3. It also gave his previous nationality as Austrian. As of 16 October 1940, his address was 63 Eaton Square, London SW1; in 1946 his business address was Associated Skin Exporters Ltd., 62-63 Queen Street, London EC4 (Prince Rupert House). Olga had arrived at Croydon the week before Otto on 9 March 1939. Even though she had been born in Bratislava, her previous nationality was also given as Austrian. As of 26 June 1939, her address was 16 Queen's Gate, London SW7 (having also been at 36 Netherhall Gardens as of 7 June). According to the Wambachs' Aliens Registration cards, neither was permitted to take any employment, paid or unpaid, under the terms of being admitted to the UK.
2. TNA KV2/730.
3. Sir Basil, the Deputy Divisional Food Officer for London (1942–44), had been awarded the KCMG in the 1925 New Year's Honours List while serving as the Assistant British Delegate to the Reparations Commission in Paris. He also served in the Transport Department of the Admiralty from 1900 to 1915. He had previously married Nancy Annie Pavitt (1881–1959) in 1906 with whom he had a daughter, Marion Birch (1925–2012), as well as a son, Temporary Captain Brian Hartley Kemball-Cook of the Intelligence Corps born on 12 December 1912 and attached to SHAEF.
4. Richard Kemball-Cook: personal communications to the author, 4 & 5 April 2018; Venn, John & J.A. Venn, *Alumni Cantabrigiensis: A Biographical List of All Known Students* (Cambridge: Cambridge University Press, 1951; 2011 digital version), Vol.2, p.13; *Who's Who, 1950* (Adam & Charles Black, London, 1950), p.590.
5. The State Department's *Foreign Service Lists* for 1939, 1940, 1941 and 1942 show no one of that name so whoever he was must have been one of the 'locally engaged' staff.
6. As of 24 June 1944 he commanded the US Army's 315th Infantry Regiment, 79th Infantry Division 'Cross of Lorraine', and wrote to her every day during the invasion of Normandy from 'Utah' beach onwards.
7. Sweet, *op.cit.*, p.336, n.18.
8. TNA KV2/730.
9. TNA KV2/730.
10. A Mrs Dare, also referred to as Deen or Deer but possibly Cicely Yvonne Deere (unconfirmed), born 1909.
11. Liddell Hart Centre for Military Archives at King's College, University of London: Letter from P. Polovtsoff to Major General Spears giving details of Tchermoieff and Col. Savitsky, views on Polish and Ukrainian questions, and the future of Russia, 11 May 1920. Spears 1/23.

12. TNA KV2/731. A fuller account of this event can be found in this file, serials 116JR and 116D.
13. TNA KV2/732.
14. The *London Gazette*, 3 December 1948, p.6340.
15. A death certificate for a Clara Bauer, born in Vienna on 24 February 1866 shows that she died on 22 September 1942 at the Theriesenstadt concentration camp of 'enteritis-darmkatarrh' (gastro enteritis). However, it is unknown whether this was the sister to whom Maurice was referring. www.holocaust.cz/en/database-of-victims/victim/47929-clara-bauer/; www.holocaust.cz/en/database-of-digitised-documents/document/83805-bauer-clara-death-certificate-ghetto-terezin/
16. The *London Gazette*, 8 February 1949, p.728. Gottlieb Moritz Bauer (1845–1936) is shown as a 'manure and commission mer[chant]' of 16 Mark Lane, EC in *Kelly's Post Office London Commercial and Professional Directory*, 1891, p.779.
17. www.elgar.org/6ccnewAF.htm; www.elgar.org/whoswho-supp1-singlepage.pdf
18. In a review of a biography of Friedelind Wagner Norman Lebrecht refers to the baroness as 'a Nazi spy – perhaps a double agent': Rieger, Eva, *Friedelind Wagner* (Boydell & Brewer, Cambridge University Press, 2013), in: *Wall Street Journal*, January 23, 2014.

Chapter 12. Major Masterman's Report

1. Sisman, Adam, *John le Carré: The Biography* (Bloomsbury, London, 2015), p.187. This was A5, listed in John Curry's official history of MI5 as 'Overseas Services, Organisation and Administration' in 1941 and in 1943 as 'Special Services'; in the 1950s it became A2a.
2. 'Fabian of the Yard', Superintendent Fabian – Robert Honey Fabian (1901–78) of New Scotland Yard. A recent history of Special Branch gives his rank as DI (Detective Inspector) in 1939, and an online article on the murder of Charles Walton as Detective Chief Inspector in 1945: Wilson, Ray & Ian Adam, *Special Branch. A History: 1883–2006* (Biteback, London, 2015), pp.197-8; https://ipfs.io/ipfs/QmXoypizjW3WknFiJnKLwHCnL72vedxjQkDDP1mXWo6uco/wiki/CharlesWalton_(murder_victim).html
3. See: TNA KV2/1297-1302; KV2/3669.
4. TNA KV2/731.

Chapter 13. 'Damn the Torpedoes!'

1. Grange airfield later became HMS *Siskin* in 1945 and HMS *Sultan* in 1956; it is now the home of the Defence School of Marine Engineering (DSMarE), the RN Air Engineering and Survival School, the Nuclear Department and HMS *Sultan* Royal Naval Volunteer Cadet Corps.
2. Taken from KV2/733 unless otherwise specified
3. TNA KV2/732.
4. *Air Force List*, May 1940, p.19a.
5. TNA KV2/733: Report (serial 187xb); the other Mills' notes (serial 187xc).
6. *Air Force List*, March 1941, pp.247; 497; *Ibid*, November 1938, column 173.
7. The only crash which occurred around about that date was on 7 January 1942 when a Bristol Beaufort Mk.IIA torpedo bomber (AW335) crashed on take-off at Gosport due to engine failure, killing the pilot, Flying Officer Harry Edgar Charles Elliott, and Aircraftman First Class (AC1) St. Clair Roderick James Andrews. https://aviation-safety.net/wikibase/wiki.php?id=192630
8. Serial number X8065. www.fortgilkicker.co.uk/torpedo.htm; https://aviation-safety.net/wikibase/wiki.php?id=158797; www.hambo.org/lancing/view_man.php?id=246. He is buried in Rowner (St. Mary) churchyard, Gosport. Commonwealth War Graves Commission: www.cwgc.org/find-war-dead/casualty/2350282/shaw,-richard-griffith/. The Commonwealth War

Graves Commission lists him as aged 35, the son of Edward Mackenzie Shaw and Emmeline Grace Shaw, and husband of Joan Mabel Shaw.
9. https://patentimages.storage.googleapis.com/bf/b1/b3/d7d23490c3cf2e/US2414928.pdf
10. TNA KV2/732.
11. TNA KV2/732.
12. TNA KV2/734. RAF Finningley in Yorkshire during the Second World War was part of Bomber Command and home to various units.
13. *Supplement to the London Gazette*, 29 November 1960, p.8146.
14. TNA KV2/734.

Chapter 14. Jean Castelain
1. TNA CO167/861/15.
2. According to the *Air Force List*, January 1943, p.17, Ferrier was with the Directorate of Intelligence (Security), Deputy Directorate of Intelligence (Security); in May 1944 he was a squadron leader: *Air Force List*, May 1944, p.17; in 1940–41 AI1Z dealt with Postal & Telegraphic Censorship: http://forum.12oclockhigh.net/showthread.php?t=26604
3. In 1947 Jacques Antonin Maurice Cochemé, AFC was a flight lieutenant: *Supplement to the London Gazette*, 1 January 1947, p.28.
4. *British Medical Journal*, 15 May 1943, p.617: www.bmj.com/content/bmj/1/4297/local/admin.pdf
5. TNA KV2/728.
6. Auxillou's son, the late Raymond Dennis Auxillou Jr., stated that 'My father was a behind the lines British Officer, French speaking spy for MI6 … He had been behind in France for two years and escaped when the Gestapo had swept up his Resistance Movement Escape Line.'[sic] After the war Auxillou was posted to Vienna as a colonel in the British Army. He immigrated to Canada in 1949, settling in Woodstock, Ontario before he died at the age of 83. https://ambergriscaye.com/raymondauxillou/. The *Supplement to the London Gazette* for 10 December 1948, p.6424, gives the following entry: 'INTELLIGENCE CORPS. War Subs. Capt. R. D. AUXILLOU (348673) relinquishes his commn., 11th Dec. 1948, and is granted the hon. rank of Maj.' He is also listed as a lieutenant, Intelligence Corps, on the staff list of IS9, No. 9 Intelligence School, part of MI9: www.arcre.com/mi9/is9apxg
7. Possibly Squadron Leader Ralph Cleland (1906–48), who had been with HQ Advanced Air Striking Force (BEF, France) for air staff training duties in 1939, and No.2 British Air Mission (with the BEF, France) as Officer-in-Charge of Eastern Detachment in 1940.
8. TNA KV2/734.
9. TNA HS9/358/5.
10. West, Nigel, *Secret War: The Story of SOE* (Hodder & Stoughton, London, 1992), p.135; republished by Pen & Sword, Barnsley, 2019, p.134. AL was the Air Operations section. DD/B was Lieutenant Colonel John Munn, Codes, Ciphers and Telegrams section, or Major Bertie Blount of the Scientific Research section.

Chapter 15. A Parting of the Ways
1. TNA KV2/730.
2. TNA2/741.
3. TNA KV2/730.
4. TNA KV2/731.
5. TNA KV2/734.
6. This may have been the solicitors Abraham Kramer (1908–96) and Jonathan Michael Kramer of 40 Portland Place, London W1.
7. TNA KV2/735.

Chapter 16. Declarations of Love
1. Hélène de Lonza Dantas was in 1942 the director of PACT (Propagande et Action Contre le Taudis – Propaganda and Action against Slums) in Lyon and editor-in-chief of *Terres et Pierres*. She also became the first Secretary-General of the Fédération PACT ARIM (Association de restauration immobilière) founded in 1951. Her uncle, Luis Martins de Souza Dantas, was the Brazilian ambassador to the Vichy government, responsible for helping hundreds of Jews to escape from France by issuing them with diplomatic visas to enter Brazil.
2. 'La commedia è finita!' Canio, in Leoncavallo's *I Pagliacci*, Act 2.
3. TNA KV2/729.
4. In February 1944 she changed her name to Hamilton. See: the *London Gazette*, 22 February 1944, p.922.

Chapter 17. 'A Person of Hostile Associations'
1. TNA KV2/733.
2. TNA KV2/733.
3. Extract from TNA HO 862944; KV2/737.
4. Second Epistle to Timothy, Chapter 4, Verse 7. The translation referred to by this author mentions a 'crown of justice': http://biblescripture.net/2Timothy.html
5. When Frank Smith first introduced potato crisps in the 1920s, they were not ready salted, but had a small twist of blue paper included in the bag, containing a small portion of salt (0.6g) to be sprinkled on the crisps at will.
6. TNA KV2/732.
7. TNA KV2/732.
8. TNA KV4/344. Jean Abel Louis Poumeau de Lafforest appeared in a Look-Up Summary from the Royal Victoria Patriotic School dated 28 July 1942: 'Possible traces in connection with Stella LONSDALE who had a paper with some notes of enquiries she was to make about KRAFT, November 1941.' See also Ch.10, n.18.
9. 'The London Divisional Signals, Royal Corps of Signals. The divisional signals were based at Signal House, 20, Atkins Road, Clapham Park, London S.W.12. The unit can trace its history back to 1861, with the formation of the 1st Tower Hamlet Militia. The unit became part of the Royal Engineers, which was then responsible for Army communications. It served in The Great War as a Telegraph Company. In 1921, the unit became part of the Royal Signals as The 56th (London) Divisional Signals': www.britishmilitaryhistory.co.uk/wp-content/uploads/sites/9/2017/12/The_London_Division__1937_38_.pdf. It is now a TA Centre (Territorial Army).
10. TNA KV2/735.
11. TNA KV2/735.
12. Brigadier General Hugh Nugent Leveson-Gower, 1900–79.
13. Count de Borchrave (1898–1993) became the head of military intelligence for the Belgian government-in-exile at 32 Eaton Square during the Second World War.
14. TNA KV2/735.
15. 'Sougne' may have been Henri Joseph Bathélemy Edouard Lambert, *dit* Henri Sougné (called Henri Sougné), a chartered accountant of Verviers, Belgium, born in Wihogne, Belgium on 6 February 1913 and later married Joséphine Louise Guillemine Lecomte, according to an adoption notice in *Belgisches Staatsblad* (Issues 182-273, 13 July 1957, p.5073), when he and his wife were adopting Michel-Eduard Ninane, born on 12 February 1955. A novel about him claims to be 90 per cent factual and states that he was a Communist alderman in Verviers in September 1940. David Armstrong. Personal communication to the author, 10 March 2019. www.enaos.net/P1240.aspx?IdPer=112869&IdEsp=556338. Ellison, Mark Stuart & Eli Ellison, *Dear Mom, Dad & Ethel: World War II Through the Eyes*

of a Radio Man. A Novel (iUniverse, New York, 2004), p.174. There was also Henri Sougne, born 4 March 1921 listed as working for SOE, who is a more likely candidate and the right sort of age to qualify as a 'lad', whose file (HS9/1394/2) is closed until 1 January 2031; and Raymond Alphonse Elvire Joseph Sougne @ Raymond Sergers, born 17 March 1916 who also worked for SOE: TNA HS9/1394/3.
16. A John Henry Marshall (1923–2009) served as a flight sergeant (1004784) with the RCAF during the war with 138 (Special Duties) Squadron.
17. TNA HS9/162/6. See note 4, Chapter 20.
18. Tremain, *Victoire*, p.110; Ch.9, pp.121-27. Lieutenant (later Captain) Jósef Rzepka @ 'Krzysztof' @ 'Znicz' (1913–51); see: https://en.wikipedia.org/wiki/J%C3%B3zef_Rzepka
19. TNA KV2/735.
20. TNA KV2/735.
21. TNA KV2/735.
22. TNA HO862944/8. This file is not available, but extracts are quoted in TNA KV2/737.
23. McLaren, *op.cit.*, p.71; see also: The *London Gazette*, 21 February 1950, p.944.
24. Mrs Christabel Sybil Caroline Nicholson, the wife of Admiral (ret'd) Wilmot Nicholson, who had been arrested in connection with the Anna Wolkoff-Tyler Kent Affair and charged under the Official Secrets Act (1911). She was acquitted, but then interned under DR.18B. See: TNA KV2/902-4; HO144/22478-9.
25. Tremain, *op.cit*, p.311.

Chapter 18. 'Well, There is Only One Lie …'
1. Young's report, dated 24 February 1942, and that of Nina, written by Cyril Mills, are taken from KV2/734.
2. Randall is mentioned in: Isenberg, Sheila, *A Hero of Our Own: The Story of Varian Fry* (iUniverse Inc., Lincoln, 2001, 2005), Ch.8. n.142, p.302.
3. Marcel Joseph Fernand Verges, born Marseille, 12 October 1914, died 13 April 1964; merchant seaman and member of FNFL: www.francaislibres.net/liste/fiche.php?index=100395
4. See Ch.6, n.7.
5. Maurois, André, *Climats* (Grasset, Paris, 1962) – a novel about love and relationships, set in the early 20th century, first published in 1928, is considered a classic of French literature.
6. TNA KV2/734.
7. Hassell H. Dick was now working at the State Department in Washington DC and was prepared to answer any questions about Stella that MI5 wished to put to him.
8. TNA KV2/734.
9. TNA KV2/732.
10. TNA KV2/733. A passenger list of Hebrew names gives the Binders' arrival in Buenos Aires on 11 August 1939 on the SS *Almanzora*, a liner formerly operated by Royal Mail Lines, but requisitioned as a troopship in 1939. Binder and his wife Laetitia Mary G.B. Binder arrived at Liverpool on 29 November 1941 on the MV *Melbourne Star* from Río de la Plata (River Plate), saying that he intended to enlist in HM Forces, and giving an address in Harrogate: www.hebrewsurnames.com/arrival_ALMANZORA_1939-08-11
11. TNA KV2/733.
12. The SS *Batory*, built in 1934 in Gdynia, was a Polish merchant ship employed mainly as a troop ship during the Second World War.

Chapter 19. Aylesbury or Bust!
1. Riddell, a member of the Right Club, and a close friend of Anna Wolkoff and American diplomat Tyler Kent, who were both convicted in 1940 under the Official Secrets Act (1911) for passing secrets to Germany, was interned under DR.18B on 29 May 1940 and

released from Holloway in 1943. This and other accounts are all taken from KV2/735 unless otherwise specified.
2. TNA KV2/1097.
3. TNA KV2/706.
4. *Daily Express*, 11 July 1942, in: TNA KV2/735.
5. For more information on Taylour see: Willetts, Paul, *Rendezvous at the Russian Tea Rooms* (Constable, London, 2016), paperback edition, pp. xvi, 219, 253, 293-4, 295, 319, 375, 392; TNA HO 45/23667/1; HO 45/23667.
6. See: TNA KV2/832-833; HO 283/65; HO 45/25731; Willetts, *op.cit.*, pp. xvi, 153, 180, 202-3, 216, 229, 231, 252.
7. Camp WX was based at Peel on the Isle of Man, in operation from 1941 to September 1942 when it was moved to Dartmoor prison; used to hold former Camp 020 inmates.
8. TNA KV2/735.
9. TNA KV2/735.
10. TNA KV2/736.
11. *The Sunday Pictorial*, 9 August 1942, in: TNA KV2/736.
12. TNA KV2/736.
13. Equal parts of water and baking soda are used. A heat source, such as a light bulb, or grape juice is used to reveal the writing.
14. TNA KV2/736.
15. TNA KV2/736.
16. Tremain, *op.cit.*, pp.284, 290-5, 297-8, 300, 302-3, 305-7, 310-12, 317, 375, 377, 379.
17. TNA KV2/737.
18. Tremain, *op.cit.*, pp.312-3. In a letter dated 21 February 1944.
19. TNA KV2/736.
20. TNA KV2/736.
21. TNA KV2/736.

Chapter 20. 'A Very Cheap Specimen of a Human Being'
1. TNA KV2/737.
2. TNA KV2/737.
3. See, Neave, *op.cit.*, p.117.
4. His SOE file (TNA HS9/162/6) states he was a commercial traveller born in Bromley, Kent, 21 March 1913. SOE Central Registry in 1943 recommended that 'We consider this man entirely unsuited for the purpose for which you want him.' Vetting forms to be stamped 'Not to be employed'; Service Historique de Défense: SHD PF GR 16 P 63100.
5. Foot, M.R.D. & J.M. Langley, *MI9* (Little, Brown & Co., Boston; Toronto, 1980), p.133; Langley, *op.cit.*, reprinted by Pen & Sword, Barnsley, 2013); Neave, *op.cit.*, no pagination in online version accessed; see also: www.conscript-heroes.com/Art21-Titania-Rosalind-960.html; www.conscript-heroes.com/Art15-Bluebottle-960.html. TNA HO334/517/954 on Ludmilla Blanchain.
6. www.christopherlong.co.uk/pub/fourcade.html
7. Nadia (1920–93), daughter of Countess Lily Pastré @ Marie-Louise Double de Saint-Lambert (1891–1974) and Count Jean André Hubert Jean Pastré (1888–1960): www.musiques-regenerees.fr/GhettosCamps/Clandestinite/PastreLily.html; https://gw.geneanet.org/wikifrat?lang=en&n=pastre&oc=0&p=nadege+claire+andree+renee+therese
8. www.christopherlong.co.uk/pub/fourcade.html. He does not appear to be Polish politician Jan Stanisław Jankowski (1882–1953).
9. Alexander Esway (1895–1947), born Sándor Ezry, in Budapest.
10. Pilot Officer (later Wing Commander) Thomas Campbell 'John' Parker whose Hurricane was shot down over St. Quentin on 20 May 1940, and evaded capture in Belgium and France: TNA WO208/3298/19.

11. A fighter ace shot down on 17 June 1941 near Fauquembergues in the Pas-de-Calais *département*, referred to as a Squadron Leader by Airey Neave. See: Neave, *op.cit.*, pp.93, 99-109, 218, and by Helen Long: Long., *op.cit.*, p.142. He became a wing commander in 1953. Obituary: www.telegraph.co.uk/news/obituaries/1422556/Wing-Commander-Taffy-Higginson.html
12. Possibly Pierre Dehillotte, who died at Buchenwald, 2 March 1945, author of *Gestapo: l'organisation, les chefs, les agents, l'action de la Gestapo à l'étranger* (Payot, Paris, 1940).
13. Possibly Mathilde Henriette Lagrange, wife of Pierre Cathala, Minister of Finance in Pierre Laval's Vichy government.

Chapter 21. The 'Pot Calling the Kettle Black'
1. See: Tremain, *op.cit.*, pp. 62, 71, Ch.6, pp.85-98. The Kraus files (TNA KV2/1727-9) are very poor, faded mimeographed copies and not very legible.
2. For more information on Graumann @ von Gröning and his relationship with Chapman see: Macintyre, Ben, *Agent Zigzag* (Bloomsbury, London, 2007) and Booth, Nicholas, *Zigzag* (Arcade Publishing, New York, 2007), trade paperback.
3. TNA KV2/456.
4. See TNA KV2/456, Chapman, Vol.2, serial 68a.
5. TNA KV2/737.
6. MI5 files on Mond and Castelain, PF.413,542 and PF.304,750 respectively, are not available from the National Archives at Kew.
7. Neave, *op.cit.*, pp.120-1,160. This was actually Fabien de Cortès, who had worked with the 'Pat O'Leary' line and was arrested at the same time as Guérisse in March 1943.
8. *German Intelligence Service Personnel of the Abwehr Stations in France*, CIA document declassified 2001 and 2007: https://numbers-stations.com/cia/German%20Intelligence%20Service%20(wwii),%20%20Vol.%201/GERMAN%20INTELLIGENCE%20SERVICE%20(WWII),%20%20VOL.%201_0004.pdf; *Sûreté de l'État, Allemands Recherchés*, p.37: www.cegesoma.be/docs/Invent/AA_1312_ListeAllemandsRecherches.pdf; TNA KV1973; KV2/560.
9. Tremain, David, *The Beautiful Spy* (The History Press, Stroud, 2019), Ch.5, pp.85-91, 112, Appx 5; TNA KV2/1293.
10. There is no evidence that she had.
11. TNA KV2/737.
12. TNA KV2/737.
13. Paillole, *op.cit.*, p.384. In 1944 Desvoges, as it is spelled in Paul Paillole's book, was head of military security in Fez, Morocco.
14. *Hansard*, 4 November 1943, Series 5, Volume 393, c849: https://api.parliament.uk/historic-hansard/sittings/1943/nov/04

Chapter 22. Stella's Circle
1. TNA KV2/739.
2. http://chateaubriant.org/560-livre-max-veper
3. Commission Féminine des Guerres 14-18/39-45 des Amis de Vieux Calais: www.resistance62.net/Gelabert%20Jeanne.pdf
4. He may have been connected to Claude Rochat who testified before a military court in Dijon on 9–13 March 1948 about fourteen former resistance fighters who appeared before the court: http://theses.univ-lyon2.fr/documents/getpart.php?id=lyon2.2000.chantin_r&part=18696
5. A Marcel Corgnet is listed as treasurer of the mutual aid society mutual help of stenodactylos and assimilated accountants in Nantes, 1934 in the *Official Journal of the French Republic. Laws and decrees*, 1934/02/15 (Year 66, No. 39).

Chapter 23. The Advisory Committee
1. Home Office files, TNA HO283/47 or HO45/25745.
2. Later Lord Morris of Borth-y-Gest.
3. The full transcript of the Committee's hearings into the case can be found in Stella's MI5 file, KV2/737.
4. TNA KV2/731. On 6 January 1944 Gordon was listed in the *Supplement to the London Gazette* as a temporary colonel (p.150), and on 18 July 1947 in the *Second Supplement to the London Gazette* as being awarded the Legion of Merit (p.3319); he was awarded the OBE on 6 January 1944. See: TNA WO373/77/466.
5. TNA KV2/732. Information on Father John Wilfred Murray, CSsR (1901–59) indicates that in 1939 he was a naval chaplain. If this was the same person, he must have transferred to the army. He was on board the *Lancastria* when it was sunk, but survived and rescued two men. This would tie in with Murray's time in Nantes. He died at the Redemptorist House of Studies at Hawkstone, Shropshire, on 6 October 1959. Very Rev. Fr. Richard Reid, CSsR, The Redemptorist Community, St. Mary's Monastery, Clapham: personal communication to the author, 20 March 2019.
6. TNA KV2/732.
7. TNA KV2/2748. Conflicting information exists about exactly who Hermann Hyman was. If he was actually Hermann Heinemann (Heinmann), who was born in Liebnau on 31 December 1870 (aged about 71 in 1941, so hardly '60 odd'), he was transported from Frankfurt-am-Main to Terezín concentration camp on 16 September 1942, and thence to Auschwitz where he died on 19 November 1943. See: www.joodsmonument.nl/en/page/122319/hermann-heinemann. Another Hermann Heinemann was born in Aachen, Germany, 4 December 1890: https://discovery.nationalarchives.gov.uk/details/r/C14916668. HO/396/34/256
8. All quotes are taken from KV2/737 unless otherwise specified.
9. Kitson, *op.cit.*, Ch.3, pp.43-56, for more information on the French intelligence services during this period.
10. *Ibid.*, pp.43-44.

Chapter 24. 'If I Had Been a Nasty Piece of Work ...'
1. West, Nigel, *Spycraft Secrets: An Espionage A-Z* (The History Press, Stroud, 2016), p.170; West, Nigel, 'Cold War Intelligence Defectors', in: Johnson, Loch K. (ed), *Handbook of Intelligence Studies* (Routledge, London; New York, 2009), p.232.
2. There is now in Nantes a Clinique Sourdille which is an ophthalmic clinic which sounds like it might be what she was referring to, although the building is new.
3. This could have been Roland Eugène Jean Alexandre, born in Jouy-à Josas, France on 30 June 1921 who was involved with the Angers/Nantes circuits, executed at Gross-Rosen in September 1944. See: Grehan & Mace, *op.cit.*, pp.14-15.
4. Listed as E. Fradet, seller of typewriters in 1930: https://app-archives-inventaires.loire-atlantique.fr/pleade/embed/functions/ead/attached/FRAD044_cadredeclassement/FRAD044_cadredeclassement_e0053871.pdf
5. Grehan & Mace, *op.cit.*, pp.142-3.
6. TNA KV2/736.
7. TNA KV2/738. Camp 020R was the Reserve Camp at Huntercombe near Nuffield, Oxfordshire.
8. For more information on Boyd see: Stephens, Robin, *Camp 020 and the Nazi Spies* (Public Record Office, London, 2000), pp.214-5; TNA WO 416/38/177.
9. TNA KV2/738.
10. TNA KV2/738.

11. West, Nigel, *MI5. British Security Service Operations 1909–1945* (Bodley Head, London, 1981), p.139; republished by Pen & Sword, Barnsley, 2019, p.99.
12. See: https://fr.wikipedia.org/wiki/Maurice_Duclos and Chapter 9.
13. Probably in Montpelier or Nice, according to his MI5 file: TNA KV2/2848.
14. Possibly Pierre Dehillotte. See Chapter 20, note 12.
15. TNA KV2/738. A book in the Deutsche Nationalbibliothek (German National Library) is a possible contender, given that its subject is Anglo-American law, and that RENÉ had studied law in the USA: Rauch, Siegfried, *Der Begriff der 'Consideration' im anglo-amerikanischen Schuldrecht* (The Concept of 'Consideration' in Anglo-American Law of Obligations), (Würzburg, 1940).

Chapter 25. 'A Fog of Falsehood and Misrepresentation'
1. Later Director General of MI5 (1953–6) and Chief of SIS (1956–68).
2. TNA KV2/738: Appendix A: Highlights the various facts and dates mentioned by witnesses in their statements; Appendix B: Statement by Marcel Dugast; Appendix C: Statement by Madame Jenny Dazy; Appendix D: Statement by Madame Mouillard; Appendix E: Statement by Madame Maud Martineau; Appendix F: Statement by Abbé Jean Luneau; Appendix G: French newspapers concerning death of Jean Platiau (*Ouest France*); Appendix H: Statement by Odette Châtenet; Appendix I: Letter from Stella Lonsdale to Odette Châtenet, 1 April 1941 – Letter from Stella Lonsdale to Odette Châtenet, Friday morning (possibly 4 April); Letter from Stella Lonsdale to Odette Châtenet, Sunday evening (possibly 6 April).
3. TNA KV2/738.
4. Appendix B of Young's report, TNA KV2/738.
5. Appendix C of Young's report, TNA KV2/738.
6. Appendices D & E of Young's report, TNA KV2/738.
7. Appendix F of Young's report, TNA KV2/738.
8. TNA KV2/456; De Zeng, Henry L. IV, *Luftwaffe Airfields 1935–45 France (with Corsica and Channel Isles)*, July 2014, p.264 et seq: www.ww2.dk/Airfields%20-%20France.pdf
9. This may have been Georges Tardy (1921–64) of Vauclaix who married Janine Pauline Fernande Hugon (1927–91) on 15 April 1939, or the painter Georges Tardy (1883–1980).
10. TNA KV2/738.
11. TNA KV2/738; see Ch.9, n.3 regarding the error in the catalogue entry for document reference HW 19/17.
12. TNA KV2/738.
13. TNA KV2/738.
14. TNA KV2/738.
15. TNA KV2/738.

Chapter 26. The Advisory Committee's Report
1. The committee's full report can be read in TNA KV2/739.
2. Talking confidentially – OED.

Chapter 27. 'The Woman Who Laughs Like a Horse'
1. Veuve (widow) Mahé was a former political detainee and signatory to a letter to Brigadier Daly at the British Embassy, Paris, of those shot in Nantes after the assassination of Karl Hotz: http://archivesnantes1941.blogspot.com/2014/02/1944-11-11-parents-general-daly.html. It is possible she is related to Henri Mahé @ Berry who was director of the school at La Baule, and full time P2 agent in the *Jade-Fitzroy* organization. See: *Cahier de lAremors*, l'Association d'Etude et de Recherche sur l'histoire du Mouvement Ouvrier de la Région de St-Nazaire, No.5, pp.21, 26, 41.

2. A Marcel Hevin, an 'agent technique' for the SNCF, is shown as living at 44, Boulevard Gabriel Lauriol. He was shot along with Hubert Caldecott. See: *Trial of the Major War Criminals Before the International Military Tribunal, Nuremberg*, Nuremberg, Germany, 1949, p.203: www.loc.gov/rr/frd/Military_Law/pdf/NT_Vol-XXXVII.pdf
3. Charles Platiau (no relative). Personal communication to the author, 1 June 2109, quoted from: Berlière, Jean-Marc & Franck Liaigre, *Le Sang des communistes* (Paris: Fayard, 2004), and: http://maitron-fusilles-40-44.univ-paris1.fr/spip.php?page=imprimir_articulo&id_article=167133, 2007–2019 © Copyright Maitron/Editions de l'Atelier – All rights reserved. http://maitron-fusilles-40-44.univ-paris1.fr/spip.php?article166993. Saunier was an insurance agent in Saint-Suliac suspected of working for Allied intelligence and another of the hostages shot at Mont-Valérien: http://maitron-fusilles-40-44.univ-paris1.fr/spip.php?article166993
4. TNA KV2/739.
5. Notable Names Database (NNDB): www.nndb.com/people/212/000114867/
6. Orwell, George & Reginald Reynolds, *British Pamphleteers. Volume I. From the 16th Century to the 18th Century* (London: Allan Wingate, 1948); Taylor, A.J.P. & Reginald Reynolds, *British Pamphleteers. Volume II. From the French Revolution to the present time* (London: Allan Wingate, 1951): https://orwellsocietyblog.wordpress.com/2016/11/19/british-pamphleteers-volumes-one-and-two/. His best-known work is *The White Sahibs in India* (Martin Secker & Warburg, London, 1937).
7. TNA KV2/739.
8. TNA KV2/739.
9. Marquess of Donegal, *Sunday Dispatch*, April 18, 1937, p.1, and *Toronto Globe and Mail*, April 21, 1937, p.10, cited in: McLaren, *op.cit.*, pp.185, 248, n.52.
10. During the Spanish Civil War Cazalet had been a strong supporter of Franco's Phalange party and served on the Friends of National Spain committee.
11. *Hansard*: https://api.parliament.uk/historic-hansard/commons/1937/may/31/spain
12. *Vapaa Sana* (*Free Press*), Toronto, April 21, 1937, pp.1,3; see also *Toronto Globe and Mail*, April 21, 1937, p.10, cited in: McLaren, *op.cit.*, pp.185-6, 248, n.53.
13. *Winnipeg Free Press*, Wednesday April 21, 1937.
14. TNA MEPO3/2030.
15. 'Jewel Theft Charges', *The Times*, London, 2 May 1939, p.11.
16. Lynden, Albert, 'Why Germany Banned Jewish Culture', in: *Blackshirt*, 25 July 1936, cited in: Gottlieb, Julie V. & Thomas P. Linehan (eds), *The Culture of Fascism: Visions of the Far Right in Britain* (: I.B. Tauris, London & New York, 2004), p.214. See also: TNA HO 144/16538 (Closed until 2033); HO 334/130/2070.
17. TNA KV2/739.
18. TNA KV2/739.
19. The *London Gazette* gives it as the South Counties Oil Company: *London Gazette*, 21 February 1950, p.944.
20. TNA KV2/739.
21. TNA HO396/100/395. Resi Clark, *née* Weltlinger, b. Berlin, 1921, arrested in 1944 for the forgery of two National Insurance stamps.
22. TNA KV2/739.
23. TNA KV2/739.
24. TNA KV2/739.
25. TNA KV2/739.
26. TNA KV2/739.
27. The Seymour Tyre & Motor Co. Ltd was dissolved in around June 1951: The *London Gazette*, 10 April 1951, p.2010: www.thegazette.co.uk/London/issue/39199/page/2010/data.pdf

Chapter 28. Stella's Statement to the Abwehr

1. TNA KV2/739.
2. Brigadier General (later Major General) Sir Hugh Keppel Biddulph Bethell: Sheffield, Gary & John Bourne (eds), *Douglas Haig War Diaries and Letters 1914–1918* (Phoenix, London, 2006), paperback edition, p.247, n.5; www.arrse.co.uk/community/threads/major-general-sir-hugh-bethell.159633/; www.greatwarforum.org/topic/113452-keppel-bethell/; www.thepeerage.com/p52455.htm
3. Likely the Right Reverend John Lonsdale, educated at Eton and King's College, Cambridge; Preacher of Lincoln's Inn (1836); the third Principal of King's College, London (1838/9–43); Bishop of Lichfield (1843–67), having turned down the appointment of Provost of Eton in 1840. Even so, he could hardly have been John's grandfather, but possibly great-grandfather.
4. *Christie's* catalogue, 30 November 2015: www.christies.com/PDF/catalog/2015/CKS10401_SaleCat.pdf, Lot 42.
5. Later Colonel Commandant of the Intelligence Corps (1952–60), and also considered for the position of Director General of MI5 after the war, but lost out to Sir Percy Sillitoe. Between 1937 and 1938 he was an instructor at the Army Staff College at Camberley; from 1939 to 1940 he was Commander, Royal Artillery (CRA) of I Corps of the BEF, and from January 1938 until September 1939 he was the GSO1 of the 2nd Infantry Division.
6. Alan 'Fred' Judge, Military Intelligence Museum, Chicksands: personal communication to the author, 25 October 2018.
7. This may have been George Edward Hicks, born in London in 1886, who is shown in the records of the Royal Aero Club to have possessed an Aviator's Certificate. Andrew Dawrant, Trustee of the Royal Aero Club: personal communications the author, 26 & 27 April 2018; George Edward Hicks: TNA AIR76/226/12. More likely it is George Rensburg (or Rhensburg) Hicks, born on 24 January 1900 in Woodford, Essex (other accounts say Walthamstow, which is close by), who was credited with eight 'kills' during his service with the Royal Flying Corps during the First World War, and died on 24 November 1951. George Rensburg Hicks: TNA AIR76/226/13; WO339/127410. In July 1927 his address was c/o Provincial Air Service, Toronto (the Ontario Provincial Air Service was formed in 1924) and living at 164 Glen Road, Toronto, Ontario, Canada. In March 1940 he was serving in the RAF Reserve as a Squadron Leader in the General Duties Branch. By 1948 he is listed as the same rank, but in the Secretarial Branch: *The London Gazette*, 5 March 1940, p.1318; *Supplement to the London Gazette*, 1 June 1948, p.3245.
8. Brevet Lieutenant Colonel William Turner Murray-Bisset (1890–1949), commanded the 6th (Banffshire Battalion), The Gordon Highlanders, part of the 153rd Infantry Brigade, 51st Highland Division, BEF, which landed at Le Havre in January 1940 and was deployed to northern France. Once in France the 6th Gordons transferred to the 2nd Infantry Brigade and were evacuated at Dunkirk. http://51hd.co.uk/tag/gordon_highlanders; Bellis, *op.cit.*, p.43.
9. No connection with the character in the Jeffrey Archer novels.

Chapter 29. The *Sunday Express* Affair

1. TNA KV2/739. 23 Belmont Court, Finchley Road, London NW3.
2. www.legislation.gov.uk/ukpga/2000/36/contents
3. KV2/739 and KV2/740.
4. Lt. Cmdr. Patrick O'Leary, 'Secret Agent. British traitor betrays three of my best men', *Daily Express*, 20 April 1947, p.2., cited in: TNA KV2/739.
5. TNA KV2/739 – 546a, dated 10.5.47 and 547a, dated 14.5.47 further to 546a. On 5 December 2018 MI5 responded to a request made by the author on 20 September 2018 for

access to those documents. Having reviewed them, MI5 decided that the documents could be released to the National Archives 'with only minor redactions' and are now included here.
6. Now known to be Sylvia Cooper-Smith.
7. TNA KV2/739, and see note 4. Pitt-Rivers' MI5 file (KV2/831) has been heavily weeded and redacted but a mention of the letter from Vivian in the minute sheet gives the date as 9 May 1947 and not 10 May.
8. TNA KV2/739, and see note 4.
9. https://en.wikipedia.org/wiki/Uriah_the_Hittite
10. TNA KV2/739, and see note 4. Unfortunately, there are no references to Willyams in the *Army List*, but since it was sent from Willyams' address in Carnanton, St Columb Minor, Cornwall, he is possibly the grandson of the late Colonel Edward Brydges Williams (1834–1916), the Liberal MP for Truro (1857–9; 1880–5) and East Cornwall (1868–74).
11. Lyman, Robert, *Operation Suicide* (Quercus, London, 2012), p.125.
12. Hinchley Cooke was referred to as 'a Colonel in His Majesty's Army, Military Intelligence, at the War Office', and Seymour Bingham of B1b was referred to as a 'civil assistant on the General Staff of the War Office': Tremain, *Rough Justice*, (Amberley, Stroud, 2016) p.193; TNA KV2/45.
13. https://swarb.co.uk/asiatic-petroleum-co-ltd-v-anglo-persian-oil-co-ltd-ca-1916/ and cited in: www.cambridge.org/core/journals/cambridge-law-journal/article/evidence-excluded-by-considerations-of-state-interest/70B4D3E69E228B92C1367A4633B5391D
14. The Treasury Solicitor's full judgement can be read in TNA KV/739, serial 565a.
15. https://api.parliament.uk/historic-hansard/commons/1939/jun/05/loss-of-his-majestys-ship-thetis. See also: TNA TS32/124-5; TS36/358; TS32/119; www.dailypost.co.uk/news/nostalgia/how-hms-thetis-sank-coast-2729422; www.dailymail.co.uk/news/article-1167547/REVEALED-How-Navy-let-99-sailors-die-avoid-damaging-stricken-sub.html
16. http://swarb.co.uk/duncan-v-cammell-laird-and-company-limited-discovery-hl-27-apr-1942/; Baber, Mary, Home Affairs Section, House of Commons Library, *Public Interest Immunity, Research Paper 96/25*, 22 February 1996, p.5, *et seq.*: researchbriefings.files.parliament.uk/documents/RP96-25/RP96-25.pdf; further discussion on Crown Privilege is in *Hansard*: https://api.parliament.uk/historic-hansard/commons/1956 /oct /26/crown-privilege-documents-and-oral
17. Davies, Philip H.J., *MI6 and the Machinery of Spying* (Frank Cass, London; Portland, 2004), paperback edition, pp.113, 126; Foot & Langley, *op.cit.*, pp.58-9.
18. https://en.wikipedia.org/wiki/Crown_Proceedings_Act_1947; www.legislation.gov.uk/ukpga/Geo6/10-11/44/section/28
19. Captain Charles Sydenham Collinson, who had previously served in Ireland 1940–44. See: O'Halpin, Eunan, *Spying on Ireland: British Intelligence and Irish Neutrality During the Second World War* (Oxford University Press, Oxford, 2008), pp.xx, 113.
20. For a discussion on the *Security Service Act*, 1989, and ministerial responsibility see: Leigh, Ian & Laurence Lustgarten, 'Legislation. The Security Service Act, 1989', in: *The Modern Law Review*, November 1989, vol.52, pp. 801-836. See also: Lustgarten & Leigh, *In From the Cold: National Security and Parliamentary Democracy* (Clarendon Press, Oxford, 1994); Thomas, Rosamund M., *Espionage and Secrecy. The Official Secrets Acts 1911–1989 of the United Kingdom* (Routledge, London; New York, 2016).

Chapter 30. 'A Champagne-loving Brunette'
1. TNA KV2/739.
2. Hart, Bradley W., *George Pitt-Rivers and the Nazis* (Bloomsbury Academic, London, 2015), p.167.

3. Anthony Pitt-Rivers: personal communication to the author, 30 May 2019.
4. TNA KV2/831.
5. See: TNA KV2/831; TS 27/514 (Treasury Solicitor and HM Procurator-General, Application for Writs of Habeas Corpus under DR.18B); HO283/58/1 (closed extracts, 3 pp); HO 45/25725; HO 283/58
6. Hart, *op.cit.*, p.170.
7. Landis MacKellar, F., 'Captain George Henry Lane-Fox Pitt-Rivers and the origins of the IUSSP', Extended Abstract F. Landis MacKellar, Population Council, and Bradley Hart, Department of History, California State University, Fresno 29 April, 2014, p.12: https://epc2014.princeton.edu/papers/141068
8. TNA KV2/831.
9. TNA KV2/831.
10. See: Tremain, *Victoire*, pp.372-81; TNA KV2/831; TS 27/514 (Treasury Solicitor and HM Procurator-General, Application for Writs of Habeas Corpus under DR.18B); HO283/58/1 (closed extracts, 3 pp); HO 45/25725; HO 283/58
11. The *London Gazette*, 22 July 1952, p.3965; Benthall, Jonathan, *The Independent*, 25 August 2001.
12. Andrew Lownie: personal communication to the author, 27 June 2018; Angela Lownie: personal communication to the author, 5 August 2018.
13. In the England & Wales, Civil Registration Marriage Index, 1916–2005 on Ancestry.co.uk it gives the date of registration as 1968 between April and June in Chelsea.
14. McLaren, *op.cit.*, p.223; Hart, *op.cit.*, pp.174,176; Sweet, *op.cit.*, pp.253-4.
15. Hart, *op.cit.*, p.176.
16. Feay, Suzi, *The Independent on Sunday*, 6 November 2011, writing about *The West End Front*.
17. *Ancestry* website gives the date as February 1994.

Afterword
1. Lyman, *op.cit.*, p.125.
2. Gelles, Dr Mike, Exploring the Mind of a Spy: https://issuu.com/eyespy/docs/the_mind_of_a_spy; www.wrc.noaa.gov/wrso/security_guide/mind.htm. See also: Schwartz, Janet Mielke, 'Exploring the Mind of a Spy': *The Forensic Examiner*, Spring 2007, pp.67-8: https://lastsummerwithoscar.com/whitecollarcorruption.com/wp-content/uploads/2012/06/MindofaSpy.pdf and: Michalak, Sebastian, 'Motives of espionage against one's own country in the light of idiographic studies': *Polish Psychological Bulletin*, 2011, vol.42(1), pp.1-4: www.degruyter.com/downloadpdf/j/ppb.2011.42.issue-1/v10059-011-0001-2/v10059-011-0001-2.pdf
3. TNA MEPO3/902, cited in McLaren, p.23.
4. TNA KV2/739.
5. Furse, Elisabeth & Ann Barr, *Dream Weaver* (Chapman, Edinburgh,1993).
6. Tremain, David, *Rough Justice*; and Ch.23, 24, 26.

Appendix 2. The 'Siegfried' Letters
1. TNA KV2/728, serial 1FFFA. This letter can also be found in KV2/739.
2. TNA KV2/728, serial 21A.

Selected Bibliography

Primary Sources
HO334/163/18538 (Bendemann); HO334/239/240 (Bendemann); HO396/8/4 (Binder); HS9/358/5 (Le Corvaisier); KV2/728-741 (Stella Lonsdale); KV2/81-2; KV2/281-2 (Meissner); KV4/469 (post-war Liddell Diaries); KV2/1328 (Bensmann); KV2/2136 (Rohleder); KV2/158 (Paulsen); KV2/2848 (Mumme); KV2/2850 (Gorman); KV2/2102-03 (Meiler); KV2/1097 (Brett-Perring); KV2/408 (Garthe); KV2/3778 (Kosyakov); KV2/1297-1302 (Schutz); KV2/3669 (Harbottle)

Secondary Sources
Andrew, Christopher, *Defence of the Realm* (Viking Canada, Toronto, 2009).
Bristow, Desmond, *A Game of Moles* (Little, Brown & Company, London, 1993).
Clutton-Brock, Oliver, *RAF Evaders* (Bounty Books, London, 2012).
Curry, John, *The Security Service 1908–1945: The Official History* (Public Record Office, London, 1999).
Darling, Donald, *Secret Sunday* (William Kimber, London, 1975).
Fitzsimons, Peter, *Nancy Wake* (Harper Collins, London, 2002), paperback edition.
Foot, M.R.D. & J.M. Langley, *MI9 Escape and Evasion 1939–1945* (Little, Brown & Company, Boston; Toronto,1980), 1st American edition.
Hart, Bradley W., *George Pitt-Rivers and the Nazis* (Bloomsbury Academic, London, 2015).
Ireland, Josh, *The Traitors* (John Murray, London, 2017).
Kahn, David, *Hitler's Spies* (Hodder & Stoughton, London, 1978; DaCapo Press, Cambridge, MA, 2000).
Kitson, Simon, *The Hunt for Nazi Spies: Fighting Espionage in Vichy France* (University of Chicago Press, Chicago, 2008).
Lochery, Neill, *Lisbon: War in the Shadows of the City of Light, 1939–1945* (Public Affairs™, New York, 2012), paperback edition.
Long, Helen, *Safe Houses are Dangerous* (William Kimber, London, 1985).
Marnham, Patrick, *Wild Mary: A Life of Mary Wesley* (Vintage Books, London, 2007), paperback edition.
McLaren, Angus, *Playboys and Mayfair Men: Crime, Class, Masculinity and Fascism in 1930s London* (Johns Hopkins University Press, Baltimore, 2017).
Neave, Airey, *Saturday at M.I.9.* (Hodder & Stoughton, London, 1969).
Neave, Airey, *Little Cyclone* (Coronet Books/Hodder & Stoughton, London, 1985), paperback edition, 4th impression.

Nichol, John & Tony Rennell, *Home Run: Escape from Nazi Europe* (Penguin Books, London, 2008), paperback edition.

Paillole, Paul, *Fighting the Nazis: French Intelligence and Counterintelligence 1935–1945* (Enigma Books, New York, 2003).

Rankin, Nicholas, *Defending the Rock* (Faber & Faber, London, 2017).

Read, Anthony & David Fisher, *Colonel Z* (Hodder & Stoughton, London, 1984).

Stourton, Edward, *Cruel Crossing* (Transworld/Random House, London, 2014), paperback edition.

Sweet, Matthew, *The West End Front* (Faber & Faber, London, 2012), paperback edition.

Tillotson, Michael (ed), *SOE and Resistance, As Told in The Times Obituaries* (Continuum, London, 2011).

Tremain, David, *Rough Justice* (Amberley, Stroud, 2016).

Tremain, David, *Double Agent Victoire* (The History Press, Stroud, 2018).

Tremain, David, *The Beautiful Spy* (The History Press, Stroud, 2019).

Weber, Ronald, *The Lisbon Route: Entry and Escape in Nazi Europe* (Ivan R. Dee/Rowman & Littlefield, Lanham, 2011).

West, Nigel, *MI5. British Security Service Operations 1909–1945* (Bodley Head, London, 1981); Pen & Sword, Barnsley, 2019.

West, Nigel (ed), *The Guy Liddell Diaries Vol.1, 1939–1942* (Routledge, London; New York, 2005).

West, Nigel, *MI6. British Secret Intelligence Service Operations 1909–45* (Weidenfeld & Nicolson, London, 1983); Pen & Sword, Barnsley, 2019.

Willetts, Paul, *Rendezvous at the Russian Tea Rooms* (Constable, London, 2016), paperback edition.

Index

Abbott, George M., 34
Abwehr, 4, 9, 21–23, 25–27, 37, 43, 56, 65, 67–71, 82, 88–89, 115, 156, 158, 163, 165, 180, 208–9, 211, 213, 215, 219, 237–40, 246–47, 255, 270, 274. *See also* German Intelligence Service
Abwehr interrogation, 211
Abwehr interrogation document, 239
Addis, Jasper John, 12–13
Admiralty, 37, 88, 218–19, 221, 225–26, 230, 264
Advisory Committee, 14, 36, 45, 50, 80, 89, 121, 124–25, 134, 143, 168–78, 184, 186, 191, 193, 195, 197, 201, 222, 238–39, 271–72
Aix-en-Provence, 50, 80, 107–8, 130, 178
Alisch, Ernst, 263
American Consul, 20, 45, 182–83, 257
American Consulate, 34, 45–46, 79–80, 110, 129, 150–51, 182
André Gars, 179
  suspected Inspector, 48
Angers, 23, 25, 27, 36, 40, 44, 56–57, 63, 65–66, 69–71, 81, 110, 151, 162, 171, 174, 177, 180–81, 184, 186–89, 198, 204–5, 208–9, 213, 238, 245, 249–50
Angoulême, 115
Anjou, 22, 177
Auxillou, Raymond Dennis, 108
Aylesbury Prison, 55, 127–28, 138–41, 143, 145, 158–60, 235, 268

Bachkiroff, Barbara, 5
Bandinel, Madame Roland, 95
Barnes, Sir Thomas, 224
Barton, Susan, 5, 12, 25, 55, 93–94, 106, 114, 117, 132, 156–58, 161, 168, 172, 240
Bashkiroff, Vladimir, 5, 7, 209
Bauer, Maurice George, 96

Beaumont-Nesbitt, Paddy, 210
BEF (British Expeditionary Force), 12, 38, 151, 169, 266, 274
Bendemann, 166, 255, 277
  Oswald, 21
Berlitz Language School, 17, 21, 69, 162–64, 167, 170, 177, 182, 185, 189, 198, 211–12, 247, 249–50
Bernard, Ervin V., 63
Bernard, Hilde, 63–64
Bethell, Sir Hugh Keppel Biddulph, 274
Biarritz, 14–15, 170, 184, 188, 195, 249
Bibby, Private Amos, 19
Binder, Francis Martin, 135–37, 268, 277
Bingham, Seymour, 275
Bingham IV, Harry, 34–35, 194
Blanchain, Francis Paul, 126
Bosio, 44, 75, 102, 115, 141, 151, 258
Bosiot, 73. *See also* Bosio
Boulanger, Christian, 48, 69, 72, 82–84, 91, 93, 95–96, 98, 102, 110, 114–15, 118–19, 124, 134–36, 178–79, 240, 245, 247–48
Bowden, Bertram Vivian, 101
Boyle, Air Commodore Archie, 159
Bradford, Leonard, 41–43, 263
Brest, 23, 33, 36, 58, 86, 88, 262–63
Brett-Perring, 55, 277
Brisson, 162–63
British Army, 9, 169, 266
British Expeditionary Force *see* BEF
British Intelligence, 18, 21, 27, 32, 36–37, 40–42, 45, 65, 90, 95, 107, 165, 167, 173, 189, 191–94, 209, 237, 275
British Secret Intelligence Service Operations, 256, 278
Brooman-White, Lieutenant Colonel Dick, 184
Bruce, Jimmy Douglas Ferrier, 94, 100–101, 104–6, 173
Bruce, Mary, 105

Bruce, Victor, 37
Buchenhagen, Erich, 23
Buckmaster, Lieutenant Colonel Maurice, 258
Burdett, Olive, 138–39
Bürvenich, Sonderführer, 65–66

Caldecott, Hubert George William, 163–64, 273
Cammell Laird, 225, 228
Campillo brothers, 130, 160–64, 166–67, 188, 198, 206, 213, 215, 250
Canaris, Admiral Wilhelm, 22, 27, 247
Carré, Mathilde, 1, 55, 88, 128, 140, 143, 145, 156–57, 159, 235, 265
Caskie, Donald, 31
Castelain, 36, 46, 108–10, 151, 158, 178, 259, 270
Castelain, Jean, 36, 107, 109, 111, 178, 266
Castelain, Jean Joseph Xavier, 107
Castelain, Manuel Alfred Xavier, 107
Castelain, Marie Thérèse Antoinette, 107
Castellain, Jean, 34, 44, 46
Castellan, Dominique, 252
Castillo, Joachim, 130, 162–63, 177, 250
Catalan, Pilar, 163
Chagall, Marc, 35
Challan-Belval, Lieutenant Joseph, 47, 50, 259
Challan-Belval, Marie-Noël, 48, 259
Chalon-sur-Saône, 57
Chapman, Eddie, 11, 63, 156–57, 186, 270, 276
Château-Thierry, 1, 122, 138–39, 159
Chatelain, Jacques, 6
Châtenet, Odette, 177, 185–89, 195, 236, 250, 272
Churchill, Clementine, 234
CIA, 22–23, 65, 255, 257, 261, 270
Cinquième Bureau. 174. *See also* French intelligence services
Claubert, Raymond, 32, 108, 110, 157
Clifton, 211–12
Clive, Ernest Robert George, 1
Clive, John Norman, 1
Clive, Norah Janet, 1
Clive, Stella, 3, 5–6, 91
Clive, Stella Howson, 1
Cobham, Viscount, 3, 12, 17, 211, 252, 254

Cochemé, Alfred Ernest, 107
Cochemé, Jacques Antonin Maurice, 266
Cole, Harold, 31, 38, 150, 238, 258
Collinson, Captain Charles Sydenham, 227, 231, 275
'Colonel Passy,' 33
'Colonel Remy,' 88, 263
Cooper-Smith, Sylvia, 217, 221, 275
Coppe, Robert, 110, 182
Corgnet, Marcel, 166, 188, 206, 270
Count Sumarokov-Elston, 7
Cowgill, Felix, 53
Crane, Leslie, 12, 91, 112–14, 116, 201
Critchley, James H., 217
Crockatt, Brigadier Norman, 226, 228
Crown Prince Alois, 25–28
Cussen, Edward, 8, 198
Cuthbert, Sister Marie, 177, 212, 249

Daily Express, 140, 217–18, 220, 235, 269, 274
Dansey, Colonel Claude, 29–30, 34, 72, 84–85, 88
Darlan, Admiral, 70, 108, 125, 130, 153, 181–82, 262
Darling, Major Donald Robert, 29–30, 141, 150, 226, 256, 277
Davidson, Major General Francis Henry Norman, 210
Dazy, 165–66, 177, 190, 204, 206, 238, 249
Dazy, Jenny, 166, 185–86, 188–89, 272
Dazy, René, 131, 164–66, 177, 187, 189–90, 206, 250
Deere, Cicely Yvonne, 264
Dehillotte, Pierre, 150, 182, 270, 272
Delbar, Yves, 79, 130, 134, 181, 262
de Naeyer, 165–66, 177, 206
DePauw University, 63–64, 67, 261
de Renzy Martin, Lieutenant Colonel Edward, 29
Dernbach, Oberstleutnant Friederich, 21–24, 44, 65–66, 69–70, 113, 134, 156, 171, 173, 193, 198, 238, 255, 257
Desimiroff, 211–13, 215
Deuxième Bureau, 17, 19–20, 37, 47–48, 70, 107, 111, 126, 131, 150, 152, 154–56, 160, 164, 173–74, 178, 187. *See also* French intelligence services
Devauges, Capitaine, 161, 163, 198

Dewavrin, Captain André, 33. *See also* 'Colonel Passy'
d'Harcourt, 148, 150, 152, 156–57, 258
Dick, Hassell H., 21, 34, 45, 134, 183, 268
Digard, Micheline, 31, 150, 153
Director of Military Intelligence (DMI), 90, 210
Dissard, Marie-Louise, 30
Dodds, Hugh 'Granny,' 34–35, 45–46, 110, 257
Dolphin Square, 90, 136, 263
Dorchester Hotel, 9, 91–92, 120, 122, 125, 135–36, 221–22
d'Orves, Etienne, 33, 88
Dowding, Corporal Kenneth Bruce, 38
DR, 55, 89, 121, 123, 140, 142, 168, 202, 225, 234, 239, 268, 276. *See also* French intelligence services
Drummond-Wolff, Lieutenant Colonel Robert, 46, 78, 259
DSDoc, 161, 198. *See also* French intelligence services
Duclos, Maurice, 62, 86, 272
Dugast, Claire, 14, 170, 184. *See also* Dugasts
Dugast, Marcel, 14, 164, 170, 184, 186–88, 272. *See also* Dugasts
Dugasts, 14–15, 170, 182, 185, 188, 195, 249
Dunderdale, Wilfred 'Biffy,' 227–28
Duprez, 38, 130
Dutour, 150, 153–55, 174, 179, 181–82

Eccles, David McAdam, 34
Ede, Colonel Bertram Montague, 181
Elgar, Sir Edward, 96
Eriksen, Vera, 1, 122
Eriksson, My, 1, 122, 138–39, 159
Ernst, Max, 35
Évian-les-Bains, 65, 67, 261

Fayyang, François, 50, 182
Feltesse, Lucien, 62
Feuchtwanger, Lion, 35
FFI, 164, 261
FFL (Forces Françaises Libre), 128
Finckenstein, 78
Fiocca, Henri, 32
Fiocca, Nancy, 146, 179

Fleming, Ian, 34, 257
FNFL, 268
Foley, Frank, 125
Forrest, Jacques, 123
Fourcade, Jean, 148–49
Franco, Generalissimo, 10, 29, 200
Free French Forces, 66, 135–36
French contre-espionage services, 74. *See also* French intelligence services
French counter-espionage network, 47. *See also* French intelligence services
French intelligence services, 174, 239, 259, 271, 278
Fry, Varian, 268
Fullerton, Hugh, 35, 43–44, 46, 79, 129–31, 181–82, 194

Gaessler, Alfred, 33–34, 36–37, 58, 84–88, 90, 193, 237, 241
Gannat, 181, 246
Garrow, Ian, 30–34, 36–44, 46, 69, 74–75, 77–81, 84–85, 99, 109, 129–34, 143, 145–58, 179, 181–82, 231–32, 256
Garrow's arrest, 38, 238
Garrow's betrayal, 238
Garrow's organization, 32, 37, 86
Gars
  earlier suspected, 179
  Raphael, 48, 179
Garthe, Colonel Friederich Alfred, 68, 262, 277
Geiger, Peter, 26, 256
Géraldy, Paul, 119
German Intelligence Service, 18, 40, 49, 57–58, 60, 62–63, 68, 84, 103, 105, 165, 168, 171, 191, 193, 219, 237, 255, 262
Gerschel, Christian, 84
Gerschel, Lucien, 179
Gestapo, 21, 28, 35, 47, 49, 58, 167, 188, 198, 206, 217–19, 221, 224, 232, 266, 270
Gillham, John Graham, 6
Glanzberg, Norbert, 148
Gneisenau, 87–88, 263
Gordon, Lieutenant Colonel Edward Anthony, 13, 169, 202, 222, 226, 231, 271, 274
Gosport, 100–103, 106, 121, 173, 265
Guérisse, Albert, 30, 217, 220, 238, 270

Haden-Guest, 30, 141
Haden-Guest, Elisabeth, 38, 41, 79, 82, 115, 130, 144, 157, 178
Haden-Guest, Leslie, 142
Hamilton Stokes, 29
Hankey, Mark John Barnard, 81–82, 263
Harley, Robert Paul, 10–11
Harmer, Christopher, 55, 156
Harvey, 120
Haylor, Ronnie, 42, 44
Heinemann, Harry, 177. *See also* Heinemann, Hermann
Heinemann, Hermann, 69, 173, 271
Hervey, Victor, 200
Hewart, Lord Chief Justice, 10–11
Hicks, George Edward, 104, 210, 274
Highland Light Infantry, 30, 256
Hill, Bernard, 218–28, 231–32, 235
Hinchley Cooke, Colonel, 143, 222–23, 275
Hitler, Adolf, 24, 28, 59–60, 79, 159, 261–62
Hoare, Sir Samuel, 29
Holloway Prison, 1, 122–24, 140–42, 159, 161, 175, 203, 235, 269
Holme, Paul Christian Boeg, 3–4, 7, 12, 77, 93, 119, 159
Home Office, 63, 89, 121, 128, 138–39, 141, 159, 164, 191, 197, 203, 222, 225, 239, 271
Hôtel Lutetia, 68, 115, 158
Hôtel Noailles, 37, 130, 147–48, 152, 179
Hotz, Oberstleutnant Karl, 164
Hyde Park Hotel, 10, 222, 234, 237

Intelligence Corps, 39, 90, 254, 264, 266, 274
IS9, 226, 266. *See also* MI9
ISOS decrypts, 65, 160, 189, 239, 260
ISRB, 42, 258. *See also* SOE
Italian Armistice Commission, 110, 148, 258

Jenkins, Peter Martin, 10–11, 253
Johns, Commander Philip, 108
Johnstone, Bobby, 107
Johnstone, Mary, 237

Kell, Sir Vernon, 31
Kemball-Cook, Lady Cecile, 93
Kennard, Sir Coleridge, 34

Kenny, 37, 41, 47, 79, 81, 109, 130, 147–54, 256
Kenny, Captain Patrick William, 31, 256
Kenny, Thomas Edward James, 31
Kenny's arrest, 79
Keswick, David, 111
Knight, Maxwell, 90, 97, 112–13
Krafft, Mathilde, 138–40, 159
Kraus, Freddy, 156
KRRC (King's Royal Rifle Corps), 10, 209

Langley, Jimmy, 25, 30, 43, 45, 47, 53, 57–58, 60, 72, 131, 226, 228, 255, 269, 277
Lavallière, Simone, 110, 153, 189–90
La Vallière, Simone, 126. *See also* Lavallière, Simone
'Leclerc,' 47–50, 58, 69, 71–72, 76, 80–82, 110, 130, 154, 174, 179, 181–82, 187
Le Corvaisier, Yves Francois, 110. *See also* Marcilly
Lenitz, 130
Lévêque, Comte André Philippe Marc, 33
Liddell, Guy Maynard, 11, 34, 59–60, 75, 83, 85–86, 91, 159, 207
Liddell Diaries, 257, 262–63, 278
post-war, 253, 277
Liechtenstein, 25–27, 256
Lithgow-Smith, Barbara, 7, 210
Little Gran, 13, 20, 115–17, 121–23, 125, 127, 161, 199, 211
Littleton, Tony, 3
London Reception Centre (LRC), 68, 126
Lonsdale, 4, 10–12, 15, 19, 22, 40, 51, 53, 60–61, 63, 85–86, 96, 113–15, 121, 123, 135, 139, 143, 152, 156, 164, 168, 176, 180–81, 184–88, 190–98, 200, 203–4, 206, 208, 216, 218, 220–21, 224, 231–32, 235, 241, 253, 260
Lonsdale, Christopher Mainwaring, 234
Lonsdale, Diana, 105
Lonsdale, Georgina Beatrice, 9
Lonsdale, Ina, 106, 114
Lonsdale, John Christopher Mainwaring, 9, 11–12, 17, 20, 59, 82, 90, 93, 105, 119, 123, 142, 165, 169, 185, 200–202, 209, 220, 237–38, 253
Lonsdale, John Claude Jardine, 9
Lonsdale, Katherine, 123, 161. *See also* Little Gran

Index 283

Lonsdale, Right Reverend John, 274
Lonsdale, Stella Clive, 52–53, 228
Lonsdale, Stella Edith Howson, 1–4, 6–98, 102, 104–6, 108, 110, 114, 116, 120–36, 140, 142, 144, 146–48, 150, 152–54, 158, 160, 164–66, 170, 172, 174, 178, 180, 182, 186–96, 200, 202–4, 206, 208, 210–32, 235–36, 238–78. *See also* Clive, Stella Howson
Lonsdale's Secret Ink & Code, 241
Lonza Dantas, Helene, 118–19, 267
Loschenski, 17. *See also* Loshensky
Loshensky, 186, 201
Luke, Billy, 208, 211
Luneau, Abbé Jean, 25, 172, 177, 185, 187, 195, 249–50, 272
Lunn, Peter Northcote, 81

Magaloff, Nickolas, 209
Mahe, Madame, 198
Mann, Heinrich, 35
Mann, Thomas, 35
Mannin, Ethel Edith, 199, 202
Marcilly, 110, 179
Marseille, 6, 10, 27, 30–32, 34–38, 40–48, 50–51, 67, 69–73, 75, 79–81, 83–84, 89, 96, 108, 110–11, 118, 123, 125, 129, 131–33, 145–52, 154, 157, 169, 173–74, 177, 179, 181–82, 187, 189, 194, 217, 219, 221, 223, 228, 231, 245, 254, 257–58
Martineau, 69, 163, 166, 170, 184, 188, 249
Martineau, Madame Maud, 164, 170, 185–86, 188, 272. *See also* Martineau
Martineau, Monsieur, 21, 163, 170, 177, 186, 212, 215. *See also* Martineau
MASSINGHAM, 110
Masterman, John, 17, 33, 97
Matheson, Dr John, 122, 127–28, 138, 203
Maumen, Raoul, 181, 235–36
Maurois, André, 114, 119, 241
Maxwell, Sir Alexander, 121
Mayfair jewellery robbery, 142, 209, 220
Meissner, Karl, 21–25, 32, 35, 48, 50–51, 55, 57, 66, 68–71, 78, 80, 85, 89, 131, 171–73, 180, 189, 193, 214, 238, 247, 251, 277
Meissner's assistant in Ast Angers, 180
Melikoff, Boris, 39, 41–44, 120, 135

Mellanby, Molly, 140–41, 143
Menzies, Sir Stewart, 40, 65, 219
MEW (Ministry of Economic Warfare), 34, 63, 235
MI5, 1–2, 5, 8–12, 17, 23–25, 27, 31, 33–34, 37, 39, 42, 44–46, 52, 54, 56–57, 59–60, 63–71, 82, 85, 88–91, 95–97, 100–101, 104, 107, 109, 112–14, 119, 121–23, 128–29, 132, 136, 141, 143, 145–46, 156, 158–60, 164, 168–70, 172–73, 178, 184–86, 191–92, 194, 196, 198, 201, 203, 208–9, 217–19, 222–23, 225–28, 231, 234, 237–40, 255, 261, 265, 268, 272, 274–75, 278
MI6, 256, 266, 275, 278. *See also* SIS
MI7a, 31
MI8, 210
MI9, 25, 29, 57–58, 86, 90, 218, 226, 228, 255, 266, 269, 277
Mills, Cyril, 9, 12–13, 18, 24, 56, 75, 92, 94, 207, 268
Milmo, Buster, 13
Ministry of Economic Warfare (MEW), 34, 63, 235
Mitchell, Graham, 203, 234
Mond, Flight Sergeant Philip, 46, 110
Monte Carlo, 4–7, 11, 17, 123, 189
Moravec, František, 39
Morrison, Herbert, 121, 161, 197, 203
Mosley, Sir Oswald, 1, 138
Mouillard, Madame, 185–86, 188, 195, 272
Muelleman, 62
Muggeridge, Major Malcolm, 161, 165, 184, 198
Mumet, 181
Mumme, Francis George Kerr, 38
Murchie, Captain Charles Plowman, 44
Murray, Father John Wilfred, 13, 18, 20, 169, 271
Murray-Bisset, Lieutenant Colonel William Turner, 211, 274

Nantes, 12–16, 18, 20–21, 25–26, 33–34, 45, 66, 70, 73, 79, 134, 156–57, 161–65, 167–70, 174, 177–78, 180, 182, 184–92, 194, 198, 202, 204–6, 211–14, 217–21, 224, 232, 249–51, 270–72
Neave, Airey (MI9), 29–30, 32, 38, 226, 256–58, 269–70, 277

Newsam, Sir Frank, 121, 197
Nicholson, Christabel Sybil Caroline, 138, 268
Nouveau, Louis Henri, 31
Nyeres, 186, 188, 250

Okolo-Kulak, Olgierd, 14–15, 17, 195
O'Leary, Patrick, 29–38, 147, 179, 218–22, 225–28, 230–32, 238, 256, 270, 274
O'Leary libel case, 235
Operation Aerial, 169
Operation Anthropoid, 158
Operation Barbarossa, 36
Operation Cerberus, 88
Operation Dove II, 262
Operation Golden Eye, 257
Operation Pastorius, 262
Operation Sea Eagle, 70
Operation Sealion, 70
Operation Suicide, 275
Operation Titania, 148
Operation Torch, 111
Oriel College, 90. *See also* Oxford University
Orléans, 190
Orwell, George, 199, 273
OSS, 67, 255, 261, 263
Oxford University, 10, 25, 55, 68, 90, 260, 263, 275

Paillole, Colonel Paul, 47–48, 259, 270, 278
Pastré, Countess Lily, 148, 269
Pastré, Count Jean André Hubert Jean, 269
Pat Line, 30, 32, 238
Paulsen, Adalbert Karl Friederich, 56
Pavie, Jacques, 258
Pavie, Jean Jacques, 258
Pavie, René Jean Jacques, 37
Pavie's activities, 181
Pembroke College, 90, 263. *See also* Oxford University
Petrie, Sir David, 88
Philby, Kim, 36, 43–44
Piaf, Edith, 148
Pilcher, Toby, 89, 100–101, 121, 144
Pioneer Corps, 13, 202, 211
Pitt-Rivers
    twice-divorced, 234
    Anthony, 234, 236, 276
    Captain George Henry Lane-Fox, 218, 220, 234–35, 275–77
    Lieutenant General Augustus Henry Lane-Fox, 236
    Michael, 236
Pitt-Rivers collection, 236
Pitt-Rivers's diatribe, 235
Platiau, 163, 166–67, 170–71, 177, 183, 193, 198, 211–13, 215–16, 238
Platiau, Charles, 261, 273
Platiau, Henry L., 198
Platiau, Jean Émile, 21, 170, 186, 188, 198, 208, 249–50, 272. *See also* Platiau
Pöel, 56–57, 113
Pöhner, Egon Adin, 51–52, 77
Prassinos, Mario Lambros Achilles, 32, 149, 231–32
Prince Franz-Josef II, 26
Prince Hans Moritz, 28
Prince Louis Metternich, 51
Prince Nikita Magaloff, 5–6
Prince Schwarzenberg, 42, 160
Princess Irina Yusupov, 7
Princess Vavara Magaloff, 5, 127
Prinz Alois, 26
Prinz Ferdinand, 26
public interest immunity (PII), 218, 227, 275

RAF Bramscote, 1
RAF Evaders, 256, 277
RAF Finningley, 266
RAF Gosport, 100
RAF Reserve, 274
RAF Ringway, 110
RAF Technical Branch, 101, 105
RAF Volunteer Reserve, 102, 252
Ramsbotham, Peter, 44
RASC (Royal Army Service Corps), 6, 44
Rauch, Sonderführer, 56–57, 63–67, 71, 78, 113–14, 144, 178, 180, 183, 204–7, 212, 215, 251, 261, 272
Renault-Roulier, Lieutenant Colonel Gilbert, 88, 263
RENÉ, 6, 22–25, 32–33, 35–36, 43–44, 46, 48–50, 55–63, 65–67, 69, 72, 77–78, 80–81, 83–84, 86, 93, 95, 98, 110, 113–15,

Index   285

122, 124, 130–32, 134–36, 143–45, 154, 156–57, 165–66, 172–73, 177–83, 185–90, 193–95, 201, 205, 211, 214, 219, 226, 232, 236, 238, 240–41, 245–46, 248, 250–51, 272
Rennes, 185, 204
Reynolds, Reginald Arthur, 199–203, 273
Rhodes, Detective Sergeant, 4, 21, 83, 100, 123
Rieth, Charlotte-Louise, 24, 66
Ritson, Corporal George, 19
Robertson, Tar, 18, 25, 37, 56, 75
Rodocanachi, Dr George, 31, 38
Rohleder, Joachim, 22, 277
Royal Army Service Corps (RASC), 6, 44
Royal Artillery, 19, 81
Royal Electrical & Mechanical Engineers, 38
Royal Engineers, 12, 19, 211, 220, 267
Royal Navy, 88, 103, 209
Royal Navy Volunteer Reserve (RNVR), 81, 108
Royal Signals, 11, 267
RVPS (Royal Victoria Patriotic Schools), 42, 44, 68, 120, 125, 137
Ryder, Iris Katherine, 140

Sainte-Croix, 25
Sainte-Luce oil installation, 193
Sainte-Luce plans, 131
Sainte-Luce-sur-Loire, 21–22
Saint-Hippolyte-du-Fort, 30, 147, 150
Saint-Nazaire, 14, 163–64, 166, 169, 182, 211–12, 272
Saint-Pierre-des-Corps, 31, 80
Saint-Valéry-en-Caux, 30
Saône-et-Loire, 57
Scharnhorst, 87–88, 263
SCR (Section de Centralisation du Renseignement), 174, 259. *See also* French intelligence services
Secret Intelligence Service, 209
Section VB4, 125, 228
Section VIII, 87
Sécurité Militaire (SM), 161, 165, 186–87, 198, 259. *See also* French intelligence services
Security Service, 224–25, 228–30, 252, 277. *See also* MI5

Selby, Sir Walford, 29
Senter, Lieutenant Commander John, 57
Service de Renseignments (SR), 37, 174–75, 198. *See also* French intelligence services
SHAEF, 184, 198, 264
Shaw, Dickie Griffith, 101
Sideroff, Nickolas, 5–9, 11–13, 17, 82, 91–94, 104, 115–17, 121–26, 142, 147, 156, 159, 169, 172, 199, 202, 209–11
Sillitoe, Sir Percy, 225, 274
SIS, 8, 25, 29, 33, 37, 42–44, 46, 53–54, 57–60, 63, 75, 81, 83–86, 88, 90, 107–8, 130, 133, 135, 144, 147, 156, 159, 161, 179, 184, 210, 218–20, 223, 225–28, 237, 255, 272
Smith-Bingham, Colonel Oswald, 34, 259
SOE, 42, 57, 61, 63, 71, 81, 90, 105, 110, 144, 146–47, 158, 237, 258, 262, 266, 268, 278
Solange, 82–83, 93
Sougné, Henri, 267
Sougne, Raymond Alphonse Elvire Joseph, 268
Speck, Walter, 167
SR (Service de Renseignments), 37, 174–75, 198. *See also* French intelligence services
SS-Sonderkommando, 43, 89, 263
Stamp, Edward Blanchard, 23, 128
Stangroom, Walter, 32, 44, 130, 132, 150–51, 157
St. Germain, 25, 69
Stuart-Bunning, George Harold, 168
Sunday Express, 217–33, 274. *See also Daily Express*
Sûreté, 34, 115, 125, 147–50, 164, 261, 270

Taylour, Fay, 140
Torpedo Development Unit (TDU), 100–102, 173–74, 240
TR (Travaux Ruraux), 47, 174, 204. *See also* French intelligence services
Treachery Act, 239

University of Colorado Colorado Springs (UCCS), 64
Unternehmen Seeadler, 70, 262

Unternehmen Seelöwe, 70
Unternehmen Taube II, 262

Veper, Max, 163
Verges, Marcel, 130
Vernon, Diana, 1, 83, 92, 100–102, 104, 114, 121
Vice Chief of SIS (VCSS), 84. *See also* Vivian, Colonel Valentine
Vichy France, 40, 43–44, 47, 50, 68, 108, 111, 130–31, 150, 153, 259, 277
VICTOIRE, 55–56, 140, 143, 145, 156–57, 159–61, 268, 276. *See also* Carré, Mathilde
Vierzon, 177
Villemorin, André, 133. *See also* Vilmorin
Vilmorin, 33, 110
Vilmorin, Roger, 179. *See also* Vilmorin
Viner, Frank, 37, 39, 42–44, 47, 59, 69, 77, 79, 81, 83, 91, 95, 110, 114, 120, 124, 130–31, 135–37, 141–43, 145, 147–49, 151–52, 157–58, 160, 179, 201–2, 240
Vivian, Colonel Valentine, 75, 86, 218–21, 223, 225–28, 230, 232, 275

Wachter, Sonderführer, 208, 216
Wake, Nancy, 31–32, 256, 277. *See also* Fiocca, Nancy
Waldorf Hotel, 47, 60, 68, 85, 91, 96, 120, 133, 136
Wambach, Israel, 264. *See also* Wambachs
Wambach, Olga, 94, 264. *See also* Wambachs
Wambachs, 92–93, 112, 264
Wandsworth prison, 9, 142
Warner, Stella Edith, 7
War Office, 12, 17, 53–54, 68, 101–2, 123, 143, 151, 170, 173, 199, 210–11, 218, 221–22, 226, 230, 235, 238, 257, 275
Wesley, Mary, 43, 277
White, Dick Goldsmith, 57, 75, 86, 184, 219
Wiener, František, 39. *See also* Viner, Frank
Willyams, Colonel Edward Brydges, 13, 220, 275
Wilmer, David, 10–11, 253
Wilson, D. Ian, 135–37, 140, 265
Wolpert, Louise Ruth, 30
Wrede, Sonderfuehrer, 158
Young, Courtenay, 55, 129, 170, 191, 198, 238

ZIGZAG, 11, 63, 156, 186, 270. *See also* Chapman, Eddie